MW00718372

Building Client/Server Applications Using TUXEDO®

Carl L. Hall

WILEY COMPUTER PUBLISHING

John Wiley & Sons, Inc.
New York • Chichester • Brisbane • Toronto • Singapore

Trademarks

OS/2, RS/6000, IMS, IMS/DC are trademarks or registered trademarks of International Business Machines Corporation.

ORACLE, ORACLE7, SQL*Net, SQL*Forms, Pro*C, PL/SQL are trademarks or registered trademarks of Oracle Corporation.

Microsoft, MS, MS-DOS, Windows are trademarks or registered trademarks of Microsoft Corporation.

Novell, TUXEDO, and UnixWare are registered trademarks of Novell, Inc.

UNIX is a registered trademark in the United States and other countries, licensed exclusively through X/Open Company Ltd.

Micro Focus and Micro Focus COBOL are trademarks of Micro Focus Limited.

Encina is a trademark or registered trademark of Transarc Corporation.

TCP/IP is a trademark or registered trademark of Defense Advanced Research Projects Administration.

All other brand and product names referenced in this book are trademarks or registered trademarks of their respective holders and are used here for informational purposes only.

Publisher: Katherine Schowalter
Editor: Robert Elliott
Managing Editor: Angela Murphy
Text Design & Composition: Publishers' Design and Production Services, Inc.

Designations used by companies to distinguish their products are often claimed as trademarks. In all instances where John Wiley & Sons, Inc. is aware of a claim, the product names appear in initial or all capital letters. Readers, however, should contact the appropriate companies for more complete information regarding trademarks and registration.

This text is printed on acid-free paper.

Library of Congress Cataloging-in-Publication Data:

Hall, Carl L.
    Building client/server applications using Tuxedo / Carl Hall.
      p.   cm.
    Includes index.
    ISBN 0-471-12958-5 (pbk. : alk. paper)
    1. Client/server computing.   2. TUXEDO System.   I. Title.
QA76.9.C55H32   1996
005.2—dc20   95-50555

Printed in the United States of America
10 9 8 7 6 5 4 3 2

Foreword

The purpose of this book is to provide the reader with an in-depth understanding of how TUXEDO can be used to solve the problems with developing distributed applications. Many client/server publications address the fundamentals of building a distributed application but this is the first book that I have had the pleasure of reading that details how to develop a working system using TUXEDO. The author makes extensive use of diagrams, figures, and examples in an attempt to present this knowledge in as simple a form as possible.

This book provides system architects, designers, developers, and administrators with a detailed understanding of how a project can be developed using TUXEDO. System architects and designers will be keenly interested in the author's description of the methodology of building TUXEDO applications. This book presents information not readily available such as the proper manner to package services and how to divide an application into distributable sub-components. The author walks the reader through the entire process of developing a simple server, configuring the TUXEDO environment, developing a client program, and then testing/debugging the application. Throughout the book, particular attention to detail is given to the various administration procedures which are needed to complete the process. This shows the author's depth of knowledge of TUXEDO and his familiarity with the pit-falls most client/server organizations fall into.

The author provides valuable insight into Novell's newest release of TUXEDO—6.1. Using this information, system managers can determine what benefits they might expect and what the impact of upgrading existing applications using older releases of TUXEDO might be. Key information about each of these features such as enhanced security, administration APIs and a Graphical User Interface (GUI) along with information about compatibility issues will be invaluable. Developers and administrators alike of TUXEDO applications will benefit through the author's description of typical problems/error messages users may encounter throughout the development and life of TUXEDO applications.

HAROLD LAVENDER
Sr. Technical Consultant, Fidelity Investments

How to Get the Most from This Book

As client/server usage has expanded, people have increasingly discovered that there is a need for an additional layer between the application on the work station and the database on the server. This layer, usually called "middleware," provides distributed application management and transaction management. Systems that supply this layer are often called enhanced client/server systems, and sometimes on-line transaction processing (OLTP) systems. TUXEDO is currently the enhanced client/server system of choice for many enterprises.

At the present time the only source of information about TUXEDO is:

- On-line documentation that comes with the system.
- Product documentation available from Decision Support, Inc.
- Training courses from various sources.

The documentation from Decision Support, Inc. is essentially a printout of the on-line documentation, so that those two sources should be considered one. Training courses are expensive both as direct cost and as loss of productivity of individuals. These training courses generally provide the same information as the on-line documentation, though the presence of a human being can make understanding easier. Training courses, while good, provide information that may be quickly forgotten once the trainee returns to work.

I learned TUXEDO the hard way, by simply working with it until I could use it efficiently. I did not get the opportunity to work with individuals who had TUXEDO experience until recently.

Even today, the number of people with TUXEDO experience is relatively rare. As a consequence, systems are all too often designed by people with a limited knowledge of the full capabilities available.

What is needed is a book on TUXEDO that explains the system in a meaningful way to application architects, application designers, application programmers, and administrators; a book that guides people through the process of defining architectures and designing systems, as well as providing the details required by programmers. The intent of this book is to fill this need.

TUXEDO is consistent with open systems concepts and its functionality and application programming interfaces are compliant with the X/Open transaction processing specifications. Readers of this book can acquire a logical understanding of open systems on-line transaction processing that will enable them to use other transaction processing systems in addition to TUXEDO, though some specifics may be different.

Many people developing client/server systems are not familiar with the general concepts of transaciton processing so a short overview of this information is included in the early chapter. The database chapter also includes a description of some techniques which have been used for a long time in transaction processing systems on mainframes. These techniques have been adapted to the open systems environment. This book is designed to explain TUXEDO to application architects, application designers, application programmers and administrators. The book does this by:

- Providing detailed design guidelines.
- Giving suggestions for achieving and maintaining high performance levels.
- Including considerable information not found in the system documentation.
- Aiding architects, designers and developers in choosing TUXEDO features to fit specific application requirements.

The reader should have some knowledge of C or C++ to get the most out of this book, since most examples are in C. Database examples use SQL.

The primary goal of the book is to show how to develop real distributed applications using TUXEDO. For most applications, no other documentation should be necessary. (Although much detail about TUXEDO functions and utilities is included, the TUXEDO documentation should, of course, be consulted as needed.) It should be noted that this book does not focus on GUI programming. For information on GUI interfaces and the specific development tools, see the manuals for those products.

This book can also be used as an ongoing reference as the user gains experience with TUXEDO. The book provides clear descriptions and examples of each feature.

All programming examples were tested using TUXEDO Release 5. The book was updated for Release 6.1 prior publication.

HOW TO USE THIS BOOK

This book should be used by anyone who wants to learn how to create applications using TUXEDO. It has been designed to present the material so that anyone who has a minimal knowledge of C and UNIX can understand the principles and details. The material concentrates on the information needed to design and create TUXEDO applications. Considerable material about administration is included to help the developer and administrator work together. It would require another book to provide full information on the administration of TUXEDO, so this book provides only sufficient information on administration to help the application designer and developer understand administration sufficient to perform their tasks.

Chapters 1 through 3 provide an overview of the material. Everyone should be thoroughly familiar with these chapters before proceeding further. Those who are knowledgeable of transaction processing principles may skip these chapters.

Chapter 4 provides important information about the relationship between TUXEDO and databases.

Chapter 5 presents the principles for designing good TUXEDO applications and makes suggestions about the procedures to use for creating a design.

Chapters 6 through 9 present detailed information about how to implement TUXEDO applications.

Chapter 10 and 11 provide information for use by TUXEDO administrators. Application developers should also read these chapters to become familiar with the administration process so that systems can be implemented for optimal administration capabilities.

Chapter 12 presents the security aspects of TUXEDO Release 5. If the security features are being used, all those involved with implementing applications should be familiar with this chapter.

Chapter 13 is for COBOL programmers who create TUXEDO clients and servers. The chapter presents methods of using COBOL and assumes knowledge of the preceding chapters.

Chapters 14 through 16 provide information on the TUXEDO features for reliable queues (/Q), X/Open interfaces, and multiple domain TUXEDO instantiations (/Domain).

Chapter 17 describes new features available with TUXEDO Release 6.1. Since this book is primarily for developers, only an overview of administrative functions are included. The Event Broker is fully discussed because this feature is expected to be programmed by application programmers. Application programmers will not use the programmed administration feature so it is described only briefly.

The appendixes provide additional information that will be useful to all. Note especially Appendix D, which contains the coding necessary to implement a sample application.

There is sufficient information in this book to implement almost any application. Some complex and advanced material that is needed only for unusual situations is not included. The reader should consult the TUXEDO product documentation for additional information.

This book is written to explain TUXEDO Release 5 and 6.1. Chapter 17 discusses the specific features of Release 6.1. This book can also be used by those working with Release 4.2.2. Some of features that Release 5 and Release 6.1 add are:

- The name of the environment variable where the TUXEDO root directory is stored was ROOTDIR on earlier releases. Release 5 changed the name to TUXDIR.
- Release 5 adds /Domain. In 4.2.2 there was only limited availability of this feature.
- Release 5 adds an interface to the Distributed Computing Environment (DCE) from the Open Software Foundation (OSF) using the X/Open transactional interface specification called TxRPC. Note that this interface is not described in this book.
- Release 5 adds runtime tracing.
- Release 5 provides a method of changing data dependent routing dynamically.
- Release 5 provides an easier method of adding and modifying buffer types than previous releases. The Release 5 method is described in Appendix A.
- Release 5 makes available on-line documentation, including access via a windowing interface and via the UNIX **man (1)** command.
- Release 5 and Release 6.1 add more security features.
- Release 6.1 adds Access Control Lists, and Event Broker feature, a programmed administration feature, and a Graphical User Interface administration tool.

Acknowledgments

This book would not have been possible without the help of Novell, Inc. TUXEDO Systems Group in the person of Dianne Langeland. Novell, Inc., supplied UnixWare and TUXEDO for use in testing so that this work could be as accurate as possible. I also want to thank the other personnel at the TUXEDO Systems Group who provided much needed support and advice.

Many thanks to George Holober for his efforts in reviewing the final manuscript for technical accuracy and appropriateness. George's comments helped focus my efforts onto certain things which make the book easier to understand.

Lee Morrow and Peter DeSart at Information Management Company (IMC) also provided invaluable help.

The COBOL samples were compiled with Micro Focus COBOL. Many thanks to the folks at Micro Focus who provided the compiler.

I also want to thank my wife, Dawn E. Hall, who used her knowledge as an English teacher to edit the manuscript.

Contents

Introduction to Client/ Server Technology

1.1   CLIENT/SERVER TECHNOLOGY

Client/server technology implements a modern computing paradigm that is made possible by a combination of powerful computer hardware and reliable, fast, and relatively low cost communications technology. Client/server technology has become popular because it:

- Allows use of lower cost hardware
- Supports scalability
- Supports better fault-tolerant systems
- Provides easier management of distributed data
- Supports GUI front ends that make user interfaces better and smarter.

Figure 1.1 illustrates a typical client/server configuration. In this example, each branch office has a local computer with necessary data, while the home office maintains central files on a larger set of servers. A properly designed client/server system can support thousands of users with high performance.

Enhanced client/server systems are built on a three-tiered architecture. These enhanced systems overcome many of the problems inherent in simpler, but less efficient client/server systems. Though database servers and file servers still have their place, any enterprise that requires support for large numbers of users must use enhanced client/ server technology to meet its goals.

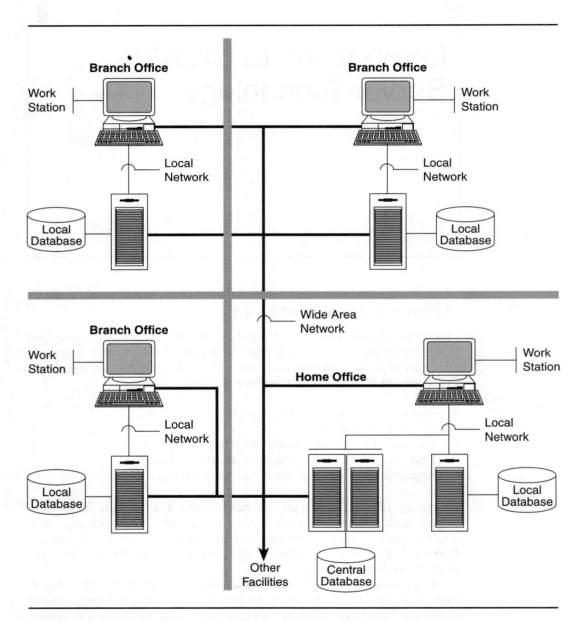

Figure 1.1   Using client/server technology in the enterprise.

Enhanced client/server technology is provided by TUXEDO from Novell, TOP END from AT&T Global Information Systems, and Encina from Transarc. CICS6000 from IBM Corporation provides a way to implement systems using the enhanced client/server paradigm, though that is not its primary purpose. Products that implement enhanced client/server systems are often included in a class of products called *middleware* because they operate between the application program and the database.

1.2   DISTRIBUTED COMPUTING

1.2.1   General Discussion

Distributed computing has different meanings to many people, and yet, its meaning is often taken for granted. Generally, distributed computing refers to the case where more than one independent computer process is used to complete a specified task. The processes used may be on the same or different computing platforms. Unfortunately, this definition is not very restrictive, because it allows a multiple step batch job to be included as a distributed computing system. Intuition says this is not right. Those who think in terms of batch can replace the word "task" with "job step" and the result will not be far from the correct definition.

This definition of distributed computing allows the term to encompass many computing paradigms, including client/server, distributed processing, and distributed databases. This book will use more exact terms, such as distributed processing and distributed database, for clarity.

1.2.2   Distributed Processing

The terms *distributed processing* and *distributed computing* are probably the most abused terms in computer science. This book does not consider distributed processing to be synonymous with distributed computing. *Distributed processing* is defined as follows:

> Distributed processing means that the processing of an application unit of work uses more than one independent computer process, where the processes included are application processes and are not part of an operating system, database, or other support system.

This definition specifically defines distributed processing as application capability, since any distribution of support processes (including database processing) is not apparent to the application developer. Only

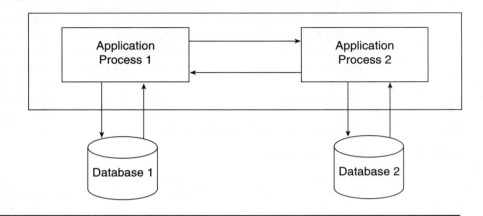

Figure 1.2   Distributed processing.

when the processing of an application can be distributed can the system be scalable and allow the use of multiple computer platforms by the application.

Distributed processing does not occur because various job steps may be done by different processes, as on so-called mainframes; it is distributed processing only when a single unit of work is being done by multiple computer processes.

A distributed processing application may use the various processes in parallel or serially, depending upon the application requirements. Further, these processes may be on different computer platforms, but processing on different platforms is not required to consider the application distributed.

Figure 1.2 illustrates distributed processing. A single application unit of work uses more than one process, in this case two. The processes cooperate to complete the task by means of a communication protocol. Each application process may access an independent database. The two databases may or may not be of the same type.

1.2.3   Distributed Database

A *database* can be defined as a collection of information permanently stored in a computer and accessible by a computer application to support application processing. This general definition has been made more specific by the use of specialized software called database management systems (DBMSs), and the more modern relational database management systems (RDBMSs).

A *distributed database* is a database where the data is divided among more than one database instance, but may be treated as a single logical database by applications. A distributed database can exist on the same platform or on multiple platforms. Usually, a distributed database is spread over multiple platforms, but distributing over multiple platforms is not required by this definition. The concept of a distributed database is essential to understanding the implications of transaction management.

Most DBMSs provide for defining multiple instances of the database management software. In these types of DBMSs, each instance is called a database. These systems often also allow the definition of multiple *spaces*, which define the physical location of the data. When multiple spaces are defined for the same database, the DBMS manages the spaces as if they were logically one space (*spanning* the spaces), and the database is not considered distributed.

The concepts of distributed database and distributed processing are very different. A distributed database spreads the *data* into various locations. Distributed processing spreads the *processing* of the business application into various locations.

Figure 1.3 illustrates a distributed database. The application process communicates with the database management system as if the

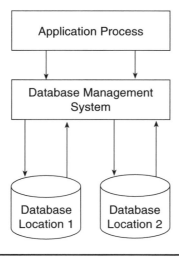

Figure 1.3   Distributed database.

database were at a single location. The DBMS manages the distribution of the data over multiple locations.

1.3   GENERAL DEFINITION OF CLIENT/SERVER

The term *client/server* refers to a relationship between two systems or processes. The *client* is the system that requests work to be done on its behalf by the *server* system. In most situations, which is client and which is server is determined by the relationship of requestor (client) to server.

Servers provide *services* to requesting clients. It is important to carefully distinguish between servers and the services they provide. Since a single server can provide several services, the designation "server" should be carefully separated from the designation "service."

It is convenient to refer to a system or process that usually receives requests as the server, and to a system or process that usually sends requests as the client. This can create some confusion, for example, when a server sends a request to another server. In later discussions, the context will serve to clearly distinguish which type of object is being discussed.

Figure 1.4 illustrates the simple client/server relationship. The client sends a service request to the server and the server responds with an appropriate reply.

1.4   HARDWARE SERVERS

It is common today to provide a variety of services from one or more networked computer systems. In this case, the machine providing the services is referred to as a server. Normally there is no end user interaction directly with the server machine. User interaction is performed with some other hardware—the hardware client. This other hardware may be a completely different type of computer, and is sometimes referred to as a *work station*.

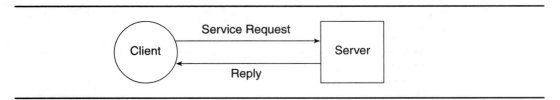

Figure 1.4   Client/server relationship.

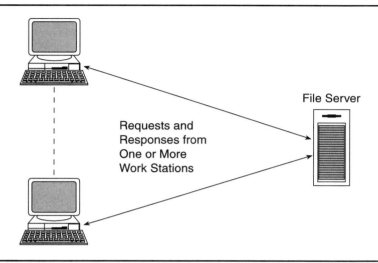

Figure 1.5   Hardware client/server.

The operating system and the network software make the hardware server function. In other words, although the machine is referred to as the server, it needs specialized software to be a server. A hardware server usually functions:

- As a print server, where printers are attached to the servers and used by everyone on the network
- As a file server, where common files are stored on the server
- As a storage mechanism supporting work stations with little or no storage capacity
- As a central storage for enterprise information

Figure 1.5 illustrates a hardware client server. One or more work stations are connected to the server. The work stations send requests to the server system and the server responds with the required response.

1.5   SOFTWARE SERVERS

Software servers are provided by special software that is designed specifically to handle requests. This special software is often provided on server hardware, but not always. It is not uncommon to find that

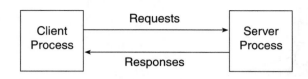

Figure 1.6   Software client/server.

the hardware that provides the software server also contains the software clients. Software servers usually provide one of the following types of service:

- Data file services
- Remote procedure call services
- Database services
- Enhanced client/server capabilities which provide a true distributed processing capability

Figure 1.6 illustrates a simple software client/server arrangement. Running programs are called *processes* in the open systems venue. The client process sends requests to the server process. The request for service names the service and includes any information required to perform the requested service. The server performs the requested service and returns the results in the form of a reply. The client and server process may be on the same hardware system or they may be on different hardware systems.

1.6   TYPES OF SERVERS

1.6.1   File Servers

A widespread use of servers is as *file servers*. Most networks today contain file servers, which are usually completely transparent to any user, including application developers. They are supported by a combination of operating system and network manager software. In some cases, the network software makes the file server services available to the operating system in such a manner that the operating system has no need to be aware of the file server services.

Two types of file services are available on many systems: file access and remote procedure call (RPC). File access services make files on the designated hardware available to the network. The physical location of these files is generally not apparent to the user, though in some cases it is necessary that the user is signed on correctly to access particular files.

The Novell NetWare file server is one popular example. This product works with several operating systems, but is most common with MS-DOS. In this case the user must sign onto the server where the desired files are located. For example, a local PC may have a disc drive designated C, where files are called **C:\dir1\file1**. NetWare servers have a mapping mechanism that maps drive designations to the local system. For instance, the local system may have a network server disc drive mapped to F. Files on it are accessed from local PCs as **F:\dir\file**. Developers must be aware of this designation; however, application users need not be aware of the location of the files.

Figure 1.7 illustrates a file server, which looks very similar to a hardware server. The file server is simplest to understand of the client/server architectures. (In a large network using many file servers, administration and use is not always as simple as the diagram seems to indicate.) File servers are implemented by software in the network or operating system so that file access requests are routed to the server system. The server system accesses the requested file on behalf of the client system and returns a reply that includes the result of the access.

Remote procedure calls are made available by a system that provides a library of application programs that can be accessed by other applica-

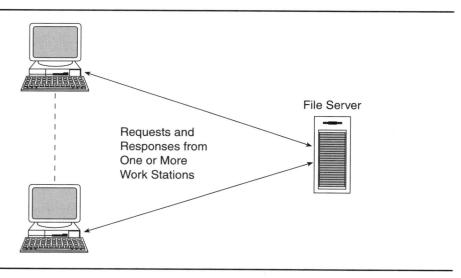

Figure 1.7   File server.

tion programs as if they were simple function calls. The following C notation calls a subroutine to print information: **printf(\n, "Hello World");**

Without RPC, the actual subroutine will be linked with the calling program by a system program called a link editor. When the main program is stored, the printf() subroutine is stored right along with it, using extra disk space in each main program where printf() is called. A system called dynamic link libraries can eliminate this situation on local machines. Discussion of this system is deferred until later. Using a combination of operating system services and network file server services, the program printf() may reside physically on some other machine. When the call is invoked at run time, the printf() routine may be loaded into the local machine and executed, or may be executed on the server.

Figure 1.8 illustrates a simple RPC configuration. The application client program issues a call to a subroutine. The RPC software intercepts the call and routes it to the location of the subroutine to be executed. RPC software at the location of the subroutine is used to cause execution of the subroutine and then route the results back to the application client program.

Some simple RPC systems simply find the required subroutine on the remote system and transfer it back for execution to the system where the application program is executing. More sophisticated RPC systems cause the subroutine to be executed where it resides and route only the results back to the client. With simple RPC systems, subroutines are written exactly the same as if they were to be linked directly with the application client. Thus, neither the application developer nor the subroutine developer need to do anything different to use the RPC system.

1.6.2   Database Servers

Major database vendors now provide software features that work within networks to provide one or more database servers. Before database servers were available, all database access on a local machine required that the database reside physically on the same machine. It was very

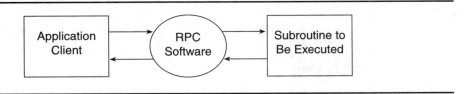

Figure 1.8   Simple RPC.

difficult, if not impossible, to access data on any machine other than where the data resided.

Database software was later designed to use file servers to store the data, but this was very costly in loss of performance and resulted in extremely high network traffic. The availability of database servers has made central and distributed storage a practical reality, and advertising by database vendors has recently made database servers and client/ server technology synonymous to many.

Database servers make database functions available on a server. File access by the database software is performed locally on the server. With database servers, the application runs on the work station, accessing the database with requests that execute database services in the server. A single database server can support a number of work stations.

Some databases provide a feature called *stored procedures* that provide a limited capability to perform application functions within the database. Stored procedures provide a pseudo-distributed processing capability that can be quite powerful.

Figure 1.9 illustrates a database server. Database software running on the client system intercepts requests for database access, and uses the network software to route the requests to the database software running on the server. Database software executes the request on the server and returns the result to the client. Since these types of

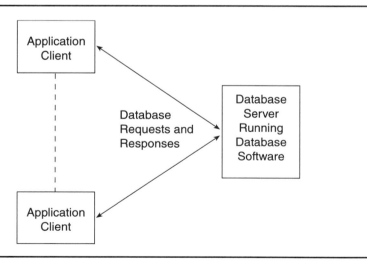

Figure 1.9   Database server.

systems require close cooperation between the network software and the database software, database vendors must write special software for each network system supported.

1.6.3   Enhanced Client/Server Processing

Enhanced client/server processing adds the following features:

- Application servers may be placed on any system in the network.
- Automatic balancing of the load among several servers performing the same service.
- Multiple application servers may be active on the same or multiple machines.
- Requests may be routed to a particular server depending on the data passed with the request.
- Application programs are never aware of the locations of services invoked.
- Multiple database types (heterogenous databases) can be used in the system with a minimal programming effort.
- New types of databases may be added, or existing database types may be changed with little or no impact on application programs.

Enhanced client/server processing is provided by distributed transaction processing systems. It is unfortunate that many people think of transaction processing as a specific requirement, when all programs that update databases are, in fact, performing transaction processing.

Figure 1.10 illustrates enhanced client/server technology. One or more clients issue requests for service that are intercepted by the name

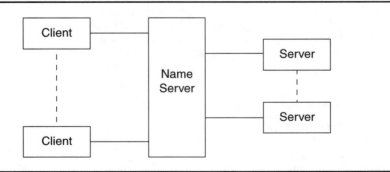

Figure 1.10   Enhanced client/server technology.

server. The name server routes the request to the appropriate server based on the name of the service and other considerations. The server performs the requested service and returns the response to the client. Multiple servers may provide the same service. The name server provides several methods to determine which server to use, including data dependent routing and load balancing. Routing and load balancing may be changed by administrative services without affecting the operation of either the clients or servers.

1.7   RPC, PEER-TO-PEER, AND CONVERSATIONAL

The traditional client/server relationship between two computer processes, RPC, was discussed earlier in this chapter. Other paradigms for cooperative distributed computing are conversational and peer-to-peer.

The *conversational* paradigm allows a process to initiate a conversation with another process. The two processes may then exchange a number of messages. Either process may terminate the conversation.

Figure 1.11 illustrates the conversational paradigm. Process 1 initiates a conversation with process 2 and exchanges a number of messages, while both processes maintain information on what has gone before in the conversation (the context). Then, in this case, process 1 terminates the conversation. Process 2 then loses context of the conversation and becomes ready to serve other processes that may need its services. Conversational capabilities are provided by some enhanced client/server products, such as TUXEDO.

The *peer-to-peer* paradigm supports communication between independent processes. Using peer-to-peer communications, any process may initiate a message exchange with any other process at any time. As many messages as desired may be exchanged on any of several peer-to-peer connections by either process; peer-to-peer processes may each

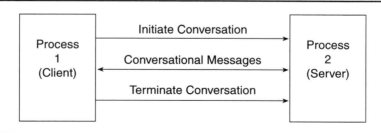

Figure 1.11   Conversational paradigm.

maintain message exchanges with as many other processes as desired. When the peer-to-peer exchange is closed, both processes may continue independently and may initiate another peer-to-peer exchange with each other or with other processes. Both processes can maintain context of their processing after completing a peer-to-peer exchange, and therefore another connection that depends on previous communications can be established.

Figure 1.12 illustrates the peer-to-peer paradigm. Process 1 initiates a peer-to-peer connection with process 2, exchanges messages, and terminates the connection. Both process 1 and process 2 may maintain context of the exchange during and after the connection is broken down. In the illustration, process 2 later initiates a peer-to-peer connection with process 1, exchanges messages, then ends the connection. Again both processes may maintain context during and after the connection is broken down. Note that both process 1 and process 2 could also have open peer-to-peer connections with other processes while exchanging messages with each other.

One product that provides peer-to-peer capabilities is the LU6.2 advanced program-to-program communications (APPC) provided by IBM

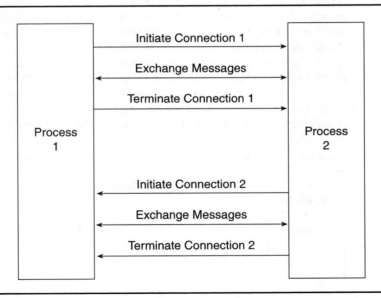

Figure 1.12   The peer-to-peer paradigm.

on many of its platforms. APPC also provides many communication capabilities including conversational and client/server, RPC-like functionality. TUXEDO does not support peer-to-peer functionality.

1.8   TRANSACTION PROCESSING

1.8.1   Definition of a Transaction

Essentially, a *transaction* is any set of operations that must be completed as a unit. A purchase transaction requires that when an item is paid for it is to be delivered. If either part of this transaction is not completed, then the part that has not been completed must be restored to its original state. If the money has not been paid, the item must be returned. If the item is not delivered, then the money must be returned. The essence of transaction processing is assuring that all parts of a transaction complete satisfactorily.

Even after the purchase has been made it is possible that the seller might deliver the wrong goods. If the articles are similar pieces of furniture it might be difficult to tell the difference immediately, but the purchaser will nonetheless be unhappy and the seller must be prepared to correct the situation. Sometimes there are attempted interferences with even simple transactions, like the purchase example. Suppose that after a person has paid for an item the seller also sells it to someone else. There is now a dilemma created because the transaction was not protected from outside sources. In this case the remedy seems simple in that the seller merely has to refund the money to the second purchaser or obtain additional merchandise. In real life things aren't always so simple. Sometimes it even takes complicated legal action to sort out the mess that occurred.

It is expected anytime a purchase is made that the buyer owns the property outright and that the transaction is completed. There are rare cases where the seller attempts to retrieve the article, perhaps by returning the money. There are also cases where the article does not meet the expectations of the buyer, in which case the buyer will attempt to return the article.

The illustration of the purchase transactions and some of the problems that can occur shows why, when transactions are defined, they are defined as exhibiting the *ACID properties*.

The ACID properties are:

Atomicity Each transaction is a complete entity, that is, all the work is either done or not done.

Consistency Any changes to the system which remain at the end of the transaction must be consistent with the rules of processing. Changes made to a database must be consistent with the rules within the database. Consistency implies that every time the same information is processed the result will be the same.

Isolation Changes made by a transaction are not affected by changes made by any other transaction running at the same time. Isolation implies that changes made during the processing of a transaction are not seen by any other transaction until the first transaction commits.

Durability All changes made during a transaction become persistent once the transaction commits. This means that once a transaction commits, changes made to a database must remain until further changes are made by another transaction.

In the purchase example, the completion of the purchase by exchanging money and delivering goods can be called the *atomic* property. That is, the transaction is complete in itself and can be discussed as a single unit. People often say that they have bought a table, for instance. Immediately everyone knows that the transaction was complete as a single unit.

The property of *consistency* says that once the transaction has completed, all expectations have been met. To assure delivery of the proper item, the seller could have immediately tagged the item with the name and address of the purchaser. Transaction processing systems ensure consistency.

Most people expect that the purchase transaction will be *independent*. That is, there will be no interference with the transaction once it has started. The seller in the example must mark the item sold so that no one else will be able to purchase it before it is delivered to the first purchaser and the transaction completed. Transaction processing systems must assure that transactions are independent by preventing changes by other transactions to any information being processed in the current transaction.

Purchase transactions are also expected to be *durable*. Neither the seller nor the buyer initiated the transaction with any other intent than that ownership would move from the seller to the buyer. Transaction processing systems must also assure that changes made during the transaction remain in place until another authorized transaction makes some other change. The purchaser, for instance expects to own the item until they sell it to someone else.

From these examples it is apparent that there is more to a transaction than the simple action of giving money and receiving goods. There is also a set of requirements that if met properly will assure that the transaction has been completed satisfactorily to all. Transaction processing systems work because they enforce these ACID properties.

The ACID properties guarantee *transaction integrity*. If any of the ACID properties are compromised, then there is danger of losing transaction integrity. Once transaction integrity has been lost it is very difficult to return the information in the system to an acceptable condition.

1.8.2   How Transaction Integrity Is Maintained

Computer systems store information in databases. Most information processing is done to update the database. Maintaining transaction integrity within the database is of paramount importance, especially if the application is mission critical. A transaction processing system will maintain transaction integrity by cooperation among the database management system (DBMS), the transaction manager (TM), and the application programs.

The popular example (the ever popular banking example) supposes that there is a single DBMS and one database. Let us suppose that the system maintains banking account records and that there is one table of checking accounts and another table of savings accounts. For this example, suppose that the application programs work properly, updating the database as expected (not always a good assumption!). Suppose also that the database system together with the storage hardware will assure that all changes remain in place. These two assumptions provide the properties of consistency and durability.

The property of atomicity is then assured by marking the beginning of a transaction in some manner, perhaps by storing a flag in memory. The system can then test this flag to determine that a transaction is in process. At the end of the transaction the flag is reset to let other programs know that the transaction has completed. Since there may be more than one transaction in progress at the same time, the flag is associated with some sort of identifier, the transaction identifier. Later chapters will discuss this identifier and show how it can be used to recover lost transactions and how it can be logged for historical purposes.

The property of isolation is maintained by the database when it sets locks that prevent another transaction from updating database elements that have been or will be updated by a transaction still in progress.

For our example, suppose that the transaction is a transfer of funds from a checking account to a savings account. The transfer application program may first ask the database to decrement the checking account balance then ask the database to increment the savings account balance. When the change to the checking account element is requested, the DBMS knows a transaction is starting, so it first locks the checking account element, then updates it. When the request for updating the savings account is received, the DBMS knows it is part of the same transaction, so it locks the savings account element, then updates it also. The transfer application then tells the DBMS that the transaction is complete. The DBMS then performs processing to assure durability, then unlocks the checking account and savings account elements. These mechanisms assure the ACID properties and maintain transaction integrity. Later chapters will include information on just how this mechanism works using TUXEDO and the DBMS.

1.8.3   Transaction Terms

Terms associated with transactions are used throughout this book and must be clearly understood.

> **Abort** Abort, in information processing, means to cease a process and remove all interim affects of the process. If a transaction has updated a database and is then aborted, the database is restored to exactly the state it was before the start of the transaction. Abort is sometimes called *rollback*.
>
> **Commit** Commit is the process by which the effects of a transaction are made permanent. When a DBMS commits, it writes the updated information to disk in the permanent storage area.
>
> **Transaction** A transaction is any group of processes that must complete, including updates to resources, in its entirety or leave no traces of ever having been attempted. A transaction is completed successfully by committing it. A transaction may be aborted. A transaction can have the following states: in-flight, in-doubt, and ended. An in-flight transaction has been started but no attempt has been made to either commit or abort it. An in-doubt transaction is one where an attempt has been made to commit the transaction, but the commit has not yet been completed. An ended transaction is one that has been committed or aborted. An ended transaction is actually not a transaction state, but it is convenient to define the term for discussion purposes.
>
> **Transaction Integrity** Transaction integrity is the term applied when work performed during a transaction was completed or not

completed in accordance with transaction rules. If transaction integrity is lost, then the user can no longer be certain that either all updates are completed or all updates have been rolled back (aborted). In more technical terms, loss of transaction integrity means that the ACID properties have been lost.

2

Enhanced Client/Server Technology

2.1   **ENHANCED CLIENT/SERVER BASICS**

2.1.1   **Characteristics of Enhanced Client/Server Systems**

TUXEDO is an enhanced client/server system and is one of a number of products called *middleware*. Middleware systems fit between the application programs and the database to provide a number of system management enhancements, such as:

- The ability to partition application processing among clients and multiple servers
- The ability to manage distributed transactions
- Improved ability to use heterogeneous database products in the same application system
- Decreasing the effort required to change database vendors

Figure 2.1 illustrates how middleware fits between the application programs and the database.

Enhanced client/server middleware is a new generation of what were previously known as on-line transaction processing (OLTP) systems. The older systems did not support the architecture required for efficient client/server functionality, and many people do not consider these older systems as client/server systems at all. Because of this inherited name of "OLTP" many of the enhanced client/server systems are called OLTP systems. Also, when X/Open created a standard for

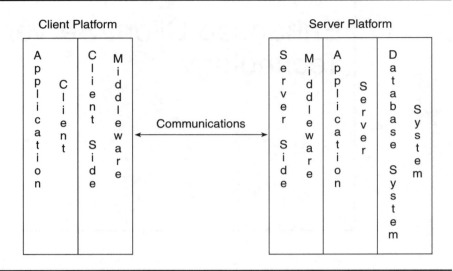

Figure 2.1   Where middleware fits.

what has become known as enhanced client/server middleware, the standard is called an OLTP specification. Most enhanced client/server products are now compliant with the X/Open OLTP specifications.

Enhanced client/server systems are separate from database systems. Therefore, they can be used to manage the client/server environment in the most efficient manner possible. Enhanced client/server systems, cooperating with database products to provide extended capabilities, provide a natural environment where application processes can be modularized into client programs and server programs that can be distributed about the network in an efficient manner.

Figure 2.2 illustrates enhanced client/server functions. In this architecture, clients request services by name. The system then routes the request to the named service. When the service has completed its work, it returns the result to the client by simply using a return function. Neither the client nor the server requires information on the location of the other. The server application programs may reside on any platform in the system, and may be moved administratively for improved efficiency without programming involvement.

On the theory that managing client/server and/or fully distributed resources cannot be easily mingled with database management, vendors have created software that concentrates on managing the client/

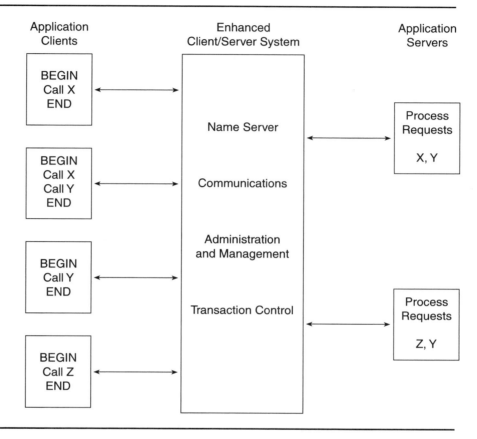

Figure 2.2   Enhanced client/server architecture.

server environment. In general, enhanced client/server software provides the following services:

- Two-phase commit management among many *resource managers* (resource managers are discussed more fully later; for now they can be considered simply as databases)
- Automatic routing of service requests to the appropriate application server
- Routing based on the contents of the message being sent with the request, called *data dependent routing*

- Automatic load balancing among multiple application servers that are assigned the same task
- Rerouting in the case of partial system failure
- Automatic restart of servers when a server fails
- Migrating servers and/or groups of servers to an alternate platform in the case of partial system failure

All of the features can be controlled administratively while the system is running and do not affect the application programming. Enhanced client/server technology allows programming and system design techniques that dramatically reduce the network load and make it much less costly to move data from one server to another or to totally reconfigure the network.

2.1.2   OLTP and Enhanced Client/Server Systems

On-line transaction processing (OLTP) has been used for many years to describe a specific type of computer usage. No real definition has ever been devised, but it is generally agreed that OLTP is characterized by:

- Rapid, interactive interfaces with users
- Support for mission-critical applications
- Transaction-oriented processing
- Support for a large number of users

As OLTP systems were developed to support fully distributed computing on open systems platforms, application developers discovered that these systems did more than provide OLTP capabilities. Managers and developers also discovered that, in fact, all production applications processed transactions! Once these discoveries were made, people using distributed computing found that the modern OLTP system provided something beyond simple client/server and OLTP, hence the designation enhanced client/server.

2.1.3   Typical Platforms

Modern enhanced client/server systems provide support for a wide range of platforms, including use of almost any UNIX-based server and MS-DOS, Microsoft/Windows, X Windows System, OS/2, and UNIX work stations. These systems have been ported in some cases to a number of proprietary platforms such as VMS, but the demand has not been sufficient to keep these ports up to date. In addition, some systems offer connectivity to CICS and IMS on IBM systems and also to other mainframes.

In the past, the work stations have typically been UNIX based, such as SUN SPARC work stations. Relatively recently, Windows and OS/2 work stations are becoming more popular. Primarily because of the inherent flexibility of the systems, more variety will become apparent as enterprises use those platforms that fit their needs.

2.1.4   The Enhanced Client/Server Model

The model described in this section has been considerably simplified and is derived from the model described in the X/Open DTP standard (1991), *Distributed Processing: Reference Model* and *Distributed Transaction Processing: The XA Specification*. Figure 2.3 depicts the X/Open OLTP or, as designated here, enhanced client/server model. The *application program* defines the operations to perform to accomplish the desired results. The application program defines the boundaries of the transaction and issues requests for service to the transaction manager, the communication manager, and one or more resource managers.

The *resource manager* provides services within the transaction as requested by the application program. Typically the resource manager is a database, but it may not always be so. Any updatable resource that must be maintained with transaction integrity must be managed by a resource manager, such as the queue to a money machine. Resource

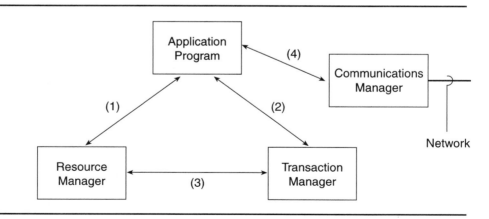

Figure 2.3   The enhanced client/server model.

managers must provide two-phase commit services for the resources they are associated with.

The *transaction manager* provides services that manage transactions, including the two-phase commit among resource managers and the communication manager. If the transaction spans more than one platform, then one transaction manager involved with the transaction will be automatically designated the control transaction manager for the transaction.

The *communication manager* provides the interface to the communication services and manages the application-level protocol. Generally, in client/server situations, the services provided are simply an interface to the data transport mechanism. Most enhanced client/server systems provide some type of conversational services through the communications manager.

This book will refer to this model often, and an understanding of the model is essential to fully understand how to efficiently utilize TUXEDO. The model is supported by interface specifications from X/Open. These interfaces are discussed in Chapter 15.

2.1.5   Available Products

There are three major enhanced client/server products:

- TUXEDO from Novell's TUXEDO System Group
- Encina from Transarc
- TOP END from AT&T Global Information Systems

TUXEDO is the oldest and most mature of the products. TUXEDO began as an in-house TP system within AT&T, and has been developed into a fully mature enhanced client/server and conversational manager.

Encina from Transarc is the newest of the offerings. It was developed based on work by the Computer Science Department at Carnegie Mellon University. Encina uses the distributed computing environment (DCE) developed by the Open Systems Foundation (OSF).

TOP END was developed by NCR (now AT&T Global Information Systems) in the early nineties as its entry into the open OLTP market, but when the design was completed, NCR found it to be a fine enhanced client/server manager. It is currently available principally on NCR UNIX platforms, but is in the process of being ported to other platforms.

CICS/6000 is a robust product, built on top of Encina, from IBM that runs on IBM's AIX operating system. AIX is a POSIX and XPG3 (X/Open operating system specification) compliant, UNIX-type operating system that for the purposes of this book can be considered UNIX, though it is slightly different is some respects. AIX is the operating system used on the RISC System/6000 computer.

There is some debate about whether CICS systems should be called client/server products; in many respects, though, CICS performs many functions required for implementing enhanced client/server systems. CICS/6000 is specifically designed to function in an open system environment with distributed computing capabilities, including a type of enhanced client/server.

2.2   TWO-PHASE COMMIT

2.2.1   Why Two-Phase Commit

Some form of two-phase commit is used by all distributed systems to assure transaction integrity. Details of two-phase commit will be discussed in later chapters as part of the practical application of enhanced client/server using TUXEDO. This summary is provided so that the reader can understand its importance and see how it fits in with the system.

Using our banking example again, suppose that the savings account table is in database A and the checking account table is in database B. Suppose that the application tells database A to commit, then tells database B to commit. There is no difficulty if everything works correctly because both databases will have permanently updated their tables. A problem occurs in the case where database A successfully commits, but database B fails in some manner before completing the commit process. In this case, the transaction would not be properly completed, the ACID properties would be compromised and transaction integrity lost.

Two-phase commit is the accepted solution to the problem of failure during the commit process.

2.2.2   How Two-Phase Commit Works

Figure 2.4 shows the sequence of events during a two-phase commit operation. The commit process begins with a call by the application to commit the transaction. When the transaction manager receives the commit request (assuming that there are no problems), the sequence is as follows:

1. The transaction manager sends a vote request to each resource manager, in this case database 1 and database 2.

2. Database 2 may send its vote first, in this case it votes OK.
3. Database 1 sends an OK vote.
4. When the transaction manager has received votes from all resource managers, it analyzes them and—in this case all are OK—it sends a final commit message to all resource managers.
5. Database 1 and database 2 complete the request process and return a message indicating that the commit was successful.

The transaction manager returns a commit OK message to the application when it is sure that all commits are complete. The most secure time to respond to the application is when the transaction manager has received good responses for a final commit from all resource managers, shown as return point 2 in Figure 2.4.

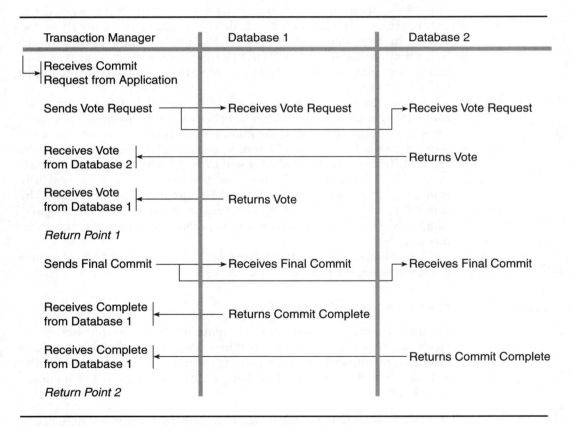

Figure 2.4   Two-phase commit sequence.

For faster response, the transaction manager may return to the application at return point 1, after all votes have been received.

Some important terms are:

- A transaction is *in-flight* until the transaction manager has sent the vote request to all resource managers.
- A transaction is *in-doubt* between the time the transaction manager requests votes and the time it has received responses from all resource managers.
- A transaction is *complete* when the transaction manager has received a final commit completion message from all resource managers, or when it has decided to abort the transaction.
- *Abort*, sometimes called *rollback*, means to remove all effects of the transaction from the resource, usually a database.
- The vote request is sometimes called *prepare*.

Each resource manager will consider the transaction in-doubt after receiving a vote request until it has received either a commit or abort (rollback) request from the transaction manager.

Recovery procedures used after a failure when using two-phase commit are discussed in detail later. The following are important points:

- The transaction manager will send final commit request to the transaction managers only if it receives all OK responses to the vote requests, otherwise it will send abort requests to all resource managers.
- Resource managers are free to abort their portion of the transaction at any time before they receive a vote request.
- Once a resource manager has responded OK to a vote request, it must remain ready to commit or abort the transaction on request from the transaction manager, under any circumstances, including a complete platform failure (after the system has resumed operation).
- If the transaction manager does not receive a response from a resource manager to a vote request, it may assume that the resource manager either has already aborted or will abort the transaction, hence the appellation *presumed abort*. Whenever this book talks about two-phase commit, it means two-phase commit with presumed abort.
- Once the transaction has reached the in doubt state, recovery is guaranteed to either abort or commit the entire transaction, unless a resource manager has unilaterally committed or aborted.

Transaction managers make an option available for the situation where there is a need (particularly in case there is a massive, long-term failure) to complete transactions on individual resource managers. When the recovery procedures are run, the transaction manager will analyze the situation, and will inform the user whether or not transaction integrity has been breached.

Since two-phase commit requires several interactions between the transaction manager and the resource managers, several optimizations are usually provided:

- The transaction manager will not invoke two-phase commit unless more than one resource manager was involved in a transaction, but will instead send a *vote-commit-now* request to the single resource manager, thus using only one interchange to complete the commit.
- A resource manager may have information that no updates were processed by it, and will in this case send an *OK-complete* return to a vote request, thus causing the transaction manager to not send any further messages to the resource manager for this transaction.
- Some transaction managers will send a vote request to all but one of the resource managers, and if all vote OK, it then sends a vote-commit-now request to the remaining resource manager. Depending on the response from that resource manager, the transaction manager will then send either a commit or abort request to the rest of the resource managers. This optimization saves one interchange.

If the transaction manager receives all vote-complete responses, it will send no more messages to the resource managers. It is important to note, though, that if the system designer knows this will always be the case, then the application should not invoke the transaction manager at all for transaction beginning or completion.

It was noted earlier that there are two points where the transaction manager can respond to the application that the transaction has been completed. Return point 1 will always be used if the transaction manager has decided to abort the transaction. If return point 1 is used when the transaction manager will (eventually) commit the transaction, it may improve the performance of the system, but leaves the problem that there could be a system failure before the resource managers have actually committed the transaction. Since the good response to the application will probably cause the application to continue with the assumption that the transaction is fully committed, there are circumstances where the application could get into trouble. Normally this cannot cause a loss of transaction integrity, but could cause a loss of information to the user for recovery purposes.

2.3   **ADVANTAGES OF ENHANCED CLIENT/SERVER SYSTEMS**

TUXEDO and other enhanced client/server systems (often called transaction processing systems) offer a large number of advantages for full enterprise client/server computing. Enhanced client/server systems can:

- Distribute processing, not just data
- Use servers to maximum
- Allow use of heterogeneous databases without major program changes
- Dramatically decrease network traffic
- Allow reconfiguration of a network without requiring application program changes
- Improve scalability to take advantage of more computing power without application program changes
- Interface with relational database management systems in a standardized way
- Allow adding new RDBMS systems with minimal disruption and program changes
- Provide a fully integrated enterprise-wide solution to distributed processing
- Provide departmental and central control and accountability, even when using distributed data
- Work with mixed networks—LANS and WANS—without program changes
- Provide great flexibility when choosing platforms on which to implement applications
- Simplify administration with dynamic application configuration and system tuning

2.4   **DISADVANTAGES OF ENHANCED CLIENT/SERVER SYSTEMS**

It is difficult to find disadvantages to the enhanced client/server system method when it appears to be the optimal solution available today for large client/server systems. Some have perceived the following as disadvantages:

- Currently only a limited number of enhanced 4GL and CASE tools are available for development in the enhanced client/server environment.

- The technology is not well known at this time (though it will become standard soon, with recognition of X/Open distributed transaction processing).
- All current users are very satisfied, but there are not as many users of this enhanced client/server as there are database server users, though more businesses are finding this environment necessary as they gain experience.

3

About TUXEDO

3.1 OVERVIEW

3.1.1 General Discussion

TUXEDO is the result of more than ten years of development, first by Bell Laboratories, and later by UNIX System Laboratories (USL), now Novell, Inc.'s TUXEDO System Group. Initially the system was developed for internal use by AT&T, but later became a part of the UNIX offerings from USL. Release 4, made fully available in 1990, was the first release to offer full distributed transaction management capabilities, allowing reliable update use of databases on several platforms in the same transaction. Release 5 offers a number of important features. TUXEDO adheres to all existing standards, most notably the XA Specification from X/Open. Release 6 offers additional features including expanded security and a GUI administration interface.

3.1.2 TUXEDO as a Development Tool

TUXEDO is actually both a development platform and an execution platform. In many ways, TUXEDO operates as an extension to the operating system. The features provided by TUXEDO also provide functionality, in the nature of a set of development tools that enhance the ability of developers to create high quality systems in less time than it would take to get the same results without TUXEDO.

TUXEDO aids developers in several important areas.

- TUXEDO is a relatively simple to use distributed computing manager.
- TUXEDO is an X/Open compliant transaction manager.
- TUXEDO provides a rich, but simple to use, application programming interface (API) called the application-transaction monitor interface (ATMI).
- TUXEDO provides powerful administration tools that decrease the amount of specific coding required for applications.

TUXEDO provides distributed computing management with the following features.

- Application developers are not required to know the location of servers, their routing, or the types of platform where they reside.
- Application servers can be written to perform required services without regard to the location the server will run or network characteristics and without regard to the source of the invoking request.
- Load balancing and distribution of service requests is completely isolated from developers.
- Application execution can be distributed among many platforms and the configuration can be changed without affecting application programs.

TUXEDO is an X/Open compliant transaction manager. As a result, a distributed system can include multiple databases from multiple vendors (heterogeneous databases). Application programs that interface with the databases use the same interface they would use if the program were not using TUXEDO. Other resource managers may also be used with TUXEDO, such as interfaces to printers, automatic teller machines, and, with the help of other vendors, several file systems other than relational databases.

The TUXEDO ATMI provides a way for the application developer to simply

- Invoke services synchronously and asynchronously
- Start a conversation between a client and a service and continue the conversation as long as necessary
- Send messages to clients without the need to invoke an application service

- Manage transactions in a manner that preserves transaction integrity, including protection against losing transaction integrity because of program failure
- Use C, C++, or COBOL as the programming language for clients and services, intermixing them among clients and servers
- Write application programs that can be used on multiple client platforms where the only coding difference is that required by the user interface

The X/Open XATMI is a large subset of the TUXEDO ATMI, so with a little care, applications developed for TUXEDO are source compatible with other X/Open compliant enhanced client/server products.

TUXEDO administration provides the ability to change the network configuration without changing programs. Administration tools also provide a means to reuse application clients and servers on many platforms with different sets of data via data dependent routing of service requests. For instance, if a database is partitioned among several platforms, the same database access service can be used on all platforms with the location of the appropriate service selected via data dependent routing. TUXEDO administration allows the administrator to define and change many parameters with minimal interruption of service to users.

Some of the important features of TUXEDO administration provide

- The ability to locate services on the platform best suited to the application
- Definition of data dependent routing transparent to the application programs
- Security capabilities that can be modified without changing application programs, though application programs must be initially developed with security capabilities
- Specification of load balancing among servers that can be changed as user needs change
- A means of defining independent administration domains, without limiting access to servers
- A means to specify resource managers that is independent of application programs

Someone has estimated that to develop an application system with the capabilities that TUXEDO provides might require 100 person years, even if a modern relational database product were available. TUXEDO makes development of large distributed computing systems within the reach of any enterprise.

3.1.3 **Features of TUXEDO**

TUXEDO is rich with features important to developing and using enhanced client/server applications. TUXEDO

- Implements the enhanced client/server model.
- Provides a fully distributed processing capability with transparent access to services from clients and other services.
- Provides both RPC and conversational client/server interaction between application processes.
- Provides a simplified application program interface (API).
- Provides dynamic administration control and management of applications.
- Supports distributed computing using standard database interfaces to control two-phase commit.
- Allows specification of application password security and also user provided authentication routines, such as Kerberos.
- Provides administrative control of data dependent routing.
- Includes important development tools for use by C and COBOL programmers.
- Includes interfaces for development of work station and mainframe interfaces.
- Provides automatic translation of messages between clients and services and between services and services to support heterogeneous hardware.
- Supports DCE by way of the X/Open TxRPC specification.
- Supports communication between UNIX and mainframes via the /HOST feature.
- Supports multiple domain communication via the /DOMAIN feature.

TUXEDO also provides special support for work stations with its /WS feature, including:

- Client side API
- Support for UNIX, MS/DOS, MS/Windows and OS/2 work stations
- Provides additional security when accessing TUXEDO from non-secure work stations

TUXEDO provides support for interfacing with mainframes, especially IBM MVS via CICS and IMS. /Host includes:

- Communication between UNIX-based TUXEDO and MVS/CICS
- Transparent data conversion between ASCII and EBCDIC
- Ability to boot and shut down /Host services from the TUXEDO UNIX system
- Ability to route requests to MVS/CICS services and/or UNIX-based TUXEDO services without regard to their location or type of platform
- Provides the same API for TUXEDO application programs to access MVS/CICS servers as it does for other TUXEDO servers

3.1.4   How TUXEDO Works

Applications developed using C, COBOL or a modern 4GL or object-oriented language will all use the same basic approach to using TUXEDO. Client programs are ordinary programs that run in their environment exactly the same as if they were not TUXEDO clients, except that client programs:

- Issue a request to TUXEDO to join or leave a TUXEDO application
- Issue requests for service to TUXEDO application servers
- Have access to a number of useful TUXEDO tools and services, once the program has joined the TUXEDO application
- Can communicate conversationally with servers, as an option
- Client programs may be part of a *client group* that includes a resource manager that participates with other resource managers in the commit controlled by the transaction manager

Client programs may use any of the services offered by the operating system they are running on, except that they may not call the functions **fork()** and **exec()** while joined to TUXEDO. It is not a good idea for a client program to access a database directly.

Service programs are written as subroutines called from TUXEDO. In other words, TUXEDO provides the main line program for servers and calls them upon request. Service programs may use platform services as desired, except that they should never spawn other programs, since service programs are always automatically joined with TUXEDO. Service programs may

- Use interfaces and APIs provided by databases to access database services (including SQL), except they may never use any connect or transaction management provided by the database (this is done by TUXEDO via the standard database interface).
- Invoke other application services as if they were clients.

- Use all TUXEDO services.
- Communicate conversationally with clients and other services.
- Participate in TUXEDO transaction management with other services.

TUXEDO provides a network gateway in such a way that application program communication is transparent. In fact, some servers may be on the same platform as the client or may be remote. Also, it is possible during the life of the application that servers may be moved or that message routing might be administratively changed. All of this is completely transparent to the application program.

Figure 3.1 shows application clients requesting services via TUXEDO from application servers. Each client first issues a BEGIN request

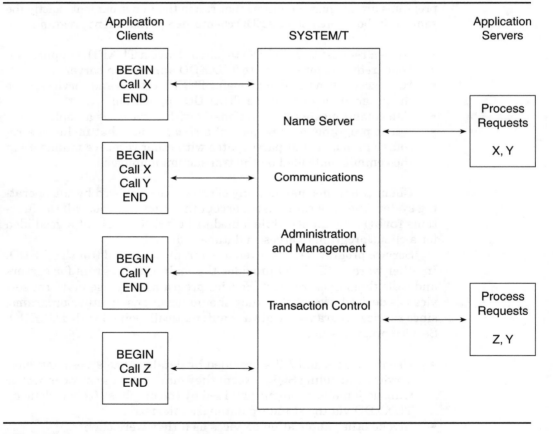

Figure 3.1   High level view of TUXEDO.

to TUXEDO, which signals that the client wants to begin processing a TUXEDO transaction. The client then issues one or more service requests. Using the name of the service, TUXEDO routes the request to the appropriate server.

Figure 3.1 indicates that a service may be provided by more than one server. If so, the application designer may use one of the following options to indicate to TUXEDO which server will provide the requested service.

- Allow TUXEDO to choose the server based on the current system load (load balancing).
- Indicate some value, contained in the service request data, that will be used to determine which server to use (data dependent routing).

The routing options may be changed by the system administrator at any time without affecting either the application clients or service programs.

Within TUXEDO, the name server receives requests for service and determines the proper routing. The communications server will move the request using information provided by the name server. The destination server may be on the same platform as the client (unless the client is on a /WS work station or a /Host platform), or the destination may be anywhere in the network, as long as the destination platform is running TUXEDO.

Transaction control is invoked when the TUXEDO function **tpbegin(3)** is issued. The TUXEDO transaction manager maintains the transaction status until the transaction has been successfully completed or aborted. When the client issues a TUXEDO commit request, **tpcommit(3)**, transaction control assures that all database updates have been reliably completed, via the XA interface with the databases used in the transaction.

TUXEDO administration management supports dynamic and static modification of the system configuration. Administration management can also be invoked if part of the system fails, to attempt to continue functionality of the application (though perhaps at a degraded performance level due to decreased resource availability), or to find and correct the problem.

3.1.5   Clients, Services, Servers, and Server Groups

It has been noted that in general, any program that requests a service from another program is a client and the program that provides the service is a server. TUXEDO modifies this conceptual view of the client/

server relationship, in that TUXEDO applications include programs that may only request services, called *clients* in the TUXEDO nomenclature. The programs that provide the services are called servers, as expected. TUXEDO allows services to request services from other services, thus making it possible for a server to be a client in the general sense. TUXEDO never refers to a server as a client, even though the services it provides may request services from another server.

TUXEDO treats clients differently than servers, and it is important to understand that a TUXEDO client is always only a client to TUXEDO and a server is always a server, no matter what type of processing is occurring.

Figure 3.2 shows the relationship of clients, services, servers, and server groups. A *service* is that part of the *server* that provides a particular named service. A server may provide one or more services. A *server group* is a group of servers, identified to TUXEDO, that use a particular resource manager. Each server group may access zero or one resource manager.

To access the same database from more than one server group, identify the resource manager as associated with each server group. Multiple types of databases (heterogeneous databases) can be used in the same TUXEDO application by establishing multiple server groups.

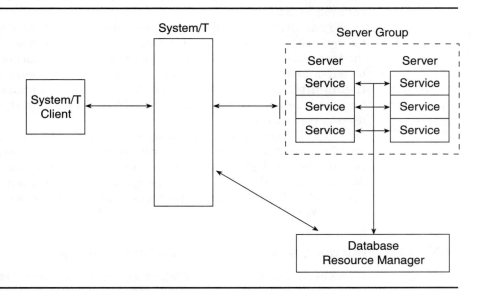

Figure 3.2   Clients, services, servers, and server groups.

All of the servers within a server group must reside on the same platform and the server group must appear to TUXEDO to be on the same platform as the resource manager associated with it. Some databases provide distributed capabilities, so that the actual database may not be on the same platform as the server group. But as long as the database has the provision to provide an interface on the same platform as the server group, TUXEDO will consider the database to be on the same platform.

3.1.6   Modes of Communication

There are multiple modes of communication between clients and services: RPC, conversational, and unsolicited notification.

In RPC mode, the client requests a service and receives a response. This is the only communication allowed between the client and service in RPC mode (except for unsolicited notification, described later).

Conversational mode allows a TUXEDO process (a TUXEDO client of a TUXEDO service) to initiate a conversation with a service designated as conversational. Once the conversation is established, multiple messages may be exchanged without losing the context of either program. Conversations are terminated when either process in the conversation executes a TUXEDO return (**tpreturn(3)**) or commits the transaction (**tpcommit(3)**). TUXEDO clients cannot initiate conversations with other TUXEDO clients.

Unsolicited notification allows a service to send an unsolicited message to a client. The client must be programmed to receive an unsolicited message. The service may use either the **tpnotify(3)** or **tpbroadcast(3)** function to send a message to the client. The client can be notified immediately or when it next invokes a TUXEDO function.

3.2   TUXEDO AND DATABASES

3.2.1   Transactions

X/Open provides a standardized interface between transaction managers and resource managers (resource managers are usually databases) defined in the X/Open document *Distributed Transaction Processing: The XA Specification*, generally known as the XA specification. This specification provides for the communication required between the transaction manager and the database to control transaction integrity. When a transaction is started, a global transaction identifier, called the

XID, is created for the internal use of the transaction manager. Whenever any application server invokes database services, the transaction manager stores that fact along with the XID. When the transaction is terminated, the transaction manager uses the XA specification interface to communicate with the database to properly terminate the database transaction. When the application requests a commit, and more than one server group was involved in the transaction, the transaction manager will use a *presumed abort two-phase commit* protocol (described earlier) to complete the transaction with assured transaction integrity. The transaction manager cooperates with the databases to accomplish the two-phase commit.

When only one server group is involved in a transaction, TUXEDO considers it a *local transaction*. The transaction manager will not use two-phase commit with a local transaction. If more than one server group is involved in a transaction, whether on the same platform or not, TUXEDO will consider it a *distributed transaction* and use the two-phase commit protocol. Generally, a transaction is considered distributed only when more than one platform is involved. In fact, any system must consider a transaction distributed if more than one resource is involved, on the same platform or not. TUXEDO detects this distribution automatically.

3.3   TUXEDO AND WORK STATIONS

3.3.1   The TUXEDO Work Station Product

The TUXEDO work station product (/WS) was described earlier. /WS provides access to all TUXEDO features without loading the work station with the overhead of the full system. It provides a smaller part of TUXEDO so that it can run in an environment with less resources. A number of useful tools for developing end user interfaces are available for /WS, including window system tools.

Figure 3.3 illustrates /WS. Each work station has a gateway that connects via the LAN to the gateway in a UNIX server. Each work station TUXEDO client has access to the full services of TUXEDO as described earlier.

Since /WS costs less per work station than a full system, and smaller work stations cost less than larger ones, using /WS on the work stations can be very cost effective. Fortunately, using work stations on a LAN with /WS provides very good performance, to the point where there is no significant difference from using the entire system on a LAN.

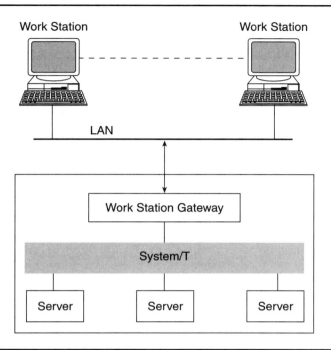

Figure 3.3   /WS architecture.

The /WS feature can be used on a WAN, and in the right circum-stances, can be very effective. /WS should be used directly on the WAN when

- There are few work stations at a remote location.
- Using the local server for a particular application is not cost effective.
- When the system is under test, and it is not desirable to use a local server.
- The work station has sufficient disk space to store the system and the application programs.

The following section will discuss some particulars about using /WS on various types of work stations.

3.3.2   UNIX Work Stations

UNIX work stations can be very powerful because

- They can provide multiple user access to a single work station.
- They provide X/Windows based GUI interfaces.
- They usually are on powerful computers.
- They are capable of running complex user interface calculations, while providing good performance.

/WS provides a solution to providing access for UNIX work stations to a TUXEDO-based application. If the work station is diskless and connected to a LAN-based file server, /WS will work with good performance characteristics, since it does not require a large amount of program reloading. /WS supports multiple users with a multithreaded gateway, and therefore does not load UNIX with multiple processes as more users are added. In some cases, using TUXEDO and /WS will improve performance over other methods because of the decreased number of UNIX processes.

3.3.3   PC Work Stations

/WS supports the following platforms: MS-DOS, MS/Windows, Windows/NT, OS/2, Macintosh, and UNIX. MS-DOS, Windows, and Macintosh usually are single-user work stations. OS/2 is sometimes used to support multiple users on the PC. With Windows and OS/2 single users may start multiple transactions that overlap. /WS provides a multithreaded gateway for these platforms, and thus does not overload the system with overhead. /WS provides support for building GUI applications on these platforms, so that the presentation of information can be very user friendly. Using /WS allows the system designer to assign user display processing to the work station and number crunching to the server, improving control and performance.

3.4   TUXEDO ADMINISTRATION

3.4.1   Introduction to Administration

TUXEDO is administered by manipulating the values in two files: ubbconfig and tuxconfig. ubbconfig is an ASCII file that can be modified with any text editor; tuxconfig is a binary file generated by TUXEDO. tuxconfig can be created (or recreated) in its entirety using ubbconfig as input, or it can be modified directly using TUXEDO interactive administration tools.

TUXEDO is administered and monitored using three methods:

- Off-line modification of ubbconfig with the text editor of choice
- On-line interactive modification of the running system, including shutting down and bringing up new servers and services
- On-line modification of the system configuration

The procedure for creating the initial configuration and making modifications is:

- Create initial ubbconfig and tuxconfig.
- Use the interactive tools to make necessary changes to tuxconfig— in most cases while the system is still running.
- Use a TUXEDO utility to store a backup of the new parameters in ubbconfig.

The items that cannot be changed with the system running are those that could affect an in-flight transaction. In many cases, these changes can still be made on-line by first shutting down the part of the system that will be affected. For instance, new servers and new services can be added at any time, but servers and their services cannot be removed without first shutting down the affected servers.

3.4.2   **Administration Tools**

3.4.2.1 Off-Line Tools.   Off-line modification is completed using the following steps:

- Modify ubbconfig with a text editor
- Create a tuxconfig binary version using the utility **tmloadcf(1)**
- Reboot TUXEDO to apply the changes

Usually this method is used to configure the system initially and to make major changes to the configuration. The interactive utilities described later will be used to make changes with the system running.

The following utilities are used to manage other aspects:

- **tmunloadcf(1)** reads the binary configuration file, tuxconfig, and creates ubbconfig
- **tmboot(1)** boots TUXEDO
- **tmshutdown(1)** shuts TUXEDO down

3.4.2.2 Monitoring the System and Modifying Service Availability.
The utility **tmadmin(1)** provides interactive services on a running system, including:

- Information on available servers, including their configuration
- Examining a number of statistics such as:
  - Number of requests outstanding on a server
  - Rate of service requests
  - Number of transactions completed
  - The status of service queues
- Moving servers from one platform to another
- Starting new servers and making their services available
- Moving all services from one platform to another in a block
- Shutting down individual servers or all servers on a platform

Changes made by **tmadmin(1)** become effective as soon as they are completed, but are not permanent; that is, they will not be in effect on the next system start after the system is shut down. **tmadmin(1)** is also useful for finding and correcting problems. It is especially useful if a portion of the network fails, since it can be used to find the failed part of the system and replace it with a backup system without taking the entire system down.

3.4.2.3 Changing the System Configuration On-Line.
TUXEDO provides the utility **tmconfig(1)** to examine and modify the system configuration file interactively while the system is running. Changes made by **tmconfig(1)** are permanent, because **tmconfig(1)** directly modifies the binary version of the configuration in the binary configuration file.

All elements of the system configuration can be examined with **tmconfig(1)**. Changes that can be added or modified while the system is running include:

- Modifying network addresses
- Adding certain elements of the server or services configuration, such as copies of servers and changing priorities
- Adding new entries to the configuration to make the addition of servers and services permanent
- Adding new platforms and all related configuration entries

Changes made using **tmconfig(1)** become effective the next time the system is started.

3.4.3   ### An Administration Example

Suppose that a new platform is to be added to an existing system to provide additional capacity and the user does not want to shut the system down to provide the new capacity. The following steps accomplish the desired results.

1. Examine the running system with **tmadmin(1)** to be sure that the system is currently executing as expected.
2. Examine the current configuration using **tmconfig(1)** to be sure that the configuration is set as expected.
3. Add the proper configuration for the new platform, including limitations of the servers so that they do not affect the running system.
4. Boot the new platform using the **tmboot(1)** option that boots only the desired platform without affecting the running system.
5. Run a test of the new platform to be sure that it is on-line properly.
6. Use **tmadmin(1)** to make the new servers available.
7. Use **tmconfig(1)** to modify the configuration to set tuxconfig so that the next system start will make the new servers generally available.
8. Run **tmunloadcf(1)** to create a new ubbconfig for backup.

After these procedures are completed, users will have access to services on the new platform and the system configuration will be backed up for future use, if required. The additional capacity will increase the performance, while system activity was not affected during the process of adding the new platform.

3.5   ### USING TUXEDO WITH A MAINFRAME

TUXEDO provides a generalized gateway called /HOST designed specifically to allow use of interfaces with any other transaction management system, including any required data conversion such as between ASCII and EBCDIC. Using /HOST, a user need only create a gateway for the desired system, allowing TUXEDO to access and use servers that are running on the proprietary platforms in the same manner as if they were on a UNIX platform. Servers provided by /HOST are available transparently to all TUXEDO clients and administered from TUXEDO in the same manner as any other servers.

One vendor, Information Management Company, currently provides *Open Transport for MVS*, which provides full TUXEDO connectivity with MVS platforms using IMS/DC and CICS. The IMS/DC version of *Open*

Transport for MVS routes the transaction to MVS via TCP/IP and places in the IMS/DC transaction queue. Only one *Open Transport for MVS* is required in the network, and any number of UNIX platforms and their counterpart MVS servers may be configured by the customer to meet access and performance requirements. The CICS version operates in a similar manner.

Using gateways such as *Open Transport for MVS* allow the TUXEDO user to access and modify DB2, IMS/DB, VSAM, or other databases stored on MVS platforms while maintaining full transaction integrity and server management capabilities provided by TUXEDO.

3.6   THE DATA ENTRY SYSTEM

TUXEDO provides a feature called the Data Entry System (DES), which is a tool used to quickly define character-oriented terminal presentations. DES includes a TUXEDO provided client called **mio(1)** (**wmio(1)** for /WS work stations) and a screen definition facility. It is possible to create screens quickly, including limited editing on fields where TUXEDO services are invoked based on input data content. DES and **mio(1)** are used very little since the advent of powerful GUI development tools and are not discussed further in this book. Full information on DES is contained in the *TUXEDO Data Entry System Guide*. **mio(1)** is described in the *TUXEDO Reference Manual*.

3.7   TUXEDO TERMS

The following terms are used in this book when referring to TUXEDO.

BBL The name given to the TUXEDO administration service that manages the TUXEDO bulletin board. Sometimes the bulletin board itself is called the BBL. The bulletin board stores the TUXEDO configuration and certain dynamic information while a domain is running. Every TUXEDO node has a bulletin board and a BBL.

DBBL The distinguished bulletin board server that runs on the MASTER platform. The DBBL is responsible for everything the BBL handles; the DBBL also runs the heartbeat of the system to check for system partitioning and other failures. All administrative activity must take place on the MASTER platform using the DBBL. If changes are made to the bulletin board on the master using TUXEDO dynamic administration tools, the DBBL propagates the changes to all BBLs in the domain.

domain A TUXEDO instance that may have many nodes. What makes it a domain is that it is a single administrative entity, supported by one configuration definition. TUXEDO documentation has traditionally called a domain an *application*. In this book the word application will apply to the set of processes that define user functionality. The word application used in TUXEDO documentation is used to mean domain.

MASTER platform Where the active DBBL resides. TUXEDO allows definition of a backup MASTER. If the platform running as MASTER fails, the backup will automatically assume the function of MASTER. The administrator can use TUXEDO administration tools to switch masters at any time.

native client A TUXEDO client that runs on the same platform where a full TUXEDO node also resides. Since TUXEDO usually is built on UNIX, a native client is usually a UNIX program. Discussions in this book assume that a native client is running on a UNIX platform with a full TUXEDO node. Note that a client running on a UNIX platform that is connected to TUXEDO via the /WS feature is not a native client.

node In this book is used in its traditional sense, with the added concept that in some types of multiprocessor computers, each processor may be treated as a node. The terms node, platform, and machine are used interchangeably when discussing TUXEDO configurations.

platform A local computing environment, consisting of hardware and the operating system software. If a computer runs more than one operating system at the same time, each operating system is a platform.

Universal Device List (UDL) Stores the location of transaction logs and queues.

TUXEDO and Databases

4.1 OVERVIEW

The enhanced client/server model was discussed in a previous chapter where it was noted that the resource manager (RM) is not necessarily a database. The principles of using XA-compliant RMs are the same whether the RM is an automatic teller machine, a flat file, or a database, so the information in this chapter is applicable in principle to any RM. This chapter will concentrate on the details of using a relational database RM within the model and specifically how to use databases with TUXEDO. In Figure 4.1 the database is specifically involved in the SQL and XA interfaces.

Application programs use SQL data manipulation language (DML) statements in the same way for TUXEDO as any program would, except that transactional statements like COMMIT WORK and ROLLBACK WORK may not be used when running under control of the XA interface. Applications running within TUXEDO should not use data definition language (DDL) statements, although they are allowed. Data control language (DCL) statements like GRANT and REVOKE should never be used within any client/server application programs. The XA interface provides a means for the transaction manager (TM) and the resource manager (RM), or in particular, the relational database management system (RDBMS) to cooperate in transactional activities.

The TX interface is defined in the X/Open document *Distributed Transaction Processing: The TX (Transaction Demarcation) Specifica-*

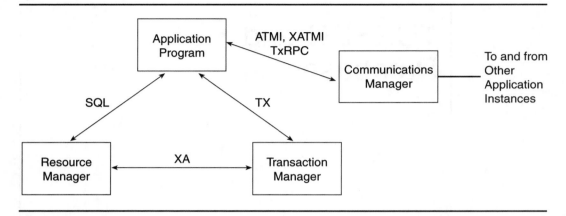

Figure 4.1 The enhanced client/server model.

tion. TUXEDO provides several means of establishing transaction demarcation, including the TX interface.

4.2 THE XA INTERFACE

4.2.1 About XA

The XA interface (XA in Figure 4.1) is the line of communication between RMs and TMs. TUXEDO servers and clients can be created with or without an XA interface. When a client or service uses a database attached to a TM, it is said that client or service is running in XA, otherwise it is said that the program is running in non-XA. All services in a server created with XA run XA; all services in a server created non-XA run non-XA.

The application designer decides where to use XA. The administrator needs to know where XA is used in order to properly describe servers, groups and clients to the system. The application programmer may need to know where the designer has defined use of XA in order to properly create server and client initialization routines and what type of transaction boundary functions to include in services and clients. The details of these procedures are described in later chapters.

When a client or service runs XA it must run in transaction mode to get the benefits of XA. The difference between running XA and non-XA is shown in Table 4.1.

Table 4.1   XA and Non-XA Functionality

Functionality	Running XA	Running non-XA
Coordinated commit among two or more services	Provided	Not provided
Coordinated commit between client and service	Provided	Not provided
Application program can use SQL transactional statements	Cannot use	Must use
Can start and end a transaction	Yes	Yes

Figure 4.2 illustrates the relationship between XA and non-XA services when invoked by a client. The client shown is non-XA, but can start and end a transaction. The sequence within the client is:

1. Start a transaction
2. Invoke XA service 1
3. Invoke non-XA service 3

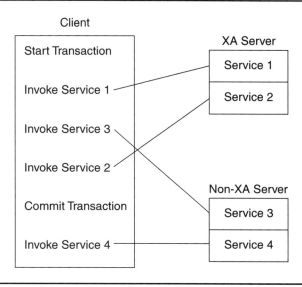

Figure 4.2   XA and non-XA within a transaction.

> **4.** Invoke XA service 2
> **5.** Commit the transaction
> **6.** Invoke non-XA service 4

When the transaction is committed, the commit of updates done by service 1 and service 2 are coordinated. Service 3, although it was executed within the scope of the transaction, is not included in the transaction commit. Service 4 was invoked outside of any transaction. Even if both service 3 and service 4 were invoked from the client while in transaction mode, any updates they might have done would not be included in the transaction commit.

4.2.2   How XA Works

There is no need for those involved in application implementation to know more about the XA interface than the functionality it provides. This information is provided so that both the developer and the administrator will have a more solid foundation.

What follows is a high level overview about how the XA works. More details are provided in the X/Open document *Distributed Transaction Processing: The XA Specification.*

The XA interface consists of a set of function calls, ten provided by the RM and two provided by the TM. The functions provided by the TM allow the RM to communicate its presence or to tell the TM that it, the RM, is no longer available. The functions provided by the RM are used by the TM to communicate transactional and recovery requests to the RM.

Some functions provided by the RM allow the TM to request the RM to

- Vote on transaction commit, that is, to prepare to commit
- Commit work done on behalf of a transaction
- Rollback work done on behalf of a transaction
- Get a list of transactions that the RM has prepared but not yet committed
- Forget transactions that were committed or aborted heuristically, that is, outside of TM control

Other functions are used to keep the RM and TM synchronized on transaction identifiers (XIDs) and status.

An RM is made available to work with TUXEDO by creating a TM service using the TUXEDO utility **buildtms(1)**. This build creates a TM server and service using libraries provided with TUXEDO and libraries provided by the RM vendor. This build attaches the RM provided functions to the TM. Instructions from the RM vendor are followed to link the TUXEDO TM functions with the RM. More details on building the TM are included in Chapter 10.

4.2.3   When XA Is Required

When a client and one or more services or multiple services modify the database, all modifications must be done within an XA global transaction to coordinate the commit. All services that require commit coordination must be XA services. Modifications done by a client that require commit coordination must be done by an XA resource manager and must be done within the transaction.

The database software, when running outside XA, holds the scope of a transaction to a single process, so the database software cannot coordinate global transactions when multiple programs modify the database. As discussed later, it is a bad idea to plan on committing a transaction in a service with the hope that the procedure will properly commit updates done in another service, even when that service is in the same server.

4.2.4   Sequence of Events in a Transaction

Figure 4.3 illustrates the sequence of events during a transaction. The client calls **tx_begin(3)**, which communicates with the transaction manager to start a transaction. The transaction manager returns the global transaction identifier, called the XID, where **tx_begin(3)** stores it for use by TUXEDO. When the client invokes service 1 and service 2, TUXEDO includes the XID in the TUXEDO message header. Service 1 calls the database resource manager to modify the database. XA functions provided by the database vendor pass the XID to the database resource manager each time the database is invoked. The first time the database is invoked, it establishes its own internal transaction and associates the XID with its internal transaction identifier. Each time the database is invoked after the first time it will associate the work with the same transaction by using the XID.

When the client has completed its processing, it calls **tx_commit(3)** to commit the transaction. **tx_commit(3)** sends a message to the transaction manager to commit the transaction, including the XID in the message. The transaction manager communicates with the database resource manager to coordinate the commit. When the commit is successfully completed, the result is returned to the client.

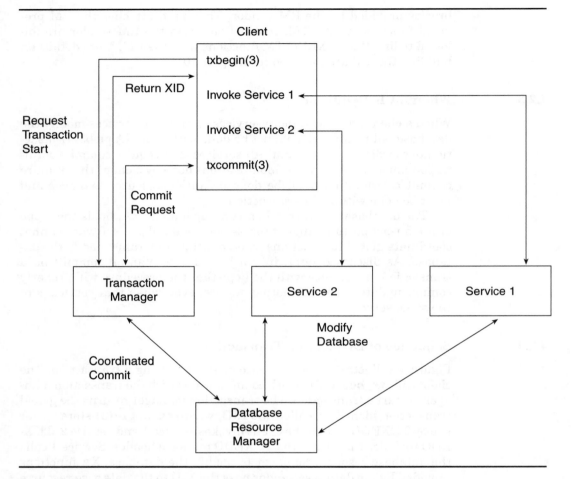

Figure 4.3 Sequence of events during a transaction.

4.3 USING SQL IN TUXEDO APPLICATION PROGRAMS

4.3.1 General Points

Data manipulation language (DML) statements may be used exactly as they would be used in any program except for transactional statements such as COMMIT and ROLLBACK. Transactional statements and those statements that open and create a connection to the database have special rules, described a little later in this section.

SQL functionality can be categorized as follows with any database:

- Opening and closing the database (CONNECT and DISCONNECT)
- Connecting to and disconnecting from the database
- Accessing the database with DML (UPDATE, INSERT, DELETE, SELECT, FETCH)
- Transaction management (COMMIT, ROLLBACK)
- Defining the database and its tables with DDL (CREATE, DROP)
- Managing database security with DCL

XA servers connect to the database during boot time using initialization programs written for the specific application. Servers disconnect from the database using shutdown procedures written for the application. The administrator provides information, called the OPENINFO, in the TUXEDO configuration file. OPENINFO is used by the TUXEDO function **tpopen(3)** to open the database. Likewise CLOSEINFO is provided in the configuration file and is used by the TUXEDO function **tpclose(3)** to disconnect from the database. The content of these strings is defined by the database vendor. Most vendors require an open string but not a close string.

4.3.2   Using SQL in Services

SQL is coded in TUXEDO services the same way it would be in any other environment. All DML statements may be used, including stored procedures. The following special rules apply.

- If the service is used in request/response invocations (via ATMI), all cursors must be closed before exiting the service.
- If the service is used conversationally, cursors may remain open during the conversation, but all cursors must be closed before exiting the service.
- If the service is an XA service, transactional statements are not allowed.
- If the service is a non-XA service, transactional statements must be used to commit or rollback any work done.
- If a non-XA service sets any read locks during execution, they must be released before the service returns. An XA service may set read locks. These locks will be held until the transaction is ended by the transaction manager or released by the service that set them.

When a request/response service is invoked, all application context is lost when the service returns its response. Databases typically retain their own context for each process to which they are attached, thus if a cursor is left open when the service returns, it will remain open. The next time the service is invoked, it will again open its cursors, adding to the number of open cursors. At some point the maximum number of cursors will be reached and the database will cease to function. There is no reasonable way to prevent the service from opening new cursors since all context is lost when a service returns. Even if context is maintained in a memory, there is no way to guarantee that the next invocation of the service will execute the same instance. More importantly, it is highly likely that the next request to the service will not be from the same source. A section that suggests some methods of retrieving larger found sets with request/response services follows later in this chapter. A conversational service may hold a cursor open during a conversation. All cursors must be closed before terminating the conversation. In any case, the service must close the cursor before exiting.

If the service is an XA service, COMMIT and ROLLBACK statements may execute without error, although some databases will return an error in this situation. Whether the database returns an error or not, the result of issuing a transactional SQL statement in an XA service will create an unknown situation. In general, there is no way to predetermine what the database will do with this type of program failure. If more information is required on this point, the documentation for the specific database should be consulted.

Databases consider the scope of a non-XA transaction as including all SQL statements issued from the same operating system process since the last transactional statement. A TUXEDO server is a single operating system process. If several services residing in the same server issue SQL statements before one of them issues a transactional statement, all of those SQL statements will be treated by the database as a single transaction. This can lead to confusion if various services in the same server have been invoked as part of separate logical transactions. For this reason it is a hard and fast rule that non-XA services that modify the database must issue a COMMIT or ROLLBACK statement before returning.

Read locks are sometimes used to hold the database rows anticipating update. It is not a good idea to set read locks within TUXEDO services. There may be times when it is essential to hold the data for update or some other purpose, but in that case the following points must be noted:

- Read locks are held for a non-XA service for the process, that is, for the server (see the discussion on cursors above). All read locks set by a non-XA service must be released before the service returns.

- Read locks set within an XA service can be released by the service before returning. If they are not released by the service, they will be held until the global transaction is ended by the transaction manager. In some cases this could be a long time in terms of on-line computing, leading to severely decreased performance or even system lockup.

Some suggestions for how to maintain data consistency while browsing for update are given later in this chapter.

4.3.3 Using SQL in Clients

There are two types of clients: work station clients and native clients. Work station clients run on a separate platform from the TUXEDO system, often on an operating system such as Windows or OS/2. Work station clients are connected (when they join the system) to TUXEDO via a network and a special listener on the platform where TUXEDO resides. Native clients run on the same platform as the TUXEDO system and are connected directly to TUXEDO when they join the system.

SQL can be used in both types of clients, but there are different considerations for both. Native clients can use SQL within a global transaction while work station clients cannot. Native clients have access to the same databases as the services on the particular platform, while work station clients have access to only those databases that may reside on the work station.

Using SQL within a client outside of global transactions is done the same as for any stand-alone program. All features of SQL are available. The important point is that any updates made in this mode will not be coordinated with updates made in any service.

Additional details about how to use an XA resource manager with a TUXEDO client are discussed in Chapter 8.

4.4 DATABASE PARTITIONING

4.4.1 Definition

It is often necessary to spread the data in a logical relational table over several physical tables. The physical tables may be placed in the same or different database instance, located on different platforms. They may even use database products from different vendors. The resulting table is called a *partitioned table*. There are two types of partitioning.

Vertical partitioning: Related columns are defined in separate tables, which must then be joined via a common column to retrieve rows of the logical table.

Horizontal partitioning: Data is placed in separate identically defined tables based on the actual values in specified columns. Individual rows can be retrieved by choosing the table based on data content.

Often a table is horizontally partitioned so that the information is locally available. Local retrieval is important when a particular location handles information based on some type of specific criteria, such as servicing customers from a specific geographical area.

A number of problems are introduced by either type of partitioning, and there are various solutions for each problem. This section addresses the problem of maintaining unique keys in a horizontally partitioned database.

The following sections contain a short review of two methods of assigning unique identifiers in the distributed environment. The implications to system design are only touched on. Each enterprise must examine how best to accomplish required results.

4.4.2   The Problem

Suppose a customer database is partitioned such that certain zip codes are placed in physical tables in local offices in multiple locations. The network might look something like Figure 4.4. Suppose further that the Dallas office wants to add a new customer. It would certainly be possible to allow Dallas to assign a locally unique customer identifier without regard to identifiers assigned in other locations. It is also possible to imagine that there might be a way to still maintain a central replication of all the customer databases from the various offices, though getting approval for such a scheme might be difficult. A serious problem occurs if the customer is transferred to another office. Consider what might happen if another office is established and the customers are realigned among the offices. Unless some method has been used to assure that the customer identifier is unique in the enterprise, it is certain that there would be a chaotic set of duplicate identifiers.

4.4.3   Partitioning Requirements

Any solution to the problem must meet the following requirements:

- The customer identifier must remain unique even if the customer is assigned to another location.

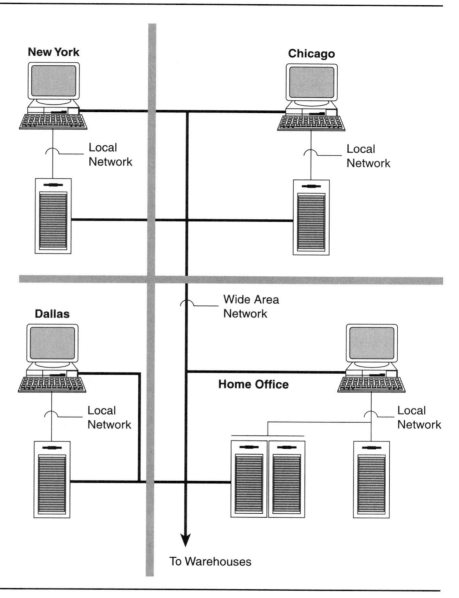

Figure 4.4   A distributed system.

- The identifier will remain unique as long as the customer is on file.
- Assignment of the identifier must be fully automatic and must be done without involvement of the end user. The algorithm used to assign the number may use information entered by the user to establish the customer.
- Impact on system and network performance must be minimal.
- Any data storage used to assure uniqueness must be included in failover mechanisms.
- The uniqueness must be assured. That is, there must be no possibility of inadvertently assigning duplicate IDs. This point is especially important when many requests for new customer IDs may be made in a short time period.

4.4.4   Partitioning Method One: Central Next Identifier

To use this partitioning method:

- Establish a central location where the last or next customer ID number is stored.
- The customer ID is a simple number with no structure.
- Use a standard table in the database to store the number.
- Include a location code in the customer master and denormalize the location code to include it in all related tables.

If the customer number is stored as an unsigned long, it will support up to 4 billion numbers. Even if there are already 10 million customers and new customers are established at the rate of 10,000 per week, there will be enough numbers for the next 7,600 years.

Using this procedure, the service that establishes new customers will invoke a service at a central location that will create the new number and return it. The new number service will run as a separate transaction, and there will be only one such service in the system, so that during the time it is running, there will be no possibility of duplication.

The location code is used to partition the database. It is a good idea to denormalize the location code and include it in all related tables.

The primary advantage of this system is that it is very simple and very sure. A second advantage is that this method provides an identifier that is independent of the enterprise organization and office location. The additional load on the network should be minimal because of the small amount of data required to support this method. The disadvantage is performance degradation if the number assignment becomes a "hot spot," causing backup of new number assignment requests.

Some databases provide a feature that can be used to assign the number instead of using the standard one-column one-row table. Use of this database feature makes it more difficult to change database vendors. Also, there is less control over how the number is managed. There is no performance comparison information between using the database feature or the application assignment method.

4.4.5   Partitioning Method Two: A Structured Identifier

This partitioning method uses a structured identifier as follows:

- The customer identifier has at least two parts: the location creating the new identifier and a generated sequential number. Additional structure can be used as required.
- The identifier is assigned locally at the place where the new customer is being established.
- Once established, the identifier is never changed, even if the customer is transferred.
- Include a current location code in the customer master.

The current location code is used for partitioning the database, and can be denormalized for performance. The location code embedded in the customer number will continue to indicate the location which originally established the customer.

This is the method used for assigning social security numbers.

This method has the advantage of having high performance characteristics, but has the disadvantage of additional complexity. It works only if the location code in the customer number is never changed.

4.4.6   Comparing the Methods

Both methods work well. Method one provides a means of using a centralized, simple unstructured number for an identifier and alleviates the danger of using parts of the identifier for unintended purposes. Method two has the advantage of performance, but introduces complexity. The complexity can be minimized by hiding the structure from the end user.

4.4.7   Retrieving Data from a Partitioned Database

The simplest method for retrieving data from a partitioned database is to request that the user include the location in all requests for data retrieval. If the user wants to retrieve information on all people from all partitions with the last name Hall, the user makes a separate entry for every possible location. This method works satisfactorily if there are only a few locations. If the inconvenience of this method is more than the user can handle, then use the following method.

To search all partitions, the client can accept an indication of "all" from the user. The client then creates a request for service for all known locations. If the client invokes the search service with TUXEDO asynchronous service invocation (**tpacall(3)**), all partitions will be searched simultaneously. The client can depend on the data dependent routing set by the administrator to cause invocation of the correct services.

4.5   SEARCHING THE DATABASE

An online interactive system requires fast response. Fast response can be prevented by inappropriate database searching. Database searches tend to use a large amount of computing resources, including both disk access and CPU time. The performance of transaction A can be severely affected when transaction B starts a long search. Some rules that help prevent problems are:

- Always search on a key.
- Limit the number of rows retrieved by a cursor.
- Use ORDER BY sparingly.
- Use joins rarely, and never use a join that requires tables from two different platforms.
- Be careful not to start a full table search inadvertently by using wild cards that cause the database to ignore the index.
- Remember that an UPDATE ... WHERE ... requires a search, and use it according to the previously stated rules.
- Avoid using FOR UPDATE OF with cursors. Every row retrieved by FETCH is locked when retrieved and the lock is held until the end of the transaction, preventing use by other transactions, even if the row has not been updated.

The system designer and the database designer should work carefully as a team to make sure the rules can be followed and still meet the functional requirements for the system. But, even with the best designs, some specific functional requirements cannot be met so easily. The most common problems are caused by the need to manage large blocks of data retrieved from the database. The two most common cases are the requirement to browse areas of the database and batch-type processing where the entire database must be scanned. The following sections discuss some techniques to help minimize problems of performance when these requirements must be met.

4.6   BROWSING THE DATABASE WITH CONVERSATIONAL SERVICES

The simplest way to browse a database is to start a conversation between the client and the retrieval service, retrieve rows until done, then end the conversation. There is some controversy about this method because both database and computing resources are held as long as the conversation lasts, which can be a long time if the user goes to lunch without closing the conversation. The controversy is about the size and impact of resources held by a conversation and the effectiveness of time-out procedures. Certainly if a large number of users are in long conversations, overall performance of the system will deteriorate. If the conversational client is a native client (that is, it is running on the same system where TUXEDO is installed), it can also place a load on the operating system, but that load would be there just because the client is in use, not because it is using the conversational paradigm.

The facts are:

* Most enterprises use work station clients, removing the client load from the TUXEDO platform.
* A server can support only one conversation at a time. If multiple conversations are allowed in the system for the same service, multiple instances of the server must be provided by the administrator. This situation can throttle down the number of simultaneous conversations to a manageable level.
* No locks are held by an open cursor unless the cursor is defined with FOR UPDATE TO.
* TUXEDO provides a means of timing out an idle client.

In many cases, browsing with the conversational paradigm will operate very well, and is recommended, unless it is likely that a relatively large number of users will be using the conversational transaction at the same time.

To browse using a conversational server:

1. The client sends the key for selecting a set of data in the message that connects with the service.
2. The service opens a cursor on the database using the key sent by the client.

3. The service retrieves a number of rows (agreed upon between the client and server) and sends the information back to the client.
4. The client sends a message to the service for the next set of data.
5. The process repeats until the client indicates to the service that the conversation is complete, the service uses the TUXEDO service completion function (**tpreturn(3)**) to close the conversation and return a final message to the client.

The service should not use a stored procedure to retrieve data, because stored procedures close cursors when they return, so context is lost.

4.7 BROWSING WITH REQUEST/RESPONSE SERVICES

4.7.1 Overview of the Techniques

The following paragraphs describe methods for obtaining and browsing large found sets using TUXEDO services when the amount of data exceeds the capacity of a single message. The responsibilities of the client using these services are to

- Save the context information returned with each "chunk" of data.
- Return the context information with each request for the next chunk.
- Supply information to the service about the maximum amount of information that should be returned as a chunk.

The client should supply the amount of data to return with each request for a chunk, and the service should return that amount of data.

There is one major "don't" about managing large amounts of data: *Don't attempt to retrieve all the data and store it in the work station.* Attempting to load all the data onto the work station at the beginning of the browse will require using the chunk retrieving method to obtain all the data, thus using up the same amount of system resources as if each individual chunk was displayed—before anything has ever been displayed.

Often expressed as "unlimited number of rows returned," the issue of browsing a database is the most perplexing of all interactive processing issues. When a service generates more data than can be returned in one reasonably sized message, usually because there are a large number of rows in the found set from a query, and using a conversational paradigm is not practical for the application, it is very difficult to find ways to satisfy the need for the user to brows the database.

There is no good solution to this problem, only a set of compromises, each with its own problems. The methods provided here have stood the test of time and seem to work as well as possible. The deficiencies of these methods are

- Loss of consistency, that is, the data that has already been retrieved may be updated immediately after retrieval by some other transaction. A method for overcoming this problem is suggested later in this chapter.
- Performance will not be super fast, because of the amount of data being retrieved and passed, but no method can overcome the problem of handling large amounts of data.

4.7.2   Method One: Advancing through Existing Keys

To use this method, the database must contain an indexed column defined unique, where the order of the values in the key is the order required by the request. To do this:

- The client invokes the GetAChunk service, passing the information used to select the data.
- The retrieved data is returned to the client along with the fact that there is more. The returned message should contain a count of some sort, such as the number of rows returned and the total number of rows available from the database.
- To retrieve the next block of data, the client invokes the service with the "get me the next row" indicator set, along with the highest key retrieved the previous time, and the key used to retrieve the data.
- The service uses the highest key retrieved the last time to request the next chunk from the database.

4.7.3   Method Two: The Snapshot Approach

In this method, the application services populate a temporary file or database table and retrieve data from it for return to the client. Assume that the following SQL describes what the application really wants to do is select all rows that meet the request requirements as if a cursor with the following SELECT was used:

```
SELECT CUSTNO, NAME, ADDRESS
FROM NAMETBL
WHERE NAME >= :LINAME
      AND NAME <= :HNAME
ORDER BY NAME;
```

Two application services will be used: GetFirstChunk and GetNextChunk.

The following discussion assumes that the data will be stored in a temporary UNIX file. The problem with using a UNIX file is that it is accessible only from the machine that wrote it (NFS should not be used in this situation). Data dependent routing can overcome the problem of location by always directing invocations of the GetFirstChunk and GetNextChunk from specific client locations to the same service location.

4.7.3.1 The GetFirstChunk Service.

The GetFirstChunk service will create a temporary file and populate it. The temporary file path and name is retrieved using the UNIX **tmpnam()**. Each record in the temporary file contains the following information:

- The value of a counter, **tmpseq**, which is actually only a record counter to assure accuracy of processing
- The data from a row in the database
- Any application-specific information required

Records in the temporary file must be fixed length for simplicity. This requirement implies that VARCHAR fields will be store in fixed length areas within records of the temporary file.

GetFirstChunk uses the form like the following SELECT in a cursor to retrieve the data:

```
SELECT CUSTNO, NAME, ADDRESS
    FROM NAMETBL
    WHERE NAME >= :LNAME
        AND NAME <= :HNAME
    ORDER BY NAME;
```

This SQL statement retrieves all the rows from the NAMETBL that are between the strings stored in LNAME and HNAME.

As each row is fetched, GetFirstChunk increments the variable **tmpseq** and writes a record to the temporary file. When the entire found set has been read, the temporary file contains the set of desired rows in sequence set up by the ORDER BY. When GetFirstChunk is finished, it uses the TUXEDO forwarding feature (**tpforward(3)**) to pass the processing to GetNextChunk, including the full path file name of the temporary file, a 0 as the last sequence number and the final value of **tmpseq**, and the original request in the message passed to GetNextChunk.

4.7.3.2 The GetNextChunk Service. GetNextChunk is an application service that will receive the last sequence number, the name of the temporary file, and the number of rows to return in its service request. Processing proceeds as follows:

1. Open the temporary file.
2. Set the file location with the C function call:

```
lseek(fd, startseq * sizeof(struct tempfile), SEEK_SET)
```

3. In a loop, read information from the temporary file and retrieve the data until the requested number of rows is retrieved.
4. Return the information.

startseq is the starting sequence number received from the invoker.

Information returned to the client includes:

- A block of information of the size requested
- The last temporary file sequence number
- The full path name of the temporary file

4.7.3.3 How the Client Uses the Browsing Services. The client invokes GetFirstChunk to start the process and retrieve the first chunk of information. After that the client will invoke GetNextChunk until the browse process is complete. When the client is finished, it will invoke an application service to clean up after the transaction. The application cleanup service might be called AppCleanUp.

When the client invokes GetFirstChunk, it provides only the application-dependent information required to define the information to retrieve. The response from GetFirstChunk includes the initial block of requested data and information needed to browse using GetNextChunk. When using GetNextChunk and AppCleanUp, the client must provide the following context information:

- The full path name of the temporary file (returned by the invocation of GetFirstChunk)
- The last temporary file sequence number (returned by both GetFirstChunk and GetNextChunk)
- Any specific information needed by the application for cleanup

For faster response to the user, the client can invoke GetFirstChunk, then use an asynchronous invocation (**tpacall(3)**) of GetNextChunk before displaying the first chunk. As each chunk is displayed, the client can use an asynchronous invocation (**tpacall(3)**) to invoke GetNextChunk while the user is looking at the previous set of data.

The sequence number is not required by AppCleanUp unless needed for some application reason.

4.7.3.4 The AppCleanUp Service.   The AppCleanUp service may do any cleanup activities required by the application; AppCleanUp *must* remove the temporary file.

4.8   **MANAGING UPDATE CONSISTENCY**

When the SQL UPDATE statement is used to update a row in a database, the database sets locks during the operation so that no other transaction can update the same row until the current transaction is complete. These locks would be sufficient if most users did not demand to see the current information before making a change. To satisfy the requirement of first retrieving the data, then later updating the same row, databases provide a means of signifying the update intent when a row is retrieved. The SQL form is the FOR UPDATE OF clause in a cursor definition. It is sufficient to say here (without getting into database theory, which is outside the scope of this book), that once a row has been fetched from the open cursor, a lock is placed on the row that prevents another transaction from updating that row, though reads of the row are usually allowed. This update intent lock remains set until the transaction is completed, whether or not the row is ever actually updated in the transaction.

Note that the finest granularity for locks in most databases is at the row level, so even though the FOR UPDATE OF clause names a column, updates to the row will usually not be allowed. The problems of performance caused by excessive locks gets even worse, because most databases provide the best performance when sector-level locks are used. A sector, or block of data, can possibly contain several rows. Some databases incur considerable performance degradation when row-level locks are used.

Since most databases allow a lock management setting that allows reading a row with an update intent lock set on it, using the FOR UP-DATE OF clause to view a row or rows then updating one or more of the viewed rows works fine when using the conversational paradigm, because the context is held until the transaction is complete. The problem with this method is that if a user makes a number of updates during the same transaction, or worse, updates some rows, then leaves the system idle without closing out the transaction, the locks may begin to interfere with the update activities of other users. Therefore, even when using the conversational paradigm, it is a good idea to use an application-developed method for assuring update consistency.

If using the request–response paradigm, and especially when using the previously described browsing methods, locks cannot be held. It should be noted that the FOR UPDATE OF clause could be used, but there is a potential for holding locks on a large number of rows, certainly interrupting the update operations of other users. Therefore, if the request–response paradigm is used to support browsing and updating of retrieved rows is allowed, it becomes essential to use an application-developed method for assuring data consistency.

Data consistency can be lost if two users retrieve the same row at about the same time, then each tries to update the row. Many update services are written to set values for all columns in the row, even if there is no actual change. Transaction and lock management will assure that one of the updates will be completed before the other, but no matter which one executes first, the odds are high that one of the updates will be overlaid by the other unless some preventive method is used in the application.

The general procedure for assuring update consistency is to include a separate column, either in the table in question or in a separate associated table, a value that will indicate to the updating service that the row has not been updated since the last time the row was read on behalf of the transaction. The column is called the *update signal column*. Every time a row is retrieved the update signal column is retrieved with it, and every time a row is updated the update signal column is updated with a new value. The sequence of events is:

1. Every time a service retrieves a row, the update signal column is retrieved.
2. The update signal column is always passed to the requesting client.
3. If the requesting client requests an update, the update signal column last retrieved is included in the update request message.
4. The update service uses a WHERE clause in the UPDATE specifying the value of the primary key for the row and the last value of the update signal column. If the update fails with an error indicating that no row was found (+100 for most relational databases), the update column has changed.
5. If the update signal column has changed, the update service retrieves the row. There are options on what can be done if there has been a change since the last retrieval by the transaction.

The value in the update signal column can be anything that can be changed by each update to signal that the update has taken place. Using the system data-time integer is a favorite; another is a simple integer that is incremented by each update. If an integer is used, the test is simply for change so that when the number wraps there is no difficulty.

The UPDATE statement would look like:

```
UPDATE table-name
    SET upd-sig-col = new-val,
        column-to-be-updated = new-val,
    .
    .
    .
    WHERE upd-sig-col = :old-val AND key-column = key-val;
```

If the update service discovers that the update signal column has changed since the last retrieval of the row, the following action can be taken:

- The new values in the row can be returned to the client with a flag indicating that the row has changed. The client can display the new values to the user for further consideration of the update.
- The update service can compare the values previously retrieved with the new values in the row. If the current update will not affect any of the columns changed by the other transaction(s), the update service can proceed with the update, being sure not to change the values currently in the row, except for the intended changes.

4.9   BATCH PROCESSING

A batch process is a process that tends to run a long time and is usually run in background. In most cases, a batch process reads all rows in some database, potentially updating some of them. Locks set during a batch process tend to be held a long time and interfere with on-line processing. The common technique for using batch processing simultaneous with on-line processing is to count the updates and commit the transaction every few updates, thus releasing the locks. Usually a file is maintained that contains information to allow restarting the batch program from the point of last commit. Often, the file is a special database table containing one row with the required information. Batch processing can be done using the same techniques when the on-line processing applications use TUXEDO.

Designing Applications

5.1 OVERVIEW

The principles of design for TUXEDO applications are different from those used for designing either mainframe OLTP systems or database client/server systems. There is a greater need for proper planning and understanding of the end user requirements and technical goals. In some ways TUXEDO is more forgiving of design error, but the nature of TUXEDO provides a great deal of leverage to move a merely adequate system to an excellent system. Proper planning and design will lead to time and money savings during development, and more importantly, will enhance the flexibility of the system, allowing lower cost and easier modification later on. Although almost any system based on TUXEDO will have enhanced scalability, when the system is properly designed, the scalability can become almost ideal. Good planning, good design, and good development techniques will make people say: "It's not just a good system, it's an amazing system."

This chapter provides specifics on what it takes to design an enhanced client/server system using TUXEDO. The reader should understand Chapters 2 through 4, which provide basic information. It is assumed that the reader understands general design principles and human–computer interface principles and has in hand a complete set of requirements for the system.

If the steps described in this chapter have been completed successfully based on a complete set of requirements, coding in any language will be very straightforward. TUXEDO supports very complex application systems by providing simple management of partitioned processes. People who have tried to skip the requirements and design steps have created many problems for themselves. It is even more important to plan and design completely and well when developing systems for this powerful tool.

The term "business" used in this chapter, such as in business rules or business requirements, is meant to mean any end-user defined rules, requirements, processes, and so on.

5.2   PROCESS PARTITIONING

5.2.1   General Discussion

Process partitioning is the means by which large processes are divided into clients and services. A single business process may be partitioned into several clients and several services. Proper process partitioning is essential to assure good scalability, flexibility of location, and high performance. In some ways, process partitioning is still somewhat of an art. This section contains information, rules, and suggestions to help bring some engineering into this effort. Simplistically, all processes not included in clients must be placed in services and vice versa. Good design technique does not allow the simplistic approach. The designer should specifically decide independently which processes to place in services and which processes to place in clients. The processes left over are the troublesome ones that press the talent and experience of the designer to make intelligent choices.

5.2.2   Process Partitioning and Data Partitioning

The efforts of process partitioning and data partitioning are difficult to separate. In some enterprises, the database designers and the application designers are in separate organizations. There are two situations: Both the database and the applications are being designed from scratch or the database already exists and is being used by other applications.

If the database already exists and is being used by other applications, the amount of change allowable to accommodate a new application is limited. If the database is being designed from scratch along with the application, then the database can be designed to optimally accommodate the requirements of the application. In either case it is necessary for the database designers and the application designers to work closely together so that the location of physical elements of the database will support near optimal partitioning of the application processes. Services should have local access to all data required to perform their functions.

If the database is new, it should be designed with horizontal partitioning capabilities. If it is an older database, then, because changes must be minimized, some method of partitioning should be examined. In some instances it might be reasonable to maintain two copies of the database, one for the older systems and one for the new systems. The new version can be designed to support the partitioning necessary for distributed processing with TUXEDO. The cost of replication is relatively high in hardware capacity and can also affect performance. The benefits should be examined closely.

5.2.3 **Functionality Types**

5.2.3.1 Overview. While partitioning processing, the TUXEDO application designer constantly asks the question "Where does this function belong?" There is no cut-and-dried answer, but there are some rules to guide the decision. These rules are based on the type of functionality being considered. This section will attempt to define a set of functionality types that can be used to aid in deciding how to do the process partitioning.

5.2.3.2 User Interfaces. The user interfaces functionality type is applied to the set of functions required to prepare data for presentation, including the functions used to actually put the information on the screen, send it to a printer, and so on. Some of the operations included in the presentation functionality type are:

- Converting data from internal format to presentation form, usually applied to operations such as formatting integers or floats to a presentation form
- Building forms
- Building screens, panels, and windows
- All GUI operations
- Interaction with a user, such as maintaining a dialogue

5.2.3.3 Data Verification. Data verification includes operations that verify that the data received is valid as tested by a set of rules. Data verification includes validating:

- Codes
- Data types, that is, numeric fields contain only numbers
- That values are within a prescribed range
- Logical, that is, when field A has a certain value, then field B must have a value within a range specified as associated with the value in field A

5.2.3.4 *Enforcing Business Rules.* Enforcing business rules is a different process from data verification. A business rule might be the requirement that a stock purchase must be a minimum number of shares. Another might be that the customer must maintain a minimum amount of credit in order to purchase stock. Business rules can become complex and require multiple accesses to the database.

5.2.3.5 *Calculation.* Calculations are not limited to numeric calculations. Some operations included in the calculation functionality type are

- Numeric calculation
- Parsing, scanning, and other language operations
- String building, such as building a message
- Any kind of data analysis

5.2.3.6 *Data Access.* The data access functionality is applied to the set of functions that access data management facilities, such as databases. Data access functionality includes issuing SQL statements and calling database stored procedures.

5.2.3.7 *TUXEDO Transaction Management.* The transaction management functionality type is applied to those operations involved in maintaining transaction integrity. With TUXEDO, transaction management includes

- Starting a transaction with either the XA begin transaction function **tx_begin(3)** or the TUXEDO begin transaction function **tpbegin(3)**
- Completing a successful transaction with either the XA commit transaction function **tx_commit(3)** or the TUXEDO commit transaction function **tpcommit(3)**
- Rolling back a failed transaction with either the XA rollback function **tx_rollback(3)** or the TUXEDO rollback function **tpabort(3)**
- Testing return codes and status from all operations to determine whether or not the transaction continues to be successful

5.2.4   **Choosing Processes to Include in Client**

The prime purpose of a TUXEDO client is to interface with the user. The following rules can help make good clients and help decide the processes included in a client.

- A client should not access data directly from the database.
- A client should control transaction boundaries using TUXEDO transaction management functions, such as **tpbegin(3)**, **tpcommit(3)**, and **tpabort(3)** or the X/Open equivalents **tx_begin(3)**, **tx_commit(3)**, and **tx_rollback(3)**.
- Clients should be the first line of security.

Begin defining client processes by including the following functionality types:

- Presentation, including all necessary interaction with presentation graphics, interaction with the user, and so on
- Data verification, when the information required is available within the work station or as input from the user
- Calculations specific to creating user presentations
- TUXEDO transaction management

Client processing may be divided into multiple client programs for a number of reasons, such as:

- The amount of data exceeds a single page of the presentation media.
- Human factors analysis results in a logical division of processing.
- The business processes logically divide the client processing within the application.

The only controlling factor from the TUXEDO environment is transaction management. The designer must be sure that all processes within a transaction are within a single-client program so that all parts of the transaction can be included between the transaction begin function calls and the transaction ending function calls. Much more detail, especially pertaining to windows environments, is included in the section entitled Designing Clients.

5.2.5   **Choosing Processes to Include in Services**

Start defining service processes by including the following functionality:

- Data verification that cannot be done in the client
- Enforcement of business rules, especially when data is required from the database

- Calculations that require information from the database
- Database integrity checks
- Data access

Once the functionality for services has been decided, the processes will usually be partitioned into multiple services. It is difficult to decide how this partitioning will be done. Partitioning into multiple services increases reusability and can simplify modification, but dividing into too many services can lead to unacceptable performance degradation by causing too many service invocations. The following suggestions help:

- Long running processes should be in separate services.
- Logically complete sets of functions should be in single services.
- Consideration should be given to putting data access into services by themselves, divided into logical table sets.
- Complex calculations, or calculations that require input from multiple tables can be put into separate services.
- Services that perform database access should do only updates or only reads. It is not a good idea to mix updates and reads in the same service.

5.2.6   Partitioning and XA

Partitioning services that access the database can be affected by whether or not XA is being used. If XA is being used, the partitioning can be done without regard to separating database access among services, as long as it is possible to minimize two-phase commit. The section on combining services into servers and groups later in this chapter discusses how to avoid two-phase commit when using XA.

Services used outside of XA will run without TUXEDO transaction management. Therefore, database access must be grouped into services such that each service contains all the database modification for transaction it supports. Generally, read-only transactions can be grouped without regard to transaction boundaries because they usually do not require transaction management.

5.3   SERVERS AND SERVER GROUPS

5.3.1   Putting Services in Servers

Services are compiled together into servers using the TUXEDO utility **buildserver(1)**. This utility compiles the servers and links them with the TUXEDO provided **main()** as well as the required elements from the

TUXEDO library. For this reason the designer should attempt to properly assign services to servers, since changing these assignments requires recompiling the affected servers as well as administrative activity.

Use the following rules to decide which services to include in a server.

- All the services in a server should run about the same length of time—that is, long running services should not be included in the same server with short running services.
- Put any very long running service into a server by itself.
- Services that update the database should not be in the same server with services that only read the database.
- Services that do not use any database access should be in servers separate from services that use the database.
- Services must not call other services in the same server.
- Any service that is used very frequently should be a server by itself.
- All services in a server that access a resource manager (for instance, a database) must access the same resource manager.

5.3.2   Putting Servers into Server Groups

This section provides information that the designer needs to know about server groups. Servers are placed in server groups by the system administrator and require no recompiling of the application.

The designer should be aware of the following:

- All servers in a group access the same resource manager.
- Individual servers that do not access a resource manager may be in a group with servers that do, but it is not recommended.
- Server groups are the smallest unit of server migration, hence the need to make sure servers contain logical sets of services.
- Servers may be booted and shut down individually.
- Server groups may be booted and shut down individually. When a group is booted or shut down all the servers in the group are affected.

While the designer does not have the direct responsibility to create server groups, it is important that the designer define servers that will meet the enterprise administration requirements.

5.4   DESIGNING CLIENTS

The primary rule in designing clients is to maintain a sharp division between the part of the program that prepares the external interface for presentation and the part of the program that does calculations, calls TUXEDO functions, and so on. As a result of this rule, there are two parts to designing clients: designing the external interface and deciding how to separate the client functionality into functions. This section provides some ideas on how to make decisions about these components.

A TUXEDO client is a standard program for the platform for which it has been created. That is, it is a Windows program, a DOS program, a UNIX program, or some other operating system program. Therefore, designing a client is very similar to designing any stand-alone program, except that it connects with TUXEDO and is therefore able to use application services via TUXEDO facilities and take advantage of TUXEDO features.

Many enterprises use a variety of work station types, including both GUI and character-based terminals. For this reason all functionality other than pure presentation should be designed such that it can be separated from the presentation part of the program. By doing this, the same source code can be used for all platforms to implement the basic functionality of the client, though the code for the user interface may change.

Almost all applications will be simpler to design and code if XA is used and transaction boundaries are controlled within the client. Some exceptions exist, such as if

- The transaction is read only and transaction management is not needed.
- XA is not being used.
- The transaction is very long running and runs in the background.
- There are special enterprise requirements.

In summary, once the processes for an individual client have been determined, the rest of the effort of designing clients is little different than from designing any well structured application program.

5.5　　DESIGNING SERVICES

5.5.1　　The Steps to Good Service Design

Properly designed TUXEDO services conform to the rules previously defined. Their design also optimizes for performance, reusability, support of administration, support for security, and minimal effort and disruption when changes are made. The secret of optimizing is in the way processes are partitioned among the services. The steps described in this section are intended to aid in the process of designing good services. The results of each step should be documented informally in order not to lose the information developed. The final design should be documented more formally as part of the development methodology. The steps to designing good services are:

1. Partition the processes assigned to services into logical sets where each set may become a service.
2. Partition each set of processes into individual functions.
3. Combine the sets defined in the previous step into services.

5.5.2   ### Step 1: Partition into Logical Sets

Start the process of service design with a clear idea of what processes will be done in services. Then carefully create sets of subprocesses, where each set has a logical meaning within the application. This step is a sort of macro step. Each application process discovered in this step will be further decomposed in the next step.

For instance, some of the processes required in an order entry system are:

- Customer information lookup
- Check accounts receivable
- Check inventory level
- Apply the enterprise credit rules
- Create or reject order

Customer information lookup can be decomposed into lookup by account id and lookup by name. Checking accounts receivable includes the subprocesses for finding the proper account in the accounts receivable tables by account number, retrieving the current balance, and aging the balance.

Note that this work may reveal a number of duplicate process requirements. For instance, if the decision is made to create an order, information such as name and address will be retrieved from the customer master. This duplicates the retrieval that might be done as a service for reporting customer information to the user. The result of this step should be a list of subprocesses with duplicates removed and annotated with the major processes each subprocess supports.

5.5.3   ### Step 2: Partition Subprocesses into Functions

Each of the subprocesses defined in step 1 should be further decomposed into functions. This step generates the question: How far should the designer go in defining functions and how much should be left to the programmer? The answer is, as always, just the right amount. This is always a judgment situation, but when designing services for TUXEDO it is very important that the designer define which functions will be created as function calls and which will be created as TUXEDO services. The essential point is that the designer must designate the functions that will be made available as reusable modules, either as function calls or as services.

The following considerations help in making these decisions.

- If a subprocess is used during execution of several major processes, it should be made a separate module, either a callable function or a TUXEDO service.
- If a subprocess is relatively small and does not database access it should be made a callable function.
- If a subprocess can be run in parallel with other subprocesses or major processes, consider making it a TUXEDO service and invoking it asynchronously.
- If a subprocess requires only one or two lines of code consider making it a macro so that it is done in-line.

5.5.4   Step 3: Combine Functionality into Services

Invoking a service to perform a function requires much more time and machine resource than calling a local function. In fact, if the function is local and the service is on the same platform, invoking a service requires approximately 1,000 times as much time and machine cycles as a simple function call. Invoking a service on another platform requires that amount of time on the local machine, plus that amount of time on the remote machine, plus network time to exchange the message both ways. When either of these is done, making the call asynchronously can improve overall performance under some circumstances. Asynchronous calls are discussed later in this chapter. The result is that it is very important to consider all factors when deciding whether a particular function will be a service or a called function.

Use the following points to help decide how to group functions into services.

- Generally, a single transaction should invoke as few services as possible consistent with proper distribution among TUXEDO nodes. Usually, a transaction should not require more than three service invocations, but this rule has many exceptions.

- Combine access to database tables into logical groups and place them in the same service.
- When certain functions must be done every time a set of tables is accessed, include these functions in the service that performs the access.
- Generally, simple calculations should be done in line in the service that requires the calculation. Complex calculations that do not require intermediate database access should be done in functions.
- If a transaction requires invoking several database access services, it is sometimes a good idea to create a control service that in turn calls the other services.
- Use the TUXEDO forwarding feature when reasonable to decrease the number of messages passed during the transaction.
- If there are several nodes in the TUXEDO domain, or the system runs on a parallel processing platform, it is sometimes a good idea to plan for more services and servers to spread the processing among the nodes and/or processors.

The customer database may contain a number of tables such as name and address, buying preferences, and so on. A single service could be created that retrieves information from the customer database under control of codes in the message from the invoker. The customer retrieve service should contain all formatting, calculations, and other processing for each table and for the combined set, which must be done every time the table or combination of tables must be retrieved. Another service could be created to modify the customer database. Again, the updating will be controlled by codes included in the message from the invoker. This service should contain all calculations, enforcement of business rules, and integrity checks that must be done every time the customer database is modified. The calculations, business rule enforcement and integrity checks might be in callable functions to allow reuse where required.

A single transaction might require access to several logical data groupings which in turn requires executing several services. Invoking these services could be done from the client, but that would result in numerous messages over the network (assuming that clients generally will be on work stations) loading the network and reducing performance. Therefore, it sometimes is a good idea to create a master service for the transaction that in turn invokes the various database access services. This service should also include any processing that is specific to the transaction it services.

The forwarding feature of TUXEDO can improve performance by

reducing the number of messages used to complete each transaction. The master service could forward the transaction to the last service called, saving a message during each transaction. In most cases, the lower-level services should not use forwarding.

Since forwarding improves performance, there is a temptation to use forwarding among all services required in a transaction instead of creating a controlling service as described above.

This method may seem a good idea when the application is originally designed as long as the forwarding sequence is simple and always the same. But when changes occur it may easily become necessary to modify the forwarding scheme or create complex methods of managing the forwarding order. When this occurs, performance may be degraded by poor and/or complex processing of the transaction. Therefore, using forwarding in this manner is not recommended.

5.6   ASYNCHRONOUS PROCESSING

TUXEDO provides two methods of asynchronous processing: the ability to invoke services asynchronously as part of the transaction and the ability to place service requests on a queue that is made reliable by an XA resource manager. The former is used during normal processing to aid transaction performance, or when a service can be invoked to run independently of the current transaction. The reliable queue method is used to invoke services that will then run independently of the current transaction. Designing for the reliable queue, called /Q, is discussed in a later section.

A service is invoked asynchronously by using the TUXEDO function **tpacall(3)** to invoke the service. The **tpacall(3)** places the request into the request queue then returns a handle for the request to the invoking process without waiting for the invoked service to complete. The asynchronous method can be used to invoke a service, continue with other processing, then check for a reply. If the reply is not yet available, the requestor can continue to process, cycling through the check for a reply until either the reply is ready or the requestor cannot process further without the results of the request.

One way to use an asynchronous request is to request several services asynchronously one after the other, thus allowing the services to operate in parallel. The invoker can then check for a reply from any request for service or a reply from a specific request.

Asynchronous processing can improve the performance of a given transaction, but it puts an additional load on the system because an additional message must be exchanged for every check for a reply. The number of messages exchanged for synchronous service invocation is two. The minimum number of messages exchanged for each asynchronous request is three—one for the initial invocation, one when a reply is checked to query the reply status, and one to return the reply. Every check for reply requires one additional message. Asynchronous processing should be used carefully because these extra messages load the resources of the platform and can have a negative affect on total system throughput, ultimately affecting the response to transactions.

Clients on work stations can use asynchronous processing to improve performance—they can continue local processing while awaiting a response from a service. This can be very efficient because the service is on another platform. For example, suppose the client must retrieve customer information from the customer master and accounts receivable information from the accounts receivable database. The client can asynchronously invoke both the customer information retrievable service and the accounts receivable retrieval service, then wait for the replies. The two services will run in parallel. This method is particularly effective when the two services are on different nodes or when running on a parallel processing platform.

A feature of TUXEDO allows the requestor to signify that no response is desired when invoking a service asynchronously. This feature is especially helpful when a service can be started to run as a background service where the results will be placed in a file for later examination by another service or utility. The difficulty with using the no-reply feature is that there is no guarantee that the service will ever run in case of failure. This feature could be called an "unreliable queue," since it is disengaged from transaction management. Since most computing platforms are relatively reliable, this type of activity can be used to maintain information that is desirable for such purposes as marketing analysis, where an occasional failure will not be critical to the enterprise.

Suppose that when a new customer is added or a customer changes address, it is necessary to perform a complex analysis of the address, such as determining who lives at a given address. It might be that a husband and wife are customers under their individual names. Suppose also that children live at the same address and are also customers. In a hypothetical situation, marketing wants to maintain information that all these people live at the same address. Complex programs exist that analyze addresses and determine fairly accurately that two different but similar addresses are actually physically at the same location. Each time a new customer is added or a customer changes address, the process that changes address can use an asynchronous invocation (**tpacall(3)**) with the proper flags set to start the complex and relatively lengthy process of analyzing the new address and associated addresses. In this way a complex and lengthy process can be queued to a background process that can run as an independent transaction with little effect on the on-line processing.

5.7   RELIABLE QUEUES

TUXEDO provides an XA resource manager that provides a reliable queue feature called /Q. Reliable queues provide a means of queuing a request for a service that will run independently of the current transaction and that will be guaranteed to run even if there is a catastrophic failure. The guarantee is implemented as a persistent queue stored in stable storage. The storage of the queue is assured as part of the requesting transaction. Specific queue elements are not permanently removed until the requested service has completed its transaction.

/Q is especially useful for reliably and asynchronously starting long running processes essential for the successful management of enterprise information. One example is an extension of the use of asynchronous processing. The enterprise must normalize all addresses in the customer master in a number of ways, requiring a long running operation to run periodically, perhaps once a day, or whenever there are 1,000 changes of address completed. /Q can be used to reliably store keys to the addresses that have changed without burdening the database. A service can be started periodically at certain times to process the accumulated changes, or a /Q feature will automatically start the service when the queue reaches a certain size.

5.8   BATCH APPLICATIONS

At first glance, the idea of running batch applications in the TUXEDO environment seems inconsistent with the purpose of using TUXEDO for on-line interactive processing. If the term *batch application* is defined as a long-running application that proceeds to completion without interaction from a user, several advantages become apparent in running batch applications as TUXEDO services.

Using multiple services to do batch processing can have the following advantages, especially when running on a computer with multiple processors.

- Several processes can be run in parallel, making the batch process run faster.
- Periodic commits can be done, forcing coordination of all processes,

thus releasing locks held but assuring that the database integrity is maintained.
- The batch programs can log their position at each commit, allowing restart in case of failure. The log can be made part of each commit.
- The transaction management used to commit will assure that all attempted updates will be properly rolled back to the last commit without any application programming effort.

Designers should examine batch processing requirements and consider running batch application systems in the TUXEDO environment.

A batch application can be started from a client. The client can first interact with the user to acquire any parameters necessary for processing, then start the processing and terminate. An alternative method is to use a dedicated client to start the process. The client can remain active and periodically check for unsolicited messages from the background process. The batch process can thus post progress of the work to the client periodically.

5.9   USING CONVERSATIONAL SERVICES

TUXEDO provides the ability to create services that may interact conversationally with clients or other services. Conversational services are useful because they maintain context during the life of the conversation, whereas all context is lost when a request/response service completes the requested service.

One important feature of most applications is to allow the user to browse through a large amount of data. The obvious method to do this is to open a cursor, present the first page of information, and upon user request present the next page. Since the request-response service loses context, and as we have seen, must close the cursor before completing the service, it is not easy to arrange for browsing. One simple way to arrange for browsing is to have the client establish a conversation with the browse service. The client and service can then work cooperatively to browse the cursor until the user signifies that the browse operation is over.

While this method seems simple, there are complications, all of which are well known to those who have created OLTP applications. These complications are not caused by any deficiency in the software, but are a direct result of the need to hold the cursor open for an indefinite period of time. These complications are:

- During a conversation the service and the server it is part of are not available to provide services to any other request.

- If the database being used holds any kind of locks on reads, these locks will be held the entire time the cursor is open, leaving the system vulnerable to the user who walks away before ending the browse.
- If the browse cursor is declared for update, every row retrieved will be locked, loading the system with many locks and again leaving the system vulnerable to large delays for the time the user works with the browse.
- Holding a cursor open can use considerable platform resources under some circumstances, degrading throughput of the entire system.

Use of conversational services should be limited to situation where all of the following conditions are true.

- The database can be browsed without setting any locks and the open cursor will not overly load the system.
- The browse is used infrequently or a sufficient number of conversational services and servers can be established without degrading total system throughput.
- The browse cursor is not declared with the FOR UPDATE OF clause.

The update browse can be used effectively in the rare case where it is necessary to lock out all updates to any rows that have been read (assuming cursor stability consistency level), and a single user will be doing the browse.

5.10   MESSAGE SIZE

The designer of a TUXEDO application has the responsibility of specifying the information included in messages for service invocation and response. Message size is important for the following reasons.

- Moving messages, even when done in memory, requires processing cycles and affects overall throughput of the system.
- If the message size exceeds three-quarters of the message size allowed by the operating system, TUXEDO will write the message to temporary disk storage.
- Transmitting messages over communication networks directly affects the performance of the system.

As a general rule, the maximum size of any message should be no more than 16Kb. Minimize message size by

- Including only required data in a message. Don't include data in a message that can be calculated from other data.
- Using FML buffer types because TUXEDO sends only the populated occurrences of each field, adjusted the message length accordingly.
- Doing as much processing as possible in services so that only results are returned from the service.

For instance, if a client needs to display the price, quantity, and extension for an item from an existing order, let the retrieving service return only the price and quantity and let the client calculate the extension. If, on the other hand, the client requires only the extension, calculate the extension in the service and do not send back the price and quantity.

When a client requests large quantities of data, such as when a user browses the customer tables, some sort of design must be implemented to allow for sending only a reasonable amount of data on each request. There are a number of browsing schemes possible, each with its own set of compromises. Some of these techniques were discussed in Chapter 4.

5.11   DESIGNING FOR FAILURE RECOVERY

TUXEDO provides administration tools that help with recovery from failure that do not affect the design of the application. Depending on the platform architecture, the designer can include a few things in the system to help.

- Clients and servers can log critical information about transactions.
- If there are multiple nodes in the domain, make sure that no files are created on a node that requires access from another node after migration of servers.
- Use transaction management where it is critical that database updates remain synchronized.

Logging information from clients and servers can provide information to help in recovery efforts and can help in determining the cause of problems. The trade off is that writing logs directly affects performance. If such logs are used, minimize the information contained in the log. The next section provides information about logs.

When there are multiple nodes in the system, TUXEDO has two features that help decrease the impact of failure.

- If the same service is offered on multiple platforms and one platform fails, TUXEDO will continue to run the application successfully by using the available services.
- Server groups and their servers can be migrated from one platform to another, allowing a platform to be shut down after migration.

In either case, the system design should not restrict the platform that a server can run on. Specifically, the following rules must be followed:

- Do not attempt to maintain context in memory between service executions.
- Do not attempt to maintain context in operating system files.
- If context must be maintained between service invocations, maintain the context in the client.

Transaction management is necessary to maintain transaction integrity. If transaction integrity is not maintained, updates may get out of synchronization creating an unreliable database. The design should either use XA or compensate in some manner in the design to assure that use of database transaction management alone is sufficient. Whatever transaction management approach is used, there will be a method of determining which transactions were in-flight when the failure occurred. The system must include some method that combines computer information and manual procedures to determine the status of each in-flight transaction and provides a means of reentering aborted transactions.

5.12   LOGS

TUXEDO provides a log, known as the userlog with the default file name ULOG.*date*. The function **userlog(3)** allows application clients and services to write to ULOG. All clients and services should write a record to this log when an unusual event happens. The log record should include an identifier of the source, the date and time, and a meaningful message that includes significant data from the transaction in process. The source identifier should include the name of the service or client, the name of the server, if applicable, the platform name, and the name of the current user. Additional logs may be kept in other files, though in most instances these files may not provide any better protection than ULOG, and require more programming to use.

When the application is using hardware that includes an internally replicated reliable disk array and there is a means that allows multiple platforms to access the files and/or databases on the array, logs may be written to disk and used during the failover process. One specific example of such a situation is the ability of some databases to access the same tables from multiple platforms. Oracle provides this capability with the Oracle Parallel Server (OPS). If OPS or its equivalent is available, special database tables can be used to log critical information that must be available to support failover. Services and native clients can use this method. It is not practical to use this method from work station clients.

When using a database for logs, the logs should be written such that they are committed separately from the rest of the transaction. If not, they will be rolled back when the transaction fails. Committing logs can affect performance considerably. Writing the log from a separate service exposes the system to loss of the log records when the system fails. If logs are critical, use /Q to invoke the logging service, but note that this can cause further degradation of performance.

In summary, writing proper logs is necessary to provide information that helps correct and recover from problems quickly. Log records can be lost, and the methods used to reliably write logs affect performance substantially. Therefore, logs must be created using some sort of compromise, and recovery procedures must recognize that log content is a guide to the problem and that logs do not necessarily contain complete information.

5.13   AUDIT TRAILS

Audit trails are an integral part of information processing. Specific audit trail content requirements should be part of the user requirement definition. The suggestions in this section do not address the content of audit trail information, but rather address the technical aspects of maintaining audit trails. Audit trails should be maintained separately from the logs mentioned previously. Though audit trail information can be used in the process of failure correction, audit trails should not be considered in the same category as trouble logs.

The following approach should be made to audit trails:

- Keep the audit trail information in a database table or tables.
- Write the audit trail information as part of the transaction that made the changes to the database.
- Minimize the number of writes to the audit trail tables consistent with accuracy.

To minimize the number of updates to the audit trail, follow these rules:

- Add information to the audit trail only for changes to the database; do not write for every access.
- Analyze the proposal for information in the audit trail to prevent redundancy. If some data will imply other information accurately, write only the basic data.
- Attempt to combine information into as few tables as possible to minimize the number of updates required.
- Do not normalize the audit trail tables with other tables.

5.14   **A SUMMARY OF THE RULES OF DESIGN**

The primary rule for any design, but especially for TUXEDO based applications is: KISS (Keep It Simple, Stupid). If too many services are executed to complete a single transaction the system can become complex. Be sure that the design is as simple as possible. The following rules apply generally:

- Explicit transaction boundaries should be set in clients.
- Conversational methods should rarely be used.

Client design should use the following rules:

- A client should not access data directly from the database.
- A client should control transaction boundaries explicitly using TUXEDO transaction management functions, such as **tpbegin(3)**, **tpcommit(3)**, and **tpabort(3)**, or the X/Open equivalents, **tx_begin(3)**, **tx_commit(3)**, and **tx_rollback(3)**.
- Clients should be the first line of security.
- Application processing should be sharply separated from user presentation processing so that application processing can be used on any work station.

Use the following rules to design services and servers:

- Logically complete sets of functions should be in a single service.
- Put data access into services by themselves, divided into logical table sets.
- Complex calculations, or calculations that require input from multiple tables, can be put into separate services.
- Services that perform database access should do only updates or only reads. Do not mix updates and reads in the same service and do not combine update services with read only services in the same

server. If database reads are necessary to verify the accuracy of data, these reads are an exception and should be put into the same service that updates the database.

- All the services in a server should run about the same length of time; that is, long running services should not be included in the same server with short running services.
- Put any very long running service into a server by itself.
- Services that do not use any database access should be in servers separate from services that do use a database.
- Services must not call other services in the same server.
- Any service that is used very frequently should be a server by itself.
- All services in a server must access the same resource manager (or none).

6

The Application-Transaction Monitor Interface

6.1   **OVERVIEW**

The application programming interface (API) with TUXEDO is the application-transaction monitor interface (ATMI). This chapter provides information about the components of the ATMI.

Not all ATMI functions are discussed in this chapter. Some are used only in clients and some are used only in services and servers. These are discussed in the chapters dealing with clients, servers, and services. There are other functions that are seldom used and are therefore not discussed. The intent of this chapter is to provide a foundation to allow the developer to work with any function provided by TUXEDO. The concepts and discussions provided should arm the reader with sufficient knowledge to extend into these rarely used functions with little difficulty.

TUXEDO clients can use functions to send messages to services, which in turn do programmed application processing and return results. Services can in turn invoke other services. In this book, sending a message to a service to cause it to perform processing will be called *invoking* a service. The client or service making the request will be called the *requestor*. Thus, a client or service invokes a service; a service is invoked by a requestor.

TUXEDO documentation calls a particular TUXEDO domain an "application." This confusing nomenclature dates from the beginning of the product when there was only one application. In this book, the noun "application" will be reserved for its usual meaning, that is, the particular set of programs that support a particular set of user functionality. The term "TUXEDO domain" or just "domain" will be used to designate a particular instance of TUXEDO.

The interface between application programs and TUXEDO is called ATMI. This interface supports C and COBOL. C++ can be used with TUXEDO by calling the functions as C functions. A subset of this interface has been adopted by X/Open as the XATMI. ATMI provides function calls that enable the application program to:

- Use request/response services synchronously and asynchronously
- Initiate and participate in conversations
- Create, manage, load, and read message buffers
- Attach and disconnect from TUXEDO (clients only)
- Establish transaction boundaries
- Server and service initialization
- Perform miscellaneous functionality

TUXEDO clients must specifically attach to TUXEDO before using ATMI functions. Clients are attached with the **tpinit(3)** function. The client then detaches from TUXEDO by calling the **tpterm(3)** function. Clients can connect and disconnect from TUXEDO as many times as the application requires.

Application programs control the boundaries of transactions by calling the **tpbegin(3)** function to start a transaction and **tpcommit(3)** or **tpabort(3)** to end a transaction.

Transactions can be controlled either in clients or services. TUXEDO also has an administrative feature that allows limited automatic transaction control.

Messages are passed and returned via buffers, called *typed buffers*. Various types of buffers are provided to enable TUXEDO to provide a number of data-dependent services. Functions are provided to allocate, free, reallocate, and load buffers. A special type, the field manipulation language (FML) buffer is supported with a rich function set that provides many features useful for applications other than sending messages.

Many ATMI calls use a **long flags** parameter. The value of **flags** modifies the behavior of calls where defined. The actual modification depends on the call. A set of TUXEDO defined names are used to set **flags**. These names may be **or**'d to create combinations in the same way that many such values are set in other C functions. For instance, using the following to set **flags** will set the three named flags true:

TPNOTRAN | TPNOREPLY | TPSIGRSTRT

TUXEDO supports a conversational mode for communicating between services and requestors. A conversation is started with a **tpconnect(3)** and terminated by a number of events. During a conversation, as many messages may be passed between the connected application processes as desired using **tpsend(3)** and **tprecv(3)**. Any client may initiate a conversation with a **tpconnect(3)**, but services must be part of a server designated administratively as a conversational server in order to participate in a conversation.

Other functions available include:

- **tpbroadcast(3)**, which a service may use to broadcast unsolicited messages to all clients
- **tpnotify(3)**, which is used to send unsolicited messages to selected clients
- **tpgetlev(3)**, to determine if a service is currently part of a transaction

The functionality discussed in the following sections is available to both clients and services. Those functions that are available only to clients are discussed in Chapter 8. Those functions that are available only to services are discussed in Chapter 9.

6.2   INVOKING SERVICES WITH THE REQUEST/RESPONSE PARADIGM

6.2.1   About the Request/Response Paradigm

Request/response services receive a request, perform the requested service, and either return the result to the requestor or forward the partial result to another service for more processing. TUXEDO servers can process only one service request at a time, even if several services are part of the server. TUXEDO services can invoke other services; TUXEDO clients cannot act as services.

The basic request/response call is the **tpcall(3)**, which returns with the result when the service has completed. Asynchronous request/response is enabled using **tpacall(3)** and **tpgetrply(3)**. Services return results to the requestor using **tpreturn(3)**. Services can also forward the request to another service with **tpforward(3)**. TUXEDO does not provide any information to a service about the requestor, including whether the request came from a client or another service, or whether the requestor used **tpcall(3)**, **tpacall(3)**, or **tpforward(3)** to invoke the service.

6.2.2   **Invoking a Service Synchronously** (tpcall(3))

Services are invoked synchronously with **tpcall(3)**. The form is:

```
int tpcall(char *svc, char *idata, long ilen, char **odata,
    long *olen, long flags)
```

tpcall(3) invokes the service named in the string *svc*, transmits the information in *idata* to it, and awaits a response. The response is placed in *odata*. The parameters *idata* and *odata* are defined as char * for convenience. They must, in fact, be pointers to a typed buffer recognized by TUXEDO. The program must use **tpalloc(3)** to allocate space for *idata* and *odata*. The value of *ilen* is ignored for those types of buffers that do not require a length to be set, such as FML. Neither *odata* or *olen* may be null.

The value of *olen* is set with the length of the returned message upon successful return. If *olen* is set to 0, then no data has been returned. It is sometimes convenient to use the same buffer area for both *idata* and *odata*, in which case *ilen* and *olen* may be set by the program with the same value. If the amount of data returned is different than the length contained in *olen* when the call was made, then *idata* is no longer a valid pointer.

The valid flags for **tpcall(3)** are:

TPSIGRSTRT The flag TPSIGRSTRT should always be specified with **tpcall(3)** to be sure that the call is reissued if processing is interrupted by a signal during the execution of the call.

TPNOTRAN The flag TPNOTRAN can be set to disconnect the service from the current transaction. See the section on transaction management later in this chapter.

TPNOCHANGE The flag TPNOCHANGE prevents TUXEDO from changing the buffer type pointed to by *odata* when the return message is received. If this flag is not set and the service returns a different type, the type of *odata* is set to the type returned by the service. When this flag is not set and the service attempts to return a buffer of a different type, the type of *odata* does not change and the request fails with error TPEOTYPE.

TPNOBLOCK The flag TPNOBLOCK will cause **tpcall(3)** to return immediately with the error TPEBLOCK without invoking the service if there is a blocking condition, such as when there is no room in the internal buffer used for messages. This flag does not prevent blocking while waiting for a reply.

TPNOTIME: The flag TPNOTIME prevents a timeout because the service does not respond. This timeout is called the blocking timeout. TPNOBLOCK and TPNOTIME are mutually exclusive. The transaction may still fail due to a transaction timeout.

tpcall(3) returns 0 for success and –1 for failure (it is a good idea to look for < 0 to check for failure). When success is returned or the failure is TPSVCFAIL, tpurcode will contain a value set by the service with **tpreturn(3)**. On failure, tperrno will contain a value to indicate the type of error. The possible errors for **tpcall(3)** are:

TPEINVAL Error TPEINVAL means that the parameters were set incorrectly, such as using NULL for *idata* or **odata*. This error also can mean that **flags** contained an invalid value.

TPENOENT Error TPENOENT indicates that the service named in *svc* is not known to the system. This error also occurs when an attempt is made to use **tpcall(3)** to invoke a server marked conversational.

TPEITYPE Error TPEITYPE indicates that the buffer allocated for *idata* is not of a type recognized by TUXEDO. Often this error indicates that the pointer has become corrupted or the program did not allocate the space with **tpalloc(3)**.

TPEOTYPE Error TPEOTYPE indicates that the buffer allocated for *odata* is not of a type recognized by TUXEDO. Often this error indicates that the pointer has become corrupted or the program did not allocate the space with **tpalloc(3)**. This error also occurs when the flag TPNOCHANGE is not set and the buffer type returned is different than the buffer type allocated.

TPETRAN Error TPETRAN occurs when the invoker is in transaction mode, the service named in *svc* cannot operate in transaction mode and the TPNOTRAN flag was not specified.

TPETIME Error TPETIME indicates that a timeout has occurred. If the process was in transaction mode when the timeout occurred, the error is a transaction timeout. A transaction timeout sets an internal flag that will prevent the transaction from being committed. A transaction which has timed out can only be aborted. If the process was not in transaction mode and the TPNOBLOCK flag was not set, error TPETIME occurs when on a blocking timeout.

TPSVCFAIL The error TPSVCFAIL is set when the service has set the TPFAIL flag in **tpreturn(3)**. If the service sent a reply with the failure, *odata* points to the reply in the same manner as if there had been no failure. The client and all services may continue to process normally, but TUXEDO will abort the transaction if **tpcommit(3)** is called.

TPSVCERR The error TPSVCERR is set when a service uses **tpreturn(3)** or **tpforward(3)** improperly, such as setting invalid parameters. No reply is received when this error occurs, that is, ***odata***, its contents, and **olen** are unchanged. The client and all services may continue to process normally, but TUXEDO will abort the transaction if **tpcommit(3)** is called.

TPEBLOCK The error TPEBLOCK means that a blocking condition was present, but the TPNOBLOCK flag was set.

TPGOTSIG Error TPGOTSIG indicates that a signal occurred during process of the function, but the flag TPSIGRSTRT was not set.

TPESYSTEM The TPESYSTEM error means that there was a failure within TUXEDO. A message describing the problem is written to the log file.

TPEOS The TPEOS error means that an operating system error has occurred. This error can occur if a message queue on another node is full, but **tpcall(3)** will still return success.

6.2.3   **Invoking a Service Asynchronously** (tpacall(3) **and** tpgetrply(3))

Services are invoked asynchronously with the **tpacall(3)**. The results are retrieved with **tpgetrply(3)**.

The form of **tpacall(3)** is:

```
int tpacall(char * svc, char *data, long len, long flags)
```

tpacall(3) invokes the service named in the string ***svc***, transmits the information in ***data*** to it and returns to the calling program. When **tpacall(3)** returns successfully, it returns a handle (called a *descriptor* in the TUXEDO documentation) that can be used to retrieve the reply with **tpgetrply(3)**. If the call fails, **tpacall(3)** returns –1.

len is the length of the message sent. The value of ***len*** is ignored for those types of buffers that do not require a length to be set, such as FML.

The parameter ***data*** is defined as char * for convenience. If ***data*** is not NULL, it must be a pointer to a typed buffer recognized by TUXEDO. The program must use **tpalloc(3)** to allocate space for ***data***.

If the flag TPNOREPLY is not set with **tpacall(3)**, the calling process must retrieve the expected response with **tpgetrply(3)**. If the process is in transaction mode and attempts to commit the transaction before retrieving all expected replies, the transaction will be aborted and all reply handles will be made invalid.

The valid flags for **tpacall(3)** are:

TPSIGRSTRT The flag TPSIGRSTRT should always be specified with **tpacall(3)** to be sure that the call is reissued if processing is interrupted by a signal during the execution of the call.

TPNOTRAN The flag TPNOTRAN can be set to disconnect the service from the current transaction. See the section on transaction management later in this chapter.

TPNOBLOCK The flag TPNOBLOCK will cause **tpacall(3)** to return immediately with the error TPEBLOCK without invoking the service if there is a blocking condition, such as when there is no room in the internal buffer used for messages.

TPNOTIME The flag TPNOTIME prevents a blocking timeout. The transaction may still fail due to a transaction timeout. TPNOBLOCK and TPNOTIME are mutually exclusive.

TPNOREPLY The flag TPNOREPLY indicates that no reply will be received from the service. The handle returned when this flag is set is 0, which is an invalid handle. If the caller is in transaction mode when this flag is set, TPNOTRAN must also be set.

The errors for **tpacall(3)** are:

TPEINVAL Error TPEINVAL means that the parameters were set incorrectly, such as using NULL for *data*. This error also can mean that **flags** contained an invalid value.

TPENOENT Error TPENOENT indicates that the service named in *svc* is not known to the system. This error also occurs when an attempt is made to use **tpacall(3)** to invoke a server marked conversational.

TPEITYPE Error TPEITYPE indicates that the buffer allocated for *data* is not of a type recognized by TUXEDO. Often this error indicates that the pointer has become corrupted or the program did not allocate the space with **tpalloc(3)**.

TPELIMIT Error TPELIMIT happens when the maximum number of outstanding asynchronous requests is reached.

TPETRAN Error TPETRAN occurs when the invoker is in transaction mode, the service named in *svc* cannot operate in transaction mode, and the TPNOTRAN flag was not specified.

TPETIME Error TPETIME indicates that a timeout has occurred. If the process was in transaction mode when the timeout occurred, the error is a transaction timeout. A transaction timeout sets an internal flag that will prevent the transaction from being committed. A transaction which has timed out can only be aborted. If the process was not in transaction mode and the TPNOBLOCK flag was not set, error TPETIME occurs when on a blocking timeout.

TPEBLOCK The error TPEBLOCK means that a blocking condition was present, but the TPNOBLOCK flag was set.

TPGOTSIG Error TPGOTSIG indicates that a signal occurred during process of the function, but the flag TPSIGRSTRT was not set.

TPESYSTEM The TPESYSTEM error means that there was a failure within TUXEDO. A message describing the problem is written to the log file.

TPEOS The TPEOS error means that an operating system error has occurred. This error can occur if a message queue on another node is full, but **tpacall(3)** will still return success.

The form of **tpgetrply(3)** is:

```
int tpgetrply(int *cd, char **data, long *len, long flags)
```

tpgetrply(3) returns the reply associated with the handle pointed to by ***cd***. If the reply is not ready, **tpgetrply(3)** waits until one is ready or there is a timeout. Two flags, TPGETANY and TPNOBLOCK, modify this behavior. The result is returned in the area pointed to by ***data***. The parameter ***data*** is defined as char * for convenience. It must, in fact, be a pointer to a typed buffer recognized by TUXEDO. The program must use **tpalloc(3)** to allocate space for ***data***.

The value of ***len*** is set with the length of the returned message upon successful return. If ***len*** is set to 0, then no data has been returned.

The parameter ***cd*** must point to a handle returned by a previous **tpacall(3)**.

All replies associated with outstanding handles set by **tpacall(3)** must be retrieved with **tpgetrply(3)**. If the process is in transaction mode and attempts to commit the transaction before retrieving all expected replies, the transaction will be aborted and all reply handles will be made invalid.

The valid flags for **tpgetrply(3)** are:

TPSIGRSTRT The flag TPSIGRSTRT should always be specified to be sure that the call is reissued if processing is interrupted by a signal during the execution of the call.

TPNOCHANGE The flag TPNOCHANGE prevents TUXEDO from changing the buffer type pointed to by ***data*** when the return message is received. If this flag is not set and the service returns a different type, the type of ***data*** is set to the type returned by the service. When this flag is not set and the service attempts to return a buffer of a different type, the type of ***data*** does not change and the request fails with error TPEOTYPE.

TPNOBLOCK The flag TPNOBLOCK causes **tpgetrply(3)** to return immediately without waiting for a reply to become available. If a reply was available, the reply is placed in ***data***. If no reply was available and this flag was set, **tpgetrply(3)** returns immediately with error TPEBLOCK. If this flag is not set and no reply is available, **tpgetrply(3)** will not return until either a reply is available or there is a timeout.

TPNOTIME The flag TPNOTIME prevents a blocking timeout. TPNOBLOCK and TPNOTIME are mutually exclusive. The transaction may still fail due to a transaction timeout.

TPGETANY If the flag TPGETANY is set, **tpgetrply(3)** ignores the handle and returns any reply that is ready. Unless TPNOBLOCK is set, **tpgetrply(3)** will wait until any response is ready or a timeout occurs. A valid handle must still be provided or **tpgetrply(3)** fails with a TPEINVAL error.

The errors possible with **tpgetrply(3)** are:

TPEINVAL Error TPEINVAL means that the parameters were set incorrectly, such as using NULL for ***data***. This error also can mean that **flags** contained an invalid value.

TPEOTYPE Error TPEOTYPE indicates that the buffer allocated for ***data*** is not of a type recognized by TUXEDO. Often this error indicates that the pointer has become corrupted or the program did not allocate the space with **tpalloc(3)**. This error also occurs when the flag TPNOCHANGE is not set and the buffer type returned is different than the buffer type allocated.

TPEBADDESC Error TPEBADDESC means the ***cd*** did not contain a valid reply descriptor.

TPETRAN Error TPETRAN occurs when the invoker is in transaction mode, the service named in ***svc*** cannot operate in transaction mode and the TPNOTRAN flag was not specified.

TPETIME Error TPETIME indicates that a timeout has occurred. If the process was in transaction mode when the timeout occurred, the error is a transaction timeout. A transaction timeout sets an internal flag that will prevent the transaction from being committed. A transaction which has timed out can only be aborted. If the process was not in transaction mode and the TPNOBLOCK flag was not set, error TPETIME occurs when there is a blocking timeout.

TPSVCFAIL The error TPSVCFAIL is set when the service has set the TPFAIL flag in **tpreturn(3)**. If the service sent a reply with the failure, *data* points to the reply in the same manner as if there had been no failure. The client and all services may continue to process normally, but TUXEDO will abort the transaction if **tpcommit(3)** is called.

TPSVCERR The error TPSVCERR is set when a service uses **tpreturn(3)** or **tpforward(3)** improperly, such as setting invalid parameters. No reply is received when this error occurs, that is *data*, its contents, and *len* are unchanged. The client and all services may continue to process normally, but TUXEDO will abort the transaction if **tpcommit(3)** is called.

TPEBLOCK The error TPEBLOCK means that a blocking condition was present, but the TPNOBLOCK flag was set.

TPGOTSIG Error TPGOTSIG indicates that a signal occurred during process of the function, but the flag TPSIGRSTRT was not set.

TPESYSTEM The TPESYSTEM error means that there was a failure within TUXEDO. A message describing the problem is written to the log file.

TPEOS The TPEOS error means that an operating system error has occurred.

6.2.4   Using Request/Reply Functions

The program using the request/response functions must carefully set up the arguments. The space for the data parameters must be space allocated by **tpalloc(3)** for a buffer type recognized by TUXEDO. TUXEDO provides a number of predefined buffer types, and developers can create additional buffer types and register them with TUXEDO. The discussion on buffers in later chapters explains these procedures in more detail.

The flag TPSIGRSTRT should be always be set for **tpcall(3)** and **tpacall(3)** to indicate that if the call is interrupted by a signal it should be retried. If TPSIGRSTRT is not specified and a signal interrupts the call, the function fails with TPGOTSIG set.

Always test the return of **tpcall(3)**, **tpacall(3)**, and **tpgetrply(3)**. If these functions return less than 0 (nominally –1), move **tperrno** to a local variable (so it won't be lost by any subsequent program action, and to help in debugging if the program terminates abnormally), then check it using the errors as defined. Never try to check the error type against a hard coded value. Use **tpstrerror(3)** to get a string describing the error.

A service is a subroutine to a TUXEDO supplied mainline. The service may, as part of the application code, call other application functions. There are two important rules to follow when using application functions in a service:

- Always call **tpreturn(3)** and **tpforward(3)** from the main part of the service, never from a called function.
- Never try to call a service as a function.

6.3 **CONVERSATIONS**

6.3.1 **Overview**

Conversations are allowed between an initiator and a conversational service. Conversations may be initiated by either clients or services. The term *initiator* will be used to designate the initiating program in this section. The service that is invoked by the initiator is called the *participating service*. The initiator initiates the conversation with a **tpconnect(3)**. Once the connection is established the initiator and the participating service may exchange as many messages as desired until the connection is ended.

Once the connection is established the conversation works in a half-duplex mode. The process in control of the conversation can only send messages; the other process can only receive messages. Each time a process sends a message it can pass control to the other process. Each process must determine if an event has occurred and thus determine if it is in control or not. How to determine if an event occurred and a list of valid events is included in the description of the conversational functions.

If the conversation is a simple exchange of messages, the sequence of calls is:

1. The initiator calls **tpconnect(3)** to establish the conversation. An initial message may be sent with **tpconnect(3)**.
2. The initiator issues a **tprecv(3)** and is blocked because no response is available yet.
3. TUXEDO chooses an available service with the name from the

tpconnect(3) and passes the initial message, if any, to it, making it the participating service.

4. The participating service processes the initial message, if any, and uses **tpsend(3)** to return the response, then calls **tprecv(3)**. Since there is no response yet, it is blocked.

5. The initiator receives the response from the participating service via the waiting **tprecv(3)** and sends the next message to the service with **tpsend(3)**, then returns to the **tprecv(3)** in step 2.

6. The cycle repeats until the connection is ended. A connection can be ended in an orderly manner only by the participating service by calling **tpreturn(3)**. Specific conditions must exist before a conversation can be ended in an orderly fashion.

The conversation described above is very simple. There are a number of variations which are controlled by the **flags** parameter in the various calls and by the status of the conversation. There are a number of situations where the conversation will be ended in a disorderly manner. If a conversation that is part of a transaction has been ended in a disorderly manner, TUXEDO will abort the transaction, even if **tpcommit(3)** is called. Ending conversations while in transaction mode is discussed in the section entitled Establishing Transaction Boundaries.

Figure 6.1 illustrates a simple conversation. The initiator (any client or service) initiates a conversation with **tpconnect(3)**. The initiator and participating service exchange messages until the conversation is logi-

Figure 6.1   A simple conversation.

cally complete. When all the desired messages have been exchanged, the participating service ends the conversation with **tpreturn(3)**. Note that each has passed control to the other with each **tpsend(3)**.

6.3.2   Variations on Conversations

The variations are controlled as follows.

- The initiator may or may not send a message with the **tpconnect(3)**.
- The initiator can indicate who sends the next message with **tpconnect(3)** using **flags**.
- The **tpsend(3)** controls who sends the next message with **flags**.
- The process waiting to receive a message may not block on **tprecv(3)** by using the TPNOBLOCK flag.

The flag TPSENDONLY, used with **tpconnect(3)**, indicates that the initiator will send the next message. The participating service receiving the message is not allowed to send, but must receive only.

The flag TPRECVONLY controls who may send the next message. When set, TPRECVONLY indicates that the sending process is the one that will receive the next message, implying that the service receiving the message is placed in control of the conversation and is expected to send the next message. This flag may be used by **tpconnect(3)** and **tpsend(3)** to transfer control of the conversation.

6.3.3   Ending a Conversation

All conversations must be ended by a participating service using **tpreturn(3)** while in control of the conversation. Otherwise the conversation will be ended in a disorderly manner. In the simplest case, the sequence is:

1. A conversation is initiated by a client with a service or service with another service.
2. Messages are exchanged.
3. The last message from the initiator passes control to the participating service.
4. The participating service terminates the conversation with **tpreturn(3)**.

A more complex situation results when the participating service initiates a conversation with another service (called the *subordinate participating service*, or simply, the *subordinate service*). The participating service must turn control over to the subordinate service, which in turn uses **tpreturn(3)** to end that conversation, then assuming the participating service is in control of the first conversation, it ends the first conversation with **tpreturn(3)**. If the secondary service calls **tpreturn(3)** before the second conversation has been ended by the subordinate service, both conversations will be ended in a disorderly manner. The participating service is not required to be in control of the first conversation before the subordinate service ends the conversation.

Figure 6.2 illustrates the sequence of events when a subordinate service is included in a conversation. The following steps take place in the figure.

1. The initiator uses **tpconnect(3)** to establish a conversation with the participating service, sending a message with the connection and passing control to the participating service.
2. The participating service processes the initial message, then establishes a conversation with the subordinate service, including data

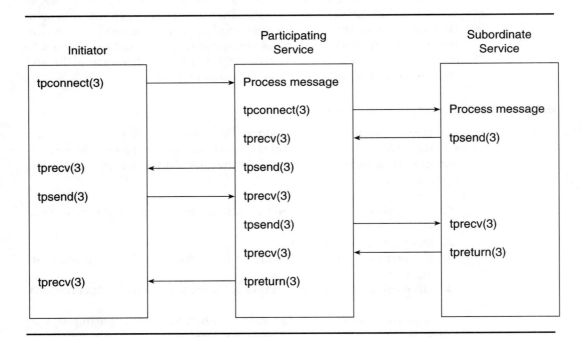

Figure 6.2   A conversation with a subordinate service.

with the connection and passing control of the subordinate conversation to the subordinate service.

3. The subordinate service sends a message back to the participating service and passes control back.

4. The participating service sends a message to the initiator passing control back.

5. The initiator sends another message to the participating service along with control.

6. The participating service sends a message to the subordinate service, passing control of the subordinate conversation.

7. The subordinate service uses **tpreturn(3)** to send the last message back to the participating service, closing the subordinate conversation.

8. The participating service uses **tpreturn(3)** to send the last message back to the initiator, closing the original conversation.

This sequence closes both conversations in an orderly manner, and if the conversations were used in transaction mode, a **tpcommit(3)** would be successful, as far as conversations are concerned.

6.3.4 Summary of Rules for Conversations

The rules for conversations are:

- Any client or service may initiate a conversation.
- Clients cannot receive connect requests.
- A participating service must be in a server identified in the configuration file as offering only conversational services.
- Conversational services cannot accept request/response requests.
- Conversational services may invoke nonconversational services with request/response calls.
- Clients may use both conversational and request/response paradigms.
- Conversational services may not use **tpforward(3)**.
- A participating service must end a conversation using a **tpreturn(3)**. The initiator cannot end a conversation, except in a disorderly manner.
- All conversations included in a transaction must be ended before the transaction can be committed (see section entitled Establishing Transaction Boundaries).

6.3.5   **Conversational Functions**

6.3.5.1 *tpconnect(3).*   The form of **tpconnect(3)** is:

```
int tpconnect(char * svc, char *data, long len, long flags)
```

tpconnect(3) initiates a conversation. Any TUXEDO client may initiate a conversation. Only conversational services that are part of conversational servers may start a conversation. The participating service is named by *svc*. If *data* is not NULL, its contents are transmitted to the participating service. *data* must be a pointer to a buffer allocated by **tpalloc(3)**. TUXEDO ignores *len* if the buffer type makes the length meaningless (such as FML), otherwise the message sent is of length *len*. The message sent with **tpconnect(3)** is acquired by the participating service in the same manner as if it were invoked as part of a request/ response sequence, that is, by using the TPSVCINFO data structure (see Chapter 9).

The parameter *data* is defined as char * for convenience. If *data* is not NULL, it must be a pointer to a typed buffer recognized by TUX-EDO. The program must use **tpalloc(3)** to allocate space for *data*.

tpconnect(3) returns a handle (called descriptor in the TUXEDO documentation) that identifies the conversation. This handle is used by other conversational functions to refer to the conversation. If **tpconnect(3)** fails, the connection is not made and **tpconnect(3)** returns −1, with the error indicator in tperrno.

flags may be a combination of the following:

TPNOTRAN Indicates that the participating service and the conversation will not be part of the current transaction (see Establishing Transaction Boundaries).

TPSENDONLY Indicates that the initiator will expect to send the next message. The participating service will be able only to receive and will not be in control of the conversation. TPSENDONLY or TPRECVONLY must be specified. They cannot both be specified.

TPRECVONLY Indicates that the initiator expects to receive the next message. The participating service can only send and has control of the conversation. TPSENDONLY or TPRECVONLY must be specified. They cannot both be specified.

TPNOBLOCK Indicates that **tpconnect(3)** should return immediately if a blocking condition exists, such as when the data buffers are full. If a blocking condition exists and TPNOBLOCK is specified, **tpconnect(3)** will fail and the connection will not be established. If TPNOBLOCK is not specified, **tpconnect(3)** will block until the condition no longer exists or there is a timeout. This flag does not apply to waiting for the acknowledgment from the server.

TPNOTIME Indicates that the blocking timeout will not occur for this execution of **tpconnect(3)**. Transaction timeouts may still occur.

TPSIGRSTRT Causes the function to be reexecuted if it is interrupted by a signal.

Errors set by **tpconnect(3)** are:

TPEINVAL Error TPEINVAL means that the parameters were set incorrectly, such as using NULL for ***svc*** or ***data*** is not a proper buffer type. This error also can mean that **flags** contained an invalid value.

TPENOENT Error TPENOENT indicates that the service named in ***svc*** is not known to the system. This error also occurs when an attempt is made to use **tpconnect(3)** to connect to a server not marked conversational.

TPEITYPE Error TPEITYPE indicates that the buffer allocated for ***idata*** is not of a type recognized by TUXEDO. Often this error indicates that the pointer has become corrupted or the program did not allocate the space with **tpalloc(3)**.

TPELIMIT Error TPELIMIT happens when the maximum number of outstanding connections is reached.

TPETRAN Error TPETRAN occurs when the invoker is in transaction mode, the service named in ***svc*** cannot operate in transaction mode and the TPNOTRAN flag was not specified.

TPETIME Error TPETIME indicates that a timeout has occurred. If the process was in transaction mode when the timeout occurred, the error is a transaction timeout. A transaction timeout sets an internal flag that will prevent the transaction from being committed. A transaction that has timed out can only be aborted. If the process was not in transaction mode and the TPNOBLOCK flag was not set, error TPETIME occurs when on a blocking timeout.

TPSVCFAIL The error TPSVCFAIL is set when the service has set the TPFAIL flag in **tpreturn(3)**. If the service sent a reply with the failure, ***data*** points to the reply in the same manner as if there had been no failure. The client and all services may continue to process normally, but TUXEDO will abort the transaction if **tpcommit(3)** is called.

TPSVCERR The error TPSVCERR is set when a service uses **tpreturn(3)** or **tpforward(3)** improperly, such as setting invalid parameters. No reply is received when this error occurs, that is **data*, its contents, and *olen* are unchanged. The client and all services may continue to process normally, but TUXEDO will abort the transaction if **tpcommit(3)** is called.

TPEBLOCK The error TPEBLOCK means that a blocking condition was present, but the TPNOBLOCK flag was set.

TPGOTSIG Error TPGOTSIG indicates that a signal occurred during process of the function, but the flag TPSIGRSTRT was not set.

TPESYSTEM The TPESYSTEM error means that there was a failure within TUXEDO. A message describing the problem is written to the log file.

TPEOS The TPEOS error means that an operating system error has occurred. This error can occur if a message queue on another node is full, but **tpcall(3)** will still return success.

6.3.5.2 *tpsend(3)*.   The form of **tpsend(3)** is:

```
int tpsend(int cd, char *data, long len, long flags,
    long *revent)
```

tpsend(3) sends a message over the conversational connection identified by *cd*. *data* must be a buffer allocated by **tpalloc(3)**. *len* is the length of the data field and is ignored if the buffer type automatically indicates length, such as FML. *data* may be NULL. **flags** may be set as described later in this section. If an event occurs, **tpsend(3)** fails, the message is not sent and an event value is placed in *revent*. **tpsend(3)** can only be called successfully by the participant in control of the conversation.

The parameter *data* is defined as char * for convenience. If *data* is not NULL, it must be a pointer to a typed buffer recognized by TUXEDO. The program must use **tpalloc(3)** to allocate space for *data*.

flags may be 0 or any combination of the following.

TPSIGRSTRT The flag TPSIGRSTRT should always be specified with **tpcall(3)** to be sure that the call is reissued if processing is interrupted by a signal during the execution of the call.

TPNOBLOCK The flag TPNOBLOCK will cause **tpsend(3)** to return immediately with the error TPEBLOCK without sending the message if there is a blocking condition, such as when there is no room in the internal buffer used for messages.

TPNOTIME The flag TPNOTIME prevents a blocking timeout. TPNOBLOCK and TPNOTIME are mutually exclusive. The transaction may still fail due to a transaction timeout.

TPRECONLY Indicates that control is transferred to the other participant. If **tpsend(3)** completes successfully with this flag set, the caller will be only able to receive and the other participant will only be able to send.

If an event occurs with **tpsend(3)**, the connection is immediately broken in a disorderly manner. The message sent with **tpsend(3)** is lost, as well as potentially other messages in the conversation. The handle for the conversation will no longer be valid. The event will be one of the following:

TPEV_DISCONIMM TPEV_DISCONIMM means that one of the following has occurred:

- **tpdiscon(3)** was called by the initiator of the conversation while a conversation was still open.
- **tpreturn(3)**, **tpcommit(3)**, or **tpabort(3)** was called by the initiator while a conversation it initiated, was still open, or a participating service had a subordinate conversation still open.
- There was a communication failure, including a network failure or a participating or subordinate service failed.

TPEV_SVCERR TPEV_SVCERR means that a participating service or a subordinate service called **tpreturn(3)** while not in control of its respective conversation. It can also mean that a **tpreturn(3)** called by a participating or subordinate service failed.

TPEV_SVCFAIL TPEV_SVCFAIL means that a participating or subordinate service called **tpreturn(3)** while not in control of the conversation, or called **tpreturn(3)** with rval set to TPFAIL or TPEXIT and *data* set to NULL.

Errors set in tperrno for **tpsend(3)** are:

TPEINVAL Error TPEINVAL means that the parameters were set incorrectly, such as when *data* does not point to a recognized buffer type. This error also can mean that **flags** contained an invalid value.

TPEBADDESC TPEBADDESC indicates that the handle in **cd** was invalid.

TPETIME Error TPETIME indicates that a timeout has occurred. If the process was in transaction mode when the timeout occurred, the error is a transaction timeout. A transaction timeout sets an internal flag that will prevent the transaction from being committed. A transaction which has timed out can only be aborted. If the process was not in transaction mode and the TPNOBLOCK flag was not set, error TPETIME occurs when on a blocking timeout.

TPEEVENT TPEEVENT means that an event occurred. The type of event is set in **revent**.

TPEBLOCK The error TPEBLOCK means that a blocking condition was present, but the TPNOBLOCK flag was set.

TPGOTSIG Error TPGOTSIG indicates that a signal occurred during process of the function, but the flag TPSIGRSTRT was not set.

TPEPROTO TPEPROTO means that **tpsend(3)** was called when the conversation did not allow the caller to send a message, such as when the caller is not in control of the conversation.

TPESYSTEM The TPESYSTEM error means that there was a failure within TUXEDO. A message describing the problem is written to the log file.

TPEOS The TPEOS error means that an operating system error has occurred. This error can occur if a message queue on another node is full, but **tpcall(3)** will still return success.

6.3.5.3 tprecv(3). The form of **tprecv(3)** is:

```
int tprecv(int cd, char **data, long *len, long flags, long
*revent)
```

tprecv(3) returns a message from the conversation identified by **cd** in the area pointed to by *data*. **len** points to the length of the data received. **flags** modify the action of **tprecv(3)**. If an event occurs, *revent* contains a value that indicates the type of event. **tprecv(3)** returns 0 upon success with no event occurrence. **tprecv(3)** returns –1 when either an error or an event occurs. Since an event can be considered a normal return, the negative value returned cannot be considered an error. The program must first check the value in **tperrno** for TPEEVENT. If TPEEVENT is in **tperrno**, **tprecv(3)** was successful, but an event occurred, with the type of event in *revent*. Note that some events may be considered a failure. If either of the events TPEV_SVCSUCC or TPEV_SVCFAIL are received, **data* contains any message that may have been sent with the **tpreturn(3)** by the participating service and **tpurcode** contains a value set by the participating service.

data and *len* may not be NULL. The area pointed to by the pointer **data* must be an area that was allocated with **tpalloc(3)**.

The following flags are valid with **tpcrecv(3)**.

TPSIGRSTRT The flag TPSIGRSTRT should always be specified to be sure that the call is reissued if processing is interrupted by a signal during the execution of the call.

TPNOCHANGE The flag TPNOCHANGE prevents TUXEDO from changing the buffer type pointed to by **data* when the return message is received. If this flag is not set and the sending participant sends a different type, the type of **data* is set to the type sent. When this flag is not set and the service attempts to return a buffer of a different type, the type of **data* does not change and the request fails with error TPEOTYPE.

TPNOBLOCK The flag TPNOBLOCK will cause **tprecv(3)** to return immediately with the error TPEBLOCK without invoking the service if there is a blocking condition. If this flag is set and there is a message available to receive, **tprecv(3)** returns immediately with the message placed in data. If this flag is not set and there is no message available, **tprecv(3)** blocks until there is a message available.

TPNOTIME The flag TPNOTIME prevents a blocking timeout. TPNOBLOCK and TPNOTIME are mutually exclusive. The transaction may still fail due to a transaction timeout.

If an event occurs, **tprecv(3)** returns −1 with the type of event in *revent*. The following events can occur with **tprecv(3)**.

TPEV_DISCONIMM TPEV_DISCONIMM means that one of the following has occurred:

- **tpdiscon(3)** was called by the initiator of the conversation while a conversation was still open.
- **tpreturn(3)**, **tpcommit(3)**, or **tpabort(3)** was called by the

initiator while a conversation it initiated, was still open, or a participating service had a subordinate conversation still open.
- There was a communication failure, including a network failure or a participating or subordinate service failed.

TPEV_SVCERR TPEV_SVCERR means that a participating service or a subordinate service called **tpreturn(3)** while not in control of its respective conversation. It can also mean that a **tpreturn(3)** called by a participating or subordinate service failed.

TPEV_SVCFAIL TPEV_SVCFAIL means that a participating or subordinate service called **tpreturn(3)** while not in control of the conversation, or called **tpreturn(3)** with rval set to TPFAIL or TPEXIT and data set to NULL.

TPEV_SENDONLY The event TPEV_SENDONLY means that the program that sent the message is passing control to the program calling **tprecv(3)**. The program receiving this event can send, but not receive.

TPEV_SVCSUCC The event TPEV_SVCSUCC means that the participating service has closed the conversation in a normal fashion. If the conversation was taking place in transaction mode, the transaction may be successfully committed, from the standpoint of the conversation. The handle, *cd*, is no longer valid after this event.

The following errors can be set in **tperrno** if **tprecv(3)** fails.

TPEINVAL Error TPEINVAL means that the parameters were set incorrectly, such as when *data* points to a buffer type not recognized by TUXEDO or **flags** is set to an invalid value.

TPEOTYPE Error TPEOTYPE indicates that the buffer allocated for *data* is not of a type recognized by TUXEDO. Often this error indicates that the pointer has become corrupted or the program did not allocate the space with **tpalloc(3)**. This error also occurs when the flag TPNOCHANGE is set and the buffer type returned is different than the buffer type allocated.

TPEBADDESC TPEBADDESC indicates that the handle in *cd* was invalid.

TPETIME Error TPETIME indicates that a timeout has occurred. If the process was in transaction mode when the timeout occurred, the error is a transaction timeout. A transaction timeout sets an internal flag that will prevent the transaction form being committed. A transaction which has timed out can only be aborted. If the process was not in transaction mode and the TPNOBLOCK flag was not set, error TPETIME occurs when on a blocking timeout.

TPEEVENT TPEEVENT means that an event occurred. The type of event is set in *revent*.

TPEBLOCK The error TPEBLOCK means that a blocking condition was present, and the TPNOBLOCK flag was set.

TPGOTSIG Error TPGOTSIG indicates that a signal occurred during process of the function, but the flag TPSIGRSTRT was not set.

TPEPROTO TPEPROTO means that **tprecv(3)** was called when the conversation did not allow the caller to receive a message, such as when the caller is allowed only to send messages.

TPESYSTEM The TPESYSTEM error means that there was a failure within TUXEDO. A message describing the problem is written to the log file.

TPEOS The TPEOS error means that an operating system error has occurred.

6.3.5.4 *tpdiscon(3).*   The form of **tpdiscon(3)** is:

```
int tpdiscon(int cd)
```

tpdiscon(3) immediately closes the conversation identified by *cd* in a disorderly manner. If the conversation is part of a transaction, the transaction will be aborted by TUXEDO, even if **tpcommit(3)** is called. Messages may be lost when **tpdiscon(3)** is called. **tpdiscon(3)** may only be called by the initiator of a conversation. If called by a participating service, **tpdiscon(3)** fails with a TPEBADDESC error without affecting the conversation.

tpdiscon(3) returns 0 for success, –1 for failure. Errors that can be set in **tperrno** are:

TPEBADDESC TPEBADDESC indicates that the handle in *cd* was invalid.

TPETIME Error TPETIME indicates that a timeout has occurred. The descriptor will not be valid if this error occurs.

TPESYSTEM The TPESYSTEM error means that there was a failure within TUXEDO. A message describing the problem is written to the log file.

TPEOS The TPEOS error means that an operating system error has occurred. The descriptor will not be valid if this error occurs.

6.4   **ESTABLISHING TRANSACTION BOUNDARIES**

6.4.1   **About Transactions**

A transaction is bounded by a *begin transaction* and an *end transaction*. The simplest method of setting transaction boundaries is to start a transaction with a **tpbegin()** function call, and end the transaction with either a successful completion, **tpcommit()**, or an unsuccessful completion, **tpabort()**. Between the begin transaction and end transaction, the application is said to be in *transaction mode*.

The **tpbegin()** function can be called from a client or any service, but the **tpcommit()** and **tpabort()** must be called from the same client or service that called **tpbegin()**.

Figure 6.3 illustrates a simple use of **tpbegin()** and **tpcommit()**. The client calls **tpbegin()**, invokes two services, then calls **tpcommit()** to end the transaction. When the **tpcommit()** is called, it causes the transaction manager to cooperate with the resource managers to commit all work done with the resources by the client and the two services.

Figure 6.4 illustrates a slightly more complex situation. In this case, the client does not control the begin and end of the transaction. Instead, the client invokes service 1, which calls **tpbegin()** to start a transaction and **tpcommit()** to end the transaction. In this situation, work done by the client will not be part of the transaction. Only work done by the three services will be included in the commit. Any resources modification by the client will be outside of the transaction.

An administrative (see Administration) value, AUTOTRAN, can be set on any service. When AUTOTRAN is set on for a service, the service always runs in transaction mode. If transaction mode was not set when the service starts, a transaction is automatically started. When the

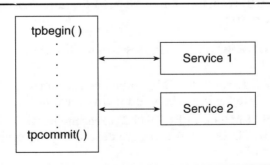

Figure 6.3   A simple transaction.

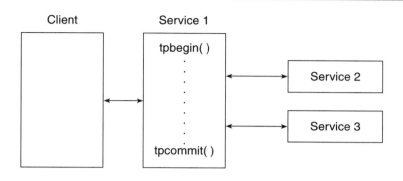

Figure 6.4   Transaction controlled in a service.

service completes (with either **tpreturn()** or **tpforward()**) the transaction is ended. If the service completed normally, the transaction is committed. If the service issued a **tpreturn()** with the TPFAIL flag set, the transaction is rolled back.

If an AUTOTRAN service invokes other services, they become part of the transaction in the same manner as if the AUTOTRAN service had explicitly started and ended a transaction.

When a service set to AUTOTRAN is invoked in transaction mode, the AUTOTRAN is ignored and the service becomes part of the existing transaction. In this case the work done by the service and any services invoked by it will be either committed or aborted by the client or service that began the transaction.

Figure 6.5 illustrates a more complex transaction structure. Service 1 is included in the current transaction. Any work done by service 1 will be committed or aborted when the transaction is ended. The first **tpacall(3)** invokes service 2 with the flag TPNOTRAN set. Service 2 will not be part of the transaction, but may be set administratively to run as a separate transaction, or service 2 may use explicit transaction start and end with **tpbegin(3)** and **tpcommit(3)** (or **tpabort(3)**). Service 2 will return its results when the client calls **tpgetreply(3)**. Service 2 must return an indication of its success or failure; even if service 2 runs in transaction mode, the success or failure of the transaction is independent of the transaction run by the client and no indication of the transaction ending condition (commit or abort) is returned with the result. The second **tpacall(3)** invokes service 3 with the flags TPNOTRAN and TPNOREPLY. Service 3 may run in transaction mode or not, in the same manner as discussed with

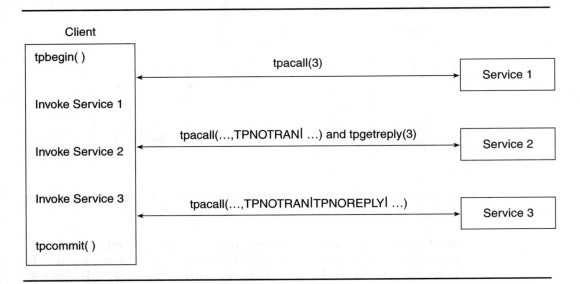

Figure 6.5   Complex transaction.

service 2, but since no reply is expected, the results will not be known by the client.

6.4.2   Transaction Management Functions

***6.4.2.1** tpbegin(3).*   Transactions are explicitly started with **tpbegin(3)**, which has the form:

```
int tpbegin (unsigned long timeout, long flags)
```

The timeout parameter is the minimum number of seconds the transaction will be allowed to run before timing out. If a transaction timeout occurs, the transaction is aborted by the system. Flags are reserved for futures and must be set to 0.

If timeout is set to 0, the system default is used for transaction timeout, which is the largest number of seconds that an unsigned long can count. When this is done, other timeouts usually prevent difficulty (such as the blocking timeout), but it is a good idea to always set the transaction timeout to a reasonable number. The timeout for transactions begun with **tpbegin(3)** cannot be affected administratively. Only transactions started administratively (AUTOTRAN—set for servers only) can be affected by administrative timeout values.

tpbegin(3) may be called by any client or any service if it is not already in transaction mode. If **tpbegin(3)** is called while the client or service is already in transaction mode, the error TPEPROTO is placed in **tperrno**. In general, it is easier to manage transactions from a client, but some application designs make it desirable to start transactions in a service. It is important to note that **tpcommit(3)** and **tpabort(3)** must be issued from the same process (in a practical sense, the same client or service), which called **tpbegin(3)**.

This function returns –1 if it fails and sets the error code in **tperrno**. The possible errors are:

TPEINVAL The error TPEINVAL means that **flags** is not set to zero.

TPETRAN Error TPETRAN occurs when **tpbegin(3)** cannot begin a transaction because of some failure.

TPEPROTO Error TPEPROTO occurs when the context is not correct for **tpbegin(3)**, for instance, the process is already in transaction mode.

TPESYSTEM The TPESYSTEM error means that there was a failure within TUXEDO. A message describing the problem is written to the log file.

TPEOS The TPEOS error means that an operating system error has occurred.

6.4.2.2 tpcommit(3). Transactions are committed with **tpcommit(3)**, which has the form:

```
int tpcommit(long flags)
```

The parameter **flags** is reserved for futures and must be set to 0.

tpcommit(3) returns –1 if it cannot commit the transaction and places a value in **tperrno** to indicate the condition that prevented successful completion. The errors returned by **tpcommit(3)** are:

TPEINVAL This error simply means that **flags** was not set to 0. The transaction is not affected.

TPETIME Error TPETIME indicates that the transaction timed out before the **tpcommit(3)** was issued. The status of the transaction is unknown, because it may have committed or aborted. Generally timeouts cause a transaction to abort. If the transaction was aborted for any reason, including timeout, the error returned will be TPEABORT.

TPEABORT Error TPEABORT means that the transaction was aborted instead of committed. This error can be caused by the following conditions:

- The transaction timed out and was aborted.
- Some service returned with TPFAIL.
- Some resource was unable to successfully commit and the transaction manager caused the transaction to abort.
- There was an outstanding reply after a **tpacall(3)**. Either the response was ready and the program did not issue a successful **tpgetrply(3)**, or the response was not ready at the time the last **tpgetrply(3)** was issued to retrieve it.
- A conversational connection was open.

TPEPROTO Error TPEPROTO indicates that **tpcommit(3)** was called in a circumstance where it is not possible to commit. Two conditions often occur that cause this error: **tpcommit(3)** is called from a participating service, rather than from the transaction initiator, or the program was not running in transaction mode when **tpcommit(3)** was called.

TPEHEURISTIC and **TPEHAZARD** These two errors occur when there has been some failure that caused manual intervention of some sort. If either of these errors occur it is not possible for the program to determine if the transaction was committed or aborted.

TPESYSTEM The TPESYSTEM error means that there was a failure within TUXEDO. A message describing the problem is written to the log file.

TPEOS The TPEOS error means that an operating system error has occurred.

6.4.2.3 tpabort(3).   If the program that started the transaction discovers a need to abort the transaction, it calls **tpabort(3)**, which has the form:

```
int tpabort(long flags)
```

The parameter **flags** is reserved for future use and must be set to 0.

It is possible for **tpabort(3)** to fail. Upon failure **tpabort(3)** returns −1 and sets **tperrno** to a value that indicates the type of failure. The possible failures are:

TPEINVAL This error simply means that **flags** was not set to 0. The transaction is not affected.

TPEPROTO Error TPEPROTO indicates that **tpabort(3)** was called in a circumstance where it is not possible to abort a transaction. Two conditions often occur to cause this error: **tpabort(3)** is called from a participating service, rather than from the transaction initiator, or the program was not running in transaction mode when **tpabort(3)** was called.

TPEHEURISTIC and **TPEHAZARD** These two errors occur when there has been some failure that caused manual intervention of some sort. If either of these errors occur, it is not possible for the program to determine if the transaction was committed or aborted.

TPESYSTEM The TPESYSTEM error means that there was a failure within TUXEDO. A message describing the problem is written to the log file.

TPEOS The TPEOS error means that an operating system error has occurred.

6.4.2.4 *tpgetlev(3)*.   The form of **tpgetlev(3)** is:

```
int tpgetlev()
```

tpgetlev(3) returns a value that indicates the transactional status of the calling process. If the return is 0, the process is not in transaction mode. If the return is 1, the process is in transaction mode. If **tpgetlev(3)** fails, it returns –1 and sets **tperrno** to indicate the type of error.

The possible errors are:

TPESYSTEM The TPESYSTEM error means that there was a failure within TUXEDO. A message describing the problem is written to the log file.

TPEOS The TPEOS error means that an operating system error has occurred.

6.5   MISCELLANEOUS FUNCTIONS

6.5.1   tptypes(3)

The form of **tptypes(3)** is:

```
long tptypes(char *msgptr, char *type, char *subtype)
```

tptypes(3) examines the buffer pointed to by ***msgptr*** and places the type of the buffer in ***type*** and the subtype in ***subtype***. ***type*** must point to a character array at least 8 bytes long, since buffer type names have a maximum length of 8 bytes. ***subtype*** must point to a character array at least 16 bytes long, since buffer subtype names have a maximum length of 16 bytes. The recommendation is to provide one extra character (9 and 17) and place a NULL in the final byte of the array. **tptypes(3)** will NULL terminate the returned string unless the name is of maximum length. If there is no subtype provided with the buffer, ***subtype*** will contain a NULL character in the first byte of the array.

tptypes(3) returns the length of the buffer upon success. If **tptypes(3)** fails, it returns –1 and sets **tperrno** to indicate the type of error. The possible errors are:

TPEINVAL TPEINVAL indicates that invalid parameters were passed with **tptypes(3)**. The most likely problem is that the buffer being tested was not allocated with **tpalloc(3)**, and is therefore not a typed buffer.

TPESYSTEM The TPESYSTEM error means that there was a failure within TUXEDO. A message describing the problem is written to the log file.

TPEOS The TPEOS error means that an operating system error has occurred.

6.5.2   userlog(3)

The form of **userlog(3)** is:

```
int userlog(char * format [,arg] ...)
```

userlog(3) appends a record to the TUXEDO user log, which has the default file name of ULOG.*date*. The record is defined by the format string and the arguments. The form of these parameters is the same as for the C function **printf()**.

The user log is a standard UNIX file. Its location and name can be controlled by the administrator. **userlog(3)** appends the following information to the beginning of each record:

- The time the record was written
- The name of the machine that **userlog(3)** was called from
- The name of the server or client that called **userlog(3)**
- The process-id that called **userlog(3)**

If **userlog(3)** is called while the process is in transaction mode, the XID is also appended.

6.5.3   **tpstrerror(3)**

The form of **tpstrerror(3)** is:

```
char *tpstrerror(int tperrno)
```

tpstrerror(3) uses *tperrno* to search the TUXEDO error library for a string that describes the error. Upon success, **tpstrerror(3)** returns a pointer to the selected string. If **tpstrerror(3)** fails, it returns NULL, but does not set **tperrorno**.

The following code fragment illustrates how **tpstrerror(3)** and **userlog(3)** can be used to report a failure.

```
#include <stdio.h>
#include "atmi.h"         /* TUXEDO Header File */
#include "fml.h"

   .
   .
   .

   char *errstr;

   if((sendbuf = (FBFR *) tpalloc("FML", NULL, sendlen)) ==
(FBFR
*)  NULL) {
       errstr = tpstrerror(tperrno);
       userlog("%s", errstr);
       tpterm();
       exit(1);
   }
```

Typed Buffers

7.1   OVERVIEW

All messages transmitted between TUXEDO application processes must use a buffer of a type known to TUXEDO. TUXEDO provides four buffer types: CARRAY, STRING, VIEW, and FML. Other types may be defined as necessary. All buffer types except CARRAY allow automatic translation and bit rearrangement of the information across platforms, including ASCII to EBCDIC as required. The need for translation or bit rearrangement between platforms is controlled administratively.

CARRAY buffers are defined as an array of characters. Any bit configuration is allowed for each character, including NULL. CARRAY buffers are transmitted bit for bit with no translation, even if crossing platforms. No data-dependent routing is provided for CARRAY buffers. X_OCTET is defined as an alias for CARRAY to support XATMI.

STRING buffers are defined as a single NULL terminated string of characters. STRING buffers are automatically translated when necessary if messages cross platforms. No data-dependent routing is provided for STRING buffers.

VIEW buffers are defined to use standard C structures for access. VIEW buffers allow both automatic translation and data dependent routing. VIEW32 functions the same as VIEW, except that VIEW32 has expanded identifiers, counter variables, and size variables. X_C_TYPE and X_COMMON are defined as aliases of VIEW to support XATMI.

Field manipulation language (FML) buffers are fielded buffers that provide a means to use a rich assortment of TUXEDO functions for manipulation. FML buffers allow for both automatic translation and data-dependent routing. FML buffers also have the advantage that the amount of data transmitted is calculated so that only significant information is actually transmitted. FML32 functions the same as FML except that FML32 has a number of expanded capabilities.

All defined buffer types, including user defined buffer types, may be used in clients and services to transmit data. FML buffers may be used independently in any program that has access to the TUXEDO libraries, using special FML allocation functions.

Buffers used for messages must be allocated with **tpalloc(3)**. Buffer sizes may be changed with **tprealloc(3)**. The required size of CARRAY, STRING, and VIEW buffers is determined within the program by the size of the space defined for the C array or structure used to load the buffer. The required size of an FML buffer can be determined using the functions described in the discussion on FML buffers. TUXEDO buffers must be freed with **tpfree(3)**. Using any of the C space allocation functions (**malloc()**, **free()**, etc.) for message buffers will cause failures.

7.2   CARRAY BUFFERS

CARRAY buffers are used to transmit binary data between TUXEDO processes. CARRAY buffers are transmitted bit for bit with no rearrangement or translation of the information. If the transmission crosses platforms, the bit and byte sequence remains identical to the original sequence. This type of buffer must be used with care if platforms requiring differing bit sequences or translation are used or could potentially be used in the system. The minimum length of a CARRAY buffer is one byte.

Create a CARRAY buffer using **tpalloc(3)** with the type set to CARRAY and the length set to the desired length. Load the buffer using any of the C copy functions (**memcpy()** is recommended because NULLs are allowed) or any other method to transfer binary data that is allowed by C.

7.3   STRING BUFFERS

A STRING buffer is useful for transmitting a string of characters. The buffer holds one NULL terminated string. This type of buffer is translated as necessary when the message moves from one platform to another. Data dependent routing cannot be used with STRING buffers. The minimum length of a STRING buffer is 512 bytes.

Create a STRING buffer using **tpalloc(3)** with the type set to "STRING" and the length set to the desired length. Load the buffer using any of the C copy functions (**strcpy()** is recommended) or any other method to transfer string data that is allowed by C.

7.4 VIEW BUFFERS

7.4.1 Overview

There are two types of VIEW buffers: those used in combination with FML buffers and independent VIEW buffers. This section discusses independent VIEW buffers. Information on FML dependent VIEW buffers is provided in the next section, which discusses FML buffers. There are two versions of VIEW: VIEW and VIEW32. VIEW uses C short integers to store field sizes, while VIEW32 uses C long integers. As a result, VIEW string and carray fields have a maximum of approximately 64Kb, while VIEW32 fields can be as large as approximately 2Mb. The utilities, environment variables, and so on associated with VIEW32 all have a "32" appended to the name, while the VIEW equivalents have no number appended. For example, **viewc(1)** compiles VIEW viewfiles, while **viewc32(1)** compiles VIEW32 viewfiles.

A VIEW buffer requires a number of preparatory steps before it can be used. (Using VIEW buffers in COBOL is similar to using them in C. Specific information on COBOL is contained in Chapter 13.) The steps are:

1. Define the VIEW by creating a VIEW in a viewfile.
2. Run **viewc(1)** or **viewc32(1)** with the **-n** option to create a compiled viewfile and a header file.
3. Use **#include** to include the header file or files in the source for application clients and servers required for the buffers used.
4. Set the environment variables VIEWFILES and VIEWDIR (or VIEWFILES32 and VIEWDIR32) before running applications using VIEW buffers.

7.4.2 Definition

The viewfile is described in the TUXEDO reference manual as viewfile(5). The VIEW compiler is listed as viewc(1). The discussion in this section provides some pointers about using VIEW buffers. The reader should consult the TUXEDO documentation for more details.

viewc(1) and **viewc32(1)** create two output files: *viewname*.V and *viewname*.h. *viewname*.V is an object version of the VIEW. *viewname*.h contains a C structure to use for accessing the VIEW.

The first line of each VIEW in the viewfile must be **VIEW *viewname***. The name of the VIEW is used in the subtype argument used in **tpalloc(3)** to allocate space for the buffer. Although the name in the viewfile may be up to 33 characters, it is a good idea to limit the name of each VIEW to 16 characters because **tpalloc(3)** allows a maximum of 16 characters for the subtype. The last line of each VIEW must be simply END.

Every field of the viewfile must be specified on the definition lines. If the default is intended, a dash (-) must be placed in the viewfile field for the element.

The type of each element may be specified as char, string, carray, long, short, int, float, double, and dec_t. All may be used in both CO-BOL and C programs. dec_t is a special format to accommodate information that was originally in packed decimal format (COBOL COMP-3 format).

size must be specified for the types carray and string. The maximum size allowed for VIEW views is 65,535 bytes. The maximum size allowed for VIEW32 views is approximately 2Mb. The maximum allowable size is the only difference between VIEW and VIEW32 files.

The following example viewfile is a VIEW file.

```
VIEW testv1
# type    cname     fbname    count    flag    size    null
char      char1     -         1        -       -       -
string    str1      -         1        -       9       -
carray    cary1     -         1        -       8       -
long      long1     -         1        -       -       -
short     short1    -         1        -       -       -
int       int1      -         1        -       -       -
END
#
VIEW testv2
# type    cname     fbname    count    flag    size    null
char      char2     -         1        -       -       -
string    str2      -         5        C       9       -
carray    cary2     -         1        L       16      -
long      long2     -         1        -       -       -
short     short2    -         1        -       -       -
int       int2      -         1        -       -       -
END
```

If the name of the above viewfile was exampview.v, **viewc(1)** created the header file exampview.h, which looks like this:

```
struct testv1 {
    char    char1;
    char    str1[9];
    char    cary1[8];
    long    long1;
    short short1;
    int     int1;
};

struct testv2 {
    char    char2;
    short C_str2;       /* count of str2 */
    char str2[5][9];
    unsigned short L_cary2;       /* length of cary2 */
    char    cary2[16];
    long    long2;
    short short2;
    int int2;
};
```

The following VIEW32 file is similar to the VIEW file above, except that the length of one string is increased.

```
VIEW testv1
# type   cname   fbname   count   flag    size    null
char     char1   -        1       -       -       -
string   str1    -        1       -       9       -
carray   cary1   -        1       -       8       -
long     long1   -        1       -       -       -
short    short1  -        1       -       -       -
int      int1    -        1       -       -       -
END
#
VIEW testv2
# type   cname   fbname   count   flag    size    null
char     char2   -        1       -       -       -
string   str2    -        5       C       100000  -
carray   cary2   -        1       L       8       -
long     long2   -        1       -       -       -
short    short2  -        1       -       -       -
int      int2    -        1       -       -       -
END
```

Assuming the name of the viewfile was the same as previously mentioned, **viewc32(1)** created exampview.h, which looks like:

```
struct testv1 {
    char    char1;
    char    str1[9];
    char    cary1[8];
    long    long1;
    short short1;
    int int1;
};

struct testv2 {
    char    char2;
    long    C_str2;     /* count of str2 */
    char    str2[5][100000];
    unsigned long L_cary2;        /* length of cary2 */
    char    cary2[16];
    long    long2;
    short short2;
    int int2;
};
```

The examples show the use of the flag options C and L. testv2 has provided for five occurrences of str2 and the C **flag** option is set. The resulting structure includes C_str2, which will contain the actual number of occurrences in the buffer. This variable is called the associated count member (ACM). When loading the buffer, the program should place the number of occurrences to be transmitted into the ACM. TUXEDO will then transmit only that amount of data. When a buffer is received and an ACM is present, the actual number of members received is placed into the ACM by TUXEDO.

The carray type named cary2 uses the L **flag** option. The resulting structure for testv2 includes the variable L_cary2. This variable is called the associated length member (ALM). When loading the buffer, the program should place the actual length of the element to be transmitted into the ALM. TUXEDO will then transmit only that amount of data. When a buffer is received and an ALM is present, the actual length received is placed into the ALM by TUXEDO.

The **flag** options may be used in combination. The options do not require a delimiter as shown in the following example, but a comma may be used.

```
VIEW showflag
# type    cname    fbname    count    flag    size      null
string    str2     -         5        CL      100000    -
carray    cary2    -         1        L       16        -
END
```

If the viewfile above was named showflags.v, then when **viewc32(1)** is run, the header file is named showflags.h and looks as follows:

```
struct showflag {
    unsigned long L_str2[5];     /* length array of str2 */
    long    C_str2;   /* count of str2 */
    char    str2[5][100000];
    unsigned long L_cary2;       /* length of cary2 */
    char    cary2[16];
};
```

Note that the length for str2 is an array, L_str2, to provide a length for each occurrence of str2.

7.4.3   Use

At runtime, TUXEDO uses the compiled output from viewc or viewc32. Each of these utilities creates a compiled viewfile with a name of the form *viewname*.V. The environment variables, VIEWFILES, VIEWDIR, VIEWFILES32, and VIEWDIR32 allow for multiple directories and files. VIEWFILES and VIEWFILES32 require comma separated lists, such as:

```
VIEWFILES32=/myappdir/myview1.V,relativevfile.V
```

The files identified with full path name will be used as they are, /myappdir/myview1.V in the example above. TUXEDO searches the directories specified by VIEWDIR or VIEWDIR32 for any file names specified in relative notation, such as relativevfile.V in the above example. If VIEWDIR or VIEWDIR32 is not in the environment, TUXEDO uses the current directory for relative file names. The list of directories with VIEWDIR and VIEWDIR32 is separated by colons, such as:

```
VIEWDIR32=/myappdir:/otherappdir
```

If **tpalloc(3)** is used with type VIEW, the system will assume VIEW buffers are being used. If **tpalloc(3)** is used with type VIEW32, the system will assume VIEW32 buffers are being used. It is best not to mix these types in the same application, but if it is necessary to do so, be careful to use the specific types mentioned. Note that when these types are used there is no conversion from VIEW to VIEW32 by the system. See the discussion on conversion from VIEW to VIEW32 in the next section, FML Buffers. The following program fragment illustrates using VIEW buffers in a client:

```
#include <stdio.h>
#include "atmi.h"          /* TUXEDO  Header File */
#include "sampview16.h"  /* view16 header file from viewc(1) */
#include "sampview32.h"  /* view32 header file from viewc32(1) */

/* some application code may be here, including tpinit(3) */

/* allocate a view16 buffer */

    if((sendbuf = (struct sampview16 *) tpalloc("VIEW",
      "sampview16", sendlen+1)) == (struct sampview16 *) NULL) {
      fprintf(stderr,"Error allocating send buffer %d\n",
          tperrno);
      tpterm();
      exit(1);
    }

/* there may be some application code here */

/* allocate a view32 buffer */

    if((sendbuf32 = (struct sampview32 *) tpalloc("VIEW32",
        "sampview32", sendlen+1)) == (struct sampview32 *) NULL) {
      fprintf(stderr,"Error allocating send 32 buffer %d\n",
      tperrno);
      tpterm();
      exit(1);
    }

/* some application code here */

/* SAMP16 is a service that expects a view16 buffer */
/* Request the service SAMP16, waiting for a reply */
    ret = tpcall("SAMP16", (char *) sendbuf, 0, (char**) &rcvbuf,
      &rcvlen, (long)0);
```

```
        if(ret == -1) {
          fprintf(stderr, "Can't send request to service
              TOUPPER\n");
          fprintf(stderr, "Tperrno = %d\n", tperrno);
          tpfree((char *) sendbuf);
          tpfree((char *) rcvbuf);
          tpterm();
          exit(1);
        }

/* application code here */

/* COUNT32 is a service that expects a view32 buffer */
/* Request the service COUNT32, waiting for a reply */
    ret = tpcall("COUNT32", (char *) sendbuf32, 0, (char**)
        &rcvbuf32, &rcvlen, (long)0);

    if(ret == -1) {
      fprintf(stderr, "Can't send request to service
          COUNT32\n");
      fprintf(stderr, "Tperrno = %d\n", tperrno);
      tpfree((char *) sendbuf32);
      tpfree((char *) rcvbuf32);
      tpterm();
      exit(1);
    }

/* final set of application code which may include tpterm(3) */
/* and exit()                                                */
```

7.5   FML BUFFERS

7.5.1   Overview

FML provides a rich set of C functions to manipulate FML buffers. This section will discuss how to create and use FML buffers. For a complete detailed discussion of all FML features see the FML Guide in the TUXEDO documentation. FML also provides a VIEW facility to map FML buffers to C headers that operate similarly to the VIEW buffers described in the previous section. As with VIEWs, there are two flavors of FML: FML16 and FML32. The discussions in this section sometimes list specific FML32 information. If simply FML is used, the discussion applies to both flavors. FML functions all come in two types: those for FML16 and those for FML32. The FML32 functions have the same names as those for FML16, but with "32" added to the name, that is, **Fchg(3)** is an FML16 function and **Fchg32(3)** is an FML32 function. The functions work identically and the descriptions here apply to both flavors equally. Note that the parameters used to pass arguments and receive results with FML32 functions require the FML32 version of all FML types.

FML functions provide a wide range of functionality, as follows:

- Field ID functions to access the fldid, the name of the field, and the attributes of the field
- Buffer management functions to determine the amount of space needed for buffers and to allocate buffer when FML is not being used for passing messages
- Functions for moving and copying entire buffers
- Functions for adding data to a buffer and changing data in a buffer
- Functions for retrieving data from a buffer
- Functions for finding data in a buffer
- Full buffer operations that allow modifying a buffer using the data in another buffer
- Indexing functions to delete and add buffer indexes
- Functions that move buffers to and from files or streams
- Boolean operation functions that evaluate boolean expressions with information in FML buffers

The steps for using FML buffers are:

1. Create FML field table files.
2. Setup FML environment variables FIELDTBLS and FLDTBLDIR and/or FIELDTBLS32 and FLDTBLDIR32.
3. Run **mkfldhdr(1)** to create header file for use in application programs.
4. At runtime, be sure the proper environment variables are set.

See the discussion on using VIEWs with FML buffers for additional steps required for this feature.

Fields in FML buffers are self-defining, that is, the information that defines the data type and length of the field is contained within the field. Each field is structured as illustrated in Figure 7.1. The fldid is a numeric value assigned when the field is defined. The length is the

Figure 7.1   FML field.

maximum length the field can be, assigned when the field is defined. The length will be present when needed, as for string and carray types. The data contains the data for one or more occurrences of the data for the field. If no occurrences of the data are in the buffer, only the fldid will be present for the field.

An FML buffer with several fields is shown in Figure 7.2. Some of the fields have a length attribute and others don't.

An FML buffer has the logical view shown in Figure 7.3. The data can be considered in columns, with each column headed by the

fldid	len	data	fldid	data	fldid	data	fldid	len	data	...

Figure 7.2   An FML buffer.

oc	field 1 Type: string Length: *n*	field 2 Type: long
0	"a string"	1234
1	*no data here*	5432
2	"another string"	6789

Figure 7.3   FML buffer logical view.

fldid and the field attributes. There may be multiple occurrences of each field, as noted in the column "oc." Each occurrence represents a logical record, shown as rows in Figure 7.3. FML manages buffers such that the data uses only as much space as needed, up to the amount of space that has been allocated. Thus field 1, occurrence 1 will take no space. Each of the strings will take only the space necessary to hold the individual string. FML functions that manipulate fields use the combination of fldid and occurrence (oc) to access the information in fields.

An empty occurrence for a field is the equivalent of a NULL. If a null value is put into an occurrence, FML routines detect it and use no space for it. When the empty occurrence is retrieved a null value is returned. Null values can be specified in the field tables for each field or the default value can be used. The defaults are 0 for numeric fields, "\0" for strings and "" for carrays.

When an FML buffer is allocated, an index is created. The index is used to access the buffer by the FML functions. Functions are provided to delete and rebuild the index so that if the buffer is transmitted to a service, the amount of data transmitted can be minimized.

7.5.2   Definition

FML buffers are defined in field table files. These files are made available to TUXEDO at run time by the environment variables FIELDTBLS and FLDTBLDIR and/or FIELDTBLS32 and FLDTBLDIR32. Access to fields is simplified by using **mkfldhdr(1)** to create header files from the field table files. A sample of a field table file is:

```
# name     fld-nbr   type       flag comment
*base 200
mystr1     1         string      -   my own first string
$ /* this comment was placed after the string definition */
achar      2         char        -   this is a char field
along      3         long        -   this is a long integer
ashort     4         short       -   this is a short integer
afloat     5         float       -   this is a floating point
adouble    6         double      -   this is a double float
acarray    7         carray      -   this is a carray
```

When **mkfldhdr(1)** is run with this file it creates the following header file:

```
/*   fname      fldid         */
/*    —        —            */
#define   mystr1    ((FLDID)41161) /* number: 201  type: string
*/
/* this comment was placed after the string definition */
#define   achar     ((FLDID)16586) /* number: 202  type: char */
#define   along     ((FLDID)8395)  /* number: 203  type: long */
#define   ashort    ((FLDID)204)   /* number: 204  type: short */
#define   afloat    ((FLDID)24781) /* number: 205  type: float */
#define   adouble   ((FLDID)32974) /* number: 206  type: double
*/
#define   acarray   ((FLDID)49359) /* number: 207  type: carray
*/
```

If the name of the field table file is sampflds, the name of the header file will be sampflds.h. Fields in FML buffers are identified by a numeric *field identifier*, called fldid in the documentation and **typdef**'d as FLDID in the header file generated by **mkfldhdr(1)**. Fields are assigned a *field number* in the field table file. FML allows up to 8,191 field numbers within a single TUXEDO domain. FML32 allows up to 33,554,431 field numbers. Field numbers 1–100 are reserved for use by TUXEDO. The rest are available for use by applications. **mkfldhdr(1)** generates the field identifier by combining a numeric field type with the field number to make a unique field identifier.

The line beginning with ***base** in the example sets the base field number, in this case 200. The field number assigned is added to the base to get the actual field number. The base number can be set to identify the field numbers for the applications in a system. For instance, the accounts receivable base might be 200, and the inventory base might be 2000, leaving 102–200 for system programmer use. Accounts receivable will thus use field numbers 200–2000 and inventory will use 2001 through some other number set by policy. This method uses a lot of numbers so use of FML32 is desirable.

The name of a field can be any legal C name. The type can be char, string, short, long, float, double, or carray. The numeric types correspond directly with the C data types of the same name. Type char is always a single character. Type string is a NULL terminated string, as in C. The type carray is a string of binary bytes and maps to a C character array. The flag column is reserved for future use. The comment area can contain any value and will be ignored by **mkfldhdr(1)**. Lines beginning with # and blank lines are ignored by **mkfldhdr(1)**. Lines beginning with $ are moved without change to the header file by **mkfldhdr(1)**. Be sure to present these lines as proper C comments.

7.5.3 **Definition of mkfldhdr(1)**

mkfldhdr(1) is a utility that creates a header file from an FML field table file. The resulting include file should be included in all programs that use the FML buffers defined in the field table file. The fields defined in the field table file are used to create #DEFINE statements that should be used to identify fields when using FML functions.

The forms of **mkfldhdr(1)** and **mkfldhdr32** are:

```
mkfldhdr [-d outdir] [field_table ...]
mkfldhdr32 [-d outdir] [field_table ...]
```

The **-d** option can be specified to name a path where the header files are written. If not specified the header files are written on the current directory.

If field table files are named on the command line the named files are processed. If no field table files are named on the command line, **mkfldhdr** uses the field table files named in the environment variable FIELDTBLS as input. A header file is created for each field table file. The name of the header file is created by adding **.h** to the name of the field table file.

7.5.4 **Allocating FML Buffers**

If buffers are going to be used for messages between TUXEDO application processes, use **tpalloc(3)** with the type set as FML to allocate the buffers. **tpalloc(3)** will properly initialize the buffer for use with FML. The TUXEDO documentation seems to indicate that buffers can be allocated using the C function **malloc()**; use **malloc()** only if the buffers are being used strictly internal to the program. Buffers for use as messages MUST be allocated with **tpalloc(3)**. Use **Falloc(3)** to allocate internal buffers that will not be used as messages to services.

The size required for the buffer can be determined using **Fneeded(3)**. This function accepts the number of occurrences of all fields and the size of the fields and returns an estimate of the amount of space needed. For instance, if there are five fields in the buffer and eight occurrences are expected for each field, the number of occurrences passed to **Fneeded(3)** will be 40. If the average length of all fields is 10, then the number of bytes for all fields is set to 400. **Fneeded(3)** estimates the amount of space required for FML overhead, combines it with the number of fields and the amount of space required for data and returns the result. If an FML buffer already exists, such as when a message is received by a service, **Fsizeof(3)** can be used to find the size of the received buffer. After data has been added to a buffer, use **Fused(3)** to find out how much space has been used. The return from **Fused(3)** can be subtracted from the amount originally allocated to see if there is enough space for additional information before a failure occurs while adding information to the buffer. If more space is required, use **tprealloc(3)** to expand the size of a message buffer, or **Frealloc(3)** to expand the size of a buffer used internally.

7.5.5   **Changing the Contents of an FML Buffer**

Use **Fadd(3)** to add an occurrence to a field. Fadd(3) creates another occurrence after the last one already in the buffer in the named field and places the data into it. **Fadd(3)** does not affect any values already in the buffer, nor will it put data into an empty occurrence of the field. **Fadd(3)** is especially useful for loading the buffer from an array, such as shown in the following code fragment.

```
int I;
long number[10];
FBFR bufptr;
. . .
for(i=0; i < 10; i++)
}
    if(Fadd(bufptr, NUMFLD, &number[i], 0)  <0)
    {
      /* Put error handling here */
    }
} /* end of for loop */
/* The values in number have been loaded into the buffer */
```

The value number[0] will be placed in occurrence 0 if there is no occurrence of the field already present. Otherwise the value in number[0] will be placed in the next occurrence.

Use **Fchg(3)** to change the value of occurrences already in a buffer. **Fchg(3)** is recommended over **Fadd(3)** for placing data into a buffer because it does not require any assumptions about the current contents of the buffer. **Fchg(3)** can be used to perform the same operation as **Fadd(3)** by using –1 for the occurrence. The following code fragment illustrates loading the same values as the illustration of **Fadd(3)**, but this time number[0] will be placed into occurrence 0 no matter what values may have been there previously:

```
FLDOCC i; /* FLDOCC is typedef'd in fml.h as an int */
long number[10];
FBFR bufptr;
. . .
for(i=0; i < 10; i++)
}
   if(Fchg(bufptr, NUMFLD, i,&number[i], 0)     <0)
   {
     /* Put error handling here */
   }
} /* end of for loop */
/* The values in number have been loaded into the buffer */
```

If **Fchg(3)** is used to change an occurrence with a number higher than the last one already in the buffer, additional occurrences of the field will be created containing null values, so that all occurrences between up to and including the new occurrence will exist. For instance, if the field STRING already contains values (perhaps null values) for the first five occurrences, the code

```
Fchg(bufptr, STRING, 10, "some string", 10);
```

will place the value "some string" into occurrence ten, and set occurrences 6 through 9 as empty.

7.5.6   Retrieving Data from FML Buffers

There are a number of functions that provide means of retrieving data from FML buffers, or that provide information about the contents of the buffer. For the client/server developer the two most useful functions are **Fget(3)** and **Fnext(3)**. These two functions return the actual contents of the buffer, rather than pointers or occurrence numbers, or other data. A number of functions, such as **Ffind(3)**, return a pointer to the data in the buffer. The pointer can be used to retrieve the information from the buffer, but should never be used to update the information in the buffer. Always use **Fadd(3)**, **Fchg(3)**, or their variants to change information in an FML buffer.

Fget(3) retrieves a specific occurrence of a specified field into an area specified by the program. The form is:

```
int Fget(FBFR *bufferptr, FLDID fldid, FLDOCC oc, char
*retvalue,
FLDLEN *maxlen)
```

Where bufferptr is a pointer to an FML buffer, fldid is the fldid to be retrieved, oc is the occurrence to be retrieved, retvalue is the location to place the retrieved data, and maxlen is the maximum length that can be placed into retvalue. The occurrence is easily specified by using the name of the field as specified in the field table file, since it is defined in the header file generated by **mkfldhdr(1)**. The following program fragment illustrates using **Fget(3)**.

```
/* uses fml16 buffer */

#include "atmi.h"          /* TUXEDO  Header File */
#include "fml.h"
#include "fmlflds.h"


. . .

FBFR *sendbuf, *rcvbuf; /* for view16 */
FLDLEN worksze; /* length of field for FML functions */
FLDOCC occ;
char workstr[100];


. . .

worksze = sizeof(workstr);
occ = 3;
if(Fget(rcvbuf, mystr1, occ, workstr, &worksze) < 0)
{
   /* put error handling here */
}

/* Occurrence 3 of mystr1 is now in workstr */
```

Fnext(3) is useful for retrieving data from a buffer to place into some array. The form of **Fnext(3)** is:

```
int Fnext(FBFR *bufferptr, FLDID fldid, FLDOCC oc, char
*retvalue, FLDLEN *maxlen)
```

where the parameters are the same as for **Fget(3)**.

Fnext(3) requires careful planning and cooperation between the program loading the buffer and the program retrieving with **Fnext(3)**. **Fnext(3)** returns the information pointed to by the specified field identifier and occurrence, if the occurrence exists (is not empty). If the occurrence does not exist, **Fnext(3)** returns the contents of the first occurrence of the field identifier. If the TUXEDO defined value FIRSTFLDID is used for the field identifier, the first occurrence of the first field is always returned, no matter what field identifier is passed to the function. **Fnext(3)** places the next field identifier–occurrence combination into fldid and oc, allowing the possibility of looping through the function to retrieve a number of occurrences simply. **Fnext(3)** sets the next occurrence/field combination into oc and fldid, so that if the program loops through the function the values are retrieved in order. When **Fnext(3)** is repeated it will retrieve all the occurrences of the current field, then all the occurrences of the next field, and so on. The order of the fields is by ascending field identifier.

The following code fragment shows a method of loading a numeric array with values from an FML buffer.

```
/* Loading an array from an FML buffer using Fnext(3) */

#include <stdio.h>
#include "atmi.h"        /* TUXEDO  Header File */
#include "fml.h"
#include "fmlflds.h"


. . .

    FLDOCC occ;
    int i;
    short number[100];
    int maxnum = 10;
    FLDID fieldid;

    . . .

    fieldid = FIRSTFLDID;
    for(i=0; i<maxnum; i++)
    {
        Fnext(rcvbuf, &fieldid, &occ, (char *) &number[i], 0);

        /* process each occurance here */
    }
    /* The number array has been loaded from the FML buffer */
    . . .
```

7.5.7   **FML, VIEWs, and C Structures**

It is possible to transfer data between C structures and FML buffers using the following steps.

1. Create a field table file for the FML buffer.
2. Run **mkfldhdr(1)** as explained above.
3. Create a view file for the view, being sure to include the FML filed name for each field.
4. Run **viewc(1)** as explained above, but without the **-n** option.
5. Allocate the buffer with **tpalloc(3)** with the type set to FML.
6. Allocate space for the structure with a C function, such as **malloc()**.
7. Use the FML VIEW functions to transfer data between the buffer and the C structure generated by **viewc(1)**. The FML VIEW functions have names that begin with "Fv".

This method of accessing FML buffers is an adjunct to the methods mentioned previously, and all rules about buffer management and use apply the same as for any other FML buffer.

Note that the structure cannot be overlaid onto the FML buffer. The program must allocate space for the structure using C functions such as **malloc()**, then transfer information from the FML buffer to the C structure using FML VIEW functions, such as **Fvftos(3)**. To update the FML buffer, put information into the C structure, then transfer the information to the FML buffer using FML VIEW functions, such as **Fvstof(3)**.

7.5.8   **FML Functions**

7.5.8.1 Overview.   FML provides a rich set of C functions to manipulate FML buffers. For a complete detailed discussion of all FML features see the FML Guide in the TUXEDO documentation. The functions most used for manipulating data in FML buffers are described here.

Data stored in FML buffers is available only to FML functions. To use the data directly in a program it is necessary to retrieve the data and place it into a C structure. One method is to define a VIEW that is associated with the FML buffer. The other method is to retrieve data with FML functions and place it into storage areas defined by the program. Data is placed into FML buffers either by populating the VIEW defined on the buffer or by using FML functions to move the data from a program defined storage area to the FML buffer. Methods for performing these tasks were previously discussed. The following sections describe several FML functions in detail. Remember that buffers used for TUXEDO messages must be allocated with **tpalloc(3)**, not with **Falloc(3)**.

The include file fml.h must be included to use FML16 functions; the include file fml32.h must be included to use FML32 functions. FML32 functions are identified with a "32" appended to the name of the function. FML16 functions have no number appended. FML functions work the same as FML16 functions. The descriptions for all functions use FML16 notation. Append a "32" as necessary to use FML32 functions.

FML functions that reference fields in buffers use a field identifier to name the field. The field identifier is specified as FLDID *fldid* (or FLDID32 *fldid*). The proper way to specify fldid is to use the values defined in an include file generated by **mkfldhdr(1)**.

7.5.8.2 *Fadd(3).*   The forms of **Fadd(3)** and **Fadd32(3)** are:

```
int Fadd(FBFR *bufptr, FLDID fldid, char *value, FLDLEN len)
int Fadd32(FBFR *bufptr, FLDID32 fldid, char *value,
    FLDLEN32 len)
```

Fadd(3) creates a new occurrence of the FML field named by *fldid* in the buffer pointed to by *bufptr*. The new occurrence is populated with the data pointed to by *value*. If the field has no occurrences, the new occurrence is numbered as zero. If there are any occurrences of the field, **Fadd(3)** creates a new occurrence numbered one higher than the highest existing occurrence. **Fadd(3)** will not place data in empty fields with occurrence numbers lower than the highest occurrence already there. *len* is the length of the data to be placed into the buffer. *len* must be specified for the field type carray. If *len* is specified for a field where the length is implied, such for field type long, it is ignored. The definition of the functions specifies *value* as char *. In fact, *value* must point to a C field of the same type as defined for the FML field named by *fldid*.

Fadd(3) returns zero on success. **Fadd(3)** returns −1 on failure with the type of error set in Ferror. The possible errors are:

FALIGNERR Error FALIGNERR means that the referenced buffer does not begin on a proper boundary. This error usually means that the buffer has been corrupted or that it was not properly allocated.

FNOTFLD Error FNOTFLD indicates that the referenced buffer is not an FML buffer. This error usually means that the buffer has been corrupted or that it was not properly allocated.

FEINVAL Error FEINVAL is caused by an invalid parameter specification. One common cause is specifying a NULL pointer for *value*.

FNOSPACE Error FNOSPACE indicates that there is no room in
the buffer for the value to be added. Use **tprealloc(3)** to increase
the space, and attempt to add the field again.

FBADFLD Error FBADFLD means that the field specified by *fldid*
is not a valid field for the specified buffer.

7.5.8.3 *Fchg(3)*.   The forms of **Fchg(3)** and **Fchg32(3)** are:

```
int Fchg(FBFR *bufptr, FLDID fldid, FLDOCC oc,
    char *value, FLDLEN len)
int Fchg32(FBFR32 *bufptr, FLDID32 fldid, FLDOCC32 oc,
    char *value, FLDLEN32 len)
```

Fchg(3) modifies the value of the occurrence specified by *oc* in the
FML field named by *fldid* in the buffer pointed to by *bufptr*. The new
value in the occurrence is populated with the data pointed to by *value*.
If the occurrence does not already exist for the field, a new occurrence is
created numbered with the value in *oc*.

len is the length of the data to be placed into the buffer. *len* must
be specified for the field type carray. If *len* is specified for a field where
the length is implied, such for field type long, it is ignored. The definition of the functions specifies *value* as char *. In fact, *value* must point
to a C field of the same type as defined for the FML field named by
fldid.

Fchg(3) returns zero on success. **Fchg(3)** returns −1 on failure
with the type of error set in Ferror. The possible errors are:

FALIGNERR Error FALIGNERR means that the referenced buffer
does not begin on a proper boundary. This error usually means that
the buffer has been corrupted or that it was not properly allocated.

FNOTFLD Error FNOTFLD indicates that the referenced buffer is
not an FML buffer. This error usually means that the buffer has
been corrupted or that it was not properly allocated.

FEINVAL Error FEINVAL is caused by an invalid parameter specification. One common cause is specifying a NULL pointer for *value*.

FNOSPACE Error FNOSPACE indicates that there is no room in
the buffer for the new value. Use **tprealloc(3)** to increase the space,
and attempt to do the operation again.

FBADFLD Error FBADFLD means that the field specified by *fldid* is not a valid field for the specified buffer.

7.5.8.4 Fcpy(3).   The forms of **Fcpy(3)** and **Fcpy32(3)** are:

```
int Fcpy(FBFR *dest_ptr, FBFR *src_ptr)
int Fcpy32(FBFR32 *dest_ptr, FBFR32 *src_ptr)
```

Fcpy(3) copies the contents of the FML buffer pointed to by *src_ptr* into the FML buffer pointed to by *dest_ptr*. Any values already in the destination buffer are destroyed.

Fcpy(3) returns zero for success. If **Fcpy(3)** fails, it returns −1 and sets the type of error into Ferror. The possible errors are:

FALIGNERR Error FALIGNERR means that the referenced buffer does not begin on a proper boundary. This error usually means that the buffer has been corrupted or that it was not properly allocated.

FNOTFLD Error FNOTFLD indicates that the referenced buffer is not an FML buffer. This error usually means that the buffer has been corrupted or that it was not properly allocated.

FNOSPACE Error FNOSPACE indicates that there is no room in the buffer for the data being copied in. Use **tprealloc(3)** to increase the space, and attempt to the operation again.

7.5.8.5 Fdel(3).   The forms of **Fdel(3)** and **Fdel32(3)** are:

```
int Fdel(FBFR *bufptr, FLDID fldid, FLDOCC oc)
int Fdel32(FBFR32 *bufptr, FLDID32 fldid, FLDOCC32 oc)
```

Fdel(3) deletes the occurrence specified by *oc* in the FML field named by *fldid* in the buffer pointed to by *bufptr*. If there are any higher occurrences, their occurrence numbers are shifted down by one. For example, if occurrences one through seven exist in the buffer before **Fdel(3)** is called, and **Fdel(3)** deletes occurrence five, the previous occurrences six and seven will become occurrences five and six respectively.

Fdel(3) returns zero on success. **Fdel(3)** returns −1 on failure with the type of error set in Ferror. The possible errors are:

FALIGNERR Error FALIGNERR means that the referenced buffer does not begin on a proper boundary. This error usually means that the buffer has been corrupted or that it was not properly allocated.

FNOTFLD Error FNOTFLD indicates that the referenced buffer is not an FML buffer. This error usually means that the buffer has been corrupted or that it was not properly allocated.

FNOTPRES Error FNOTPRES indicates that the field occurrence specified by *oc* is not present for the field named by *fldid* in the buffer pointed to by *bufptr*.

FBADFLD Error FBADFLD means that the field specified by *fldid* is not a valid field for the specified buffer.

7.5.8.6 *Fdelall(3)*. The forms of **Fdelall(3)** and **Fdelall32(3)** are:

```
int Fdelall(FBFR *bufptr, FLDID fldid)
int Fdelall32(FBFR32 *bufptr, FLDID32 fldid)
```

Fdelall(3) deletes all occurrences of the field named by *fldid* in the buffer pointed to by *bufptr*. An error is returned if no occurrences are found to delete.

Fdelall(3) returns zero on success. **Fdelall(3)** returns −1 on failure with the type of error set in Ferror. The possible errors are:

FALIGNERR Error FALIGNERR means that the referenced buffer does not begin on a proper boundary. This error usually means that the buffer has been corrupted or that it was not properly allocated.

FNOTFLD Error FNOTFLD indicates that the referenced buffer is not an FML buffer. This error usually means that the buffer has been corrupted or that it was not properly allocated.

FNOTPRES Error FNOTPRES indicates that the field occurrence specified by *oc* is not present for the field named by fldid in the buffer pointed to by *bufptr*.

FBADFLD Error FBADFLD means that the field specified by *fldid* is not a valid field for the specified buffer.

7.5.8.7 *Fdelete(3)*. The forms of **Fdelete(3)** and **Fdelete32(3)** are:

```
int Fdelete(FBFR *bufptr, FLDID fldid_array)
int Fdelete32(FBFR32 *bufptr, FLDID32 fldid_array)
```

Fdelete(3) deletes all occurrences of the fields named included in *fldid_array* in the buffer pointed to by *bufptr*. *fldid_array* is an array where each element contains a valid field identifier, except the last element, which must contain BADFLDID.

Fdelete(3) returns zero on success. **Fdelete(3)** returns –1 on failure with the type of error set in Ferror. The possible errors are:

FALIGNERR Error FALIGNERR means that the referenced buffer does not begin on a proper boundary. This error usually means that the buffer has been corrupted or that it was not properly allocated.

FNOTFLD Error FNOTFLD indicates that the referenced buffer is not an FML buffer. This error usually means that the buffer has been corrupted or that it was not properly allocated.

FBADFLD Error FBADFLD means that the field specified by *fldid* is not a valid field for the specified buffer.

7.5.8.8 Fget(3).   The forms of **Fget(3)** and **Ffget32(3)** are:

```
int Fget(FBFR *bufptr, FLDID fldid, FLDOCC oc,
    char *value, FLDLEN len)
int Fget32(FBFR32 *bufptr, FLDID32 fldid, FLDOCC32 oc,
    char *value, FLDLEN32 len)
```

Fget(3) retrieves the value of the occurrence specified by *oc* in the FML field named by *fldid* in the buffer pointed to by *bufptr*. The value in the occurrence is placed the data area pointed to by *value*. *len* specifies the length of the receiving field. When **Fget(3)** returns successfully, the actual length of the data retrieved is placed in *len*. If the length of the data to be retrieved is greater than *len*, an FNOSPACE error is returned. If *len* is specified as zero, no check of the length is done by **Fget(3)**.

The definition of the functions specifies *value* as char *. In fact, *value* must point to a C field of the same type as defined for the FML field named by *fldid*.

Fget(3) returns zero on success. **Fget(3)** returns –1 on failure with the type of error set in Ferror. The possible errors are:

FALIGNERR Error FALIGNERR means that the referenced buffer does not begin on a proper boundary. This error usually means that the buffer has been corrupted or that it was not properly allocated.

FNOTFLD Error FNOTFLD indicates that the referenced buffer is not an FML buffer. This error usually means that the buffer has been corrupted or that it was not properly allocated.

FNOSPACE Error FNOSPACE means that the length of the data retrieved was greater than *len*, and *len* was not zero.

FNOTPRES Error FNOTPRES indicates that the occurrence specified by *oc* was not present for the field specified by *fldid* in the buffer pointed to by *bufptr*.

FBADFLD Error FBADFLD means that the field specified by *fldid* is not a valid field for the specified buffer.

7.5.8.9 *Fneeded(3)*.   The forms of **Fneeded(3)** and **Fneeded32(3)** are:

```
int Fneeded(FLDOCC fnbr, FLDLEN len)
int Fneeded32(FLDOCC32 fnbr, FLDLEN32 len)
```

Fneeded(3) calculates the size of the FML buffer required to store the number of occurrences specified by *fnbr* where each occurrence is of length *len*. **Fneeded(3)** adds the size of FML overhead to *len* and multiplies by *fnbr*. Use **Fneeded(3)** to calculate the size required for a buffer by using estimates for *fnbr* and *len*. Neither *fnbr* nor *len* must reflect any actual values defined for a buffer. Use the result in **tpalloc(3)** to allocate the buffer.

Upon success, **Fneeded(3)** returns the results of its calculations. If **Fneeded(3)** fails, it returns –1 and sets Ferror to the type of error. A possible error is:

FEINVAL Error FEINVAL means that one of the parameters supplied to the function are invalid. This error is returned if *fnbr* or *len* is negative, if either is zero, or if *fnbr* is greater than 65,534.

7.5.8.10 *Fnext(3)*.   The forms of **Fnext(3)** and **Fnext32(3)** are:

```
int Fnext(FBFR *bufptr, FLDID fldid, FLDOCC oc,
    char *value, FLDLEN len)
int Fnext32(FBFR32 *bufptr, FLDID32 fldid, FLDOCC32 oc,
char *value, FLDLEN32 len)
```

Fnext(3) retrieves the value of the occurrence specified by *oc* in the FML field named by *fldid* in the buffer pointed to by *bufptr*. The value in the occurrence is placed the data area pointed to by *value*. *len* specifies the length of the receiving field. When **Fnext(3)** returns successfully, the actual length of the data retrieved is placed in *len*. If the length of the data to be retrieved is greater than *len*, an FNOSPACE error is returned. If *len* is specified as zero, no check of the length is done by **Fnext(3)**.

Fnext(3) increments *oc* by one after retrieving the specified value. When *oc* exceeds the largest occurrence of the current field, the next field is chosen. When **Fnext(3)** returns, the occurrence and field identifier for the data retrieved is in *fldid* and *oc*. If *fldid* is set to FIRSTFLDID, **Fnext(3)** retrieves the first field in the buffer. The definition of the functions specifies *value* as char *. In fact, **Fnext(3)** assumes that *value* points to a C field of the same type as defined for the FML field retrieved.

If **Fnext(3)** is retrieving from the last field in the buffer and *oc* is larger than the highest occurrence of the field, **Fnext(3)** returns the last occurrence of the last field without error. If a loop is used to retrieve all the occurrences in a field, use **Foccur(3)** to determine the number of occurrences and stop the loop when all occurrences have been retrieved. If retrieving values from all fields in the buffer, use some terminating value stored in the buffer to determine that all occurrences from all fields have been retrieved.

Fnext(3) returns zero on success. **Fnext(3)** returns –1 on failure with the type of error set in Ferror. The possible errors are:

FALIGNERR Error FALIGNERR means that the referenced buffer does not begin on a proper boundary. This error usually means that the buffer has been corrupted or that it was not properly allocated.

FNOTFLD Error FNOTFLD indicates that the referenced buffer is not an FML buffer. This error usually means that the buffer has been corrupted or that it was not properly allocated.

FNOSPACE Error FNOSPACE means that the length of the data retrieved was greater than *len*, and *len* was not zero.

FEINVAL Error FEINVAL indicates that one of the parameters specified for **Fnext(3)** was invalid, such as specifying NULL for *bufptr* or *oc*.

7.5.8.11 Foccur(3).   The forms of **Foccur(3)** and **Foccur32(3)** are:

```
FLDOCC Foccur(FBFR *bufptr, FLDID fldid)
FLDOCC32 Foccur(FBFR32 *bufptr, FLDID32 fldid)
```

Foccur(3) returns the number of occurrences of the field named by *fldid* in the buffer pointed to by *bufptr*. If **Foccur(3)** fails, it returns –1 and sets Ferror to the type of error. The possible errors are:

FALIGNERR Error FALIGNERR means that the referenced buffer does not begin on a proper boundary. This error usually means that the buffer has been corrupted or that it was not properly allocated.

FNOTFLD Error FNOTFLD indicates that the referenced buffer is not an FML buffer. This error usually means that the buffer has been corrupted or that it was not properly allocated.

FBADFLD Error FBADFLD means that the field specified by *fldid* is not a valid field for the specified buffer.

7.6   BUFFER SPACE MANAGEMENT FUNCTIONS

7.6.1   Overview

Buffer space for messages for both the request/response and conversational paradigm require that the buffer space must be allocated with the TUXEDO function **tpalloc(3)**. TUXEDO also provides **tprealloc(3)** to increase the space for a buffer. All clients and servers should be sure that any buffers allocated are freed with **tpfree(3)** before exiting, unless the buffer is freed automatically by the system (such as buffers allocated by service routines and used to return data with **tpreturn(3)**).

Buffers allocated with **tpalloc(3)** must be freed with **tpfree(3)**. They may also be reallocated with **tprealloc(3)**. Never use **malloc()** to allocate TUXEDO buffers. Never use **free()** or **realloc()** on buffers allocated with **tpalloc(3)**.

7.6.2   tpalloc(3)

The form of **tpalloc(3)** is:

```
char *tpalloc(char * type, char *subtype, long size)
```

tpalloc(3) allocates and initializes space for a message buffer. The buffer type will be the type specified by *type*. *subtype* may be non-NULL only for VIEW type buffers. The recommendation is not to use subtypes. The size of the buffer is specified in *size*. The type of the pointer returned by **tpalloc(3)** will be the type for the specified buffer. The call to **tpalloc(3)** must be type cast to the specific type expected. Note that the data area of the buffer is not to be set to all zeros by **tpalloc(3)**.

tpalloc(3) returns a pointer to the allocated space when successful. If **tpalloc(3)** fails it returns a NULL and sets **tperrno** to indicate the type of error. The possible errors are:

TPEINVAL Error TPEINVAL means that the parameters were set incorrectly, such as using NULL for *type*.

TPENOENT Error TPENOENT indicates that the buffer type named in *type* is not known to the system. This error is also returned if *subtype* is not NULL and the subtype is not defined to the system.

TPESYSTEM The TPESYSTEM error means that there was a failure within TUXEDO. A message describing the problem is written to the log file.

TPEOS The TPEOS error means that an operating system error has occurred.

7.6.3   tpfree(3)

The form of **tpfree(3)** is:

```
void tpfree(char *ptr)
```

tpfree(3) releases the buffer space pointed to by *ptr* and clears all state and associated data for the buffer. *ptr* must point to a buffer space allocated by **tpalloc(3)**. *ptr* should be cast to the appropriate buffer type. **tpfree(3)** does not return any value.

7.6.4   tprealloc(3)

The form of **tprealloc(3)** is:

```
char *tprealloc(char *ptr, long size)
```

tprealloc(3) reallocates space for the buffer pointed to by *ptr* and returns a pointer to a new buffer. *size* specifies the new size for the buffer. **tprealloc(3)** may allocate the new buffer in the same space as the original buffer or may place the new buffer in a new location. Data in the buffer previous to calling **tprealloc(3)** is preserved in its entirety unless *size* is smaller than the original size of the buffer, in which case the data past *size* is lost. The buffer type is not changed by **tprealloc(3)**. *ptr* must point to a buffer allocated with **tpalloc(3)** and must be cast to the proper type for the buffer type.

The primary use of **tprealloc(3)** is to resize a buffer when the current buffer is full. **tprealloc(3)** preserves data already in the buffer so that buffer loading can continue uninterrupted after resizing.

When **tprealloc(3)** completes successfully, it returns a pointer to the new buffer. If **tprealloc(3)** fails, it returns NULL and sets **tperrno** to the type of error. The possible errors are:

TPEINVAL Error TPEINVAL means that the parameters were set incorrectly. If *ptr* does not point to a buffer originally allocated by **tpalloc(3)**, **tprealloc(3)** will fail and set TPEINVAL.

TPESYSTEM The TPESYSTEM error means that there was a failure within TUXEDO. A message describing the problem is written to the log file.

TPEOS The TPEOS error means that an operating system error has occurred.

8

Creating Client Programs

8.1   OVERVIEW OF CLIENTS

A TUXEDO client is an application program written for its own platform. The difference between a TUXEDO client program and any other program written for the platform is that the TUXEDO client contains code to attach it to TUXEDO. There are two flavors of client:

- Those that run on a platform with a TUXEDO domain and attach locally to that domain are called *native clients*.
- Those that run on a platform which does not itself contain a TUXEDO domain. These clients run using the work station feature (/WS) and are called */WS clients*.

The design, coding, and operation of both types of client are the same, being affected only by the specific platform each is intended to run on. The ATMI for both flavors is identical. There are several differences in the way the clients are compiled, which are explained in the sections in this chapter for each flavor.

A client can be in two states with regard to TUXEDO: attached or not attached. Note that the TUXEDO documentation calls the process of attaching to TUXEDO "joining the application." This book will use the more accurate term "attaching to TUXEDO." The initial state of a client is not attached. A client attaches to TUXEDO by calling **tpinit(3)**, or by calling one of the common ATMI functions, such as **tpalloc(3)** or **tpcall(3)**. It is a good policy to require all clients to attach using **tpinit(3)** rather than using the automatic attachment feature. Once attached, the client can detach by calling **tpterm(3)**. A client can attach and detach repeatedly.

A client enters transaction mode by calling either **tpbegin(3)** or its X/Open equivalent, **tx_begin(3)**. With the exception of an X/Open variation called *chained transactions*, the client leaves transaction mode by calling **tpcommit(3)**, **tpabort(3)**, or their X/Open equivalents.

The following rules apply to developing all clients.

- Any function available for the platform, including **fork()** and **exec()** (or equivalent) can be used while the client is not attached to TUXEDO.
- It is bad practice to use **fork()** and **exec()** while the client is attached to TUXEDO, although it sometimes works properly.
- Never use **fork()** or **exec()** while the client is in transaction mode.
- Avoid using **sleep()** or equivalents while the client is in transaction mode.
- It is possible to use XA compliant resource managers in native clients, but good design avoids this practice.

Native clients can be created for X/Windows based GUIs such as Motif and OPEN LOOK. /WS clients are supported for DOS, Windows, Windows/NT, Macintosh, and OS/2. A number of development tools are available also on most of these platforms. In general, any development tool that supports calling C functions can be used to develop clients of either flavor.

This chapter concentrates on presenting information on building native clients. Everything that applies to native clients also applies to /WS clients, so the section on /WS clients will concentrate on describing the specifics for the various platforms.

8.2 SUGGESTIONS FOR CLIENT DESIGN

8.2.1 General Design Suggestions

Good client design is essentially the same as for any well designed program. This discussion points out some specific points that apply to TUXEDO clients.

Since clients may be run on a variety of platforms, and since most enterprises use a number of these platforms, it is important to design clients so that as much as possible of the program code can be used on any platform without change. Clients written in C, C++, or COBOL should be designed according to the principles in this chapter. If development is being done with a tool that operates on all anticipated platforms, the client design should be modified to match the tool being used while following the spirit of the principles in this chapter.

In general, clients should not use databases or any other type of resource manager. It is possible for any client to use a resource manager outside of the transaction managed by TUXEDO. In this case, the application code is responsible for maintaining transactional integrity. Any client that accesses a resource manager is also exposed to problems of portability.

Native clients can access XA compliant resource managers, in which case TUXEDO will manage transaction integrity. More information on this capability is provided in the section on native clients in this chapter.

There is really only one rule for making the TUXEDO part of the client portable:

Put all the portable code into callable functions.

Place calculations and TUXEDO access into separate functions or even into a single function that can be called from the main part of the program. Keep the user interaction code completely separate from the calculations and TUXEDO access. Design a function that controls attaching to and detaching from TUXEDO with **tpinit(3)** and **tpterm(3)**. This function can also control transaction beginning and ending.

Presentation processing can be done while the client is attached to TUXEDO with no performance penalty. It is a good idea to attach the client to TUXEDO when the client starts and to keep the client attached to TUXEDO until just before the client program ends. Although the overhead of attaching to TUXEDO is small, security must generally be invoked while the client is attached, and the overhead of security is not small.

Presentation processing should not be done while the client is in transaction mode, since presentation processing is not small, and the transaction may time out. Also, database locks will be held the entire time the client is in transaction mode, further affecting overall system performance. Of course, the client should never wait for human response while in transaction mode.

A client should have the following basic logical flow:

```
General initialization
Attach to TUXEDO and do Security
Present first screen
Do until done:
{
    Retrieve data from screen
    Start transaction
    Invoke TUXEDO services
    End transaction
    Present next screen
}
Detach from TUXEDO
End.
```

8.2.2   **Transaction Management in Clients**

The following rules should be followed when starting and ending transactions in a client.

* Call **tpbegin(3)**, **tpcommit(3)**, and **tpabort(3)** in the same code
  segment.
* Be sure to do an explicit **tpabort(3)** if the transaction fails.
* Test for failure of **tpbegin(3)** and **tpcommit(3)**.
* Be sure all replies to **tpacall(3)** have been received before calling
  tpcommit(3) or **tpabort(3)**.

If the client is a C main() program, call **tpbegin(3)**, **tpcommit(3)**,
and **tpabort(3)** in main(). If the TUXEDO part of the client is written
for portability as described earlier, put these functions in the controlling function between the **tpinit(3)** and **tpterm(3)**. Logically calling
tpbegin(3) from **tpcommit(3)** (or **tpabort(3)**) from different functions
will cause multiple maintenance problems, often resulting in failure to
issue the calls in the proper sequence. Suppose that main() calls a user
written **beginit()** function, which in turn calls **tpbegin(3)**. Then, if
main() calls a user written **endit()** function that calls **tpcommit(3)**,
the principle of calling both **tpbegin(3)** and **tpcommit(3)** from the
same logical object has been followed.

TUXEDO transaction management features protect transactions
against inappropriate commits by causing an automatic abort of the

commit when the transaction is in a state that does not allow committing. Most of these conditions, such as failure to receive a reply from all outstanding **tpacall(3)**s, failure of a database modification, timeouts, and so forth, can be detected by the application program. The client designating transaction boundaries should be sure to test for all these conditions by examining the return from all services. It should call **tpabort(3)** when these conditions occur.

It is good general practice to check for function failure. It becomes even more important to check for failure of transaction boundary functions so that the user can be properly notified. Known failures can often be corrected without catastrophe; unknown failures can lead to disaster. Always check for failure of **tpbegin(3)** and **tpcommit(3)**. **tpabort(3)** has limited failure possibilities, but it doesn't hurt to check for failure of this function also.

Getting replies from **tpacall(3)**s has been already mentioned. If a service has been called with **tpacall(3)** and the reply has not been received, the transaction will automatically be aborted if **tpcommit(3)** is called. Such a situation should be considered a disorderly transaction end, because it is out of the control of the application program. Therefore, unless a **tpacall(3)** was called with the TPNOREPLY flag set, be sure to get the reply before ending the transaction.

8.3   FUNCTIONALITY COMMON TO ALL CLIENTS

8.3.1   Attaching to TUXEDO

Clients use **tpinit(3)** to attach to TUXEDO. The form of **tpinit(3)** is:

```
int tpinit(TPINIT * info)
```

info points to a typed buffer of type TPINIT. If used, it must be allocated by **tpalloc(3)** before **tpinit(3)** is called. *info* may be NULL. TPINIT is a typed structure that contains the following fields:

```
char    usrname[MAXTIDENT+2];    /* client user name */
char    cltname[MAXTIDENT+2];    /* application client name */
char    passwd[MAXTIDENT+2];     /* application password */
char    grpname[MAXTIDENT+2];    /* client group name */
long    flags;                   /* initialization flags */
long    datalen;            /* length of app specific data */
long    data;                    /* placeholder for app data */
```

usrname, cltname, passwd , and data are used for security and for identifying the client to invoked services. How they are used for security is discussed in Chapter 12. usrname and cltname are also used to direct unsolicited messages. The section on unsolicited messages in this chapter explains these more fully. These two fields are also used to retrieve statistics for administrative use. Native clients use grpname to identify the group that supports client use of resource managers. This is discussed in detail in the section on native clients in this chapter. The use of flags is different than for other ATMI functions. **flags** affect how unsolicited messages are received and the mode of system access. Normally flags should be set to 0 (the default). Unsolicited messages and flags are discussed later in this chapter.

If **tpinit(3)** is not used to attach, then the first ATMI call (with some exceptions) will execute **tpinit(3)** with a NULL initialization buffer on behalf of the client. **tpinit(3)** returns –1 if it fails, and sets **tperrno** to indicate the type error. The possible errors are:

> **TPEINVAL** Error TPEINVAL means that the parameters were set incorrectly. If info is not NULL and does not point to a buffer of type TPINIT, **tpinit(3)** fails and sets **tperrno** to TPEINVAL.
>
> **TPENOENT** Error TPENOENT indicates the client cannot attach to TUXEDO because there is not enough space. The most common problems are lack of space in the bulletin board or maximums set by the administrator have been reached.
>
> **TPEPERM** Error TPEPERM means that security has been violated. This error can be caused by improper passwords, invalid user identification or failure of authentication by the authentication service.
>
> **TPEPROTO** Error TPEPROTO means that **tpinit(3)** was called in an improper context. One possibility is that **tpinit(3)** has been called from a server.
>
> **TPESYSTEM** The TPESYSTEM error means that there was a failure within TUXEDO. A message describing the problem is written to the log file.
>
> **TPEOS** The TPEOS error means that an operating system error has occurred.

The following code fragment attaches a client with a NULL initialization buffer.

```
. . .

#include "atmi.h"          /* TUXEDO  Header File */

main(argc, argv)
int argc;
char *argv[];

{

    . . .

    /* Attach to System/T as a Client Process */

    if (tpinit((TPINIT *) NULL) == -1) {
        /* put error handling here */
    }
```

The following code fragment attaches a client with an accessible initialization buffer and put user identification and client name into it.

```
. . .

#include "atmi.h"          /* TUXEDO  Header File */
#include <sys/types.h>
#include <unistd.h>
#include <stdlib.h>

main(argc, argv)
int argc;
char *argv[];
{

    . . .

    uid_t myid;
    char myname[100];
    char myinit[5];
    TPINIT *initbuf;
```

```
/* Attach to System/T as a Client Process */
/* allocate space for init buffer */
if ((initbuf = (TPINIT *) tpalloc("TPINIT", 0, 0)) == (TPINIT
*) NULL) {
    /* put error handling here */
}

getpw(getuid(), myname);
memcpy(initbuf->usrname, myname, 3);
/* copied only three chars - change approach here */

if (tpinit(initbuf) == -1) {
    /* put error handling here */
}

initbuf->usrname[3] = NULL;
strcpy(initbuf->cltname, "testprog");

    . . .
```

usrname and cltname can be any null terminated string. The exact values in these fields will be determined by the administrator and system designer working together. Commonly, usrname is the sign-on string, as the sample code shows. The system the sample was tested on used a three character sign-on name. **getpw()** returns a string containing a number of values and uses colon for a delimiter. The string returned by **getpw()** in the example above was:

```
clh:x:101:1:Carl L. Hall:/home/clh:/usr/bin/sh
```

grpname is used in a native client to attach the client to a group associated with an XA compliant resource manager. If grpname is zero length (the default), the client is associated with a group automatically maintained by TUXEDO for clients.

8.3.2   Detaching from TUXEDO

Clients must detach from TUXEDO by calling **tpterm(3)** before exiting. The form of **tpterm(3)** is:

```
int tpterm(void)
```

tpterm(3) detaches a client from TUXEDO and decrements the user count. **tpterm(3)** returns –1 if it fails and sets **tperrno** to the type of error. The possible errors are:

TPEPROTO Error TPEPROTO means that **tpterm(3)** was called in an improper context. One possibility is that **tpterm(3)** has been called from a server.

TPESYSTEM The TPESYSTEM error means that there was a failure within TUXEDO. A message describing the problem is written to the log file.

TPEOS The TPEOS error means that an operating system error has occurred.

8.3.3 **Unsolicited Messages**

8.3.3.1 Overview. Unsolicited messages can be received by clients on any supported platform. Unsolicited messages can be received from execution of **tpnotify(3)** or **tpbroadcast(3)** and from administrative action. Messages are addressed to the client by **tpbroadcast(3)** and by administration with the usrname and cltname in the initialization buffer. The unsolicited message works well only if these names are carefully controlled and documented. Although a hard programmed literal was used for cltname in the example in the last section, some installations might require more dynamic creation of cltname.

There are two methods for a client to detect unsolicited messages: DIPIN and SIGNAL. The SIGNAL method works only on those platforms that provide a signaling method like that provided by UNIX. Also, the SIGNAL method can only notify those clients running with the same user identification as the administrator. For these reasons, the SIGNAL method is not recommended for general use. The DIPIN method detects unsolicited messages whenever the client calls a TUXEDO function call and makes the messages available to the function named by **tpsetunsol(3)**. This chapter will describe how to code a client to receive messages. The function **tpchkunsol(3)** detects unsolicited messages without performing any other function.

The following steps are necessary to allow a client to accept messages.

1. The client is enabled to receive messages either by administrative default or by setting a flag in the initialization buffer.

2. Values must be placed in usrname and cltname fields of the initialization buffer to receive messages sent by **tpbroadcast(3)** or by the administrator.
3. The client must contain a function to receive messages.
4. The client provides a pointer to the message subroutine using **tpsetunsol(3)**.

An administrator can set to system with a default that enables all clients to receive unsolicited messages unless they set a flag in the initialization buffer to ignore unsolicited messages. A client can enable itself to receive unsolicited messages even if the administrator has not set the system default by setting a flag in the initialization buffer to receive messages. Set **flags** in the initialization buffer to TPU_DIP to receive unsolicited messages by the DIPIN method. If **flags** is set to TPU_IGN, no unsolicited messages will be sent to the client.

Services send messages back to a client using **tpnotify(3)** using an identifier generated by TUXEDO. **tpbroadcast(3)** and administrator tools send messages to clients using the name of the platform, usrname and cltname. The name of the platform is set by the administrator. usrname and cltname must be set by **tpinit(3)** as illustrated previously.

8.3.3.2 The Message Handler Function. The application function to receive messages must have the form:

```
void msghandler (char *data, long msglen, long flags);
```

The name of the function msghandler is application defined. The data of the message will be stored by the system in _data_. The length of the message will be stored in _msglen_. _flags_ should be ignored. _data_ will be a typed buffer of the type set by the service sending the message. STRING is recommended, but not necessary for application generated messages. Administrator unsolicited messages are type STRING. The function must be coded to recognize the type of data in order to process it properly. The buffer is freed by the system following return.

If it is possible to receive unsolicited messages with multiple buffer types, the message handler function should use **tptypes(3)** to determine the type of the message buffer before attempting to process the message.

The message handler function may use FML functions to retrieve the message if the message was sent using an FML type buffer. Other FML functions may also be used within the function. The only other ATMI functions that may be used in the message handler are:

```
tpalloc(3)      tpgetlev(3)     tprealloc(3)
tptypes(3)      tpfree(3)
```

The client uses **tpsetunsol(3)** to provide a pointer to the message handler. Any messages received before the client calls **tpsetunsol(3)** will be ignored and lost.

8.3.3.3 tpsetunsol(3). The form of **tpsetunsol(3)** is:

```
void tpsetunsol(*msghandler)
```

tpsetunsol(3) sets a pointer that is used to direct unsolicited messages to the function named in *msghandler*. *msghandler* must be defined with the form previously discussed. To determine that **tpsetunsol(3)** succeeded or failed, set **tperrno** to 0 before calling **tpsetunsol(3)**, then test **tperrno** for non-zero after calling **tpsetunsol(3)**. Possible errors are:

TPEPROTO: Error TPEPROTO means that **tpsetunsol(3)** was called in an improper context. One possibility is that **tpsetunsol(3)** has been called from a server.

TPESYSTEM: The TPESYSTEM error means that there was a failure within TUXEDO. A message describing the problem is written to the log file.

TPEOS: The TPEOS error means that an operating system error has occurred.

The following code fragment shows a way to code a client to receive unsolicited messages.

```
#include <stdio.h>
#include <sys/types.h>
#include <unistd.h>
#include <stdlib.h>

#include "atmi.h"          /* TUXEDO  Header File */

. . .

char *msg;
long msglen;
```

```
void msghand(char*, long, long);
void (*msghptr)() = msghand;

main(argc, argv)
int argc;
char *argv[];
{

    . . .

    int ret, i;
    uid_t myid;
    char myname[100];
    char myinit[5];
    TPINIT *initbuf;

    /* allocate an initialization buffer */
    if ((initbuf = (TPINIT *) tpalloc("TPINIT", NULL, 0)) ==
(TPINIT *) NULL)
    {
        printf("tpalloc fail on tpinit, %d\n", tperrno);
    }
    /* Attach to System/T as a Client Process */
    if (tpinit(initbuf) == -1) {
        tpfree(initbuf);
        fprintf(stderr, "Tpinit failed\n");
        exit(1);
    }

    /* put user id string into initialization buffer */
    getpw(getuid(), myname);
    memcpy(initbuf->usrname, myname, 3);
    initbuf->usrname[3] = NULL;
    strcpy(initbuf->cltname, "testprog");

    . . .

    /* set up ready for an unsolicited message */
    (*tpsetunsol) (msghptr);

    . . .
```

```
    /* detach from TUXEDO */
    tpterm();
} /* end of main */
```

A sample message handler function follows.

```
/* The message handler function */
void msghand(char *msg, long msglen, long flags)
{
    char workstr[200];
    memcpy(workstr, msg, msglen);
    /* message has been copied into workstr and can now */
    /* be processed                                     */
    return;
} /* end of message handler */
```

8.3.3.4 *tpchkunsol(3)*. **tpchkunsol(3)** checks for unsolicited messages. The form of **tpchkunsol(3)** is:

```
int tpchkunsol(void)
```

The DIPIN method for receiving unsolicited messages causes each TUXEDO function call to detect unsolicited messages and execute the message handler service if any are present. It is not always convenient for a client to wait to call a function, such as **tpcall(3)**, to detect unsolicited messages. If there are any messages waiting, **tpchkunsol(3)** returns the number of messages after executing the message handler. If **tpchkunsol(3)** detects no messages, it returns zero. If **tpchkunsol(3)** fails, it returns –1 and sets **tperrno** to the type of message. The possible errors are:

TPEPROTO Error TPEPROTO means that **tpchkunsol(3)** was called in an improper context. One possibility is that **tpchkunsol(3)** has been called from a server.

TPESYSTEM The TPESYSTEM error means that there was a failure within TUXEDO. A message describing the problem is written to the log file.

TPEOS The TPEOS error means that an operating system error has occurred.

8.3.4   **Using** tpbroadcast(3)

Clients and services can use **tpbroadcast(3)** to send unsolicited messages to clients. The form of **tpbroadcast(3)** is:

```
int tpbroadcast(char * lmid, char *usrname, char * cltname,
char *data, long datalen, long flags)
```

lmid is the name of the platform where the receiving client resides. *usrname* is the user name placed into the initialization buffer by the receiving client. *cltname* is the client name placed into the initialization buffer by the receiving client. (See the previous section on attaching to TUXEDO). *data* is the message being sent.

The value for *lmid* must be obtained from the system administrator. *usrname* and *cltname* are available from design documentation. *lmid*, *usrname*, and *cltname* may each be set to NULL, which will be used by the system as a wild card.

data points to a typed buffer and may be any type that the receiving client recognizes in its message handler function. *data* must be allocated by **tpalloc(3)**. *datalen* is the length of the buffer being sent and may be zero if the buffer is a type that automatically supplies length (such as FML). A STRING type buffer is recommended.

Valid flags for **tpbroadcast(3)** are:

TPSIGRSTRT The flag TPSIGRSTRT should always be specified with a TUXEDO function to be sure that the call is reissued if processing is interrupted by a signal during the execution of the call.

TPNOBLOCK The flag TPNOBLOCK will cause **tpbroadcast(3)** to return immediately with the error TPEBLOCK without sending the message if there is a blocking condition, such as when there is no room in the internal buffer used for messages.

TPNOTIME The flag TPNOTIME prevents a blocking timeout. TPNOBLOCK and TPNOTIME are mutually exclusive. The transaction may still fail due to a transaction timeout.

8.4   **NATIVE CLIENTS**

8.4.1   **Overview**

Native clients are clients that attach directly to TUXEDO on a node of the domain. Native clients have capabilities that are not available to /WS clients. In addition to the capabilities available to all clients, native clients can use XA compliant resource managers, and use the SIGNAL method for unsolicited messages.

This section will discuss how to use XA compliant resource managers, especially databases, in native clients. Unsolicited messages were discussed in an earlier section of this chapter.

8.4.2   Accessing an XA Compliant Database from a Native Client

This section concentrates on databases, but the principles apply to any XA compliant resource manager. The steps for using an XA compliant database from a native client are:

1. Put the proper group name into grpname of the initialization buffer used with **tpinit(3)**.
2. Start a transaction with **tpbegin(3)** and end it with **tpcommit(3)** or **tpabort(3)**.
3. Include database access statements in the client program.

Put the name of the group with the appropriate resource manager into grpname. The group name will be provided by the system administrator. If no group name is provided when **tpinit(3)** is called, TUXEDO attaches the client to a special client group automatically assigned. The default client group does not allow use of resource managers.

A client using an XA resource manager must control the transaction boundaries. Any database access done by the client while in transaction mode will be included in the transaction, as long as the database accessed is the one associated with the group named in grpname. Since a client can be associated with only one group at a time, only one XA resource manager can be used by a client in a single transaction.

As with any XA compliant resource manager, the database access statements are the same ones used even when not using the XA feature, the most common being SQL. If the database access by the client must be part of a transaction managed by TUXEDO, these statements must be used while the client is in transaction mode, that is, between the time **tpbegin(3)** is called and the transaction is ended. If the client uses the X/Open form of transaction begin and end, the main point remains the same: The client must begin and end transactions and the database access must be done while in transaction mode.

For example, to use SQL in a global transaction from a native client, create the client with **buildclient(1)**, except include the name of the RM in the -r option. The client must execute the following functions in the given order when running.

1. Populate the grpname in the TPINIT buffer with a group name provided by the TUXEDO administrator.
2. Call **tpinit(3)**.
3. Call **tpopen(3)**.
4. Start a global transaction by calling **tpbegin(3)** or **tx_begin(3)**. SQL statements used in a client cannot be included in a transaction started by a service.

After the program has executed the above steps, the client may use any SQL DML statements except transactional statements. See the rules for XA services. A client may leave cursors open as long as desired, but must close all cursors before ending the transaction. Open cursors may set locks and can cause performance problems, so there is a practical limit on how long cursors can remain open.

Clients that use SQL in global transactions must call **tpclose(3)** before calling **tpterm(3)**. The section on **tpsvrdone(3)** in Chapter 9 contains more information on **tpclose(3)**.

8.4.3   **Compiling Native Clients**

Native clients are compiled using the utility **buildclient(1)**. If clients do not use a resource manager, are written in C, and do not use any embedded language, such as SQL, they can be compiled with the command line:

```
buildclient -o cltname -f cltsource
```

cltname is the name of the resulting executable module. *cltsource* is the name of the source file. Some of the example code in this book was compiled with the command line:

```
buildclient -o testcl -f testcl.c
```

Other options are similar to those used by the UNIX C compiler, cc, and the linker ld as follows:

-v Causes buildclient to run in the verbose mode.

-w Indicates that buildclient should use the work station libraries. The **-r** option is not valid with the **-w** option. If **-w** is not used, buildclient builds a native client. This option will be discussed further in the section on /WS clients.

-r rmname This option links the resource manager libraries with the client. Available only for native clients. rmname is the name of the resource manager to use. rmname must be present in the udataobj/RM file.

-o exname exname is the name of the executable module to create. If this option is not specified the name of the executable module is a.out.

-f string This is the "first files" option. string is a space delimited list of files to be included before TUXEDO libraries. If more than one file is named, the list must be enclosed in quotation marks.

-l string This is the "last files" option. string is a space delimited list of files to be included after TUXEDO libraries. If more than one file is named, the list must be enclosed in quotation marks.

-C This option causes buildclient to invoke a COBOL compiler instead of the C compiler.

buildclient will use information in several environment variables if they are present. For C compilation, these variables are:

CC This environment variable contains the name of the C compiler to be executed. If this environment variable is not present or contains a NULL, the default compiler is used. On UNIX the default compiler is cc(1).

CFLAGS If this environment variable is present and not NULL, its contents are passed to the C compiler as command line options.

If a native client uses a resource manager, the **-r** option must be used to identify it. If the resource manager requires a precompiler that must be run before the C compiler, the precompiler must be run before buildclient. The command lines used if the client is using embedded SQL from Oracle might be (in order):

```
proc iname=rmclient.pc oname=rmclient.c
buildclient -o rmclient -f  rmclient.c -r ORACLE
```

8.5 /WS CLIENTS

8.5.1 General Discussion

/WS clients use the same TUXEDO functions as native clients. They are limited in that they cannot use XA compliant resource managers. All the rules for developing clients previously apply the same to /WS clients.

UNIX /WS clients are developed in the exact same way as native clients. They are compiled using **buildclient(1)** in the same manner as for native clients, except that the **-w** option is specified, and the **-r** option cannot be used. If a UNIX client will be run on a windowing system, it should be developed the same as any other program for the windowing system, then compiled using **buildclient(1)**.

Some details of client development change for DOS, Windows, Windows/NT, OS/2, and Macintosh clients because of the varying ways these operating systems work. The developer should consult the TUXEDO/Workstation Guide for details on how to develop clients for these platforms.

A version of **buildclient(1)** called **buildclt(1)** is used on DOS, Windows, Windows/NT, and OS/2 platforms. It is used in much the same way as **buildclient(1)**. There is no **-w** option with **buildclt(1)** because it only builds /WS clients. Additional options are provided in **buildclt(1)** for use in these environments. They are:

- The **-c** option designates the compiler to use, rather than an environment variable.
- The uppercase options **-W**, **-O**, and **-P** designate the environment as Windows or Windows/NT, OS/2 character mode, and OS/2 Presentation Manager respectively.
- The uppercase **-C** option causes a COBOL compile.

Note that various compilers are available on these platforms. For each compiler and each platform certain compiler flags are necessary as documented in the TUXEDO/Workstation Guide.

8.6   SPECIAL WORK STATION FUNCTIONS

8.6.1   Functions Available on All Work Stations

The functions described here help manage environment variables on platforms that do not readily support environment variables in a manner necessary to support TUXEDO clients. These functions are also useful when the values for environment files are stored in a file on the local network and must be retrieved for the specific work station. There are three functions:

- **tuxgetenv(3)**, which retrieves a named environment variable from a location within TUXEDO
- **tuxputenv(3)**, which adds or changes an environment variable in the local TUXEDO environment

- **tuxreadenv(3)**, which reads a set of environment variables from a file and loads them into the TUXEDO environment

Use of these functions is not limited to work stations. They can be used in application utility programs to be sure that environment variables are properly distributed in a multinode domain. These functions require that atmi.h is included in any program that calls them.

The form of **tuxgetenv(3)** is:

```
char *tuxgetenv(char * var_name)
```

tuxgetenv(3) searches the environment for the environment variable named by *var_name* and returns a pointer to its contents. If the environment variable is not found, **tuxgetenv(3)** returns NULL. The search is case sensitive, and the recommendation is always use upper case names for environment variables.

The form of **tuxputenv(3)** is:

```
int tuxputenv(char * var)
```

var is a string of the form *name=value*. **tuxputenv(3)** populates the environment variable *name* with *value*. The recommendation is to always use upper case names on all platforms. **tuxputenv(3)** can be used to define environment variables in on a platform that usually does not support environment variables. **tuxputenv(3)** returns zero for success. **tuxputenv(3)** returns non-zero if it could not allocate sufficient space to store the environment variable.

The form of **tuxreadenv(3)** is:

```
int tuxreadenv(char * filename, char *label)
```

tuxreadenv(3) reads environment variables from *filename* and loads them into the local TUXEDO environment. *label* provides a means to select portions of the file for loading. *filename* should be a string containing a valid full path file name. If *filename* is specified as NULL, the following default file names are used:

For DOS, Windows, and NT: C:\TUXEDO\TUXEDO.ENV

For MAC: TUXEDO.ENV in the system preference directory

For NetWare: SYS:SYSTEM\TUXEDO.ENV

For Posix (most UNIX platforms): /usr/tuxedo/TUXEDO.ENV or /var/opt/tuxedo/TUXEDO.ENV

The environment file may contain one global section and multiple labeled sections. The global section is at the beginning of the file and has no label. The global section is always loaded. Labeled sections are selected for loading using the *label* parameter in **tuxreadenv(3)**. If *label* is specified NULL, only the global section is loaded. Labeled sections begin with a label in the form: [*labelname*]. *labelname* may contain only alphabetic characters and underscore. An example of a valid label specification is:

```
[MYVARIABLES].
```

Variables are specified in the form: *varname=value*. They can also be specified in the form: **set** *varname=value*. *varname* is the name of the variable to be set and *value* is the intended contents of the variable. *varname* may contain only alphabetic characters and underscore.

An example of an environment file is:

```
TUXDIR=/home/tuxdir; export TUXDIR
[HOMEOFFBR]
TUXCONFIG=/home/clh/dombk/hbconfig
BDMCONFIG=/home/clh/dombk/BDMHB

[DALLAS]
TUXCONFIG=/home/clh/dombk/dalconfig
BDMCONFIG=/home/clh/dombk/BDMDAL
```

The recommendation is that all environment variable names be specified in upper case. **tuxreadenv(3)** converts all environment variable names to uppercase for DOS, WINDOWS, OS/2, and NetWare platforms.

8.6.2   Windows Functions

8.6.2.1 AEWisblocked(3). The form of **AEWisblocked(3)** is:

```
int far pascal AEWisblocked(void)
```

AEWisblocked(3) returns 1 if there is a blocking function awaiting completion, otherwise 0.

The ATMI DLL must sometimes relinquish control of the CPU to allow other processes to run while waiting for a blocking call to complete. As a consequence, an application program may be reentered while waiting for a blocking call to complete. **AEWisblocked(3)** can be used in the application program to determine if the blocking call has completed or not. TUXEDO only allows one blocking call waiting for each thread of control.

8.6.2.2 *AEWsetunsol(3).* The form of **AEWsetunsol(3)** is:

```
int far pascal AEWsetunsol(HWND hWnd, WORD wMsg)
```

AEWsetunsol(3) is used to direct unsolicited messages to a specific window identified by *hWnd. wMsg* specifies the type of message to post when unsolicited messages are received. **AEWsetunsol(3)** does not replace **tpsetunsol(3)**, but rather, provides an additional function. **tpsetunsol(3)** sets a return point to a function within the current client. **AEWsetunsol(3)** allows receiving unsolicited messages by another application program running in a different window.

AEWsetunsol(3) returns –1 if it fails and sets **tperrno** to the type of error. The possible errors are:

TPESYSTEM Error TPESYSTEM indicates that a TUXEDO error has occurred. Information on the failure is written to the log.

TPEOS Error TPEOS means that there has been an operating system failure.

Note: Programs using **AEWsetunsol(3)** must include both atmi.h and windows.h.

8.6.3 OS/2 PM Functions

8.6.3.1 *AEPisblocked(3).* The form of **AEPisblocked(3)** is:

```
int far pascal AEPisblocked(void)
```

AEPisblocked(3) returns 1 if there is a blocking function awaiting completion, otherwise 0.

The OS/2 PM ATMI DLL must sometimes relinquish control of the CPU to allow other processes to run while waiting for a blocking call to complete. As a consequence, an application program may be reentered while waiting for a blocking call to complete. **AEPisblocked(3)** can be used in the application program to determine if the blocking call has completed or not. TUXEDO only allows one blocking call waiting for each thread of control.

8.7   **DEBUGGING CLIENTS**

Bugs in clients are found and fixed in the same manner as for any program on the client platform. There are several things that can be done to simplify complexities caused by attaching to TUXEDO. Here are some suggestions.

1. For initial testing replace TUXEDO function calls with local functions that return values that can be tested.
2. Test clients as much as possible before attaching to TUXEDO.
3. If the services that the client uses are not available, use a simple service in a debug domain to return values to the client.
4. Make the final tests of the client with its required services in a debug domain.

TUXEDO calls can be replaced with a set of #define's from a header file. The name of the header file can be different for the test functions than for the real functions. Only the header file name requires change when the client is changed from using test functions to using the real functions. The file defining the test functions could be called testdef.h and the file defining the real functions could be called realdef.h.

testdef.h could include the following:

```
#define TPINITD(A) testinit(A)
#define TPCALLD(A, B, C, D, E, F) testcall(A, B, C, D, E, F)
```

realdef.h could include the following:

```
#define TPINITD(A) tpinit(A)
#define TPCALLD(A, B, C, D, E, F) tpcall(A, B, C, D, E, F)
```

A good way to prevent confusion is to use the name of the TUXEDO function in upper case, appended with a *D*. The appended letter is not necessary, but serves to help developers remember that it is a **#define** definition, not an actual function call.

The following code fragment shows how these files could be used:

```
#include <stdio.h>
#include <string.h>
#include <termio.h>
#include "atmi.h"        /* TUXEDO  Header File */
#include "app.h"
```

```
#include "realdef.h"    /* This file has the real functions */
/*

#include "testdef.h"    /* This file has the test functions */
*/

main(int argc, char *argv[])
{
   .
   .
   .

   /* Attach to System/T as a Client Process */

/*   if ((ret = tpinit(initbuf)) == -1) { */
   if ((ret = TPINITD(initbuf)) == -1) {
      fprintf(stderr, "tpinit failed %d\n", tperrno);
      exit(1);
   }

   if (tpinit((TPINIT *) NULL) == -1) {
      fprintf(stderr, "Tpinit failed\n");
      exit(1);
   }
   .
   .
   .

   /* Request the service APPSVC, waiting for a reply */
   ret = TPCALLD("APPSVC", sendbuf, 0, &rcvbuf, &rcvlen,
(long)0);

   if(ret == -1) {
      fprintf(stderr, "Can't send request to service APPSVC\n");
      fprintf(stderr, "Tperrno = %d\n", tperrno);
      if(tpurcode == SECFAIL)
      {
          printf("ticket no good\n");
      }
      tpfree(sendbuf);
      tpfree(rcvbuf);
      tpterm();
```

```
      exit(1);
   }
   .
   .
   .

   /* Free Buffers & Detach from System/T */
   tpfree(sendbuf);
   tpfree(rcvbuf);
   tpterm();
}
```

A debug domain is described in Chapter 9.

Creating Servers and Services

9.1 OVERVIEW

This chapter is about how to develop services and create servers containing services. The discussions will provide information about the structure of a server, information on how to code services, and information on how to initialize a server and how to provide cleanup functionality when a server is shut down. Information on **tpforward(3)** and **tpnotify(3)** is included as part of the section on developing services because they are available only to services.

Servers are created by linking services with a TUXEDO provided server mainline. Servers also contain initialization and completion functions. The function **tpsvrinit(3)** is executed when a server is booted and the function **tpsvrdone(3)** is executed when the server is shut down.

The following steps are required to build a server.

1. Code the service(s) that will be included in the server.
2. Code **tpsvrinit(3)** if necessary.
3. Code **tpsvrdone(3)** if necessary.
4. Use **buildserver(1)** to create the server.

A default **tpsvrinit(3)** and **tpsvrdone(3)** are provided in the TUXEDO library. The default functions can be used unless there is some application specific functionality that is required. These functions are described later in this chapter.

9.2   **SERVERS**

9.2.1   **Overview**

Servers are started when a TUXEDO domain is booted. In UNIX terms, servers are processes called *daemons*, waiting to service requests. When a server is booted, it will do the following (not necessarily in the order listed):

- Call **tpsvrinit(3)**, which in turn calls **tpopen(3)**. If an XA resource manager is being used with the server, **tpopen(3)** connects to the resource manager using OPENINFO from the configuration file.
- Register itself with the bulletin board as available for receiving requests.
- Wait on the event of a message being available.

When a message is received, the TUXEDO provided mainline in the server examines the message header for the name of the service to invoke and calls the function designated as providing that service.

When a server is shut down it invokes **tpsvrdone(3)**, which in turn calls **tpclose(3)**. If a close is required by an attached resource manager, **tpclose(3)** performs the necessary processing using CLOSEINFO from the configuration file.

If the server offers services that will participate in an X/Open transaction started with **tx_begin(3)**, **tpsvrinit(3)** must use **tx_open(3)** instead of **tpopen(3)**, and **tpsvrdone(3)** must use **tx_close(3)** instead of **tpclose(3)**. See Chapter 15.

Servers are either request/response servers or conversational servers. All services in a request/response server must be request/response services; all services in a conversational server must be conversational services. A request/response server can process only one request at a time, no matter how many services are included in it. If a server is contained in a group attached to an XA resource manager, it can process requests in transaction mode. A server may handle several requests for the same transaction, and may handle requests for several transactions, one after another. It is important for the developer to understand that transactions exist separately from service requests. Completion of work on a single request has no implication on the state of a transaction. Conversational servers can process only one conversation at a time that is initiated from a service in another server or from a client. A conversational service, once connected to a conversation, can initiate multiple conversations with other services, but not with a service in the same server. TUXEDO provides an administrative capability to start multiple copies of the same server to meet performance requirements.

9.2.2 **Structure of a Server**

When a service is invoked, TUXEDO attaches a message header to the message provided by the application in the typed buffer, then sends the message to the local bulletin board service. The local bulletin board service determines if the service is in a local server or not and either sends to the proper local server or sends the request to the bulletin board on the platform where the server resides.

Earlier chapters have described how services are grouped into servers. A requestor invokes a service with the name of the service as a parameter. The TUXEDO main() in the server receives the message and invokes the service by calling the service as a function. The structure of a server is shown in Figure 9.1.

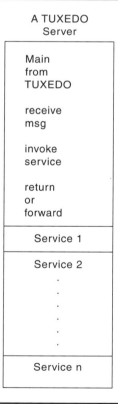

Figure 9.1   Server structure.

The main line of a TUXEDO server is provided by TUXEDO. When TUXEDO is booted, servers are started and then await a message to perform a service. In Figure 9.1, the server is waiting at the receive msg point. When a request arrives, the mainline examines it, saves the address of the requestor, determines which service to invoke and issues a function call to the selected service. Services complete with either a **tpreturn(3)** or a **tpforward(3)** function. These functions return control to the main line where the TUXEDO code returns the result to the requestor for a **tpreturn(3)** or sends a message to invoke another service for a **tpforward(3)**. In the case of **tpforward(3)** the address of the original requestor is included in the message header sent to the next service.

9.3   SERVER INITIALIZATION AND CLEANUP

When a server is booted, the TUXEDO mainline calls **tpsvrinit(3)**. A version of this function is provided in the TUXEDO libraries, but an application specific **tpsvrinit(3)** may be used. The default **tpsvrinit(3)** calls **tpopen(3)** to initialize any XA resource manager that may be present and calls **userlog(3)** to log the fact that the server has started. If an application **tpsvrinit(3)** is used, it must call **tpopen(3)** and should call **userlog(3)** to log that the server has started. **tpopen(3)** should be called, even if the server is not associated with a group using an XA resource manager; future releases may include additional initialization functionality in **tpopen(3)**. Use a C **return()** to end **tpsvrinit(3)**, not **tpreturn(3)**.

Application **tpsvrinit(3)** may call any TUXEDO function available to a service and may enter transaction mode. Conversations may be used in **tpsvrinit(3)** only if the server is a conversational server. If either **tpreturn(3)** or **tpforward(3)** is called in **tpsvrinit(3)** they return success without doing anything.

TUXEDO allows the administrator to specify the order in which servers are started, so some services may not be available when **tpsvrinit(3)** is run; all requests for service must be to services available at this time. If any conversations are left open, if there are any outstanding replies from **tpacall(3)**s, or if the transaction has not been committed when **tpsvrinit(3)** returns, the boot of the server will be aborted with a message placed in the log.

When a server is shut down, the TUXEDO mainline calls **tpsvrdone(3)** before exiting. An application specific **tpsvrdone(3)** may be used. The default **tpsvrdone(3)** calls **tpclose(3)** to close XA resource managers and **userlog(3)** to log the fact that the server has been shut down. Application **tpsvrdone(3)** programs must call **tpclose(3)**

and should call **userlog(3)**. The rules for using TUXEDO functions in
tpsvrdone(3) are the same as for **tpsvrinit(3)**.

    tpsvrinit(3) has the form:

```
int tpsvrinit(int argc, char **argv)
```

where argc and argv have the same meaning as they do with a C
main().

    The argv elements are populated by the CLOPT parameter speci-
fied for the server in the configuration file. The method of population is
explained in Chapter 10. argv is used by TUXEDO to store its own
startup parameters, so optind is set to point to the first application
argument when **tpsvrinit(3)** is called by the TUXEDO mainline.

    The following code fragment illustrates how to write an application
specific **tpsvrinit(3)**.

```
#include <stdio.h>
#include <ctype.h>
#include <Uunix.h>
#include <atmi.h>     /* TUXEDO Header File */
#include <userlog.h>      /* TUXEDO Header File */
 .
 .
 .

tpsvrinit(int argc, char *argv[])
{
    int argno, orgargc, orgopti, userarg;
    char arg1[30], arg2[30];
    char *errstr;

    argno = optind;
    userarg = argc - optind;

    /* Get arguments from configuration file. */
    /* It could be looped but since there are at most
       two arguments in this appl, use the simple method */
    if(userarg > 0)
    {
        strcpy(arg1, argv[argno]);
    }
```

```
                 argno++;
                 if(userarg > 1)
                 {
                    strcpy(arg2, argv[argno]);
                 }
                 .
                 .
                 .

                 /* call tpopen to open and connect to the database */
                 if(tpopen() < 0)
                 {
                    errstr = tpstrerror(tperrno);
                    userlog("fmlserv failed to open database because");
                    userlog("    %s", errstr);
                    return(-1);
                 }
                 .
                 .
                 .

                 /* note that server is starting and report arguments */
                 userlog("The fml16 sample server is starting");
                 userlog("arg1 is %s arg2 is %s", arg1, arg2);
                 return(0);
              }
```

9.4   CREATING REQUEST/RESPONSE SERVICES

9.4.1   Overview

A request/response service has the following characteristics:

- It can receive one request at a time and return or forward one result.
- It cannot receive any requests while working on another.
- It must terminate by either sending the result back to the requestor or by forwarding the request to another request/response service.

There are three parts to a request/response service:

- Retrieving the message and initializing the service
- Process the request

- Completing the service by returning the result or forwarding the request

The following rules must be followed when creating a service.

- Always call **tpreturn(3)** and **tpforward(3)** from the main part of the service, never from a called function.
- Never try to call a service as a function.
- Never use **tpcall(3)** or **tpacall(3)** to invoke a service in the same server; doing so will lock up the server.
- Using **tpforward(3)** to invoke a service in the same server works but is not recommended since it defeats some of the purpose of using **tpforward(3)**—that is, to free up the server to process more requests.

9.4.2   Retrieving the Message and Initializing the Service

The TUXEDO mainline passes a pointer, rqst, to the service. This pointer addresses a structure **typedef**'d as TPSVCINFO. The service uses this pointer to retrieve the message it received and other information. The following code fragment illustrates how to retrieve the data portion of the message for the service FMLSAMP. This is an FML buffer, so the pointer is type cast to FBFR.

```
FMLSAMP(rqst)
TPSVCINFO *rqst;
{

    . . .

    FBFR *bufptr; /* pointer to data area for FML buffer */

    . . .

    bufptr = (FBFR *) rqst->data; /* get location of data */
/* bufptr is now available for use in FML functions to */
/* access the buffer */
```

In this fragment, the pointer bufptr is used to address the data portion of TPSVCINFO.

The structure associated with TPSVCINFO has the following elements:

```
char    name[32];       /* svc name invoked */
long    flags;          /* trans and reply status */
char    *data;          /* message from requestor */
long    len;       /* length of message from requestor */
int     cd;        /* not used at this time */
long    appkey;    /* security code - application dependent */
CLIENTID cltid;       /* TUXEDO defined client identifier */
```

name contains the name used to invoke the service. flags indicates if the service was invoked in transaction mode or if a reply is expected by the invoker. If the field contains TPTRAN, the service was invoked in transaction mode. If the field contains TPNOREPLY, no reply is expected by the requestor. Both flags may be set. The presence of TPTRAN does not indicate that the service was invoked on behalf of a transaction initiated by some other process, only that the service has been invoked in transaction mode. Transaction mode will be set either because the service was invoked on behalf of a transaction initiated by another process or because the service was set to AUTOTRAN by the administrator.

data points to the message buffer, and is used as illustrated above. len is the actual length of the message received. If, as is recommended, this buffer is used to return or forward the result of the service, this value can be used to determine if the result will fit. appkey is a value used for security. Its contents depend on the type of security used by the application. More information about this field will be provided in Chapter 12. cltid is a TUXEDO defined client identifier. It is not from the client initialization buffer. This field will be discussed later in this section in the discussion on **tpnotify(3)**. The service should not modify any of these fields except the area pointed to by data, since they are placed there as information only.

The system does not maintain service context between invocations of services. For this reason, the service must be written to initialize any values as required. In particular, the service must close all database cursors before terminating. Therefore, cursors must be opened each time the service is invoked.

9.4.3   Processing the Request

A service processes a request by retrieving data from the message buffer and performing prescribed functionality on the data. A service may use any UNIX functions and capabilities except:

- Do not use fork() or exec() because TUXEDO cannot follow these types of processing trees.
- Do not use sleep() because the entire server is unavailable until the service completes its current request. Use of sleep() will degrade performance immensely.
- Avoid writing data to the UNIX file system (so-called "flat files"). These files are not controlled by a resource manager, so cannot be included in transactions. Also, unless the program flushes the buffers after each write, the last set of information may not be written to the disk if the system fails. Flushing buffers after each write can degrade performance.

If a service is invoked multiple times on behalf of the same transaction, each invocation may use a physically different instance of the server (and therefore the service) on the same platform, or the requests may be processed on different platforms. Services should be designed to work in this environment. If there is a need to maintain some type of context between invocations of the same service, or between multiple services, include the information in the return buffer and place responsibility for context maintenance in the client.

9.4.4 Completing the Service

When a server has completed processing a request, it may use either a **tpreturn(3)** or a **tpforward(3)** to pass on the results. The **tpreturn(3)** sends the results from the service to the original service requester. The **tpforward(3)** sends the results from the service to another server for further processing.

Figure 9.2 illustrates the possible paths through servers. Message 1 is a request from a client or another service. Service A sends message 2 to Service B with a **tpcall(3)** or **tpacall(3)** while processing the request. Since message 2 was sent with a **tpcall(3)** or **tpacall(3)**, the **tpreturn(3)** called by Service B returns its results to Service A. When Service A is finished processing, more processing is required to finish the request, so Service A uses a **tpforward(3)** to send the request with the partial results to Service C. Service C completes the processing and returns the final result to the original requester using a **tpreturn(3)**. Using **tpforward(3)** judiciously reduces the number of messages passed and frees up servers more quickly, increasing performance of the system.

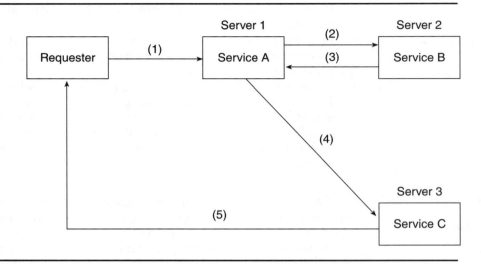

Figure 9.2   The path of a request.

9.4.5   Returning and Forwarding from a Service

This section discusses how to return or forward from a service when using the request/response paradigm. See the later section on conversational services to learn about returning from a conversational service. Forwarding is not allowed from a conversational service.

A service may return the result to the requestor with **tpreturn(3)** or may forward the result to another service with a **tpforward(3)**. These two functions are the only ones that may be used to return from a service. If a standard C return is attempted, or the processing "falls out" of the service, the system will log a failure and return a TPESVCERR to the original requestor.

The form of **tpreturn(3)** is:

```
void tpreturn(int rval, long rcode, char *data, long len, long
flags)
```

tpreturn(3) completes the service and sends the contents of the area pointed to by *data* to the original requestor. If the service was run in transaction mode, **tpreturn(3)** indicates to the transaction manager that this portion of work was completed, and that it may be committed or rolled back when the transaction ends. **tpreturn(3)** does not commit or abort the transaction, but only indicates that the service has been completed.

The service sets *rval* to indicate the status of the result to both TUXEDO and the requestor. The contents of *rval* can be set by using names defined in atmi.h. The valid *rval* names are:

TPSUCCESS Indicates that the service completed successfully. If the service was executed in transaction mode, TPSUCCESS indicates to TUXEDO that the work done by the service was acceptable and that the transaction may be committed as far as this execution of the service is concerned.

TPFAIL Indicates that during processing the service determined that the transaction must be aborted. TPFAIL does not cause the transaction to immediately abort, but indicates to TUXEDO that only abort is allowed. The **tpcall(3)** or **tpgetrply(3)** that receives the response will indicate failure with **tperrno** set to TPESVCFAIL. The return message is returned to the requestor.

TPEXIT Indicates the same as TPFAIL, with the addition that the server containing the service is shut down. If the administrator has set the server as restartable, TUXEDO will automatically restart it.

rcode is set by the service to an application dependent value. It may be set on any call to **tpreturn(3)**. The value in *rcode* is returned to the invoker in urcode.

data points to the message to send to the requestor. *data* may be NULL. If *data* is not NULL, it must point to an area previously allocated with **tpalloc(3)**. The buffer pointed to by *data* will be freed by TUXEDO during the execution of **tpreturn(3)**. *data* may point to the same buffer that was passed to the service. *len* specifies the length of *data*. If the buffer type used for the return message is a type which implies the length, such as FML, *len* is ignored. *flags* must be specified, but are ignored. It is good practice to set flags to 0. No errors can be returned by **tpreturn(3)**, because this function exits the application portion of the service. If **tpreturn(3)** fails, the invoking function fails, and the invoking program can test tperrno for the type of failure.

The form of **tpforward(3)** is:

```
void tpforward(char * svc, char *data, long len, long flags)
```

tpforward(3) indicates to TUXEDO that the service has completed, then invokes the service named by *svc*. If the service was run in transaction mode, **tpforward(3)** indicates to the transaction manager that this portion of work was completed, and that it may be committed or rolled back when the transaction ends. **tpforward(3)** does not commit or abort the transaction, but only indicates that the service has been completed. **tpforward(3)** passes information required so that the **tpreturn(3)** called by the service at the end of the forwarding chain will return to the invoker of the first service in the chain.

data points to the message to send to the requestor. *data* may be NULL. If *data* is not NULL, it must point to an area previously allocated with **tpalloc(3)**. The buffer pointed to by *data* will be freed by TUXEDO during the execution of **tpforward(3)**. *data* may point to the same buffer that was passed to the service. *len* specifies the length of *data*. If the buffer type used for the forwarded message is a type that implies the length, such as FML, *len* is ignored. *flags* must be specified, but are ignored. It is good practice to set flags to 0.

No errors can be returned by **tpforward(3)** because this function exits the application portion of the service. If **tpforward(3)** fails, the invoking function fails and the invoking program can test **tperrno** for the type of failure.

9.5   CREATING CONVERSATIONAL SERVICES

A service becomes a conversational service by being included in a server marked conversational by the administrator. While any client may initiate a conversation, request/response services may not participate in conversations in any way, including being an initiator. A conversational service

- Receives a message buffer when initiated in the same manner as a request/response service, except any data received was sent by the initiator with the **tpconnect(3)** function.
- May send and receive multiple messages with the initiator, following the conversational protocol.
- May initiate conversations with other conversational services.
- May use any TUXEDO function that other services use except **tpforward(3)**.
- Must end the conversation with the initiator with a **tpreturn(3)** while in control of the conversation.

Conversations were discussed fully in Chapter 6.

9.6   SENDING UNSOLICITED MESSAGES

There are two methods available to services for sending unsolicited messages to clients: **tpbroadcast(3)** and **tpnotify(3)**. **tpbroadcast(3)** can be used by both clients and services and was discussed in Chapter 8. **tpnotify(3)** is available only to services.

The form of **tpnotify(3)** is:

```
int tpnotify(CLIENTID * clientid, char *data, long len,
long flags)
```

tpnotify(3) sends the information in *data* to the client identified by *clientid*. The service must make sure that the value of clientid retrieved from TPSVCINFO. **tpnotify(3)** cannot be used to send unsolicited messages to services, even if the current service was invoked by a service. *clientid* is available in TPSVCINFO when a service is invoked by a client. It may be retrieved and saved for later use. *data* must point to a typed buffer allocated by **tpalloc(3)** and the receiving client must be prepared to retrieve data from the type of buffer used in **tpnotify(3)** by the service. Any typed buffer known to the system can be used, but STRING is recommended. *len* is the length of the typed data buffer. *len* may be 0 if the system has knowledge of the length of the *data*, such as when *data* is an FML buffer.

Valid flags are:

TPSIGRSTRT The flag TPSIGRSTRT should always be specified with TUXEDO functions to be sure that the call is reissued if processing is interrupted by a signal during the execution of the call.

TPNOBLOCK The flag TPNOBLOCK will cause **tpnotify(3)** to return immediately with the error TPEBLOCK without sending the message if there is a blocking condition, such as when there is no room in the internal buffer used for messages.

TPNOTIME The flag TPNOTIME prevents a blocking timeout. TPNOBLOCK and TPNOTIME are mutually exclusive. The transaction may still fail due to a transaction timeout.

If **tpnotify(3)** fails, it returns –1 and sets **tperrno** to a value that indicates the particular error. The possible errors are:

TPEINVAL Error TPEINVAL means that the parameters were set incorrectly. This error can mean that *flags* contained an invalid value.

TPETIME Error TPETIME indicates that a timeout has occurred. If the process was in transaction mode when the timeout occurred, it was a transaction timeout. A transaction timeout sets an internal flag that will prevent the transaction from being committed. A transaction that has timed out can only be aborted. If the process was not in transaction mode and the TPNOBLOCK flag was not set, error TPETIME occurs when on a blocking timeout.

TPEBLOCK Error TPEBLOCK indicates that a blocking error was found and TPNOBLOCK was set. The message is not sent when this error occurs.

TPGOTSIG Error TPGOTSIG indicates that a signal was received that affected **tpnotify(3)** and the flag TPSIGRSTRT was not set. The message is not sent when this error occurs.

TPEPROTO Error TPEPROTO means that **tpnotify(3)** was called in a situation where it is not proper. Calling **tpnotify(3)** from a client will fail with the error TPEPROTO.

TPESYSTEM The TPESYSTEM error means that there was a failure within TUXEDO. A message describing the problem is written to the log file.

TPEOS The TPEOS error means that an operating system error has occurred. This error can occur if a message queue on another node is full, but **tpcall(3)** will still return success.

If a service intends to notify a particular client, it may save clientid for later use. It might be that a specific client or even a set of clients will be notified if some unusual event happens, but that the service is often invoked by other services. The service can use the saved clientid to notify the selected client of the situation using **tpnotify(3)**. Note that the fields used to store clientid must be typed as CLIENTID, which is defined in atmi.h.

```
#include <stdio.h>
#include <ctype.h>
#include <atmi.h>    /* Always include this TUXEDO file */
. . .
void
UNSOL(TPSVCINFO *rqst)
{

    . . .

    long size = 100;
    char *notdata;

    workptr = (struct simpview *) rqst->data;
```

```
        . . .

        /* send a message to the client which called this service */

        tperrno = 0;
        if((notdata = tpalloc("STRING", 0, size)) == NULL)
        {
            userlog("tpalloc failure for msg %d", tperrno);
        }
        strcpy(notdata, "my message");
        tperrno = 0;
        if(tpnotify(&rqst->cltid, notdata, size, TPSIGRSTRT) < 0)
        {
            tpfree(notdata);
            userlog("tpnotify failure in UNSOL %d", tperrno);
        }


        . . .

        tpfree(notdata);
        tpreturn(TPSUCCESS, 0, rqst->data, 0L, 0);
}
```

9.7 ACCESSING DATABASES IN SERVICES

9.7.1 Using SQL in Services

All services may use all SQL data manipulation language (DML) statements except for transaction boundary statements, such as COMMIT or ROLLBACK. Use of transaction boundary statements is discussed in the next section.

Services should not use any data definition language (DDL) or data control language (DCL) statements. Defining tables using ALTER and other DDL statements is time consuming and may violate application system security rules. Using GRANT and other such statements certainly violates security rules and should never be used in services. Services may use any DML type tools provided by the database vendor, such as stored procedures (example: Oracles PL/SQL).

Services must close all cursors before terminating with **tpreturn(3)** or **tpforward(3)**. If cursors are not explicitly closed, they will remain open, and the next invocation of the service will open another set, leading to many open cursors. Eventually the maximum allowable number of open cursors will be reached. Services cannot set values to be invoked again on behalf of the same transaction with the intent of using already open cursors, because there is no guarantee that the next invocation of the service will be routed to the same physical process. It might even be routed to another platform. Conversational services may leave cursors open for the duration of the conversation, but must close them before calling **tpreturn(3)** to end the conversation.

9.7.2   Transaction Management

Resource managers that are XA compliant can be used to allow TUX-EDO to manage transactions when they span multiple services. If a single service is used in a transaction, there is no need to use XA capabilities because the database provides a sufficient method to manage transactions. Most databases can manage a transaction, using, for instance, the SQL statement COMMIT WORK, when all the SQL statements are issued from a single UNIX process. If the transaction spans multiple services, multiple processes will be involved and use of XA capabilities is required to coordinate the transaction commit.

All the services in a server can access a database, or other resource manager, using XA compliant methods or directly without using XA. This section will use the term "XA" to designate use of XA compliant methods. All services in a server that access a database must either use XA or not because the determination is made at server initialization time. Server initialization is discussed later in this chapter, including how to cause the server to run with an XA compliant resource manager.

All services, whether in an XA server or not, may use all SQL DML statements except for transaction boundary statements, such as COM-MIT or ROLLBACK. Services in XA servers may not use transaction boundary statements. Services in non-XA servers must use the resource manager provided transaction management statements, such as COM-MIT or ROLLBACK. Use of XA or not has no other affect on services. Note that using XA does not imply that a two-phase commit will be used by the system, only that the commit of all database access in the transaction will be coordinated.

9.8   COMPILING SERVICES INTO SERVERS

Services are compiled into servers using the utility **buildserver(1)**. In the simplest case, where a server contains only one service and there are no other modules required, the server can be compiled with the command line:

```
buildserver -o servername -f srcfile -s svcname
```

servername is the name of the resulting executable module. *srcfile* is the name of the source file. *svcname* is the name of a service for this example. Some of the example code in this book was compiled with the command line:

```
buildserver -o fmlserv -f fmlserv.c -s FMLSAMP
```

Other options are similar to those used by the UNIX C compiler, cc, and the linker ld.

-v Causes buildserver to run in the verbose mode.

-o ***exname*** *exname* is the name of the executable module to create. If this option is not specified the name of the executable module is a.out.

-f ***string*** This is the "firstfiles" option. *string* is a space delimited list of files to be included before TUXEDO libraries. If more than one file is named, the list must be enclosed in quotation marks.

-l ***string*** This is the "lastfiles" option. *string* is a space delimited list of files to be included after TUXEDO libraries. If more than one file is named, the list must be enclosed in quotation marks.

-C This option causes buildserver to invoke a COBOL compiler instead of the C compiler.

-s ***svcname,svcname[:funcname]*** This option names the services offered by the server. The list is comma delimited without spaces. *funcname* provides a means of offering a service from a function of a different name or to use several service names with the same function.

buildserver will use information in several environment variables if they are present. For C compilation, these variables are:

CC This environment variable contains the name of the C compiler to be executed. If this environment variable is not present or contains a NULL, the default compiler is used. On UNIX the default compiler is cc(1).

FLAGS If this environment variable is present and not NULL, its contents are passed to the C compiler as command line options.

Other environment variables common to most operations using TUXEDO must also be set. These environment variables should be set by the administrator. Other environment variables must be set when using COBOL to create services. See Chapter 14.

Any service in the server requires that a precompiler that must be run before the C compiler (for example, embedded SQL) must be run before buildserver. The command lines used if the client is using embedded SQL from Oracle might be (in order):

```
proc name=oserver.pc oname= oserver.c
buildserver -o oserver -f  oserver.c -s oservice
```

9.9   **DEBUGGING SERVICES**

9.9.1   **Using** tmtrace(5)

tmtrace(5) provides a trace of TUXEDO events in both servers and services. **tmtrace(5)** can be turned on to start tracing a client by setting the environment variable **TMTRACE=on** and exporting it before starting the client. When the trace is on, information about all ATMI and other TUXEDO events are written to the ULOG. Only the events that occur as a result of the execution of the specific client are traced.

tmtrace(5) can be turned on for server groups while the domain is running by using the **tmadmin(1)** command **changetrace**.

tmtrace(5) provides a number of filters that allow tracing individual ATMI calls, server groups, and various combinations. These filters can be supplied in the environment variable TMTRACE to trace client and related activity or by using the **tmadmin(1)** command **changetrace**.

9.9.2   **The** ud(1) **Utility**

The utilities **ud(1)** and **ud32(1)** are TUXEDO native clients that send FML buffer information to services and report what the service returns. Use **ud(1)** for services using FML16 buffers, **ud32(1)** for services using FML32 buffers. To use **ud(1)**:

1. Be sure the environment variable FLDTBLDIR includes $TUXDIR/ udataobj.
2. Be sure the environment variable FIELDTBLS includes Usysflds for FML16 buffers; for FML32 buffers, set FIELDTBLS32 to Usysfl32.
3. Create an input file for **ud(1)** in the proper format.
4. Execute **ud(1)** with the command line **ud <udinput**.

The format for each line of the **ud(1)** input file is:

```
[flag]fldname<tab>fldval
```

where: The optional *flag* can be used to control the usage of the FML buffer within **ud(1)**; *fldname* is the name of an FML field required for the service to be tested; *fldval* is the value to place in the field.

The input file can contain information for several executions of services. Each execution can be a different service. Each set of data must be followed by a newline character (**\n**) and a blank line. The first line for an execution must specify the service name as follows:

```
[flag]SVRCNM<tab>servicename
```

where: The optional *flag* can be used to control the usage of the FML buffer within **ud(1)**; SVRCNM must be spelled exactly as shown; *servicename* is the name of the service to be tested.

If no options or flags are used, **ud(1)** accumulates the occurrences in its FML buffer and reports a growing list of values. It is usually a good idea to use the flag **+** to indicate that the buffer should be cleared before placing the current value into the buffer.

If the following input file is used:

```
SRVCNM      FMLSAMP
mystr1      string1
\n

+SRVCNM     FMLSAMP
+mystr1     string2
\n
```

The output from **ud(1)** from a test service is:

```
SENT pkt(1) is :
SRVCNM      FMLSAMP
mystr1      string1

RTN pkt(1) is :
SRVCNM      FMLSAMP
mystr1      mystr1 = string1

SENT pkt(2) is :
SRVCNM      FMLSAMP
mystr1      string2
```

```
RTN pkt(2) is :
SRVCNM    FMLSAMP
mystr1    mystr1 = string2
```

9.9.3 Other Methods

Most modern UNIX debugging tools can dynamically trace UNIX daemons. Any of these can be used to debug TUXEDO services. Use the instructions that come with the tool for stepping through or tracing daemons. When using these tools, be sure to set the required options in the environment variable CFLAGS before using **buildserver(1)** to compile the server that is to be tested.

The simplest, and perhaps best, method of tracing is to use the **userlog(3)** function to write significant information to ULOG and to use **ud(1)** to run the various services. If the services do not use FML buffers for communication, application developers must create simple clients to exercise the services.

9.10 A SIMPLE DEBUGGING DOMAIN

Developers can set up a simple domain for testing. The simple domain shown here can be set up by each developer to test a single service without placing an overly heavy load on the debugging platform. Replace fields shown in italics with values specific to the test environment.

The test ubbconfig might be:

```
*RESOURCES
IPCKEY        123456

#Example:
#IPCKEY       123456

MASTER        mydebug
MAXACCESSERS  5
MAXSERVERS    5
MAXSERVICES   10
MODEL         SHM
LDBAL         N

*MACHINES
DEFAULT:
```

```
          APPDIR="/home/clh/mydebugdir"
          TUXCONFIG="/home/clh/mydebugdir/mydebugconfig"
          TUXDIR="/home/tuxdir"

unix1                 LMID=mydebug

*GROUPS
GROUP1
     LMID=mydebug   GRPNO=1   OPENINFO=NONE

*SERVERS
DEFAULT:
          CLOPT="-A"

myserver        SRVGRP=GROUP1 SRVID=1

*SERVICES
myservice
```

A script to set the environment might be:

```
TUXDIR=/home/tuxdir; export TUXDIR
TUXCONFIG=/home/clh/testapp/mytestcon; export TUXCONFIG
PATH=$TUXDIR/bin:/home/clh/testapp:$PATH; export PATH

VIEWFILES=fmlview.V; export VIEWFILES
VIEWDIR=/home/clh/testapp; export VIEWDIR
VIEWFILES32=fmlview32.V; export VIEWFILES32
VIEWDIR32=/home/clh/testapp; export VIEWDIR32

FLDTBLDIR=/home/clh/testapp:$TUXDIR/udataobj; export
FLDTBLDIR
FIELDTBLS=fmlflds,Usysflds; export FIELDTBLS
FLDTBLDIR32=/home/clh/testapp:$TUXDIR/udataobj;
     export FLDTBLDIR32
FIELDTBLS32=fmlflds32,Usysfl32; export FIELDTBLS32

LD_LIBRARY_PATH=$TUXDIR/lib:$LD_LIBRARY_PATH;
export LD_LIBRARY_PATH
```

This environment is set up to enable using **ud(1)** or **ud32(1)** to debug a service that uses FML16 or FML32 type buffers respectively.

To start the test domain, set the environment variables, then execute the command:

```
tmboot -y
```

To shut down the test domain, execute the command:

```
tmshutdown -y
```

10

Administration Part 1

OVERVIEW

Chapters 10 and 11 cover how to define and maintain a TUXEDO domain using TUXEDO command line utilities. This chapter describes the basic elements of TUXEDO administration. Chapter 11 includes suggestions on how to manage the system after it has been initially defined. TUXEDO configuration is determined by a configuration file that can be defined from a source file. To manage system behavior effectively, the administrator must understand these files and how they affect the operation of the system. This chapter discusses how to create and manage these files as well as the significance of the values in the files.

Once a domain has been initially defined, two utilities are available to dynamically change the configuration and manage system and application resources. They are **tmadmin(1)** and **tmconfig(1)**. This chapter describes how these interactive utilities are used.

Nothing is as simple as it seems, so various factors that are not immediately obvious affect the performance of TUXEDO applications. Therefore, there is a section devoted to managing a running system dynamically. Failures sometimes happen, so the administrator's part in minimizing the effect of failure on the system is discussed. The chapter concludes with methods of recovery from catastrophe.

10.2   **TUXEDO CONFIGURATION FILES**

The TUXEDO system uses a single file to define a domain at boot time. The generic name for this file is tuxconfig, which is a binary form usable only by TUXEDO software. A source version of tuxconfig, generically called ubbconfig, is provided as a human interface. ubbconfig can be created and maintained using any text editor that works with a standard text file. The ubbconfig file is compiled into the binary configuration file, tuxconfig, with **tmloadcf(1)**. The following ubbconfig is an example of a very simple ubbconfig file.

```
#Simplest possible ubbconfig file.

*RESOURCES
IPCKEY          123456

MASTER          example
MODEL           SHM

*MACHINES

unix1
            LMID=example
            APPDIR="/home/clh/testapp"
            TUXCONFIG="/home/clh/testapp/admconfig"
            TUXDIR="/home/tuxdir"

*GROUPS
GROUP1
        LMID=example GRPNO=1      OPENINFO=NONE

*SERVERS
DEFAULT:
            CLOPT="-A"

fmlserv    SRVGRP=GROUP1 SRVID=1

*SERVICES
FMLSAMP
```

This ubbconfig was used to run some of the sample clients and servers in this book. The components are discussed in the next section.

The line of note in the example ubbconfig for this section is the line beginning with **TUXCONFIG**. There is also a required environmental variable with this name. Environmental variables are described later in full, but this one needs to be discussed here. The environmental variable

TUXCONFIG contains the full path name of the tuxconfig file because the domain is used to boot TUXEDO. Using this mechanism, the name of the tuxconfig file can be anything the administrator desires. The actual name of the ubbconfig can also be anything. It is recommended that the ubbconfig be named ubb*somename* and the tuxconfig *somename*config to keep from confusing the name of these files with other files. The full path name in the environment variable TUXCONFIG must match the full path name for TUXCONFIG in the ubbconfig. **tmloadcf(1)** checks this match and will not compile the ubbconfig if they are different.

In theory, every user can use a different tuxconfig and thus a different domain, even if they are all on the same platform. In some circumstances giving each developer his or her own domain works out well. Production users should all be running on single domain, unless there is reason to keep them separated, such as when they are using independent applications. This subject is discussed further in the section on performance tuning.

10.3 ENVIRONMENT VARIABLES

Except for those using workstation clients (/WS clients), every TUXEDO user must set environment variables. For application users, the environment variables should be set for them in default profile files. Developers may require their own approaches, such as a set of shell scripts that set the variables for various test domains. Setting environment variables for /WS client users is discussed in the section on /WS administration later in this chapter.

A typical environment contains variables as follows:

```
# Variables for the system
TUXDIR=/home/tuxdir; export TUXDIR
TUXCONFIG=/home/clh/testapp/admconfig; export TUXCONFIG
PATH=$TUXDIR/bin:/home/clh/testapp:$PATH; export PATH

# Variables for VIEW type buffers
VIEWFILES=fmlview.V; export VIEWFILES
VIEWDIR=/home/clh/testapp; export VIEWDIR
VIEWFILES32=fmlview32.V; export VIEWFILES32
VIEWDIR32=/home/clh/testapp; export VIEWDIR32

# Variables for FML buffers
FLDTBLDIR=/home/clh/testapp; export FLDTBLDIR
FIELDTBLS=fmlflds; export FIELDTBLS
```

```
FLDTBLDIR32=/home/clh/testapp/bin; export FLDTBLDIR
FIELDTBLS32=fmlflds32; export FIELDTBLS

# COBOL variables
COBCPY=:$TUXDIR/cobinclude; export COBCPY
COBOPT="-C ANS85 -C ALIGN=8 -C NOIBMCOMP -C TRUNC=ANSI -C
OSEXT=cbl"; export COBOPT

# The following variable must be present if using dynamic
# load libraries
LD_LIBRARY_PATH=$TUXDIR/lib:$LD_LIBRARY_PATH;
        export LD_LIBRARY_PATH
```

Those familiar with Bourne shell scripts will recognize the form of this example as a script. Developers can use this type of script, adapted for their favorite shell, to set up test domains.

The variables in the first section must be set for everyone using TUXEDO. The variables for VIEW type buffers must be set for all users of applications that use VIEW type buffers. The variables for FML buffers must be set for all users of applications that use FML buffers. The variables in the COBOL section are required for COBOL developers. The dynamic load library variable must be set for all users of applications that access dynamic libraries.

Additional variables required specifically by developers are explained in the chapters about creating clients and creating servers and services.

TUXCONFIG was explained in the section on configuration files.

TUXDIR is the directory where the TUXEDO system is loaded. The example shows TUXDIR as /home/tuxdir. There are a number of directories within TUXDIR, such as bin and include. TUXDIR can be any directory that is convenient for the administrator, but none of the directories under TUXDIR may be changed. Some installations prefer to place TUXEDO in its own file system. For instance, TUXDIR might be set simply to /tuxdir.

PATH must include the path to the TUXEDO executables that are in $TUXDIR/bin. PATH must also include paths to the binaries for all services to be booted as part of the domain. It is also a good idea to include the paths to native clients here, unless they are already set by default.

The variables for VIEW type and FML type buffers are explained in Chapter 7.

LD_LIBRARY_PATH must be specified if applications are using UNIX dynamic load libraries. This variable must contain the full path to the directory containing the TUXEDO libraries.

10.4   **UBBCONFIG**

10.4.1   **Overview**

ubbconfig is a text version of tuxconfig. A TUXEDO domain must be initially defined with a ubbconfig file. Once the domain has been defined and booted, **tmconfig(1)** can be used to modify or add most configuration items. The administrator should be familiar with the limitations on what can be added or changed with **tmconfig(1)**, so that ubbconfig can be properly configured.

There are seven sections in ubbconfig:

RESOURCES The RESOURCES section contains information pertaining to all resources in the domain, such as maximum number of groups, servers, and services, and other resource items such as frequency of heartbeat checks, and maximum number of processes that can access to a TUXEDO server node at any one time. This section also defines security.

MACHINES The MACHINES section contains information pertaining to a platform (server node). Items include full path names of TUXDIR, TUXCONFIG, and APPDIR.

GROUPS The GROUPS section provides information that applies to all servers in a group and the resource manager associated with the group, or the fact that there is no resource manager. If a resource manager is provided, the GROUPS section defines the open and close strings for it.

NETWORK The NETWORK section provides network information, such as addresses, for a multinode domain.

SERVERS The SERVERS section names the servers in a group and information about each server. This section can be used to control the order in which servers are booted.

SERVICES The SERVICES section names the services and can be used to associate each service with a server group. Other optional information such as the type of buffer the service uses can also be included.

ROUTING The ROUTING section sets up data dependent routing criteria.

There are limitations on the order in which the sections are specified. For practical reasons they should always be specified in the order listed above. TUXEDO requires RESOURCES, MACHINES, and GROUPS sections to boot. A practical single-node system should include all sections except NETWORK and ROUTING. A multinode system requires the NET-WORK section. The SERVICES section should be provided to document the services provided to facilitate future administration activities.

ubbconfig has the following format:

- Each section begins with a line containing an asterisk (*) in the first character, for instance, *RESOURCES. The first character may be a nonsignificant character, such as space or tab, but putting the * in the first character of the line is recommended.
- identifiers are used to name components (machine, group, server, etc.). identifiers must always be followed by white space (space, tab, or newline) or punctuation character (comma, pound sign, etc.). Identifiers are written with standard C language rules.
- Parameters in all sections except for those in the RESOURCES section are keyword parameters. They are of the form: *KEYWORD = parameter*. An example is:

```
APPDIR = /home/clh/testapp/bin.
```

- A feature called DEFAULT can be used within every section except RESOURCES. Parameters set by DEFAULT remain in effect until another DEFAULT or the end of the section is reached. Parameters set by DEFAULT are overridden by explicit setting of the parameter in a line that is not a DEFAULT line. The form of DEFAULT is:

```
DEFAULT: parameter list
```

where parameter list is a white space delimited set *KEYWORD = value* clauses.
- All values adhere to C programming languages. *numeric_values* can be decimal, hexadecimal, or octal, using the C language notation to specify the number base. (The prefix 0x is hex, 0 is octal, and decimal values have no prefix.) The recommendation is to use decimal whole numbers for *numeric_values*. All *string* values are enclosed in double quotes. An integer number must be treated as a *string*.
- Within a line, the pound sign (#) begins a comment. A comment may be placed after a parameter on the same line. Comments end at the end of the line.
- Comments and blank lines are ignored.

It is not the purpose of this book to repeat the information in the TUXEDO reference manual, so the discussion that follows provides information and clarification on the most important items in each section. Some parameters not listed in the description of ubbconfig contents are referred to and explained in the section on performance tuning. Parameters that are used for security purposes are explained in Chapter 12.

10.4.2 The RESOURCES Section

The RESOURCES section begins with *RESOURCES. Three parameters are required in the RESOURCES section: **IPCKEY**, **MASTER**, and **MODEL**. All other parameters are optional.

IPCKEY *numeric_value*: **IPCKEY** provides a numeric key that TUXEDO uses to identify its bulletin board, message queues, and semaphores. It is also used to derive a number of other addresses, such as the name of bulletin boards in a multinode system.

MASTER *string1[,string2]*: *string1* is the **MASTER** machine name. *string2* is the backup **MASTER** machine name. Both string1 and string2 must appear in the MACHINES section as values for the **LMID** parameter. The master tuxconfig file is on the **MASTER**. When the system is booted, the master tuxconfig is used to boot the system and build the DBBL. A multinode system may also have a backup **MASTER** that will be booted if the **MASTER** fails.

MODEL {SHM | MP}: **MODEL** indicates the type of system. SHM indicates that the system will run on a single platform. **MP** indicates that there will be multiple nodes in the system.

OPTIONS *identifier[,identifier]*: **OPTIONS** is a comma delimited list of options. Two options are currently available. The **LAN** option indicates that this is a networked domain. This option is usually set when using an **MP** system. The **MIGRATE** option specifies that server groups are to be migrated. This process is discussed further in the section on failure management. If the **MIGRATE** option is specified, the **LAN** option must also be specified unless the system is running on a single multiprocessor platform.

SYSTEM_ACCESS FASTPATH | PROTECTED [,NO_OVER-RIDE]: SYSTEM_ACCESS specifies the method TUXEDO will use to store its internal tables. If FASTPATH is specified, the tables are stored in shared memory for best performance. FASTPATH does not protect the TUXEDO tables from access and corruption by application programs. PROTECTED causes TUXEDO to store its tables in protected mode, which decreases performance, but protects the tables from corruption by application programs. If NO_OVERRIDE is specified, the SYSTEM_ACCESS value cannot be overridden by an application program.

MAXGTT *numeric_value*: *numeric_value* specifies the maximum number of simultaneous XA transactions which can be processed. The default is 100.

SCANUNIT *numeric_value*: **SCANUNIT** sets the time between scans of the system to test for transaction and blocking timeouts. The time may be set in five second intervals from five to 60. Other time parameters are set in number of **SCANUNIT**s.

MAXDRT *numeric_value*: *numeric_value* specifies the maximum number of data dependent routing criteria that can be specified. The default is the number of criteria defined in the current configuration file. **MAXDRT** allows specifying additional space to support adding new criteria dynamically.

MAXRFT *numeric_value*: *numeric_value* specifies the maximum number of data dependent routing ranges that can be specified. The default is the number of ranges defined in the current configuration file. **MAXRFT** allows specifying additional space to support adding new criteria dynamically.

MAXRTDATA *numeric_value*: *numeric_value* specifies the maximum number of bytes that can be used to define data dependent routing ranges. Range definitions are stored in a string pool, and *numeric_value* specifies the size of the pool in bytes. The default is a value sufficient to contain the ranges defined in the current configuration file. **MAXRTDATA** allows specifying additional space to support adding new criteria dynamically.

SANITYSCAN *numeric_value*: **SANITYSCAN** sets the time between heartbeat checks of the system. It is set as a multiple of **SCANUNIT**. If **SCANUNIT** is 10 and **SANITYSCAN** is 6, then the integrity of the system is checked every 60 seconds. The scan checks the usability of the bulletin boards and servers on all nodes in the system. The section in this chapter on failure management contains more information on the heartbeat check.

BBLQUERY *numeric_value*: **BBLQUERY** sets the time between checks by the DBBL with bulletin boards on other nodes. The DBBL notes all messages from each of the other bulletin boards and if it has not received a message from one of them it sends a message to check. If a response is not received, the DBBL assumes that some failure has occurred that prevents use of the other bulletin board and therefore partitions it from the system. **BBLQUERY** is set to the number of **SCANUNIT**s between these checks. If **BBLQUERY** is not specified, the default is a value that causes the check every 300 seconds.

NOTIFY {DIPIN | SIGNAL | IGNORE}: **NOTIFY** sets the default method of notifying clients of unsolicited messages. This parameter can be overridden by flag values specified in the initialization buffer used with **tpinit(3)**.

10.4.3   The MACHINES Section

The MACHINES section begins with *MACHINES. Four parameters are required in the MACHINES section: **LMID, TUXCONFIG, TUX-DIR**, and **APPDIR**. These parameters must be provided for each node in the system. All other parameters are optional. This section provides a logical name for each node in the system and provides TUXEDO with the paths and/or file names for **TUXCONFIG, TUXDIR**, and **APPDIR**.

The parameters for each node have the form:

```
ADDRESS required parameters [optional parameters]
```

where **ADDRESS** is the value returned by the UNIX command **uname -n**. Multiple platforms may be specified only for the **MP** model.

The parameters in the MACHINES section are:

LMID = *string*: **LMID** associates the TUXEDO logical platform name with the name of the physical platform. *string* is the name that TUXEDO uses to identify the platform. *string* must not contain a comma.

TUXCONFIG = *string*: *string* is the full path file name of the tuxconfig file on the platform. Although this parameter is required for every platform, TUXEDO will use the tuxconfig specified on the platform designated **MASTER** and synchronize the tuxconfig files in the rest of the domain.

TUXDIR = *string*: *string* is the path to the directory where TUX-EDO is installed on the platform. This path may be different on each platform.

APPDIR = *string*: *string* is the path to the directory where application servers reside. *string* may be a colon-separated list of paths.

NETLOAD = *numeric_value*: *numeric_value* sets the additional load for use in computing the cost of sending a message over the network. This value is added to the load factor by the load balancing process for a service that is accessed over the network. For instance, suppose the load factor for service A is 50 and **NETLOAD** is set to 1,000 for the machine. When the service is invoked, the load factor 50 will be used by the load balancing process for a local access; 1,050 will be used for remote access.

TYPE = *string*: *string* identifies the type of representation used by the platform. *string* may be any value of 15 or fewer characters. When TUXEDO sends messages from one platform to another it first compares the types of the machines. If the types are different, TUXEDO will transform information appropriately for those buffer types that allow translation. If the types are the same, there will be no translation.

TLOGDEVICE = *string*: *string* is the name of the device containing the **TLOG**. The **TLOG** is used by TUXEDO while managing distributed XA transactions. This parameter is required if using an XA resource manager on the platform. See the section in this chapter on setting up a TUXEDO domain for more information about the **TLOG**.

ENVFILE = *string*: *string* is the full path name of a file that sets environment variables to be used by clients and servers on the machine. The environment is set by the TUXEDO mainline when the first server is booted on the platform, before **tpsvrinit(3)** is executed. This parameter in the MACHINES section affects all servers and clients on the platform, but may be overridden for by the **ENVFILE** parameter in the SERVERS section.

10.4.4   The GROUPS Section

The GROUPS section defines groups and associates them with particular platforms that were named in the MACHINES section. The parameters **LMID** and **GRPNO** are required parameters; all others are optional. If an XA resource manager is being used, it is associated with a group in the GROUPS section. Each group can be associated with zero or one resource managers.

The definition of each group in the GROUPS section begins with a *GROUPNAME* followed by the parameters for that group. The form for each group is:

```
GROUPNAME parameters
```

The parameters are:

LMID = *string*: *string* is the name of the platform this group is on. The name must match a name specified in the **LMID** parameter in the MACHINES section.

GRPNO = *numeric_value*: *numeric_value* is used to identify the group in other sections. It must be a number greater than zero and less than 30,000. **GRPNO** must be unique among all groups in the domain.

TMSNAME = *string*: *string* is the name of the transaction manager server that is to be used with this group. Each XA resource manager will have a transaction manager server associated with it. Naming the transaction manager server implies a specific resource manager. This parameter associates the group with a resource manager and allows servers or native clients in the group to use the facilities of the associated resource manager in a global transaction. If this parameter is not present, the servers in the group cannot use an XA resource manager.

TMSCOUNT = *numeric_value*: *numeric_value* is the number of transaction manager servers that will be started for the group. The number must be in the range of 2 through 10. If this parameter is not specified, the default is 3.

OPENINFO = *string*: *string* is specified by the resource manager vendor. This string is passed to the resource manager by **tpopen(3)** to initialize and connect to the resource manager. For instance, if the resource manager is an Oracle database, **OPENINFO** might be:

```
OPENINFO = "ORACLE:Oracle_XA+
    Acc=P/dir1/dir2+SesTm=30+
    LogDir=/logpath/xa+SQLNET=P:value"
```

The administrator must consult the vendor documentation to determine the exact form of **OPENINFO** for each resource manager. The first characters of the string up to the first colon identify the resource manager and must find a match in $TUXDIR/udataobj/ RM. This parameter may be set to a NULL string ("") or left out if the resource manager does not require an open string.

CLOSEINFO = *string*: *string* is specified by the resource manager vendor. *string* is passed to the resource manager by **tpclose(3)** to close the resource manager. Many resource managers do not require **CLOSEINFO**. The administrator must consult the vendor documentation to determine the exact requirement. If the resource manager does not require a close string, this parameter may be set to NULL string ("") or left out.

10.4.5 **The NETWORK Section**

The NETWORK section provides information necessary to allow TUXEDO to communicate between defined domain nodes. A multinode system requires one set of NETWORK parameters per node.

Each set of parameters in the NETWORK section begins with an *LMID* followed by the parameters for that node. The form is:

```
LMID parameters
```

where **LMID** is a platform logical name that matches the **LMID** for some node defined in the MACHINES section.

The only parameter required by TUXEDO is **NADDR**, but other parameters may be required depending on the type of network being used.

The parameters are:

NADDR = *string*: *string* is a network address for the bridge process on the node. It must be in a form appropriate to the type of network being used.

BRIDGE = *string*: *string* is a device name that will be used by the bridge process.

NLSADDR = *string*: *string* is the network address for the **tlisten(1)** process on the node. Even though the TUXEDO documentation calls this an optional parameter, it is required in most cases. For instance, if the network is TCP/IP, use the following steps to determine **NADDR**:

1. Run the UNIX command **uname -n**, which will return *node_name*.
2. Run **grep *node_name* /etc/hosts**, which will return an address such as: **182.11.108.107 node_name**.
3. Convert returned dotted decimal address into eight hexadecimal digits. The dotted decimal form **182.11.108.107** becomes hexadecimal **00B60006006C006B**.

10.4.6 **The SERVERS Section**

The SERVERS section associates servers with groups and provides information to TUXEDO about servers.

The form of the SERVERS section is:

```
servername parameters
```

where *servername* is the name of the server and *parameters* are the parameters specified for the server. *servername* must be an executable program created by **buildserver(1)**. The required parameters for each server are **SVRGRP** and **SRVID**.

The parameters are:

SVRGRP = *string*: *string* is the name of the group this server is part of. *string* must match the name of a group defined in the GROUPS section. Associating the server with a group will cause the server to run on the machine named in the **LMID** parameter of the GROUPS section. If the named group is associated with a resource manager, the server may use the facilities of that resource manager.

SRVID = *numeric_value*: *numeric_value* identifies a server within a group. *numeric_value* must be unique for the server within its group. If more than one instance of a server will be started, leave gaps in the assigned **SRVID**s to allow TUXEDO to assign numbers to the additional instances without duplication. See the descriptions of **MIN** and **MAX**.

CLOPT = *string*: *string* is a set of values defined in the *TUXEDO Reference Manual* under **servopts(5)**. The options include means of specifying services offered, parameters to be passed to the server when it is booted, and other options. **servopts(5)** is discussed in a later section in this chapter.

SEQUENCE = *numeric_value*: *numeric_value* is a number that specifies the sequence in which the servers should be booted. Servers with an assigned sequence number are booted first in the order of the sequence number, then all other servers in the order they are listed in the configuration file. If two servers have the same number they will be booted in parallel. If no servers have sequence numbers, they are booted in the order they are listed in the configuration file. *numeric_value* must be in the range 1 and 9999.

MIN = *numeric_value*: *numeric_value* is the minimum number of instances of the server to start. If **MIN** is not specified, the default is one. If multiple instances are started, the numeric identifier of the first one started will be as specified by **SRVID**. TUXEDO will generate an identifier for each additional instance by adding one to **SRVID**. For instance, if **MIN** is 3 and **SRVID** is 5, three instances will be started with identifiers 5, 6, and 7. If multiple instances of a server are started and **RQADDR** is specified for the server, the instances automatically form an MSSQ set.

MAX = *numeric_value*: *numeric_value* is the maximum number of instances to the server than can be started. If the server is a request/response server, additional instances may be started at any time using the **-i** option of **tmboot(1)** to specify the numeric identifier of the additional instances. If the server is a conversational server, TUXEDO will automatically start additional instances up to the number specified by **MAX**.

ENVFILE = *string*: **ENVFILE** specified for a server overrides the **ENVFILE** parameter in the MACHINES section. If the server is in a group that is defined on more than one platform and **MIGRATE** has been specified as an option in the RESOURCES section, *string* must be identical on all platforms where the server is defined.

CONV = {Y | N}: **CONV** indicates the type of server. N means the server is a request/response server, Y means the server is a conversational server. If **CONV** is not specified, the default is N.

RQADDR = *string*: *string* is a symbolic name to use for the message queue to use for the server. If two servers have the same **RQADDR** they will share the message queue. Servers that share the same message queue must be in the same group. Servers that share a message queue form an MSSQ set.

REPLYQ = {Y | N}: By default, or if **REPLYQ** is set to Y, replies to requests from services share the same message queue as requests to the services in the server. If a server contains services that make requests, **REPLYQ** should be set to Y.

MAXGEN = *numeric_value*: *numeric_value* is the maximum number of times that the server can be restarted in the period specified by **GRACE**. If **MAXGEN** is 1, the server cannot be restarted. *numeric_value* must be greater than 0 and less than 256.

GRACE = *numeric_value*: If the server is restartable, it can be restarted **MAXGEN** times in *numeric_value* seconds. If **GRACE** is set to 0, it means that there is no limit to the number of times the server can be restarted, unless **MAXGEN** is set to 1. If **GRACE** is not specified, the default is 86,400 seconds, or 24 hours.

RESTART = {Y | N}: **RESTART = Y** means that the server is restartable. If the server is in a group that is specified on more than one platform and the **MIGRATE** option is specified in the RESOURCES section, **RESTART** must be set to Y. If **RESTART** is not specified, the default is N.

10.4.7   **The SERVICES Section**

The SERVICES section provides information to TUXEDO about services.

The form of the SERVICES section is:

```
servicename parameters
```

where *servicename* is the name of the server and *parameters* are the parameters specified for the service. There are no required parameters for this section. While TUXEDO does not require listing services in this section, the administrator should list all servers here for future ease of maintenance. Some parameters not listed here are discussed in the section in this chapter on performance tuning.

Some important parameters are:

SRVGRP = *string*: *string* is the name of a group defined in the GROUPS section. The service named by *servicename* above must be offered by a server in the named group. If this parameter is specified, parameters for the service apply only to the service as offered in the named group.

ROUTING = *string*: *string* is the name of a routing criteria specified in the ROUTING section. If **ROUTING** is not specified, data dependent routing cannot be applied to the service.

AUTOTRAN = {Y | N}: If **AUTOTRAN** is set to Y, the service will always run in transaction mode. If a request is made to the service from a requestor already in transaction mode, this parameter is ignored and the transaction proceeds normally and the service will be performed as part of the requestors transaction. If the service is requested by a requestor not in transaction mode, or is called with the TPNOTRAN flag set, a new transaction will be automatically started before the service is performed. The transaction will be automatically committed if the service completes   normally   by   calling   **tpreturn(3)**   with   the TPSUCCESS flag set. If the service completes by calling **tpreturn(3)** with the TPFAIL flag set, the transaction will be aborted. The transaction will be aborted if the service fails to complete, that is if it abnormally terminates. If **AUTOTRAN** is not specified, the default is N.

10.4.8   **The ROUTING Section**

The ROUTING section provides the criteria for data dependent routing. TUXEDO buffer types FML, VIEW, X_C_TYPE, or X_COMMON support data dependent routing.

The form of the ROUTING section is:

```
CRITERION_NAME parameters
```

where *CRITERION_NAME* is a string that names a specific criterion. All parameters are required for each criterion.

The parameters are:

FIELD = *fldname*: *fldname* is the name of the field to be tested to determine routing. The value of *fldname* must match a field defined in an FML field table file or a viewfile. Note that these files require running **mkfldhdr(1)** for FML field tables or **viewc(1)** for viewfiles before the information they contain is available to TUXEDO.

RANGES = *string*:

- *string* provides the values to be used for routing and a group naming the location where the request is directed when the specified values match those in the buffer. The form of string is a comma separated list of range and target groups. Each range and associated target group has the form:

```
range:group
```

- *range* may be a single value, a pair of values, or a wild card character (*). Values in *range* are matched against the value in the field named by *fldname*. When a match is found, the request is sent to the service in the server group named by *group*. The service chosen in the group is the service that has named *CRITERION_NAME* in its **ROUTING** parameter.
- If an element of *range* is a single value, the routing is done when the value in the buffer matches the value of the element. If two values are specified they must be in the form:

```
firstvalue - secondvalue
```

where *firstvalue* is lower in the collating sequence than *second-value*. When two values are specified, the routing is done when the value in the buffer is equal to or greater than *firstvalue* and less than or equal to *secondvalue* in the collating sequence for the data type.

* The wild card character (* without quotes) may be specified to provide a default routing when other routing criteria do not match the value in the buffer. The wild card character may be used only once in each *range* and must be specified last in the *range*.

* Numeric values may be of any type allowed for ubbconfig and may be signed with a single plus (+) or minus (–). String values within range must be enclosed in single quotes ('). If a single quote is enclosed in a string, it must be preceded by two back-slashes (\ \ ). The type of value specified in range must be the same as specified for the field named by *fldname*. A value may be specified as **MIN** or **MAX**, without quotes. TUXEDO will substitute the lowest value for the data type for **MIN** and the highest value for **MAX**.

* *group* is a name that matches a group name specified in the GROUPS section. *group* may be specified with the wild card character (*), in which case a match on the *range* allows TUX-EDO to choose the named service from any group offering it.

BUFTYPE = *string*: *string* is a list of buffer types and subtypes. Within the list, subtypes are listed with each buffer type as a comma separated list and are separated from the buffer type by a colon. The list of types with their subtypes is in turn a semicolon-separated list. The form is:

```
type1[:subtype1[,subtype2,...]][ ;type2[:subtype3
    [,subtype4,...]]]...
```

type can be FML, VIEW, X_C_TYPE or X_COMMON. No *subtype* can be specified with type FML.

A criterion in the ROUTING section might be:

```
LOCATE
    FIELD=custloc
RANGES="'AL - MI':*,'TX':DALGRP,
    'CA-MO':WESTGRP,*:ALLGRP"
BUFTYPE="FML"
```

10.4.9   **Utilities Used with ubbconfig**

Two batch utilities are used with ubbconfig: **tmloadcf(1)** compiles ubbconfig into tuxconfig; **tmunloadcf(1)** decompiles tuxconfig and creates a new version of ubbconfig. **tmloadcf(1)** must be used to initialize the tuxconfig that defines a domain. **tmunloadcf(1)** is useful for getting a clear text version of the tuxconfig used in a domain after it has been modified by interactive utilities **tmadmin(1)** and/or **tmconfig(1)**.

    tmloadcf(1) is used to generate a tuxconfig file from the ubbconfig file. Most installations use the standard UNIX file system to store the tuxconfig file, and this book will not discuss the option of using a raw device for tuxconfig. The environment variable TUXCONFIG should be set before running **tmloadcf(1)**.

    The common command line used for **tmloadcf(1)** is:

```
tmloadcf -y ubbname
```

where *ubbname* is the name of the **ubbconfig** file to use as input. This command line will parse *ubbname*; if there are no errors, it will create a tuxconfig with the name specified in both the ubbconfig and TUXCONFIG. If there are any errors detected during parsing, messages are presented to the user.

    If the **-n** option is specified, **tmloadcf(1)** parses ubbname but does not create tuxconfig. This option is useful for checking the validity of a new or changed ubbconfig.

    If the **-c** option is specified, **tmloadcf(1)** calculates an estimate of the IPC requirements to support the domain. This option is especially useful when a new system is being started or when extensive changes have been made to ubbconfig. Most UNIX systems require rebooting to change IPC parameters, so setting them large enough for the domain is important. Note that the later versions of IBM's AIX automatically readjust IPC parameters dynamically as required, so this step is not necessary for AIX.

    The security features of **tmloadcf(1)** will be discussed in Chapter 12.

    The tuxconfig file for a domain can be changed dynamically by **tmconfig(1)** or by the **tmadmin(1) conf** command. It is a good idea to run **tmunloadcf(1)** periodically to create an equivalent updated version of ubbconfig for review by the administrator. The environment variable TUXCONFIG must point to the tuxconfig to decompile when **tmloadcf(1)** is run.

    The command line for running **tmunloadcf(1)** is:

```
tmunloadcf  >  ubbnew
```

where *ubbnew* is the generated ubbconfig.

10.5   **SPECIFYING SERVER OPTIONS (SERVOPTS(5))**

Server options modify the behavior of a server when it is booted and when it is running. The section in the TUXEDO reference manual called **servopts(5)** describes these options. Server options can be specified in the **CLOPT** parameter of the SERVERS section of ubbconfig, and can be changed with **tmconfig(1)**.

The available options are:

-A This option causes all services offered by the server to be available when the server is booted.

-s *services* This option lists the set of services that will be offered by the service when it is booted. A simple list is a comma separated list of service names. If a simple list is provided, the service offered must be the name of a function linked with the server. A simple list might be:

```
-s service1,service2, ...
```

The **-s** option allows assigning alias service names. The form of an alias name is:

```
-svc1,svc2,...:funcname
```

The service can then be invoked by the names *svc1*, *svc2*, and so on. *funcname* is the name of the function that implements the service. An alias service option might be:

```
-s svca,svcb:mysvcname, service1,svcc,service2:service2
```

The **advertise** command of **tmadmin(1)** can be used to change which services are offered by a service and any aliases.

-e *filename* This option specifies a file name for any stderr output generated by services in the server. *filename* must be a full path name. If the **-e** option is not specified, stderr output is directed to the file stderr in $APPDIR.

-h If this option is supplied, the server will be subject to hangups caused by the hangup signal. Normally, a server does not react to the hangup signal.

-l [t | d | p] The **-l** option causes the operating system to lock the server in real memory. The **t** parameter locks only the text. The **d** parameter locks only the data part of the server. The **p** parameter locks both the text and the data. The **-l** option will fail unless the server is being run as root. See plock(2) in UNIX documentation for more details. Using this option does not necessarily improve the performance of the system.

-n *priority* The **-n** option sets the operating system of the server to *priority*. *priority* is specified as a negative number. This option is often called the "nice" option. See the UNIX documentation on nice(2) for more information.

-o *filename* This option specifies a file name for any stdout output generated by services in the server. *filename* must be a full path name. If **-o** is not specified, stdout will be directed to the file stdout in $APPDIR.

-r The **-r** option causes a record of all services performed to be written to the file specified as stderr for the server. A utility **txrpt(1)** can be used to print out an analysis of this record. Do not set the ULOGDEBUG variable to y if this option is in use.

— The — indicates the end of TUXEDO server options. Values for argv can be specified after the —.

10.6 MONITORING THE SYSTEM WITH TMADMIN(1)

tmadmin(1) provides 51 interactive commands that allow the administrator to monitor a TUXEDO domain performance, make temporary modifications to the configuration, and troubleshoot and correct problems. A **tmadmin(1)** command, **config**, invokes the interactive configuration utility **tmconfig(1)** described later in this chapter.

tmadmin(1) commands are described in the *TUXEDO Reference Manual*. The *TUXEDO Administrator's Guide* explains some uses for **tmadmin(1)** and provides examples of how to use this powerful utility. The new administrator should practice using **tmadmin(1)** as soon as possible; that is the only way to become aware of its capabilities.

Examples of using **tmadmin(1)** are used in this book to explain how to accomplish certain tasks. The security implications are discussed in Chapter 12.

10.7   **MODIFYING THE CONFIGURATION DYNAMICALLY WITH TMCONFIG(1)**

tmconfig(1) is an interactive command line interpreter that allows the administrator to examine and modify the tuxconfig files for the domain. Changes made to tuxconfig are propagated to all nodes and will take effect as soon as logically possible. Nearly all parameters in the tuxconfig file (as documented with ubbconfig) can be modified. In most cases the new configuration can be implemented without rebooting the domain.

tmconfig(1) is documented in the *TUXEDO Reference Manual*, and the *TUXEDO Administrator's Guide* contains an explanation of how to use **tmconfig(1)**. The new administrator should practice using **tmadmin(1)** as soon as possible.

Novell will be providing a GUI interactive administration interface for a future release of TUXEDO that will dynamically change administration and will be much easier to use than **tmconfig(1)**. The following hints will help those who use **tmconfig(1)**. Be sure the environment variables are set properly and the target domain is booted. If the variables are not set correctly or there is no domain running, **tmconfig(1)** returns a TUXEDO system error.

If vi is chosen as the editor the following sequence is necessary to properly modify or add to tuxconfig:

1. Start **tmconfig(1)** from the command line.
2. Choose section.
3. Choose retrieve.
4. On request "Enter editor to add/modify fields [n]?" answer n.
5. On request "Perform operation [y]?" answer y. **tmconfig(1)** will respond with some of its own status information and a list of current settings in the section, followed by a request for the desired section.
6. Choose section.
7. Choose add or update.
8. On request "Enter editor to add/modify fields [n]?" answer y.
9. Change as desired, save file, and exit. Be sure not to change the file name as provided from **tmconfig(1)**.
10. On request "Perform operation [y]?" answer y. **tmconfig(1)** will respond with some of its own status information and a list of current settings in the section with the changes incorporated, followed by a request for the desired section.
11. Repeat procedure for each section where changes are needed.

Changes are stored in the tuxconfig file pointed to by the environment variable TUXCONFIG. **tmconfig(1)** provides the opportunity to decompile the current tuxconfig into a ubbconfig format into the file designated by the user.

Once the changes have been made, procedures with **tmadmin(1)** are necessary to make them effective. TUXEDO documentation provides some information about how to do this. The section in this chapter on setting up a domain provides some specific examples.

10.8 SETTING UP A NEW DOMAIN

The steps required to set up a new domain are:

1. Create a script file to set the basic TUXEDO environment variables TUXDIR and TUXCONFIG and set PATH and LD_LIBRARY _PATH.
2. Create an ENVFILE.
3. Create a ubbconfig.
4. Set the TUXEDO environment variables by executing the script from step 1.
5. Run **tmloadcf**.
6. Propagate the tuxconfig to all nodes.
7. Propagate the ENVFILE to all nodes.
8. Be sure that the binaries for all required servers exists on all nodes.
9. Set the TUXDIR environment variable and execute **tlisten(1)** in the root initialization of every node.
10. Run **tmboot(1)** to boot the system.

The script file to set the environment variables is useful for administering several domains. TUXEDO environment variables can be set as defaults in the profiles, but the administrator often needs to support multiple domains, so scripts should be created to set the environment for each one.

The ENVFILE allows setting application specific environment variables without involving an extra step each time the domain is used. It also eliminates the need to set the environment for each user of the system. All production systems should use this feature. Use available tools to propagate the tuxconfig, the ENVFILE, and required server binaries to the nodes in the system.

tlisten(1) must be running on every node in a multinode domain before the domain is booted. **tlisten(1)** starts a daemon called **tagent**, which listens on the network for TUXEDO traffic. **tlisten(1)** can also be run periodically by the UNIX **cron** process to be sure it is restarted in case of failure. **tlisten(1)** will gracefully fail to start a duplicate daemon. The following lines are suggested for inclusion in the root initialization file:

```
TUXDIR=tuxedo_path;export TUXDIR
$TUXDIR/bin/tlisten -d /dev/ device -1 nlsaddr -u adminid
```

where *tuxedo_path* is the path to TUXEDO. *device* is the name of the network device, such as tcp. *nlsaddr* is the network address used for TUXEDO and must be the same as specified in the **NLSADDR** parameter in the NETWORK section for the machine. *adminid* is the identifier of the administrator. It may be specified as either uid-*nbr* or uid-*admname*, where *nbr* is the numeric user id and *admname* is the sign-on name.

tmboot(1) is the TUXEDO utility that starts a domain. It is a good idea to test new domains by booting only one node and making sure it works properly, then gradually adding the various nodes. The best way to do this is to create a test ubbconfig that contains only the information for the **MASTER** node, follow the steps above, then run **tmboot(3)** with the command line:

```
tmboot -y
```

The **-l** option of **tmboot(1)** starts server groups only on the machine identified, but starts all administrative servers on all nodes in the domain. If everything works properly with the single node test, use the **-l** option to incrementally bring up the domain and test the system as each node is booted. Once the entire system is working properly, the entire domain can be brought up from scratch by using the command line above.

Use of **tmboot(1)** and the utility **tmshutdown(1)**, which shuts down a domain or part of a domain, to manage the system is discussed in Chapter 11.

10.9   SETTING UP FOR AN XA RESOURCE MANAGER

The steps to set up an XA resource manager are:

1. Add a line to $TUXDIR/udataobj/RM to define the resource manager to TUXEDO.
2. Run **buildtms(1)** to build the transaction manager server to interface with the resource manager.

3. Set the environment variable TLOGDEVICE.
4. Create the **TLOG** device.
5. Define one or more groups that use the resource manager.

The form of each line in $TUXDIR/udataobj/RM is:

`rm_name:rm_structure_name:library_names`

where *rm_name* is the name of the resource manager. *rm_structure _name* is the name of the xa_switch_t structure provided by the resource manager vendor. *library_names* is a list of libraries supplied by the resource manager vendor.

The following is a fragment of one instance of a $TUXDIR/udataobj/ RM entry:

```
ORACLE:xaosw:${ORACLE_HOME}/lib/libxa.a ${ORACLE_HOME}/lib/
libsql.a
${ORACLE_HOME}/lib/libocic.a ${ORACLE_HOME}/lib/osntab.o ...
```

buildtms(1) has the form:

```
buildtms [-v] -o srvname -r rm_name
```

where *srvname* is the name to use for the transaction manager server. This name will be used in the **TMSNAME** parameter in the GROUPS section. *rm_name* is the name of the resource manager. *rm_name* must be the same as the *rm_name* on a line in $TUXDIR/udataobj/RM.

The command line to build a transaction manager server might be:

```
buildtms -o ORATM -r ORACLE
```

The environment variable TLOGDEVICE must be set the same as the entry for TLOGDEVICE in the MACHINES section of ubbconfig for each machine.

A device must be created for the **TLOG** before booting a domain that uses an XA resource manager. To create a **TLOG** device:

1. Be sure the domain is shut down and the proper environment variables are set.
2. At the command line on the master node invoke **tmadmin -c**.
3. Use the **crdl -z *device* -b *blocks*** to create the TLOGDEVICE.

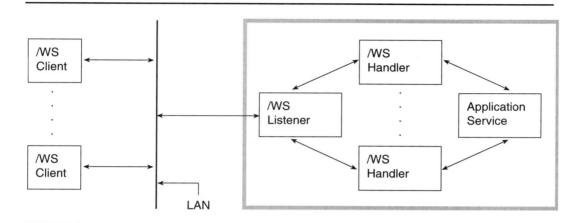

Figure 10.1 A diagram of /WS.

4. Repeat the above steps on each machine in the domain, unless there is a mirroring feature that makes it unnecessary.

device must be the full path name of the device and must match the environment variable TLOGDEVICE for the machine.

blocks specifies the number of blocks to allocate for the **TLOG**. The number of blocks required depends on the number of simultaneous active transactions the domain must support. Experimentation has shown that the minimum is about 500 blocks. 5,000 blocks will most likely support a thousand users, but the actual requirement depends on the frequency and duration of transactions.

10.10 SETTING UP TO SUPPORT WORK STATIONS

10.10.1 How /WS Works

Work stations are able to connect to TUXEDO using a feature known as /WS. /WS provides software on a number of work station platforms to allow TUXEDO clients to use TUXEDO functionality exactly the same as if they were located on the same platform as the TUXEDO domain. Chapter 8 explains how to build client applications for /WS. This section will describe the administrative functions required to set up a TUXEDO domain to service /WS clients. /WS clients can use all the features that any

TUXEDO client can use, including both the request/response and conversational paradigms.

Figure 10.1 illustrates how /WS operates. Each work station contains /WS software that places each client service request on the network addressed to the /WS listener on a platform that is a node of a full TUXEDO domain. The listener receives the request and places it in a queue for the /WS handler. The handler process passes the request to the service in the same manner that a native client would. In a real sense, the handler acts as a surrogate for the /WS client. The response is returned via the handler to the listener. The listener places the response on the network addressed to the original client. /WS handlers are special UNIX daemons started by a listener process. /WS listeners are called WSL in the TUXEDO documentation and are described in the WSL(5) section of the TUXEDO reference manual. /WS handlers are called WSH in the TUXEDO documentation.

Each node of the domain contains one or more /WS listener processes. The listener process starts handler processes as necessary to handle the current request load. When the load decreases, the listener will kill handlers that are not required. Each /WS listener can support multiple /WS clients. Each handler can in turn, handle multiple requests simultaneously. The figure shows a handler passing a request to a service. In fact, the request is processed by the TUXEDO bulletin board service exactly the same as if the request came from any source, routing it to the appropriate server based on values in the configuration file. The figure shows the response returning by a different handler. In fact, both the request and the response may be handled by any handler.

The administrator manages /WS clients from the full TUXEDO domain in a manner similar to managing any client. The /WS listener and /WS handler are servers containing services and are managed the same as any TUXEDO servers and services.

10.10.2   Configuring /WS

A domain requires certain entries in the configuration file to support /WS clients. The entries as they appear in ubbconfig are discussed in the following paragraphs.

10.10.2.1 The RESOURCES and MACHINES Sections. The **MAXWSCLIENTS** parameter is required in the MACHINES section to support /WS clients. If **MASWSCLIENTS** is not specified for some machine, no /WS clients are allowed to use the domain. Be sure to increase the value for **MAXACCESSERS** in either the RESOURCES section and/or the MACHINES section to accommodate the additional clients represented by **MAXWSCLIENTS**.

In the MACHINES section specify **MAXWSCLIENTS** as:

```
MAXWSCLIENTS=number
```

where *number* is the maximum number of /WS clients that may be active at the same time. The value supplied for **MAXWSCLIENTS** reserves the number of /WS clients specified from the value supplied for **MAXACCESSERS** and makes those slots unavailable for native clients.

10.10.2.2 The SERVERS Section. The /WS listener is defined in the SERVERS section the same as any TUXEDO server. /WS handlers are defined with the listener server option parameters. The /WS listener server is called **WSL**. **WSL** must be specified in the SERVERS section and must be associated with a server group defined for the domain. A **CLOPT** parameter must be specified to supply the options required. The form of the **CLOPT** parameter is:

```
CLOPT -A [other servopts] — -n netaddr [-d device] [-w
WSHname]
     [-t timeout] [-T client_timeout] [-m minWSH] [-M maxWSH]
     [-x mpx_factor]
```

The **WSL** parameters are:

-n *netaddr* *netaddr* is the network address used by the /WS listener. Messages from /WS client will be directed to this address. This parameter is always required.

-d *device* *device* is the file name used for network access. *device* is required only if the network interface in use requires it. For instance, sockets does not require a device name, but TLI does. There is no default for this parameter.

-w *WSHname* *WSHname* is the name of the /WS handler executable that this listener should use. If this parameter is not provided, the default is **WSH**, which is the name of the /WS handler provided with TUXEDO. /WS handlers can be customized with **buildwsh(1)** in order to specify custom buffer types.

-t *timeout* The /WS listener will time out any client that does not complete initialization quickly enough. The time starts when the client calls **tpinit(3)** and ends when the listener returns the result to the client. The actual time period is in seconds and calculated as timeout multiplied by **SCANUNIT**. The default for timeout is 3. The allowed range is 1 through 255. The value specified with **-t** has no effect on a client after it has completed initialization.

-T *client_timeout* *client_timeout* is time allowed for the client to remain idle before WSL breaks the connection with the client. *client_timeout* is specified in minutes. The timeout period is reset each time a client makes a request to the domain. If this parameter is not specified, this timeout is not used. The timeouts specified by **-t** and by **-T** are independent.

-m *minWSH* *minWSH* specifies the minimum number of /WS handlers this listener should start and maintain. The /WS listener initially start the number of handlers specified by *minWSH*. As clients request services, the listener starts additional handlers as necessary to handle the load, up to *maxWSH* specified by the **-M** option. If the load decreases, the listener will kill idle handlers, but will maintain at least *minWSH* handlers. The default value for **-m** is 0. The allowed range is 0 through 255. If 0 is specified by default or explicitly, the listener will start handlers as required to process requests; if the system goes idle, the listener will kill all handlers.

-M *maxWSH* *maxWSH* specifies the maximum number of /WS handlers that can be started by the /WS listener. *maxWSH* must be equal to or greater than *minWSH*. The valid range for *maxWSH* is 1 through 32767. The default is **MAXWSCLIENTS** divided by *mpx_factor* plus 1. *maxWSH* times *mpx_factor* determines the maximum number of clients that this listener can handle simultaneously.

-x *mpx_factor* *mpx_factor* specifies the maximum number of clients each /WS handler is allowed to process simultaneously. The default is 10. The valid range is 1 through 32767.

11

Administration Part 2

11.1 OVERVIEW

The previous chapter described the essentials of TUXEDO administration and the tools used to perform the operations. This chapter includes the following information:

- How to boot a domain or parts of a domain
- How to shut down a domain or parts of a domain
- Suggestions for initial settings of some configuration parameters
- How to dynamically modify the configuration of an existing system
- How to add servers or replace servers with updated versions
- How to tune the system for performance
- Failure management

11.2 STARTING A TUXEDO DOMAIN

Starting a domain is called booting the domain in TUXEDO nomenclature. An entire domain may be booted with a single command, or parts of the domain may be selectively booted. The command used for booting is **tmboot(1)**. **tmboot(1)** uses the environment variable TUXCONFIG in the local environment to determine the name and location of the tuxconfig file to use for booting.

tmboot(1) may be used only on the master machine identified by the **MASTER** parameter in the RESOURCES section. If the domain is defined as an MP model, **tmboot(1)** may be run from the backup master acting as master, but only if the backup DBBL is already running, that is, after executing the **master** command with **tmadmin(1)**. Only the person signed on with a **UID** equal to the UID parameter, or a user with root privileges can execute **tmboot(1)**.

When **tmboot(1)** is run with no options, it boots all servers and services in the domain, except as they are controlled by the contents of the configuration file. The DBBL is booted first, followed by the BBL on each machine, then any TMS and gateway servers designated in the GROUPS section, then the application servers defined on each machine. The order of booting application servers is controlled by the **SEQUENCE** parameter, if present. All servers with a **SEQUENCE** parameter defined are booted before servers without the **SEQUENCE** parameter. If the **SEQUENCE** parameter is not present, application servers are booted in the order of server entries in the configuration file. If **tmboot(1)** options limit which parts of the domain are booted, the sequence is preserved within the limitations imposed by the options. **tmboot(1)** will start the number of copies of each server specified in the **MIN** parameter.

If **tmboot(1)** cannot boot a server, a message is placed in **ULOG** and also to stdout (usually the terminal where **tmboot(1)** was executed), and **tmboot(1)** continues to attempt the rest of the operation. If the DBBL cannot be booted, **tmboot(1)** quits after logging information on the failure. If a specific BBL fails to start, **tmboot(1)** will not attempt to boot any servers associated with it.

tmboot(1) uses the server parameters **CLOPT**, **SEQUENCE**, **SVRGRP**, and **SRVID** when booting servers. TUXEDO code in each server reads the configuration file to load the server options specific to the server and make them available.

The environment for each server is set by **tmboot(1)** by passing the values from TUXDIR, TUXCONFIG, and APPDIR to the server. If the environment variable LD_LIBRARY_PATH is present it also is passed to the server. All of the above steps are taken before control is passed to the **tpsvrinit(3)** function in the server.

The options for **tmboot(1)** are:

-l *lmid* The **-l** option limits the booting operation to the machine specified by *lmid*.

-g *grpname* The **-g** option limits the booting operation to the group with the name specified by *grpname*.

-i *srvid* The **-i** option causes **tmboot(1)** to boot only servers with a **SRVID** equal to *srvid*.

-s *exec_name* The **-s** option limits the booting operation to servers with an executable module name of *exec_name*.

-o *seqnbr* The **-o** option limits the booting operation to servers with a **SEQUENCE** number equal to *seqnbr*.

-S The -S option causes **tmboot(1)** to boot all servers in the servers section.

-A When **tmboot(1)** is executed with the -A option, only the administrative servers are booted.

-B *lmid* The **-B** option limits the booting operation to the administrative servers on the machine identified by *lmid*.

-M The **-M** option limits booting to the administrative processes on the machine identified by the **MASTER** parameter in the RESOURCES section. The servers started include a DBBL and a BBL. A BRIDGE is started if the system model is MP, and the **LAN** option and a NETWORK entry are specified in the configuration file.

-T *grpname* The **-T** option causes **tmboot(1)** to boot only the TMS servers associated with the group identified by *grpname*.

-e *command* The **-e** option causes **tmboot(1)** to execute the program, script, or commands named by *command* if there is a failure during the boot process. *command* may be a list of commands.

The commands will be executed in the shell named by the SHELL environment variable on the platform where **tmboot(1)** was executed.

-w The **-w** option causes **tmboot(1)** to bring up servers in parallel. Normally **tmboot(1)** waits for each server to complete the booting process before starting the next server. This option is useful for speeding up the boot process. The **-w** option should not be used unless the DBBL and all other BBLs are already booted, or when application servers must be booted in a specific sequence.

-y If **tmboot(1)** is executed without any options, it will request a response to confirm that all administrative process should be started. The **-y** option suppresses the confirmation.

-q **tmboot(1)** normally prints information about the execution progress on stdout. The **-q** option suppresses these messages. The **-q** option also suppress the confirmation for booting administration processes.

-n When the **-n** option is specified, nothing is booted, but the sequence of booting is printed to stdout.

-c When the **-c** option is specified, **tmboot(1)** reads the configuration file, calculates the minimum IPC resources required to support the configuration and prints the results to stdout. Nothing is booted when this option is specified.

The **-l**, **-g**, **-i**, **-o**, and **-s** options may be used in any combination to limit the part of a domain that is booted. When multiple limiting options are specified, booting is limited to those servers that satisfy all specified conditions. TMS servers are booted for the groups where servers are started if any of the **-l**, **-g**, **-s**, and **-T** options are used. If any of the **-l**, **-g**, and **-s** options are used, gateway servers are also started. The following command line boots an entire domain without asking for confirmation as to whether to start administrative servers or not:

```
tmboot -y
```

The following command line boots the server with an executable module name of custupdsv in a group called CUSTGRP on a machine called DALLAS:

```
tmboot -l DALLAS -g CUSTGRP -s custupdsv
```

11.3   **SHUTTING DOWN A TUXEDO DOMAIN**

An entire domain may be shut down with a single command, or parts of the domain may be shut down selectively. The command used for shutting down a domain is **tmshutdown(1)**. **tmshutdown(1)** uses the environment variable TUXCONFIG in the local environment to determine the name and location of the tuxconfig file to use for controlling the shutdown process.

tmshutdown(1) may be used only on the master machine identified by the **MASTER** parameter in the RESOURCES section. If the domain is defined as an MP model, **tmshutdown(1)** may be run from the backup master acting as master. Only the person signed on with a UID equal to the **UID** parameter, or a user with root privileges can execute **tmshutdown(1)**.

When **tmshutdown(1)** is executed with no options, it shuts down the entire domain. Application servers with no **SEQUENCE** defined are shut down first in the reverse order that they appear in the configuration file. The servers that have a **SEQUENCE** defined are shut down in reverse sequence number order. After all application servers are shut down, the gateway servers, TMS servers, and administrative servers are shut down. **tmshutdown(1)** prints the progress of the shutdown on stdout unless the **-q** option is used.

The options for **tmshutdown(1)** are:

-l *lmid* The **-l** option limits the shutdown operation to the machine specified by *lmid*.

-g *grpname* The **-g** option limits the shutdown operation to the group with the name specified by *grpname*.

-i *srvid* The **-i** option causes **tmshutdown(1)** to boot only servers with a **SRVID** equal to *srvid*. Never use a *srvid* above 30,000, because system processes use **SRVID**s with these values.

-s *exec_name* The **-s** option limits the shutdown operation to servers with an executable module name of *exec_name*.

-o *seqnbr* The **-o** option limits the shutdown operation to servers with a **SEQUENCE** number equal to *seqnbr*.

-S The **-S** option causes **tmshutdown(1)** to shut down all servers in the servers section.

-A When **tmshutdown(1)** is executed with the **-A** option, all administrative servers are shut down.

-B *lmid* The **-B** option causes **tmshutdown(1)** to shut down the administrative servers on the machine identified by *lmid*.

-M The **-M** option causes **tmshutdown(1)** to shut down the administrative processes on the machine identified by the **MASTER** parameter in the RESOURCES section. If the system model is MP, both the DBBL and BBL on the MASTER machine are shut down. The BRIDGE is shut down if the system model is MP, and the **LAN** option and a NETWORK entry are specified in the configuration file.

-T *grpname* The **-T** option causes **tmshutdown(1)** to shut down the TMS servers associated with the group identified by *grpname*.

-w *time* If the **-w** option is not specified, **tmshutdown(1)** waits indefinitely for a shutdown confirmation from each server. The **-w** option causes **tmshutdown(1)** to force servers down after a delay of *time* seconds even if they have not sent a confirmation. **tmshutdown(1)** forces shutdown by first sending a SIGTERM signal, then a SIGKILL signal.

-y If **tmshutdown(1)** is executed without any options, it will request a response to confirm that all administrative process should be shutdown. The **-y** option suppresses the confirmation.

-q **tmshutdown(1)** normally prints information about the shutdown progress on stdout. The **-q** option suppress these messages. The **-q** option also suppresses the confirmation for shutting down administration processes.

-n When the **-n** option is specified, nothing is shut down, but the sequence of shutting down is printed to stdout.

-R The **-R** option cause **tmshutdown(1)** to shut down servers at their original location without deleting their bulletin board entry. The **-R** option is used to prepare for migrating servers, and must be used in combination with the **-l** and/or the **-g** option.

-c The **-c** option forces **tmshutdown(1)** to shut down BBLs even when clients are still attached.

-P *lmid* This option causes **tmshutdown(1)** to partition the bulletin board on the machine named by *lmid* from the DBBL and the rest of the domain. **tmshutdown(1)** then shuts down the administrative and application servers on *lmid*. **tmshutdown(1)** must be run on the platform named by *lmid* to use the **-P** option.

The **-l**, **-g**, **-i**, **-o**, and **-s** options may be used in any combination to limit the part of a domain that is shut down. When multiple limiting options are specified, the shutdown is limited to those servers that satisfy all specified conditions. TMS servers are shut down for the groups where servers are shut down if any of the **-l**, **-g**, **-s**, and **-T** options are used. If any of the **-l**, **-g**, and **-s** options are used, gateway servers are also shut down.

If any global transactions are in progress when **tmshutdown(1)** is executed, in-flight transactions (those at a state where **tpcommit(3)** has not been called) will be aborted. In-doubt transactions (those at a state where **tpcommit(3)** has been called, but the commit has not yet been completed) will be completed (committed or aborted, depending on the contents of the transaction log) when the TMS servers in the domain are booted again.

The following command line shuts down an entire domain without asking for confirmation as to whether to start administrative servers or not:

```
tmshutdown -y
```

The following command line shuts down the server with an executable module name of custupdsv in a group called CUSTGRP on a machine called DALLAS:

```
tmshutdown -l DALLAS -g CUSTGRP -s custupdsv
```

11.4   INITIAL CONFIGURATION PARAMETERS

11.4.1   Overview

This section makes some suggestions about the initial values for some of the TUXEDO configuration parameters along with short explanations of the factors that guide the choices made. It is important that the administrator work closely with the development personnel to understand how the application system will function and what the requirements are. It is inevitable that some experimentation will be necessary and that continuous adjustments, usually minor, are required for the life of the system. If the administrator makes appropriate choices about the initial values, making adjustments not only becomes easier, but in some cases can prevent the need to reboot the domain to effect the changes.

Changing most parameters requires restarting the components affected by the change. TUXEDO provides methods for restarting machines (platforms), groups, and servers individually. The goal is to minimize the amount of the system requiring restart by changes.

Rebooting an entire domain results in making the applications on the domain completely unavailable for a period of time. Depending on the number of nodes in the system (not counting work stations) the time can range from a few minutes to an hour. Every effort should be made to prevent rebooting the domain. Values set for security purposes are not discussed in this chapter. Chapter 12 provides information on these values.

11.4.2   Initial RESOURCES Values

If the domain has multiple nodes, always specify an alternate **MASTER**. If there is no alternate **MASTER** specified, it will be necessary to reboot the domain if the **MASTER** fails.

Always specify a **DOMAINID** even if not currently using the /DOMAIN feature of TUXEDO. Make sure that the **DOMAINID** is unique among all domains. The current version of /DOMAIN does not use this value, but it provides a means to associate the configuration with the name assigned in the dmconfig file for use by the administrator (see Chapter 16).

Set **MAXACCESSERS** sufficiently large to allow for expansion. This parameter affects the amount of memory used by the bulletin boards in every node, so setting it to the maximum might overload the memory available and cause page thrashing. Setting it to double the anticipated number is usually sufficient. This parameter cannot be changed in the RESOURCES section without rebooting, but can be overridden in the MACHINES section for each machine. Entries in the MACHINES section can be changed by rebooting TUXEDO on that platform without rebooting other nodes.

Set **MAXSERVERS**, **MAXSERVICES**, and **MAXGROUPS** to values sufficient to handle planned expansion. These values also directly affect the amount of memory used by bulletin boards, so care must be used not to make them overly large. The entire domain must be rebooted to change these values.

Set **MAXQUEUES** to a value larger than twice **MAXSERVICES**. This value will allow changing the **REPLYQ** parameter for every server without rebooting the domain. The value of **MAXQUEUES** plays a major role in using up message queue resources. If running on a smaller system, a lower value for this parameter may be required to increase performance.

It is a good idea to set **MODEL** to **MP** even if only one node exists currently. If set to **MP**, new nodes can be added without rebooting the current node.

LDBAL should be set to **Y**. Statistics about service usage are available only when **LDBAL** is set to **Y**. There is a minor performance penalty if there is only one instance of every server, but this is a very unusual situation. Generally, if multiple instances are not being used, the system is small enough that performance is not a problem anyway.

Always set **OPTIONS** to **MIGRATE**, even if no migration is planned. **OPTIONS** cannot be changed without rebooting the system.

Set **MAXGTT** to a value large enough to support the anticipated number of simultaneous transactions. The number of transactions cannot be exactly calculated, but is a result of combining the number of users with the length of each transaction and the time each user will be inactive between transactions. In most cases a setting of approximately 10 percent of the number of users will be sufficient.

This parameter can be overridden on individual platforms in the MACHINES section. **MAXGTT** has no meaning if no XA resource managers are being used.

Set **MAXDRT** to a value at least three times the number of ROUTING criteria. If no ROUTING criteria are specified, set it to at least 10 so that there is room to add ROUTING criteria if this becomes required. This parameter cannot be changed without rebooting the domain.

Set **MAXRFT** to a value at least three times the number of *range* settings in the routing section. If there are no ROUTING criteria, set it to 30 to allow adding ROUTING criteria.

Set **MAXRTDATA** to a value three times the number of characters in the ROUTING section. If no ROUTING criteria are currently used, set it to 1000 to allow adding ROUTING criteria.

Note that **MAXDRT**, **MAXRFT**, and **MAXRTDATA** create memory space to allowing adding new ROUTING criteria. If they are not specified, or the space is used up, it is not possible to add ROUTING criteria without rebooting the domain. None of these parameters can be changed without rebooting the domain.

If the domain uses XA resource managers, set **CMTRET** to **LOGGED** for maximum performance or **COMPLETE** for maximum protection of transaction integrity. When **CMTRET** is set to **LOGGED**, the transaction manager returns the response to a commit request as soon as responses have been received from all resource managers, but before the final commit has been sent to the resource managers (Return Point 1 in Figure 2.4). When **CMTRET** is set to **COMPLETE**, the transaction manager waits until all resource managers have responded to the final commit before returning the response (Return Point 2 in Figure 2.4). The setting **LOGGED** will protect transaction integrity through all failures as long as no resource manager unilaterally commits or aborts a transaction after responding to the prepare request. The setting **COMPLETE** will prevent most problems that occur when the resource manager unilaterally commits or aborts after responding to the prepare request, but in some unusual conditions the state of the transaction may be unknown to the system and require manual analysis and correction.

11.4.3   Initial MACHINES Values

Set **NETLOAD** to some reasonable value; 500 seems to work well. If this value is not set, the TUXEDO load balancing algorithm will consider using services over the network as equal with using the local service. See the section in this chapter on performance tuning for the factors involved.

Set the compression limits with **CMPLIMIT**. **CMPLIMIT** has the form:

```
CMPLIMIT=string1,string2
```

where *string1* is the compression limit for network communication. *string2* is the compression limit for local messages.

Good starting values for **CMPLIMIT** are:

```
CMPLIMIT=1024,16384
```

These values cause compression of all network messages over 1024 bytes and local messages over 16,384 bytes.

Compression is not always required for local messages. If the UNIX message size is sufficiently large to accommodate the largest anticipated message, do not use compression. Remember that TUXEDO will use a temporary file to pass local messages when the message size exceeds three-quarters of the maximum message size set for UNIX. The use of the temporary file can be prevented by use of compression, up to the point where the compressed message is too large.

Do not specify TLOGOFFSET. This feature is there to support older approaches to file management and creates unnecessary complications.

Use the ENVFILE feature to save effort in setting up the environment for users and to assure a consistent environment for all machines. ENVFILE must be specified to use services written with Micro Focus COBOL.

11.4.4   Initial GROUPS Values

The only tunable parameter in the GROUPS section is **TMSCOUNT**. This parameter may be changed dynamically, but the new value does not take effect until the group and all its servers are stopped and restarted.

11.4.5   Initial SERVERS Values

It is usually not necessary to specify the **SEQUENCE** number. If there are any services that must be started to support the **tpsvrinit(3)** function in other servers, set those servers to **SEQUENCE** numbers lower than for other servers. The same result can be obtained by listing the required services first.

Values for **MIN** and **MAX** have a direct impact on system performance and are discussed in the section on performance tuning.

Specifying the same **RQADDR** value for multiple servers creates a multiple server, single queue (MSSQ) set and causes the servers to service the same message queue. This approach decreases the number of message queues required to support the domain and may relieve system resources. If MSSQ sets are used, the size of individual queues may grow as requests are received. Usually, MSSQs should be used among differing servers only if there is a specific reason to use them. Note that if multiple instances of servers are started, they share the same message queue and form a MSSQ set (see the description of **MIN** and **MAX** in Chapter 10). There is more information on this subject in the section in this chapter on performance tuning.

If it is possible to predict whether or not a server contains services that invoke other services, set **REPLYQ** accordingly. That is, if a service in the server will invoke other services, set **REPLYQ** to **Y**, otherwise to **N**. If it is not possible to make the prediction, set **REPLYQ** to **Y**. If message queue resources are limited on the platform, set this parameter carefully because setting the value to **Y** increases the number of required message queues.

Use **RCMD** to execute a separate program when the server is restarted automatically. The program could, for instance, notify some human of the event, or simply log the event in some distinguished manner. The administrator can use the information provided by this program in addition to **ULOG** to monitor the frequency and nature of restarts. Remember that this program will have no access to TUXEDO information other than **GRPNO** and **SVRID**.

Set **MAXGEN** and **GRACE** to allow servers to be restarted to protect against occasional failures. Be sure to set both to a reasonable number to prevent restarting a server repeatedly for a long time. Good values are **MAXGEN = 5** and **GRACE = 600** (10 minutes). Remember that sometimes a server fails on the same data repeatedly and the user may continue to attempt the failed transaction. Restarting a server uses system resources heavily and repeatedly restarting a server can adversely affect the performance of everything running on the platform.

Set **RESTART** to **Y** for all servers to minimize outages and be sure to set **MAXGEN** and **GRACE** to reasonable values.

SYSTEM_ACCESS should be set to **FASTPATH** for well tested production systems to maximize performance. **SYSTEM_ACCESS** should be set to **PROTECTED** for test systems and early production usage to protect against program errors that might inadvertently modify TUXEDO system tables.

11.5   CHANGING A RUNNING DOMAIN

11.5.1   General Hints

The simplest, but least practical way, to change the configuration of a production system is to change ubbconfig, create a tuxconfig, and reboot the domain. Since this method stops all production, it should only be used in emergencies. Most changes to an existing system can be changed by using **tmadmin(1)** and **tmconfig(1)**. In fact, it is possible to use only **tmadmin(1)** and call **tmconfig(1)** with the **config** command. This section provides some suggestions on how to accomplish changes with minimum disruption to production applications.

The easiest way to stop and start a part of a domain is with **tmshutdown(1)** and **tmboot(1)**, using the options that stop and start a part of a domain. The **tmadmin(1)** command **shutdown** invokes **tmshutdown(1)**, and the command **boot** invokes **tmboot(1)**.

The following rules must be followed when modifying a running domain:

- A new machine may be added any time without shutting down any part of the existing domain.
- A new group may be added, but the machine it is running on must be rebooted.
- New servers may be added to a group without shutting down any part of the existing domain.
- New services may be added only by adding a new server or by shutting down the existing server and starting the new one.
- Changes to the NETWORK section only take effect when the associated machine is rebooted.
- Changes to any section (other than NETWORK and ROUTING) take effect when the effected element is rebooted.
- Criteria added to the ROUTING section take effect immediately.

11.5.2   Adding a Group

The steps for adding a new group are:

1. Use **tmconfig(1)** to add the group, its servers, and its services to the tuxconfig file.
2. Use **tmshutdown(1)** to shut down the machine where the group resides.
3. Restart the machine with **tmboot(1)**.

The command line to shut down a machine is:

```
tmshutdown -l lmid
```

where *lmid* is the name of the machine to shut down.

The command line to start or restart a machine is:

```
tmboot -l lmid
```

11.5.3   Adding a Server

The steps to adding a new server are:

1. Use **tmconfig(1)** to add the server and the services it provides to the tuxconfig file.
2. Use **tmboot(1)** to start the new server.

The command line to start a server is:

```
tmboot -i srvid
```

where *srvid* is the numeric server identifier assigned to the server.

11.5.4   Changing Routing Criteria

TUXEDO allows adding new routing criteria and changing the routing name in the affected services to the name of the new routing criteria. The steps to changing routing criteria are:

1. Add new routing criteria using **tmconfig(1)**.
2. Shut down the servers containing the effected services.
3. Change the routing name for the effected services using **tmconfig(1)**.
4. Restart the servers containing the effected services.

Adding new routing criteria is a little tricky because the format of RANGES is a little different than in the ubbconfig. Enter the editor after clearing the buffer, then add the new criteria. The following example illustrates a single criterion as entered with **vi**:

```
TA_ROUTINGNAME      route2
TA_BUFTYPE          FML
TA_FIELD            mystr1
TA_RANGES           MIN - 'j':GROUP1,*:GROUP2\00
```

Note the absence of double quotes around the RANGES string and the termination with a NULL (\00). This is the format required by **tmconfig(1)**. Within the string, the format is exactly as in ubbconfig.

11.6   MONITORING TUXEDO ACTIVITY

Use **tmadmin(1)** to monitor a running domain. The most useful commands for monitoring a running system are listed here. Consult the *Reference Manual* for a complete list of commands.

To monitor the system, invoke **tmadmin(1)** and then run the following commands.

- **psr** will display server information.
- **psc** will display service information.
- **pq** will display queue information.
- **pclt** will list the clients that are currently attached to the domain.

- **pnw** will display network information.
- **pt** will display transaction information.

tmadmin(1) provides a means of displaying information about specific machines, groups, servers, and services. The default machine for an MP system is the DBBL. Before any meaningful statistics can be retrieved about application servers and clients, set the default to either a specific machine or **all**.

A few examples follow; see the *TUXEDO Administrator's Guide* for additional examples. The ubbconfig for the domain of the examples is:

```
# ubbconfig for testing routing features
*RESOURCES
IPCKEY      123456
MASTER      carl
MAXACCESSERS     5
MAXSERVERS  5
MAXSERVICES 10
MODEL       MP
LDBAL       Y
SCANUNIT         5
BLOCKTIME        2
MAXDRT      20
MAXRFT      60
MAXRTDATA        9000

*MACHINES
DEFAULT:
    APPDIR="/home/clh/testapp"
    TUXCONFIG="/home/clh/testapp/rteconfig"
    TUXDIR="/home/tuxdir"

unix1          LMID=carl

*GROUPS
GROUP1
   LMID=carl   GRPNO=1    OPENINFO=NONE

GROUP2
   LMID=carl   GRPNO=2    OPENINFO=NONE

*SERVERS
DEFAULT:
    CLOPT="-A"
```

```
             rteserv1  SRVGRP=GROUP1 SRVID=1
             rteserv2  SRVGRP=GROUP2 SRVID=2

             *SERVICES
             FMLSAMP          ROUTING = "route1"

             *ROUTING
             route1           FIELD = mystr1
                 RANGES = "MIN - 'hello':GROUP1,*:GROUP2"
                 BUFTYPE = "FML"
```

tmadmin(1) was run as follows:

```
> d -m all
all> psr
Totals for all machines:
a.out Name    Queue Name   Grp Name    ID RqDone Load Done Machine
----------    ----------   --------    -- ------ ---- ---- -------
BBL           30002.00000  carl         0   11        550 carl
DBBL          123456       carl         0   27       1350 carl
rteserv1      00001.00001  GROUP1       1    1         50 carl
rteserv2      00002.00002  GROUP2       2    2        100 carl


all> psc
Totals for all machines:
Service Name Routine Name a.out Name Grp Name ID Machine  # Done Status
------------ ------------ ---------- -------- -- -------   ------ ------------
_TMIB_TM_0   _TMIB_TM     BBL        carl      0  carl         0 AVAIL
_TMIB_TM     _TMIB_TM     BBL        carl      0  carl         0 AVAIL
ADJUNCTBB    ADJUNCTBB    BBL        carl      0  carl        13 AVAIL
_TMIB_TM_SET _TMIB_TM     DBBL       carl      0  carl         0 AVAIL
_TMIB_TM_GET _TMIB_TM     DBBL       carl      0  carl         0 AVAIL
MASTERBB     MASTERBB     DBBL       carl      0  carl        31 AVAIL
FMLSAMP      FMLSAMP      rteserv1   GROUP1    1  carl         1 AVAIL
FMLSAMP      FMLSAMP      rteserv2   GROUP2    2  carl         2 AVAIL

all> pq
a.out Name     Queue Name  # Serve Wk Queued  # Queued  Ave. Len   Machine
----------     ----------  ------- ---------  --------  --------   -------
rteserv2       00002.00002     1       -          0        -        carl
rteserv1       00001.00001     1       -          0        -        carl BBL
               30002.00000     1       -       0           -      carl DBBL
     123456                 1       -       0           -      carl
all> q
```

Notes on the examples:

1. The servers BBL and DBBL and their services are TUXEDO servers and services.
2. The Load Done column for the services is a value calculated by TUXEDO to indicate the size of the load on the system. The calculation is done by multiplying the number of times a service is invoked (# done in the service report) times the load of the service, then adding up all these values for a server.
3. The domain was not being used when the queue report was created, so the number queued is 0.
4. The columns in the queue report Wk Queued (work queued) and Ave. Len (average length) are marked with a dash (-) because they are not available with an MP system.

These displays and the network display (not shown) provide information on the current status of a system. The administrator can use this information over a period of time to determine how the system is behaving.

If the domain contains XA resource managers, use the **pt** command to find the status of incomplete transactions. In most cases **pt** will return a message that there are no transactions because transactions usually complete too quickly. If a transaction is still in process or has reached some sort of invalid state **pt** will return information that may be used to determine the problem and take corrective action.

The following **pt** output was created by placing a **sleep()** into a service that updated the database, then querying the status after invoking the service.

```
all> pt

all> pt
>> index=0      gtrid=x0 x2fc0ec39 x1
:  Machine id: carl, Transaction status: TMGACTIVE
   Group count: 1

all> v
Verbose now on.

all> pt
>> index=0      gtrid=x0 x2fc0ec39 x1
:  Machine id: carl, Transaction status: TMGACTIVE
```

```
Group count: 1, timeout: 30, time left: 29
Known participants:
 group: GROUP1, status: TMGACTIVE, local, coord

all> q
```

11.7   PERFORMANCE

The initial values for ubbconfig and the default values for other parameters will provide satisfactory performance in most cases. If performance,
measured by response time, is not as high as required, the administrator
should monitor the system to determine the bottleneck and change parameters as necessary. The following paragraphs provide some hints on
how to improve performance, assuming that the initial values are set as
previously described.

    If most transactions respond quickly enough, but there are some
that are too slow, do the following:

1. Determine the services that the slow transactions use.
2. Examine the services to see if they are slow because of their nature.
   For instance, if they make a large number of database accesses or
   retrieve a large amount of data, there may be no way to speed them
   up. If this is the case, look into tuning the database. To get a general
   idea of how long a service runs each time it is invoked, examine the
   service and note the number done over a period of time.
3. Use **tmadmin(1)** to monitor the offending services and their queues.
   If a queue is filling up with a number of waiting service requests,
   increase the number of instances of the servers providing the services.
4. If step 3 does not solve the problem, examine the servers and make
   sure that the services are not badly mixed in the same server. A
   long running service should be in a server by itself.

    If the entire system is running too slow, there may be a fundamen-
tal problem, such as not enough power in the server platform or the
network may be overloaded. Some of the steps that can be taken are:

1. Examine the queues. If the queues are not very full, the problem is
   most likely the network.
2. Examine the network usage by TUXEDO by using **tmadmin(1)** to
   report network usage. If there is not much shown, then the network
   is being used for other purposes, which are blocking it.

3. If the problem is not the network, use UNIX monitoring to determine the load on the server platform. If the platform is heavily loaded, the problem is that the server platform is loaded too heavily.

If the server platform seems to be too heavily loaded it may be that a more powerful platform must be provided, but some steps can be taken within TUXEDO to help, as follows:

- Be sure that a service does not use too many CPU cycles. If so, redesign the service, if possible.
- Increase the value for **SCANUNIT**. Setting **SCANUNIT** to maximum minimizes the load, but increases the time before problems are detected. Try various values to find the best compromise.
- Examine ULOG to determine if a server is being restarted often. Restarting a server loads the system heavily. In this case, there is probably a problem with some service in the server. Fix the problem to prevent the server from abnormally terminating.

If these steps do not correct the problem, consider the following:

- Examine the database and make sure that it is properly tuned and that the data is properly spread over the available disk drives. Try to place heavily accessed tables on a disk drive where little other activity exists.
- If multiple server platforms are available, spread the services among them, and partition the database accordingly.
- Try to move activity not directly related to the TUXEDO application onto other platforms.
- When all else fails, increase the power of the server platform by adding processors and/or disk drives.

Some of the most common mistakes that result in poor performance are:

- Mixing long running services with short running services in the same server.
- Using the priority feature improperly. The priority of a service should be left at the default level unless the service must run ahead of some other service in the same server. Such a service should be provided its own service instead of setting PRIO.
- Failing to specify **REPLYQ=Y** for a server that contains services that invoke other services.

- Building a server in which a service calls another service in the same server. This mistake becomes obvious because it will cause timeouts when the event occurs. If coupled with maximum timeouts, this mistake can cause the system to gradually slow down until it stops.
- Using the multiple server, single queue feature inappropriately. Unless there is a severe restriction on the number of message queues allowed for the platform, this feature should not be used. Use of this feature can cause a backup in the queue involved. Note that multiple instances of the same server are on the same message queue by default.
- Using conversations unnecessarily. Conversations should not be used unless there is some highly important reason to do so. Conversations hold database resources, and more importantly, the locks set for the transaction, preventing other transactions from progressing. Every attempt should be made to eliminate use of conversational mode.

New installations often have problems with UNIX message queues and how they are related to the size of messages sent by TUXEDO application programs. If the UNIX IPC parameters (shared memory, message queues, and semaphores) are too small, the system will not run. There is a point where the message queue parameters are large enough to allow the system to run, but not large enough to support high performance. If any message is larger than that allowed for a single message by the operating system, TUXEDO will write the message to a file and send only an address. The receiving process will read the message from the file. The administrator must work with the designer and UNIX administrator to assure that as few messages as possible are written to files instead of being simply stored in the message queue in platform memory. See Appendix D for more information.

If an application uses one or more XA databases, other performance problems occur as follows:

- Some database vendors have introduced as much as a 25 percent performance degradation with their XA implementations.
- The architecture of the system may be causing two-phase commit processing where it is not necessary.

The administrator cannot control the use of XA databases. If use of XA transactions is a problem, the system requires redesign (see Chapters 4 and 5).

The administrator must minimize use of two-phase commit with XA resource managers. TUXEDO will use two-phase commit only if more than one XA resource manager was used by a transaction. Two-phase commit can be prevented by placing each individual resource manager in its own group. The administrator must remember that the TUXEDO reliable queue feature (/Q) is a resource manager and that if a transaction both updates a database and uses /Q in the same transaction it will always require two-phase commit. If a transaction uses resource managers on two different platforms, it also requires two-phase commit. The administrator must work with the designer to minimize these situations.

11.8 MINIMIZING THE EFFECT OF FAILURES

The administrator must work with the application designer to be sure that the application is designed to minimize the effect of failures and to enable fast and accurate recovery. Chapter 5 discusses how to design applications for high reliability and availability. This section discusses only how to set up the configuration to minimize the effect of failure. The next section discusses recovery.

To minimize the effect of failures, set up the configuration with:

- **RESTART = Y** in the SERVERS section. Be sure to set **MAXGEN** and **GRACE** to reasonable values, as noted earlier in this chapter.
- Set **MIN** in the SERVERS section to at least 2 so that even if a server crashes there will be an instance available to service requests during restart.
- If the domain is on multiple nodes, include a backup **MASTER** in the RESOURCES section.
- On multiple nodes, set the **MIGRATE** option in the RESOURCES section.

If the application design requires use of XA resource managers, be sure that the servers are grouped properly with the resource managers. The TUXEDO administrator will work with the database administrator to assure proper recovery.

If the application design relies on the transaction management capability of resource managers, the TUXEDO administrator must work with the database administrator to be sure that the database is properly set up to support reliable transaction management and recovery.

11.9   RECOVERING FROM FAILURES

11.9.1   Logs

Three logs are maintained by the TUXEDO system to assist the administrator in identifying and correcting problems. The user log file (known as ULOG) is written to APPDIR unless the **ULOGPFX** parameter is used to specify a different path and contains information written by the function **userlog(3)**. The TUXEDO main for servers writes to ULOG when each server starts and when any unusual occurrence happens. Application **tpsvrinit(3)** and **tpsvrdone(3)** functions should also write to ULOG. Application services should write to ULOG whenever an unusual event occurs. Entries in the file contain the time, the executable that wrote the entry, a catalog number, and the error message itself. It may be necessary to search back several entries to find the real cause of the problem. A new ULOG is created each day. The administrator must monitor the existing ULOGs and purge old ones manually.

The daemon started by the **tlisten(1)** command write log, named **ttlog**, which is written by default in $TUXDIR/udataobj. This name and location can be changed with the **-L** option on the command line. Entries are written to this log when the listener is started and when the listener is contacted. If there is no evidence that the BRIDGE tried to contact the listener at boot time then it is probably listening on the wrong network address.

The TAGENT process is started on a remote site at boot time to get commands from the master site to start the application. The TAGENT process will write to the log TAGENT.date, by default in $TUXDIR/udataobj, but only when it encounters a problem. The environment variable TAGENTLOG can be set to change the path for the TAGENT log. The most frequent entry in this file are messages indicating permission problems on the remote site.

11.9.2   Using tmadmin(1) **to Locate Problems**

The reports from **tmadmin(1)** can be used to detect problems as described in the following paragraphs.

The output from the **psr** command can be used to check for stuck services. If a service is shown as being active and the requests done does not change, then the service is hung up on some sort of problem.

The output from the **psc** command can be used to determine if there are services that are not receiving any requests. If a system is not responding to requests to the service and the service is not doing any processing, the server platform may be partitioned from the platform servicing the client. This condition also will occur when a server is hung up.

The output from the **pclt** can be used to check for inactive clients. If a client is inactive, it can mean that the user has left the client on and is not using it. If the client is using resources that prevent other clients from attaching to TUXEDO, the administrator must notify someone to stop the offending client. The administrator can stop a native client by using the UNIX command **kill()** to stop the client.

Use the **pc** command to identify a client that is tying up a conversational server.

Use the **pnw** command to check for partitioned networks and an indication of network activity. Even when a network is not partitioned, the activity may show that nothing is happening with a particular machine, thus giving some indication of where the problem might be. The speed of increase of the number of messages sent and received can indicate the rate of messages the network is handling.

Use the **pt** command to check for XA transactions that may need to be committed or rolled back manually.

11.9.3   Corrective Action

The administrator can perform a number of corrective tasks while the domain is running; servers can be restarted and entire machines can be brought down. This section contains the procedures for using the **tmadmin(1)** command to keep the application running. Some of these actions are done automatically by TUXEDO during scans by the DBBL. Each action that happens automatically is marked "auto."

11.9.3.1 Restarting a Server That Has Failed (auto). The server that is to be restarted must be marked as restartable in the configuration file. To restart a server manually, use the **bbclean** command in **tmadmin(1)** to remove the entry for the dead server. When this is done, the server will be restarted by TUXEDO.

11.9.3.2 Migrating a Group of Servers. If both machines are available, use the following steps to migrate a group of servers from one machine to another:

1. The servers must be marked as restartable in the configuration file.
2. The server executables must exist in the APPDIR on the backup machine.

3. Shut down the group with the **stop -R** command. This will shut the servers down and leave the entry in the bulletin board.
4. The group can now be migrated with the **migg *group*** command. This will boot the servers on the backup machine and all the statistics in the bulletin board will be moved to the bulletin board on the backup machine.

If the primary machine is not available, use the following steps to start the group on another machine:

1. The servers must be marked as restartable in the configuration file.
2. The server executables must exist in the APPDIR on the backup machine.
3. Run the **pclean *PRIMARY SITE*** command. This will remove the entry from the bulletin board.
4. Migrate the group with the **migg *group*** command. This will mark the servers as migrated to the backup machine but does not boot the servers. All the statistics from the primary bulletin board are lost by this procedure.
5. Boot the servers with the **boot -g *GROUP*** command.

The following steps migrate all groups on a machine to another machine when both machines are available:

1. All servers must be marked as restartable in the configuration file.
2. The server executables must exist in the APPDIR on the backup machine.
3. Shut down all groups on the primary machine with the **stop -R -l** command. This will shut the servers down and leave the entry in the bulletin board.
4. Migrate the machine with the **migm *PRIMARY_MACHINE***. This will boot the servers on the backup machine and all the statistics in the bulletin board will be moved to the bulletin board on the backup machine.

The following steps migrate all groups on a machine to a backup machine when the primary machine is not available:

1. All servers must be marked as restartable in the configuration file.
2. The server executables must exist in the APPDIR on the backup machine.

3. Run the **pclean** *PRIMARY SITE* command. This will remove the entry from the bulletin board.
4. Migrate the machine with the **migm** *PRIMARY_MACHINE* command. This will mark the servers as migrated to the backup machine but does not boot the servers. All the statistics from the primary bulletin board are lost by this procedure.
5. Boot all the servers on the new machine with the **boot -l** *LMID* command.

11.9.3.3 Replacing an Application Server. To replace an application server without losing service requests, do the following:

1. Replace the server on the backup machine.
2. Migrate the server group to the backup machine.
3. Replace the server on the primary machine.
4. Migrate the server group back to the primary machine.

11.9.3.4 Switching the MASTER to the Backup MASTER. To switch the MASTER machine to the backup machine if both machines are available or if the MASTER machine is not available, do the following:

1. Run the **tmadmin(1) master** command from the backup machine.
2. Answer **y** to the prompt.

11.9.3.5 Reconnecting a Failed Node. To reconnect a machine with a transient network problem (auto), run the command **rco** *non-partitioned-machine partitioned-machine*.
To reconnect a machine with a severe network problem (auto):

1. Run the command **pclean** *LMID* on the partitioned machine.
2. Run **tmboot -B** *LMID* **-l** *LMID* when the problem has been corrected.

To reconnect the MASTER node when it has failed:

1. Run the **master** command from the backup MASTER to switch to the backup master.
2. Run **pclean** *ORIGINAL_MASTER_LMID* to remove the entry.
3. Run **tmboot -B** *ORIGINAL_MASTER_LMID* to boot the administrative servers on the machine.
4. Switch the MASTER back to the original master site with the **master** command.
5. Boot or migrate the application servers on the original MASTER.

To reconnect a non-MASTER node that has failed:

1. Run **pclean** *LMID* to remove the entry.
2. Run **tmboot -B** *LMID* to boot the administrative servers on the machine.
3. Boot or migrate the application servers.

11.9.3.6 Miscellaneous Corrective Procedures.

The following steps migrate the transaction log:

1. Shut down the application servers on the problem machine.
2. Run the **dumptlog** command to write the transaction to a text file.
3. Copy the text file to the backup machine.
4. Run the **loadtlog** command to load the text file into the transaction log on the backup machine.
5. Run the **logstart** command to load the transactions into the transaction table.
6. Migrate the servers to the backup machine.

To suspend a service, run the command **susp -s** *servicename*.
To resume a suspended service run the command
   res -s *servicename*.
To unadvertise a service:

1. Run the **susp** command to suspend the service.
2. Run the **unadv** *servicename* command.

To advertise a service run the command **adv** *servicename*.

11.9.3.7 Shutting down Parts of a Domain.

A domain can be shut down in its entirety or in pieces. The command to do this is **tmshutdown(1)**. All of these commands can also be run from **tmadmin(1)**. Some of the variations are:

- Run **tmshutdown -y** to shut down an entire domain.
- Run **tmshutdown -l** *LMID* followed by **tmshutdown -B** *LMID* to shut down a machine.
- Run **tmshutdown -S** to shut down all application servers in the domain.
- Run **tmshutdown -s** *servername* to shut down all instantiations of an application server.

- Run **tmshutdown -g** *GROUPNAME* to shutdown a group and all its servers.
- Run **tmshutdown -i** *SERVERID* to shut down an individual server instantiation.

12

TUXEDO Release 5 Security

12.1   OVERVIEW

TUXEDO Release 5 provides three levels of security as well as a means to add additional security such as Kerberos. The enterprise that desires using Kerberos or other security package with TUXEDO should get information about the product and how to use it with TUXEDO from the product vendor. It is also possible to use security services developed by the enterprise. This chapter describes the security facilities provided with TUXEDO Release 5 and makes some suggestions about how to build custom security services. Release 5 features are fully compatible with TUXEDO Release 6.1; programs written to use these features will work properly with Release 6.1. Information on TUXEDO Release 6.1 is provided in Chapter 17.

There are three levels of security in Release 5:

Level one: Level one security is provided by the usual UNIX security. This security places restrictions on who can use clients and who can boot the system. This level of security is available with all releases of TUXEDO.

Level two: Level two security is provided with TUXEDO. This level requires the user of a client to enter a valid password before the client is allowed to attach to TUXEDO. This level of security is available with TUXEDO Release 4.2 and later.

Level three: Level three security provides an authentication service that checks for the combination of user identification, password, and client name before the client is allowed to attach to TUXEDO. The authorization service provides a ticket that can be used in services to further restrict the user. This level is available with Release 5 and later.

When level three is specified in the configuration file, **tpinit(3)** will invoke the service named as the authorization service. If authorization is certified by the authorization service, TUXEDO will place the value returned by the authorization service into appkey for every service invoked directly or indirectly by the client.

The three levels are cumulative, that is, if level three security is turned on, the user must meet the following combination.

- Authorization must be provided by UNIX (or whatever operating system the client is running on) in order to execute the client.
- The client must request a user id and password and place them in the proper place in the initialization buffer.
- The password must match the password set by the TUXEDO administrator.
- The combination of client identification, password and client name must pass the requirements of the authorization service.

It is possible to require more than one user identification and password before the user is allowed to use the client: a user identification and password for the operating system, a password for level two, and a user identification and password for the authorization service.

When passwords are entered into level three clients, they are placed into a buffer in "clear" format, that is, without encryption. Passwords transmitted from /WS clients are encrypted for transmission. If passwords must be encrypted within the client, the enterprise must customize the authentication service provided with TUXEDO, or use enterprise specific authorization services.

Security starts with a client. In order to use a TUXEDO application with level three and custom security, the user must:

1. Have physical access to a hardware platform that contains application clients.
2. Successfully sign on to the platform with a known user name and password.
3. Have permission to use the selected client, based on platform security rules.

4. Enter a valid user name and password when prompted by the client.

5. The user name and password must be accepted by the validation service invoked by **tpinit(3)** before the client is allowed to attach to TUXEDO.

6. If a custom security system is in place, the ticket returned by the validation routine must be valid for any services used by the client.

12.2   SECURITY ADMINISTRATION

The administrator control security for level two and level three in the ubbconfig file. The entries in the RESOURCE section are:

UID *number* *number* is a number user ID that will be associated with the IPC structures used by TUXEDO, and thereby limiting who can access TUXEDO services. If **UID** is not specified, the **UID** of the person running **tmloadcf(1)** is used.

GID *number* *number* is a number group ID that will be associated with the IPC structures used by TUXEDO, and thereby limits who can access TUXEDO services. If **GID** is not specified, the **GID** of the person running **tmloadcf(1)** is used.

PERM *number* *number* is the numeric permission used to control access to the IPC structures used by TUXEDO, limiting the users who can access TUXEDO services. The value can be any valid UNIX permission value. If **PERM** is not specified, the value is set to **0666**.

UID, **GID**, and **PERM** set global access values. All users of the system must meet the requirements set by these parameters. Normally these values are not set, since they all default to values which allow the administrator access to the system. **UID**, **GID**, and **PERM** may be overridden for individual platforms in the MACHINES section.

SECURITY APP_PW If this parameter is present, the user must enter a password and the client must place it in the initialization buffer before calling **tpinit(3)**. The client cannot attach to the system unless the password matches the password entered when **tmloadcf(1)** was run. This parameter sets up level two security.

AUTHSVC *"string"* *string* is the name of the authorization service invoked by **tpinit(3)**. TUXEDO provides an authorization service with the name AUTHSVC, which is provided by the TUXEDO server **AUTHSVR(5)**. *string* should be enclosed in quotes to prevent confusion with key words used in the system. This parameter sets up level three security.

When **tmloadcf(1)** is run using a ubbconfig with **SECURITY APP_PW** set, it asks for a password input. The password entered into **tmloadcf(1)** becomes the password all client programs must provide in the initialization buffer to be allowed to attach to TUXEDO.

If an authorization service is named in AUTHSVC, the server providing the authorization service must be defined in the SERVERS section. For example, the entries in the RESOURCES section might be:

```
SECURITY         APP_PW
AUTHSVC          "AUTHSVC"
```

The entry in the GROUPS section might be:

```
AUTHGRP          LMID=unix1      GRPNO=2    OPENINFO=NONE
```

The entry in the SERVERS section might be:

```
AUTHSVR          SRVGRP="AUTHGRP" SRVID=100 RESTART=Y GRACE=0
                 MAXGEN=2 CLOPT="-A — -f /home/clh/secapp/passwd"
```

AUTHSVR can be in any group, but it is a good idea to put it into a group by itself to make it easier to change its characteristics if required. The TUXEDO authorization service, AUTHSVC, makes it possible to require individual identification and passwords for users of TUXEDO separately from those that have access to the platform operating system. Another feature of AUTHSVC makes it possible to associate users with specific clients to further restrict access to applications.

The example shows how to set up the authorization service provided by TUXEDO via the server AUTHSVR(5). The file /home/clh/secapp /passwd is a UNIX style password file that has been generated by the TUXEDO utility **tpaddusr(1)**. The documentation for AUTHSVR(5) says that this file can be set to the UNIX file /etc/passwd, but tests have shown that this does not work with all versions of UNIX. It is safer, and perhaps more secure, to use a separate file for TUXEDO access.

The TUXEDO password file has four fields:

- Username, which contains the user identification assigned by the administrator. This name may be the same as used with the operating system, but is not required to be so.

- Client name, which is the name of a client that the user is allowed to use. Client name may be a wild card, indicated by a NULL.
- Password, which contains the password for the user–client name combination. It is possible to use a different password for each combination of user–client name.
- The numeric user identifier, which contains a user identifier to serve as a ticket to services. The **uid** in the TUXEDO security file may be the same as in the operating system file, but is not required to be so. A different user identifier may be used for each user name–client name combination.

AUTHSVC uses the user name and client name passed in the initialization buffer to find matching records in the specified password file. If no match is found, an attempt is made to find the user name associated with a wild card client name. If no match is found with a wild card client name, the request to attach to TUXEDO fails. If a match is found, AUTHSVC uses the password passed in the data area of the initialization buffer to match against the password in the record. If it matches, the client is allowed to attach to TUXEDO, otherwise the request is rejected.

The TUXEDO access password file is managed with the utilities **tpaddusr(1)**, **tpdelusr(1)**, and **tpmodusr(1)**. The TUXEDO access password file may be modified at any time using the supplied utilities, even when the domain is active. The next time AUTHSVC is invoked after the file is modified, it will use the modified file.

tpaddusr(1) has the form:

```
tpaddusr username filename [clientname [uid]]
```

username is a string used to identify the user. *filename* is the full path name of the TUXEDO password file. Any file name can be used to store security information. For easier migration to Release 6.1, use $APPDIR/tpusr for the file name. *clientname* is a string that names a client that the user has access to. *uid* is a number that identifies the user. *clientname* and *uid* are optional. *uid* cannot be entered unless *clientname* is also entered. *uid* may be the same as the uid for the user in the operating system, but it is not required to be so.

tpaddusr(1) adds a user name and associated fields to the TUXEDO password file named on the command line. If the file does not exist, **tpaddusr(1)** creates it. No check is made for duplicates. AUTHSVC uses the first match found in the file, so care must be taken to assure there are no duplicates or false security violations may be generated. Remember that AUTHSVC matches on the user name–client name combination.

The following line adds the user "clh" with the uid "101" and client "seccl" to the named file:

```
tpaddusr clh /home/clh/secapp/passwd seccl 101
```

When this command line is executed, **tpaddusr(1)** requests a password, then a repeat of the password to confirm it before adding the user to the file.

The form of **tpdelusr(1)** is:

```
tpdelusr username filename clientname
```

username, *filename*, and *clientname* are specified as above.

tpdelusr(1) does not request a password entry when it is executed. **tpdelusr(1)** finds the record in the named TUXEDO password file that matches the combination of *username* and *clientname*, then deletes the found record. If no *clientname* is specified on the command line, **tpdelusr(1)** matches only with a record that contains a matching *username* and a wildcard *clientname* and does not touch other records.

The form of **tpmodusr(1)** is:

```
tpmodusr username filename clientname
```

username, *filename*, and *clientname* are specified as above.

tpmodusr(1) requests a password entry when it is executed. **tpmodusr(1)** finds the record in the named TUXEDO password file that matches the combination of *username* and *clientname*, then changes the password in the found record to the password entered. If no *clientname* is specified on the command line, **tpmodusr(1)** matches only with a record which contains a matching *username* and a wildcard *clientname* and does not touch other records.

12.3 MORE INFORMATION ABOUT AUTHSVR(5)

AUTHSVR(5) provides the service AUTHSVC, which can be used to check user authorization and return the numeric user identification for use as a ticket sent to services by the client. Since **tpinit(3)** invokes the authorization service specified in the configuration file, AUTHSVC causes **tpinit(3)** to fail if authorization fails.

AUTHSVC requires a TPINIT type buffer for the invoking message. The username field in the buffer must contain the proper user identification. The cltname field must contain the name of a client authorized to the user, if cltname is to be checked. The password for the username–cltname combination must be in the data field. AUTHSVC checks the username, cltname, and password against the file specified in the configuration file. If a match is found, **AUTHSVC** returns the uid if present. If the uid is not present, a –1 is returned as the **uid**.

If AUTHSVC cannot verify the username–cltname combination or the password is incorrect, it returns with TPFAIL, causing **tpinit(3)** to fail.

The uid passed back by AUTHSVC is made available to services invoked by the client in the field appkey. The ticket is passed to all services called by a client and all services called by such services to any depth of nesting.

12.4   SECURITY IN CLIENT PROGRAMS

For security level two (set by the **SECURITY APP_PW** parameter), the client must provide a valid password in the initialization buffer field passwd before calling **tpinit(3)**. The password in this field is compared by **tpinit(3)** with the password provided by the administrator to **tmloadcf(1)**. If the password does not match, **tpinit(3)** fails and the client is not allowed to attach to TUXEDO.

If the application is using AUTHSVC as provided by TUXEDO, the client program must place the user name in the field usrname and the password in the data field without encryption before calling **tpinit(3)**. **tpinit(3)** will call AUTHSVC to validate the user. AUTHSVC will match the value in **usrname** and the password in the buffer with the user name and password in the file it is directed to. If there is no match, AUTHSVC will return with TPFAIL, causing **tpinit(3)** to fail, thus preventing the client from attaching to TUXEDO.

If the TUXEDO security file was set up to contain the name of the client, the client must also place its own name in the buffer field cltname. AUTHSVC will require that the combination of usrname and cltname is contained in its security file before returning with TPSUCCESS.

The client has no responsibility for the uid.

If **tpinit(3)** fails because either the password did not match the SECURITY APP_PW password, or AUTHSVC validation fails, **tpinit(3)** will return a negative value with tperrno set to TPEPERM.

Note that the password placed in passwd and the password placed in data do not need to be the same. In fact, it is a good idea to require them to be different. It is also not a good idea to use the operating system user name for the initialization buffer field usrname. The client should obtain both the user name and password by either directly requesting them, or by way of some application-specific mechanism. The client should assure that when the password is typed in by the user, it does not echo on the screen.

The following code illustrates how a client can get and use the user name and password from a UNIX terminal:

```c
#include <stdio.h>
#include "atmi.h"              /* TUXEDO  Header File */

main(int argc, char *argv[])
{

    int ret;
    long initbufsz;
    char userid[30], pswd[30], *usrptr;
    TPINIT *initbuf;
    .
    .
    .


    /* allocate space for init buffer */
    initbufsz = sizeof(struct tpinfo_t) + sizeof(pswd) + 10;
    if ((initbuf = (TPINIT *) tpalloc("TPINIT", 0, initbufsz)) ==
(TPINIT *) NULL) {
        /* put error handling here */
    }

    /* get user id and password */
    printf("enter user id ");
    usrptr = gets(userid);
    strcpy (initbuf->usrname, userid);

    printf("\nenter SECURITY APP_PW password ");
    if(getpass(pswd) < 0) /* getpass src is in the Appendix */
    {
        printf("getpass failed");
    }
    strcpy (initbuf->passwd, pswd);
```

```
printf("\nenter application password ");
if(getpass(pswd) < 0) /* getpass src is in the Appendix */
{
     printf("getpass failed");
}
strcpy (&initbuf->data, pswd);
printf("\n");

strcpy (initbuf->cltname, "seccl");

/* Attach to System/T as a Client Process */

if ((ret = tpinit(initbuf)) == < 0) {
    /* put error handling here */
}
 .
 .
 .
/* do whatever the client is supposed to do */
 .
 .
 .
tpterm();
}
```

12.5   SECURITY IN APPLICATION SERVICES

If a ticket was returned by the authorization service, application services can include code to validate the ticket. The ticket is available to the service in the TPSVCINFO field appkey.

The following code fragment illustrates how this might be done:

```
#include <stdio.h>
#include <ctype.h>
#include <atmi.h>   /* TUXEDO Header File */
#include <userlog.h>     /* TUXEDO Header File */
#include "app.h"

appsvc(TPSVCINFO *rqst)
{
```

```
        int i, ret;

        if(usersec(rqst->appkey) != 0)
        {
            userlog("Ticket not valid %s", rqst->name);
            tpreturn(TPFAIL, SECFAIL, NULL, OL, 0);
        }
        .
        .
        .
        /* do application service functionality here */

        /* Return results to the requestor. */
        tpreturn(TPSUCCESS, 0, rqst->data, OL, 0);
}
```

The ticket in this case is the user numeric identifier returned by AUTHSVC. Note that the user defined value, SECFAIL (defined in app.h), is set into the rcode of the **tpreturn(3)** to send the failure reason back to the invoker. The function **usersec()** is an application-specific function that validates the ticket.

The client that invokes the service should check the rcode returned in tpurcode to determine that the reason for the failure of the **tpcall(3)** was a security violation. The client code might be:

```
#include <stdio.h>
#include "atmi.h"              /* TUXEDO  Header File */
#include "app.h"

main(int argc, char *argv[])
{

    int ret;

    long initbufsz;
    char userid[30], pswd[30], *usrptr;
    TPINIT *initbuf;
    .
    .
    .

    /* allocate space for init buffer */
```

```
        initbufsz = sizeof(struct tpinfo_t) + sizeof(pswd) + 10;
        if ((initbuf = (TPINIT *) tpalloc("TPINIT", 0, initbufsz)) ==
(TPINIT *) NULL) {
              /* put error handling here */
        }

        /* get user id and password */
        printf("enter user id ");
        usrptr = gets(userid);
        strcpy (initbuf->usrname, userid);

        printf("\nenter SECURITY APP_PW password ");
        if(getpass(pswd) < 0) /* getpass src is in the Appendix */
        {
              printf("getpass failed");
        }
        strcpy (initbuf->passwd, pswd);

        printf("\nenter application password ");
        if(getpass(pswd) < 0) /* getpass src is in the Appendix */
        {
              printf("getpass failed");
        }

        strcpy (&initbuf->data, pswd);
        printf("\n");

        strcpy (initbuf->cltname, "seccl");

        /* Attach to TUXEDO */

        if ((ret = tpinit(initbuf)) == < 0) {
              /* put error handling here */
        }

              .
              .
              .

        /* call to a service which checks the ticket */

        ret = tpcall("appsvc", sendbuf, 0, &rcvbuf, &rcvlen,
(long)0);
```

```
                   if(ret == -1) {
                       if(tpurcode == SECFAIL)
                       {
                            /* handle invalid ticket here */
                       }
                       else
                       {
                       /* other error handling here */
                       tpfree(sendbuf);
                       tpfree(rcvbuf);
                       tpterm();
                       exit(1);
                   }
                   /* do whatever the client is supposed to do */
                   .

                   .

                   .

                   tpterm();
               }
```

12.6   SUGGESTIONS FOR CUSTOMIZING SECURITY

The simplest way to provide customized security is to modify AUTHSVC in AUTHSVR.c. The source for AUTHSVR.c is provided in $TUXDIR/ lib. Some of the changes that can be made within AUTHSVC are adding encryption of the password at the client level and encrypting the uid.

Encryption of the password in UNIX systems can be done using the UNIX function **crypt()**. If the client is a /WS client, some other encryption function might be required. Be sure to examine AUTHSVR.c to determine how to compare the password with the encrypted password in the TUXEDO password file or use an application dependent password file.

The TUXEDO version of AUTHSVC puts a clear version of the uid in appkey. It would improve security if the uid were encrypted. Developers can modify AUTHSVR.c to encrypt the uid, and use an encrypted version as a ticket in services. The difficulty is that appkey is defined as a C long, meaning that the encryption must be customized, since **crypt()** works with strings. The alternative is to pass an encrypted version of the uid back in the data field, placing the responsibility of passing the ticket in the message on the client and every service that calls other services.

TUXEDO provides the necessary support of Kerberos, so that the enterprise can purchase Kerberos from one of several vendors and use it to get very good security. If Kerberos is considered, performance should be checked very carefully to assure that performance requirements will be met with the product purchased.

12.7   A FUNCTION TO GET THE PASSWORD

The people at Information Management Company (IMC) provide this code to retrieve the password. The function sets the terminal so that the information is not echoed, retrieves the password, then resets the terminal to its former settings. The function does not protect against receiving a string larger than the data area provided.

The form of **getpass()** is:

```
int getpass(*password)
```

Where password is the data area to receive the password. If **getpass()** fails, it returns –1, leaving the UNIX error value in errno.

The source for **getpass()**:

```
#include <stdio.h>
#include <string.h>
#include <termio.h>

int getpass(char *password)
{
    struct termios attrs;
    int c, handle;
    FILE *file;
    long flags;

    /* Open the terminal */
    if ((file = fopen("/dev/tty", "r")) == NULL)
        return (-1);

    /* Set unbuffered IO */
    setbuf(file, NULL);

    /* Get the file handle */
    handle = fileno(file);

    /* Get the current terminal attrs */
```

```
(void)tcgetattr(handle, &attrs);

/* Save the attributes */
flags = attrs.c_lflag;

/* Disable echo bits */
attrs.c_lflag &= ~(ECHO | ECHOE | ECHOK | ECHONL);

/* Set the new attributes */
(void)tcsetattr(handle, TCSAFLUSH, &attrs);

/* Prompt and enter password */
(void) fputs("Enter the password: ", stdout);
while ((c = getc(file)) != EOF && c != '\n')
    *password++ = (char)c;

(void) putc('\n', stdout);
*password = '\0';

/* Restore the old terminal attributes */
attrs.c_lflag = flags;
(void) tcsetattr(handle, TCSAFLUSH, &attrs);

/* Close the terminal device */
(void)fclose(file);

/* Return success */
return (0);
}
```

COBOL

13.1   INTRODUCTION TO TUXEDO COBOL PROGRAMMING

The purpose of this chapter is to provide information to help COBOL programmers create TUXEDO clients and services using COBOL. The reader should be familiar with the material in previous chapters. A reader with no knowledge of C can ignore the samples in the previous chapters, but must understand the principles presented, especially the general architecture of TUXEDO and the structure of client and service programs.

There are several differences between COBOL and C that make writing programs in COBOL different than C, and that affect the way that the ATMI functions are structured. These differences are

- COBOL does not provide the concept or functionality of pointers.
- Typed buffers used in C are called typed records for COBOL.
- FML functions are not provided for COBOL.
- COBOL clients and services can use FML buffers as records only via the **view** mechanism.
- Data structures in COBOL are defined differently.
- The function calling protocol for COBOL is different than for C.

TUXEDO provides copy books and specific COBOL functions to hide these differences from the programmer.

The examples in this chapter were tested using Micro Focus COBOL on a UnixWare platform.

13.2   SAMPLE COBOL PROGRAMS

The COBOL functions used with TUXEDO are described later in this chapter. A simple set of programs illustrate how to use TUXEDO, and an understanding of them will help the reader use the rest of the chapter easier. The following code illustrates a COBOL client.

```
 1.           IDENTIFICATION DIVISION.
 2.           PROGRAM-ID. CSAMPCL.
 3.           AUTHOR. TUXEDO DEVELOPMENT.
 4.           ENVIRONMENT DIVISION.
 5.           CONFIGURATION SECTION.
 6.           WORKING-STORAGE SECTION.
 7.
*****************************************************
 8.           * TUXEDO copy books
 9.
*****************************************************
10.           01  TPTYPE-REC.
11.               COPY TPTYPE.
12.           *
13.           01  TPSTATUS-REC.
14.               COPY TPSTATUS.
15.           *
16.           01  TPSVCDEF-REC.
17.               COPY TPSVCDEF.
18.           *
19.           01  TPINFDEF-REC.
20.               COPY TPINFDEF.
21.
*****************************************************
22.           * Define messages to log
23.
*****************************************************
24.           01  MSG-TO-LOG.
25.               05  FILLER          PIC X(8) VALUE  "CSAMPCL:".
26.               05  LOG-MSG-INFO    PIC X(50).
27.           01  MSG-TO-LOG-LEN      PIC S9(9)  COMP-5.
28.           *
```

```
29.          01  MY-STUFF-REC  PIC X(75).
30.          01  STUFF-SENT       PIC X(30) VALUE SPACES.
31.          01  STUFF-RECEIVED   PIC X(100) VALUE SPACES.

32.
**********************************************************
33.          * Place to put user id and passwords
34.
**********************************************************
35.          01  USRPASSWD.
36.              05  USRID        PIC X(30).
37.              05  GEN-PASSWD   PIC X(30).
38.              05  AUTH-PASSWD  PIC X(30).
39.
**********************************************************
40.          * Begin csampcl and get command line input
41.
**********************************************************
42.          PROCEDURE DIVISION.
43.          BEGIN-CSAMPCL.
44.              MOVE LENGTH OF MSG-TO-LOG TO MSG-TO-LOG-LEN.
45.              PERFORM GET-ID.
46.              ACCEPT STUFF-SENT FROM COMMAND-LINE.
47.              DISPLAY "STUFF-SENT:" STUFF-SENT.
48.
49.              PERFORM ATTACH-TO-TUX.
50.              PERFORM INVOKE-SVC.
51.              DISPLAY "STUFF-RECEIVED in csampcl:"
     STUFF-RECEIVED.
52.              PERFORM DETACH-FROM-TUX.
53.              PERFORM END-OF-CSAMPCL.

54.
**********************************************************
55.          * Get the user id and two passwords
56.
**********************************************************
57.          GET-ID.
58.              DISPLAY "ENTER USER ID".
59.              ACCEPT USRID.
60.              DISPLAY "ENTER GENERAL SECURITY PASSWORD".
61.              ACCEPT GEN-PASSWD.
```

```
62.                    DISPLAY "ENTER AUTHORIZATION PASSWORD".
63.                    ACCEPT AUTH-PASSWD.
64.
65.
****************************************************
66.          * Attach to TUXEDO
67.
****************************************************
68.          ATTACH-TO-TUX.
69.              MOVE USRID TO USRNAME.
70.              MOVE "CSAMPCL" TO CLTNAME.
71.              MOVE GEN-PASSWD TO PASSWD.
72.              MOVE SPACES TO GRPNAME.
73.              MOVE 30 TO DATALEN.
74.              MOVE AUTH-PASSWD TO MY-STUFF-REC.
75.              SET TPU-DIP TO TRUE.
76.          *
77.              CALL "TPINITIALIZE" USING TPINFDEF-REC
78.                  MY-STUFF-REC
79.                  TPSTATUS-REC.
80.
81.              IF NOT TPOK
82.                  MOVE "TPINITIALIZE Failed" TO LOG-MSG-INFO
83.                  PERFORM WRITE-USERLOG
84.                  PERFORM END-OF-CSAMPCL
85.              END-IF.
86.
87.
****************************************************
88.          *   Invoke a service
89.
****************************************************
90.          INVOKE-SVC.
91.              MOVE 30 TO LEN.
92.              MOVE "STRING" TO REC-TYPE.
93.
94.              MOVE "csampsv" TO SERVICE-NAME.
95.              SET TPBLOCK TO TRUE.
96.              SET TPNOTRAN TO TRUE.
97.              SET TPNOTIME TO TRUE.
98.              SET TPSIGRSTRT TO TRUE.
99.              SET TPCHANGE TO TRUE.
```

```
100.
101.            CALL "TPCALL" USING TPSVCDEF-REC
102.                TPTYPE-REC
103.                STUFF-SENT
104.                TPTYPE-REC
105.                STUFF-RECEIVED
106.                TPSTATUS-REC.
107.
108.            IF NOT TPOK
109.                MOVE "TPCALL Failed" TO LOG-MSG-INFO
110.                PERFORM WRITE-USERLOG
111.            END-IF.
112.
113.
****************************************************
114.        * Detach from TUXEDO
115.
****************************************************
116.            DETACH-FROM-TUX.
117.                CALL "TPTERM" USING TPSTATUS-REC.
118.                IF  NOT TPOK
119.                    MOVE "TPTERM Failed" TO LOG-MSG-INFO
120.                    PERFORM WRITE-USERLOG
121.                END-IF.
122.
123.
****************************************************
124.        * Put messages out to the user log
125.
****************************************************
126.            WRITE-USERLOG.
127.                CALL "USERLOG" USING MSG-TO-LOG
128.                    MSG-TO-LOG-LEN
129.                    TPSTATUS-REC.
130.
131.
****************************************************
132.        *Stop csampcl
133.
****************************************************
134.            END-OF-CSAMPCL.
135.                MOVE "Ended" TO LOG-MSG-INFO.
```

```
136.          PERFORM WRITE-USERLOG.
137.          STOP RUN.
```

Lines 10 through 20 retrieve the copy books to support the TUX-EDO functions used in this program. TPTYPE defines the area to contain information about the message record being used. TPSTATUS defines an area where TUXEDO functions place the return status of calls. TPSTATUS also contains 88 level definitions of the return values. TPSVCDEF defines areas to place flags used by TUXEDO functions and 88 levels to aid in their use. TPINFDEF defines the area to build the initialization buffer.

Lines 23 through 27 are developer defined to use in writing to the TUXEDO user log file.

Lines 30 through 31 define the messages the program will use to communicate with the service invoked. STUFF-SENT will be loaded with the value from the command line and sent to the service. STUFF-RECEIVED will contain the result from the service and will be displayed on the terminal.

Lines 35 through 38 define areas to contain the user identification and passwords entered on request. USRID will contain the user identification. GEN-PASSWORD will contain the password required for all users of the domain. AUTH-PASSWORD will contain the password required for users of this client.

The paragraph GET-ID, lines 57 through 63, requests and retrieves the user identification information. Unfortunately, this code will display the passwords on the terminal. To prevent showing the passwords on a dumb terminal, see the information in the chapter on security. If using a GUI terminal, use the facilities provided by the GUI system to suppress showing the password. See Chapter 12 for information on how the security used in this program functions.

Lines 68 through 85 attach the client to TUXEDO. Note that the password to authorize the user for this client is placed in MY-STUFF-REC and passed as a parameter in the call to TPINITIALIZE.

Lines 90 through 111 set up the parameters and invoke a TUXEDO service with the name "csampsv". The code for csampsv follows a little later in this section. Line 92 sets the message record type to STRING. The SET verbs in lines 95 through 99 set the flags used to invoke TPCALL. See the discussion of typed records later in this chapter. The contents of the message sent to the service are in STUFF-SENT and were loaded earlier in the program. The flags must always be set. See the explanation of each flag in the description of the various calls later in this chapter.

The following code illustrates a COBOL service:

```
1.          IDENTIFICATION DIVISION.
2.          PROGRAM-ID. csampsv.
3.          AUTHOR. TUXEDO DEVELOPMENT.
4.          ENVIRONMENT DIVISION.
5.          CONFIGURATION SECTION.

6.          WORKING-STORAGE SECTION.
7.          ******************************************************
8.          * Tuxedo copy books
9.          ******************************************************
10.         01  TPSVCRET-REC.
11.         COPY TPSVCRET.
12.         *
13.         01  TPTYPE-REC.
14.         COPY TPTYPE.
15.         *
16.         01 TPSTATUS-REC.
17.         COPY TPSTATUS.
18.         *
19.         01  TPSVCDEF-REC.
20.         COPY TPSVCDEF.
21.         ******************************************************
22.         * Define user log message area
23.         ******************************************************
24.         01  MSG-TO-LOG.
25.             05  FILLER        PIC X(10)
                    VALUE    "csampsv :".
26.             05  MSG-INFO  PIC X(50).
27.         01  MSG-LEN        PIC S9(9)  COMP-5.
28.         ******************************************************
29.         * Define receive and send records
30.         ******************************************************
31.         01 DATA-GOT        PIC X(30).
32.         01 DATA-SENT.
33.            05  ADDED-DATA   PIC X(25).
34.            05  RECVD-DATA   PIC X(30).

35.         LINKAGE SECTION.
36.         *
37.          PROCEDURE DIVISION.
```

```
38.          *
39.            BEGIN-CSAMPSV.
40.                MOVE LENGTH OF MSG-TO-LOG TO MSG-LEN.
41.                MOVE "Started" TO MSG-INFO.
42.                PERFORM WRITE-USER-LOG.

43.          ********************************************************
44.          * Pick up what was sent from the client
45.          ********************************************************
46.                MOVE LENGTH OF DATA-GOT TO LEN.
47.                CALL "TPSVCSTART" USING TPSVCDEF-REC
48.                     TPTYPE-REC
49.                     DATA-GOT
50.                     TPSTATUS-REC.
51.                IF NOT TPOK
52.                    MOVE "TPSVCSTART Failed" TO MSG-INFO
53.                    PERFORM WRITE-USER-LOG
54.                    PERFORM LEAVE-CSAMPSV
55.                END-IF.

56.                IF TPTRUNCATE
57.                    MOVE "Data was truncated" TO MSG-INFO
58.                    PERFORM WRITE-USER-LOG
59.                    PERFORM LEAVE-CSAMPSV
60.                END-IF.

61.                MOVE DATA-GOT TO RECVD-DATA.
62.                MOVE "DATA RECEIVED IN csampsv" TO ADDED-DATA.
63.
64.                MOVE "Success" TO MSG-INFO.
65.                PERFORM WRITE-USER-LOG.
66.                SET TPSUCCESS TO TRUE.
67.                MOVE 55 TO LEN.
68.                COPY TPRETURN
69.                    REPLACING DATA-REC BY DATA-SENT.

70.          ********************************************************
71.          * Put out a message to the user log
72.          ********************************************************
73.            WRITE-USER-LOG.
74.            CALL "USERLOG" USING MSG-TO-LOG
```

```
75.                MSG-LEN
76.                TPSTATUS-REC.
77.          ******************************************************
78.          * Leave csampsv because of failure
79.          ******************************************************
80.          LEAVE-CSAMPSV.
81.              MOVE "Failed" TO MSG-INFO.
82.              PERFORM WRITE-USER-LOG.
83.              SET TPFAIL TO TRUE.
84.              COPY TPRETURN REPLACING
85.                  DATA-REC BY DATA-GOT.
```

Lines 10 through 20 copy the TUXEDO copy books required to support the service. TPTYPE and TPSTATUS are discussed above. TPSVCDEF defines an area where TUXEDO will place the information received from the invoker of the service.

Lines 32 through 35 define the messages received and returned. DATA-GOT will contain the message received; DATA-SENT will contain the results of the execution of the service.

Note the empty LINKAGE SECTION in line 36. All TUXEDO services are executed from a TUXEDO main program and require an empty LINKAGE SECTION.

Lines 41 through 43 write out an announcement that the service has started to the user log. Production applications should not write the log except to write out failure information.

Lines 47 through 56 retrieve the message sent from the invoker. The code in lines 47 through 51 must be executed before the service can begin processing the message received. Lines 52 through 56 are used in case there is a catastrophic error during TPSVCSTART. The program must exit if NOT TPOK.

Lines 57 through 61 illustrate an optional method of handling the condition where the message received is less than the length in **LEN**. The program may continue when condition TPTRUNCATE is present, but must handle the condition where the message has been truncated on the right. **LEN** contains the actual number of bytes received upon return from TPSVCSTART.

Lines 67 through 70 show how to end a service when it has been executed successfully. Line 67 sets the return flag to TPSUCCESS. The length of the return message is placed in **LEN** in line 68. The TPRETURN should be included using the provided copy book as shown in lines 69 and 70. TPRETURN should always be included in the service by means of the copy book. The code in the copy book contains an EXIT PROGRAM statement that returns control to the TUXEDO main program after returning the message to the invoker.

13.3   **COMPILING COBOL CLIENTS AND SERVICES**

COBOL clients are compiled using the utility **buildclient(1)** with the -C option; COBOL servers are compiled using the utility **buildserver(1)** with the -C option. (Note: Releases prior to Release 5 provided the utilities CBLDCLNT to build clients and CBLDSRVR to build servers.) The following environment variables must be set before running **buildclient(1)** or **buildserver(1)**:

- TUXDIR must contain the root directory for the TUXEDO system. For example: /home/tuxdir.
- COBOPT must be set with any COBOL compiler options required.
- COBCPY is an option variable that may be set to point to the location of application specific COBOL copy books.
- LD_LIBRARY_PATH must contain the path to shared libraries used by the COBOL compiler.

The sample programs in this chapter were compiled using the Micro Focus COBOL compiler on UnixWare. The **buildclient(1)** command line was:

```
buildclient -C -o csampcl -f csampcl.cbl
```

The **buildserver(1)** command line was:

```
buildserver -C -o csampsv -s csampsv -f csampsv.cbl
    f TPSVRINIT.cbl
```

The following script was executed to set up the environment:

```
TUXDIR=/home/tuxdir; export TUXDIR
TUXCONFIG=/home/clh/sampapp/sampconfig; export TUXCONFIG
PATH=$TUXDIR/bin:/home/clh/sampapp:$PATH; export PATH

COBCPY=:$TUXDIR/cobinclude; export COBCPY
COBOPT="-C ANS85 -C ALIGN=8 -C NOIBMCOMP -C TRUNC=ANSI -C
OSEXT=cbl"; export COBOPT

LD_LIBRARY_PATH=$TUXDIR/lib:/opt/lib/cobol/coblib:/lib:$LD_LIBRAR
Y_PATH; export LD_LIBRARY_PATH
```

COMPILING COBOL CLIENTS AND SERVICES

The environment COBDIR (required by the Micro Focus COBOL compiler) was set by the system startup to /opt/lib/cobol.

The source for TPSVRINIT (TPSVRINIT.cbl) is included in the command line for **buildclient(1)** as the most convenient method to include an application specific version of this function. TUXEDO provides a default **TPSVRINIT(3)**, which is used if there is no application specific version supplied. The code used for **TPSVRINIT(3)** with the sample program follows.

```
IDENTIFICATION DIVISION.
PROGRAM-ID.  TPSVRINIT.
ENVIRONMENT DIVISION.
CONFIGURATION SECTION.
*
DATA DIVISION.
WORKING-STORAGE SECTION.
*
01  USR-LOG-FIELDS.
    05  FILLER          PIC X(11) VALUE  "TPSVRINIT :".
    05  MSG-IN-LOG      PIC X(50).
01  USR-LOG-LEN          PIC S9(9)  COMP-5.
*
01 TPSTATUS-REC.
COPY TPSTATUS.
*********************************************************
LINKAGE SECTION.
01  ARG-DEFS.
   05 ARGC  PIC 9(4) COMP-5.
   05 ARG.
      10 ARGS PIC X OCCURS 0 TO 9999 DEPENDING ON ARGC.
*
01  SAMPSV-INIT-STATUS.
COPY TPSTATUS.
*********************************************************
PROCEDURE DIVISION USING ARG-DEFS SAMPSV-INIT-STATUS.
START-INIT.
    MOVE LENGTH OF USR-LOG-FIELDS TO USR-LOG-LEN.
*********************************************************
* No command line parameters are used in this version
*********************************************************
IF ARG NOT EQUAL TO SPACES
    MOVE "TPSVRINIT in csampsv failed" TO MSG-IN-LOG
```

```
                    CALL "USERLOG" USING
                            USR-LOG-FIELDS
                            USR-LOG-LEN
                            TPSTATUS-REC
              ELSE
                  MOVE "Welcome to a sample of a COBOL server"
                      TO MSG-IN-LOG
                  CALL "USERLOG" USING
                            USR-LOG-FIELDS
                            USR-LOG-LEN
                            TPSTATUS-REC
              END-IF.
          *
              SET TPOK IN SAMPSV-INIT-STATUS TO TRUE.
          *
              EXIT PROGRAM.
```

13.4   TYPED RECORDS

13.4.1   Overview

Typed records are used to create messages between clients and servers. The types supported for COBOL are: CARRAY, STRING, VIEW, VIEW32, X_OCTET, and X_COMMON. Communication using FML buffer types is possible using a special VIEW type.

The data in CARRAY records may be any character. The X_OCTET record type is the equivalent of CARRAY. The number of bytes in the message must be sent into LEN IN *TPTYPE_REC* when using CARRAY records to send messages.

The data in STRING records may be any character except LOW-VALUE. LOW-VALUE may be set as the last character of a string. The number of bytes in the message must be sent into **LEN** IN *TPTYPE_REC* when using STRING records to send messages.

The record type VIEW supports use of application defined structures to allow TUXEDO to provide data translation between machines using different data representation methods. VIEWs are defined outside the program. TUXEDO provides a utility, **viewc**, that will create the COBOL structure representing the VIEW. VIEW type records can be mapped to FML messages to allow COBOL clients and services to interoperate with C clients and services using FML buffers. VIEW buffers support the common COBOL data types. X_COMMON is the same as the VIEW record type, but limits the use of COBOL data types to

PIC S9(4) COMP-5, **PIC S9(9) COMP-5** and **PIC X(n)**. The record type VIEW32 is the same as VIEW but supports larger fields, more fields in a record, and larger records.

FML buffers used to communicate with C programs can be used by building special VIEW records.

13.4.2   Using CARRAY and STRING Record Types

From a COBOL point of view, the only difference between CARRAY and STRING records is that STRING records cannot contain embedded LOW-VALUES. X_OCTET is a synonym for CARRAY, and can be used wherever CARRAY can be used. To use either CARRAY or STRING records to send messages:

1. Define the record in the normal COBOL manner, beginning with the 01 level.
2. Put the desired data into the record.
3. Move the literal "STRING" for string records, or "CARRAY" for CARRAY records into REC-TYPE, which is defined in the copy book TPTYPE.
4. Move the length of the message to **LEN** in the copy book TPTYPE.
5. Set up and call the appropriate function, such as **TPCALL(3)**.

To receive a CARRAY or STRING type record in a service:

1. Define an area in WORKING-STORAGE to store the record.
2. Use the name of the defined area as a parameter in the call to TPSVCSTART.

When TPSVCSTART returns successfully, the message will be in the specified area and the actual size of the message will be in **LEN**.

The earlier example client and server used STRING type records for messages.

13.4.3   Using VIEW Type Records

Chapter 7 describes how to use VIEWs with TUXEDO in Section 7.4, VIEW Buffers. All the steps and their significance are explained there. Some of the information is repeated here, with COBOL specifics, but the reader should refer to that section for more detail.

The steps required to use VIEW type records in COBOL are:

1. Define the VIEWs in viewfiles (see description of viewfiles in Chapter 7).
2. Run **viewc** with the **-C** and **-n** options.
3. Include the resulting COBOL copy book in programs using the view.
4. Set up the environment for using VIEWs.

Client programs must set SUB-TYPE to "VIEW" and SUB-TYPE to the name of the view to use. **LEN** can be set either to the actual size of the data to be sent, or set to 0 to indicate that the length is the length of the VIEW. Services receive the VIEW by using the record containing the VIEW copy book. The length of a VIEW record returned may be either 0 or the length of the VIEW record.

The following client program illustrates using a VIEW type record:

```
IDENTIFICATION DIVISION.
PROGRAM-ID. cvsampcl.
AUTHOR. TUXEDO DEVELOPMENT.
ENVIRONMENT DIVISION.
CONFIGURATION SECTION.
WORKING-STORAGE SECTION.

******************************************************
* TUXEDO copy books
******************************************************
 01  TPTYPE-REC.
 COPY TPTYPE.
*
 01  TPSTATUS-REC.
 COPY TPSTATUS.
*
 01  TPSVCDEF-REC.
 COPY TPSVCDEF.
*
 01  TPINFDEF-REC.
 COPY TPINFDEF.


******************************************************
* Define the view
******************************************************
 01 MYVIEW-REC.
 COPY SAMPVIEW.
```

```
      ******************************************************
      * Define messages to log
      ******************************************************
       01  MSG-TO-LOG.
           05  FILLER       PIC X(8) VALUE  "CSAMPCL:".
           05  LOG-MSG-INFO  PIC X(50).
       01  MSG-TO-LOG-LEN    PIC S9(9)  COMP-5.
      *
       01  MY-STUFF-REC         PIC X(75).
       01  STUFF-SENT       PIC X(30) VALUE SPACES.
       01  STUFF-RECEIVED       PIC X(100) VALUE SPACES.


      *******************************************************
      * Place to put user id and passwords
      *******************************************************
       01  USRPASSWD.
           05  USRID        PIC X(30).
           05  GEN-PASSWD   PIC X(30).
           05  AUTH-PASSWD  PIC X(30).
      *******************************************************
      * Begin cvsampcl and get command line input
      *******************************************************
       PROCEDURE DIVISION.
       BEGIN-CVSAMPCL.
           MOVE LENGTH OF MSG-TO-LOG TO MSG-TO-LOG-LEN.
           PERFORM GET-ID.
           ACCEPT MYSTR1 FROM COMMAND-LINE.
           DISPLAY "MYSTR1-SENT:" MYSTR1.

           PERFORM ATTACH-TO-TUX.
           PERFORM INVOKE-SVC.
           DISPLAY "MYSTR1 returned in cvsampcl:" MYSTR1.
           DISPLAY "MYSTR2 returned in cvsampcl:" MYSTR2.
           PERFORM DETACH-FROM-TUX.
           PERFORM END-OF-CSAMPCL.


      *******************************************************
      * Get the user id and two passwords
      *******************************************************
       GET-ID.
           DISPLAY "ENTER USER ID".
```

```
          ACCEPT USRID.
          DISPLAY "ENTER GENERAL SECURITY PASSWORD".
          ACCEPT GEN-PASSWD.
          DISPLAY "ENTER AUTHORIZATION PASSWORD".
          ACCEPT AUTH-PASSWD.


     ******************************************************
     * Attach to TUXEDO
     ******************************************************
      ATTACH-TO-TUX.
          MOVE USRID TO USRNAME.
          MOVE "CSAMPCL" TO CLTNAME.
          MOVE GEN-PASSWD TO PASSWD.
          MOVE SPACES TO GRPNAME.
          MOVE 30 TO DATALEN.
          MOVE AUTH-PASSWD TO MY-STUFF-REC.
          SET TPU-DIP TO TRUE.
     *
          CALL "TPINITIALIZE" USING TPINFDEF-REC
              MY-STUFF-REC
              TPSTATUS-REC.
          IF NOT TPOK
              MOVE "TPINITIALIZE Failed" TO LOG-MSG-INFO
              PERFORM WRITE-USERLOG
              PERFORM END-OF-CSAMPCL
          END-IF.


     ******************************************************
     *   Invoke a service
     ******************************************************
      INVOKE-SVC.
          MOVE 200 TO LEN.
          MOVE "VIEW" TO REC-TYPE.
          MOVE "sampview" TO SUB-TYPE.

          MOVE "cvsampsv" TO SERVICE-NAME.
          SET TPBLOCK TO TRUE.
          SET TPNOTRAN TO TRUE.
          SET TPNOTIME TO TRUE.
          SET TPSIGRSTRT TO TRUE.
          SET TPNOCHANGE TO TRUE.
```

```
CALL "TPCALL" USING TPSVCDEF-REC
    TPTYPE-REC
    MYVIEW-REC
    TPTYPE-REC
    MYVIEW-REC
    TPSTATUS-REC.

IF NOT TPOK
    DISPLAY "TPCALL FAILED"
    DISPLAY "ERROR WAS " TP-STATUS
    MOVE "TPCALL Failed" TO LOG-MSG-INFO
    PERFORM WRITE-USERLOG
END-IF.


*****************************************************
* Detach from TUXEDO
*****************************************************
DETACH-FROM-TUX.
    CALL "TPTERM" USING TPSTATUS-REC.
    IF  NOT TPOK
        MOVE "TPTERM Failed" TO LOG-MSG-INFO
        PERFORM WRITE-USERLOG
    END-IF.


*****************************************************
* Put messages out to the user log
*****************************************************
WRITE-USERLOG.
    CALL "USERLOG" USING MSG-TO-LOG
        MSG-TO-LOG-LEN
        TPSTATUS-REC.


*****************************************************
*Stop csampcl
*****************************************************
END-OF-CSAMPCL.
    MOVE "Ended" TO LOG-MSG-INFO.
    PERFORM WRITE-USERLOG.
    STOP RUN.
```

Note this program uses the same data area for both the sending and receiving message.

The following code illustrates a service called from the client shown above:

```
IDENTIFICATION DIVISION.
PROGRAM-ID. csampsv.
AUTHOR. TUXEDO DEVELOPMENT.
ENVIRONMENT DIVISION.
CONFIGURATION SECTION.

WORKING-STORAGE SECTION.
********************************************************
* Tuxedo copy books
********************************************************
 01  TPSVCRET-REC.
 COPY TPSVCRET.
 *
 01  TPTYPE-REC.
 COPY TPTYPE.
 *
 01 TPSTATUS-REC.
 COPY TPSTATUS.
 *
 01  TPSVCDEF-REC.
 COPY TPSVCDEF.


********************************************************
* Define view area
********************************************************
 01 MYVIEW-REC.
 COPY SAMPVIEW.
********************************************************
* Define user log message area
********************************************************
 01  MSG-TO-LOG.
     05  FILLER    PIC X(10) VALUE
         "csampsv :".
     05  MSG-INFO  PIC X(50).
 01  MSG-LEN       PIC S9(9)  COMP-5.
********************************************************
* Define receive and send records
********************************************************
 01  DATA-GOT       PIC X(30).
```

```
01  DATA-SENT.
    05  ADDED-DATA      PIC X(25).
    05  RECVD-DATA      PIC X(30).


************************************************************
* Some working areas
************************************************************
01  RETURN-MSG.
    05 VAR-MSG          PIC X(19).
    05 VAL-RCVD         PIC X(79).

 LINKAGE SECTION.
*
 PROCEDURE DIVISION.
*
 BEGIN-CSAMPSV.
     MOVE LENGTH OF MSG-TO-LOG TO MSG-LEN.
     MOVE "Started" TO MSG-INFO.
     PERFORM WRITE-USER-LOG.


************************************************************
* Pick up what was sent from the client
************************************************************
     MOVE LENGTH OF MYVIEW-REC TO LEN.
     CALL "TPSVCSTART" USING TPSVCDEF-REC
         TPTYPE-REC
         MYVIEW-REC
         TPSTATUS-REC.
     IF NOT TPOK
         MOVE "TPSVCSTART Failed" TO MSG-INFO
         PERFORM WRITE-USER-LOG
         PERFORM LEAVE-CSAMPSV
     END-IF.

     IF TPTRUNCATE
         MOVE "Data was truncated" TO MSG-INFO
         PERFORM WRITE-USER-LOG
         PERFORM LEAVE-CSAMPSV
     END-IF.

     MOVE "MSG IN MYSTR1 WAS " TO VAR-MSG.
     MOVE MYSTR1 TO VAL-RCVD.
```

```
              MOVE RETURN-MSG TO MYSTR1.
              MOVE "MYSTR1 WAS RECEIVED IN cvsampsv" TO MYSTR2.

              MOVE "Success" TO MSG-INFO.
              PERFORM WRITE-USER-LOG.
              SET TPSUCCESS TO TRUE.
              MOVE LENGTH OF MYVIEW-REC TO LEN.
              COPY TPRETURN
                  REPLACING DATA-REC BY MYVIEW-REC.


        ******************************************************
        * Put out a message to the user log
        ******************************************************
         WRITE-USER-LOG.
              CALL "USERLOG" USING MSG-TO-LOG
                  MSG-LEN
                  TPSTATUS-REC.
        ******************************************************
        * Leave csampsv because of failure
        ******************************************************
         LEAVE-CSAMPSV.
              MOVE "Failed" TO MSG-INFO.
              PERFORM WRITE-USER-LOG.
              SET TPFAIL TO TRUE.
              COPY TPRETURN REPLACING
              DATA-REC BY MYVIEW-REC.
```

The viewfile used for these examples was:

```
VIEW sampview
# type cname      fbname      count      flag size null
string mystr1      -      1      -      100  -
string mystr2      -      1      -      100  -
END
```

The following script was run to set the environment.

```
TUXDIR=/home/tuxdir; export TUXDIR
TUXCONFIG=/home/clh/sampapp/sampconfig; export TUXCONFIG
PATH=$TUXDIR/bin:/home/clh/sampapp:$PATH; export PATH

COBCPY=:$TUXDIR/cobinclude; export COBCPY
COBOPT="-C ANS85 -C ALIGN=8 -C NOIBMCOMP -C TRUNC=ANSI -C
```

```
OSEXT=cbl"; export COBOPT
LD_LIBRARY_PATH=$TUXDIR/lib:/opt/lib/cobol/coblib:/lib:
    $LD_LIBRARY_PATH; export LD_LIBRARY_PATH
```

13.4.4   Using FML Type Records

COBOL clients and services cannot work directly with FML records. If both the service invoker and the service are written with COBOL, they should use CARRAY, STRING, or VIEW records. TUXEDO provides procedures to convert VIEW records to FML when a COBOL client or service must communicate with a C client or service that uses FML buffers. The FML field definitions will already exist to support the C programs, so the steps necessary to interface COBOL clients and services with C clients and services that use FML are:

1. Be sure that both the FML and VIEW environment variables are set correctly.
2. Create a viewfile that matches the FML field definitions. The FML field names must be specified for each field in the VIEW.
3. Run **viewc(1)** with the **-C** option, but not the **-n** option.
4. Include the resulting copy book in the COBOL programs.
5. Define an area for the FML record. See the example and discussion below for more information on how to define the FML record.
6. Include the copy book FMLINFO in the program beneath an 01 level record.
7. Include code in the COBOL programs to convert the VIEW data to FML and back again as necessary for proper communication with the C client or service.

A COBOL client or service converts between FML and VIEW by including:

1. The copy book generated by **viewc(1)** as described above within an 01 level record.
2. A record to contain the FML version of the data.
3. A call to FINIT if the program is the initiator of the buffer.
4. A call to FVSTOF to convert the VIEW to FML before invoking the service which requires an FML buffer.
5. A call to FVFTOS to convert a returned FML buffer to a VIEW record after receiving an FML buffer.

The following rules apply.

- Whenever the program originates the FML buffer, it must call FINIT to initialize the buffer. Set the length of the FML record into FML-LENGTH before calling any of the FML functions.
- COBOL programs interfacing with FML buffers must define an FML record. The record must be defined large enough to contain the largest expected amount of data. The data portion must be aligned on a full word boundary. One technique is to place a field defined as **PIC S9(9) COMP** immediately in front of the data portion.
- A COBOL service that receives an FML buffer must receive it into an area defined as above and convert the buffer to a VIEW record before using it.
- A COBOL client invoking a service requiring an FML buffer must convert a VIEW to FML before invoking the service.
- Any COBOL program that receives an FML buffer, must convert the data received to a VIEW record before using the information in the record.

The following client program illustrates how a COBOL client communicates with C service that requires an FML buffer for its invoking message and that returns an FML buffer:

```
1.              IDENTIFICATION DIVISION.
2.              PROGRAM-ID. cvsampcl.
3.              AUTHOR. TUXEDO DEVELOPMENT.
4.              ENVIRONMENT DIVISION.
5.              CONFIGURATION SECTION.
6.              WORKING-STORAGE SECTION.
7.
****************************************************
8.              * TUXEDO copy books
9.
****************************************************
10.             01  TPTYPE-REC.
11.             COPY TPTYPE.
12.             *
13.             01  TPSTATUS-REC.
14.             COPY TPSTATUS.
15.             *
16.             01  TPSVCDEF-REC.
17.             COPY TPSVCDEF.
18.             *
19.             01  TPINFDEF-REC.
```

```
20.          COPY TPINFDEF.

21.          01  FML-REC.
22.          COPY FMLINFO.
23.
*******************************************************
24.          * Define the view
25.
*******************************************************
26.          01 MYVIEW-REC.
27.          COPY SAMPFVIEW.
28.
29.          01 FML-DATA-REC.
30.             05 FML-ALIGN        PIC S9(9) COMP.
31.             05 FML-DATA         PIC X(728).

32.
*******************************************************
33.          * Define data area for authorization
34.
*******************************************************
35.          01 MY-STUFF-REC        PIC X(100).

36.
*******************************************************
37.          * Define messages to log
38.
*******************************************************
39.          01 MSG-TO-LOG.
40.             05 FILLER           PIC X(8) VALUE  "CSAMPCL:".
41.             05 LOG-MSG-INFO     PIC X(50).
42.          01 MSG-TO-LOG-LEN      PIC S9(9)  COMP-5.

43.
*******************************************************
44.          * Place to put user id and passwords
45.
*******************************************************
46.          01 USRPASSWD.
47.             05  USRID           PIC X(30).
48.             05  GEN-PASSWD      PIC X(30).
49.             05  AUTH-PASSWD     PIC X(30).
```

```
50.
**********************************************************
51.          * Begin cvsampcl and get command line input
52.
**********************************************************
53.          PROCEDURE DIVISION.
54.          BEGIN-CVSAMPCL.
55.              MOVE LENGTH OF MSG-TO-LOG TO MSG-TO-LOG-LEN.
56.              PERFORM GET-ID.
57.              ACCEPT MYSTR1(1) FROM COMMAND-LINE.
58.              DISPLAY "MYSTR1-SENT:" MYSTR1(1).
59.
60.              PERFORM ATTACH-TO-TUX.

61.              MOVE LENGTH OF FML-DATA-REC TO FML-LENGTH.
62.              CALL "FINIT" USING FML-DATA-REC FML-REC.
63.              IF NOT FOK
64.                  DISPLAY "FINIT FAILED" FML-STATUS
65.                  PERFORM END-OF-CSAMPCL
66.              END-IF.

67.              MOVE "MYSTR1(2)" TO MYSTR1(2).
68.              MOVE "MYSTR2(1)" TO MYSTR2(1).
69.              MOVE "MYSTR2(2)" TO MYSTR2(2).


70.
**********************************************************
71.          * CONVERT VIEW TO FML
72.
**********************************************************
73.              SET FUPDATE TO TRUE.
74.              MOVE "sampfview" TO VIEWNAME.
75.              CALL "FVSTOF" USING
76.                  FML-DATA-REC
77.                  MYVIEW-REC
78.                  FML-REC.
79.              IF NOT FOK
80.                  DISPLAY "FVSTOF FAILED" FML-STATUS
81.                  PERFORM END-OF-CSAMPCL
82.              END-IF.
83.
84.              PERFORM INVOKE-SVC.
```

```
85.              CALL "FVFTOS" USING
86.                 FML-DATA-REC
87.                 MYVIEW-REC
88.                 FML-REC.
89.              IF NOT FOK
90.                 DISPLAY "FVSTOF FAILED" FML-STATUS
91.                 PERFORM END-OF-CSAMPCL
92.              END-IF.
93.

94.              DISPLAY "MYSTR1(1) returned:" MYSTR1(1).
95.              DISPLAY "MYSTR1(2) returned:" MYSTR1(2).
96.              DISPLAY "MYSTR2(1) returned:" MYSTR2(1).
97.              DISPLAY "MYSTR2(2) returned:" MYSTR2(2).
98.              PERFORM DETACH-FROM-TUX.
99.              PERFORM END-OF-CSAMPCL.

100.
*****************************************************
101.         * Get the user id and two passwords
102.
*****************************************************
103.         GET-ID.
104.             DISPLAY "ENTER USER ID".
105.             ACCEPT USRID.
106.             DISPLAY "ENTER GENERAL SECURITY PASSWORD".
107.             ACCEPT GEN-PASSWD.
108.             DISPLAY "ENTER AUTHORIZATION PASSWORD".
109.             ACCEPT AUTH-PASSWD.

110.
111.
*****************************************************
112.         * Attach to TUXEDO
113.
*****************************************************
114.         ATTACH-TO-TUX.
115.             MOVE USRID TO USRNAME.
116.             MOVE "CSAMPCL" TO CLTNAME.
117.             MOVE GEN-PASSWD TO PASSWD.
118.             MOVE SPACES TO GRPNAME.
119.             MOVE 30 TO DATALEN.
120.             MOVE AUTH-PASSWD TO MY-STUFF-REC.
```

```
121.              SET TPU-DIP TO TRUE.
122.        *
123.              CALL "TPINITIALIZE" USING TPINFDEF-REC
124.                  MY-STUFF-REC
125.                  TPSTATUS-REC.
126.
127.              IF NOT TPOK
128.                  MOVE "TPINITIALIZE Failed" TO LOG-MSG-INFO
129.                  PERFORM WRITE-USERLOG
130.                  PERFORM END-OF-CSAMPCL
131.              END-IF.
132.
133.
***************************************************
134.        *  Invoke a service
135.
***************************************************
136.        INVOKE-SVC.
137.              MOVE LENGTH OF FML-DATA-REC TO LEN.
138.              MOVE "FML" TO REC-TYPE.
139.              MOVE SPACES TO SUB-TYPE.
140.
141.              MOVE "FMLSAMP" TO SERVICE-NAME.
142.              SET TPBLOCK TO TRUE.
143.              SET TPNOTRAN TO TRUE.
144.              SET TPNOTIME TO TRUE.
145.              SET TPSIGRSTRT TO TRUE.
146.              SET TPNOCHANGE TO TRUE.
147.
148.              CALL "TPCALL" USING TPSVCDEF-REC
149.                  TPTYPE-REC
150.                  FML-DATA-REC
151.                  TPTYPE-REC
152.                  FML-DATA-REC
153.                  TPSTATUS-REC.
154.
155.              IF NOT TPOK
156.                  DISPLAY "TPCALL FAILED"
157.                  DISPLAY "ERROR WAS " TP-STATUS
158.                  MOVE "TPCALL Failed" TO LOG-MSG-INFO
159.              END-IF.
```

```
160.              IF TPTRUNCATE
161.                  DISPLAY "RETURN MESSAGE TRUNCATED - CANNOT
     CONTINUE"
162.                  DISPLAY "LEN RETURNED" LEN
163.                  PERFORM END-OF-CSAMPCL
164.              END-IF.
165.
166.
****************************************************
167.       * Detach from TUXEDO
168.
****************************************************
169.       DETACH-FROM-TUX.
170.           CALL "TPTERM" USING TPSTATUS-REC.
171.           IF  NOT TPOK
172.               MOVE "TPTERM Failed" TO LOG-MSG-INFO
173.               PERFORM WRITE-USERLOG
174.           END-IF.
175.
176.
****************************************************
177.       * Put messages out to the user log
178.
****************************************************
179.       WRITE-USERLOG.
180.           CALL "USERLOG" USING MSG-TO-LOG
181.               MSG-TO-LOG-LEN
182.               TPSTATUS-REC.
183.
184.
****************************************************
185.       *Stop csampcl
186.
****************************************************
187.       END-OF-CSAMPCL.
188.           MOVE "Ended" TO LOG-MSG-INFO.
189.           PERFORM WRITE-USERLOG.
190.           STOP RUN.
```

Lines 29 through 31 define the FML record. FML-ALIGN causes the proper alignment to a full four byte word boundary. FML-DATA provides the additional space required to store the FML-RECORD. The size of this area must be large enough to store the largest record expected. Additional space must also be provided for FML overhead. A good method to calculate the space is to:

1. Determine the actual maximum number of message bytes the FML record must contain, in this case, 600.
2. Multiply the value from step 1 by 1.25, in this case, 725.
3. The size of the data is the next highest value divisible evenly by 4, in this case, 728.

Note that FML records must begin and end on a four-byte word boundary.

Lines 61 through 62 initialize the FML record. It is essential to move the length of the data area into FML-LENGTH before calling FINIT.

Lines 73 through 78 convert the VIEW record to an FML type and place it into the FML record. The VIEW named in VIEWNAME must exist in a viewfile found in the environment.

Lines 85 through 89 convert the FML record received from the service to a VIEW type and place it into the VIEW record.

Line 138 sets the record type to FML before calling TPCALL to invoke the service.

The FML buffer was defined as follows:

```
# name   fld-id type    flag   comment
*base 100
mystr1f  1     string    -     my own first string
mystr2f  2     string    -     my own second string
```

The VIEW was defined as follows:

```
VIEW sampfview
# type cname      fbname      count    flag size null
string mystr1     mystr1f     3          - 100   -
string mystr2     mystr2f     3          - 100   -
END
```

The COBOL copy book created by viewc(1) was:

```
*         VIEWFILE: "sampfview.v"
*         VIEWNAME: "sampfview"
    05 MYSTR1 OCCURS 3 TIMES    PIC X(100).
*         NULL="\0"
```

```
      05 MYSTR2 OCCURS 3 TIMES      PIC X(100).
*         NULL="\0"
```

The script used to set the environment was:

```
TUXDIR=/home/tuxdir; export TUXDIR
TUXCONFIG=/home/clh/sampapp/sampfconfig; export TUXCONFIG
PATH=$TUXDIR/bin:/home/clh/sampapp:$PATH; export PATH

VIEWFILES=sampview.V,sampfview.V; export VIEWFILES
VIEWDIR=/home/clh/sampapp; export VIEWDIR

FLDTBLDIR=/home/clh/sampapp:$TUXDIR/udataobj; export
FLDTBLDIR
FIELDTBLS=cfmlflds,Usysflds; export FIELDTBLS

COBCPY=:$TUXDIR/cobinclude; export COBCPY
COBOPT="-C ANS85 -C ALIGN=8 -C NOIBMCOMP -C TRUNC=ANSI -C
OSEXT=cbl"; export COBOPT
LD_LIBRARY_PATH=$TUXDIR/lib:/opt/lib/cobol/coblib:
      /lib:$LD_LIBRARY_PATH; export LD_LIBRARY_PATH
```

13.5 COBOL ATMI FUNCTIONS

COBOL ATMI functions work the same as the corresponding C functions. COBOL clients and services are built using the same principles as C clients and functions. The COBOL versions are, in fact, COBOL overlays that internally call the equivalent C functions. To use the COBOL functions:

- Include the copy books specified by the reference manual.
- If the function is specified using a COPY statement, use that copy statement to include the function in the program.
- Be sure to replace the name of records with the name of the equivalent record in the application.

The rules for using the functions in COBOL are the same as previously discussed for the C versions. Conversations may be used with COBOL clients and services following the same rules as for C. COBOL clients and services may invoke C services, and C clients and services may invoke COBOL services as long as the COBOL message record types match the expected C buffer types correctly.

TPCALL(3) and **TPRETURN(3)** are discussed here as examples of how to use the COBOL versions of ATMI functions.

The form of **TPCALL(3)** is:

```
01 TPSVCDEF-REC.
    COPY TPSVCDEF.
01 ITPTYPE-REC.
    COPY TPTYPE.
01 IDATA-REC.
  Place application data structure here.
01 OTPTYPE-REC.
    COPY TPTYPE.
01 ODATA-REC.
  Place application data structure here.
01 TPSTATUS-REC.
    COPY TPSTATUS.
CALL "TPCALL" USING TPSVCDEF-REC ITPTYPE-REC IDATA-REC
    OTPTYPE-REC ODATA-REC TPSTATUS-RE C.
```

TPCALL invokes the service named in SERVICE-NAME. The data in *IDATA-REC* is sent to the service. The service returns the result in *ODATA-REC*.

Before calling TPCALL, the application program must:

- Place the name of the service to be invoked in SERVICE-NAME in *TPSVCDEF-REC*.
- Put the length of *IDATA-REC* in **LEN** in *ITYPE-REC*.
- Put the type of message record *IDATA-REC* is defined as (for instance "STRING") into REC-TYPE in *ITYPE-REC*.
- If the record type is VIEW, put the view name into SUB-TYPE in *ITYPE-REC*, otherwise put spaces in SUB-TYPE.
- Repeat the above steps for *OTYPE-REC*. (Note that the examples use the same record for both *ITYPE-REC* and *OTYPE-REC*.)
- Set the flags in TPSVC-DEF-REC. In COBOL, the flags that apply to a function should be set explicitly before each call to the function. COBOL flags are defined in pairs. The application should set the flags TRUE by name using either the positive or negative name. For instance the blocking flag should be set by setting either TPBLOCK or TPNOBLOCK to TRUE. For TPCALL, the flags are:

```
TPBLOCK or TPNOBLOCK
TPTRAN or TPNOTRAN
```

```
TPTIME or TPNOTIME
TPNOSIGRSTRT or TPSIGRSTRT
TPCHANGE or TPNOCHANGE
```

The meaning of each flag is the same as previously described for the C function **tpcall(3)**.

The form of **TPRETURN(3)** is:

```
01 TPSVCRET-REC.
COPY TPSVCRET.
01 TPTYPE-REC.
COPY TPTYPE.
01 DATA-REC.
Place return message structure here.
01 TPSTATUS-REC.
COPY TPSTATUS.
COPY TPRETURN REPLACING
     TPSVCRET-REC BY TPSVCRET-REC
     TPTYPE-REC BY TPTYPE-REC
     DATA-REC BY DATA-REC
     TPSTATUS-REC BY TPSTATUS-REC.
```

TPRETURN completes a service and returns the message in DATA-REC to the original invoker.

Before calling TPRETURN, the application program must:

- Place a value in TP-RETURN-VAL. This value must be one of the following: TPSUCCESS, TPFAIL, or TPEXIT. Other values are defined for TP-RETURN-VAL, but these are reserved for TUXEDO usage.
- An application defined value may optionally put into APPL-CODE.
- Put the length of *IDATA-REC* in **LEN** in *ITYPE-REC*.
- Put the type of message record *IDATA-REC* is defined as (for instance "STRING") into REC-TYPE in *ITYPE-REC*.
- If the record type is VIEW, put the view name into SUB-TYPE in *ITYPE-REC*, otherwise put spaces in SUB-TYPE.

Note: If the same data area and message record type are being returned as were received by TPSVCSTART, there is no need to modify *TPTYPE-REC* before calling TPRETURN.

The copy book TPRETURN includes an EXIT PROGRAM statement. No application code can be executed after calling TPRETURN.

Because of the EXIT PROGRAM statement in TPRETURN, this function must be called within the main service program.

This function performs the same processing as the C function **tpreturn(3)**.

13.6   OTHER COBOL CONSIDERATIONS

13.6.1   Managing Transactions in COBOL Programs

TUXEDO provides the same set of both **TP*** and **TX*** functions for managing transactions in COBOL as were provided for C. Transactions are managed from COBOL clients and services in the same manner as from C clients and services and application transactions can execute any mix of COBOL and C programs.

The COBOL programmer should remember that a service can work one request at a time. A subsequent request might be for the same or different transaction. No context is saved by TUXEDO once a TPRETURN has been executed.

13.6.2   Conversations and COBOL

TUXEDO provides the same set of functions for using conversations in COBOL as were provided for C. Any mix of C and COBOL may be used in conversations as long as the rules for TUXEDO conversations are followed. The COBOL programmer should remember the requirement to convert between FML and VIEW type records if attempting to communicate with a C program that uses FML for messages.

13.7   SUMMARY OF RULES FOR COBOL

This chapter has provided an overview of using COBOL with TUXEDO. The COBOL programmer should read the rest of the book, or at least the chapters relative to the application at hand, before attempting to create COBOL clients or services. The following rules summarize how to use COBOL with TUXEDO.

- Always use the copy books provided by TUXEDO. Do not attempt to modify them or create a variant.
- When the TUXEDO reference manual specifies a copy book for a function, use the copy book as specified. Do not attempt to modify the copy book or create a direct call to the function.
- Always specify the **LEN** for data records.

- Always test for TPOK or FOK as appropriate after calling TUX-EDO functions.
- Always test for TPTRUNCATE after receiving a record (after TPCALL, TPGETRPLY, TPSVCSTART, etc.)
- If transactions are managed, use either the **TP*** functions or the **TX*** functions. **TP*** and **TX*** cannot be mixed in the same transaction. If COBOL and C programs are being mixed in the same transaction, the rule extends to the C programs also.

Reliable Queues

14.1 OVERVIEW

TUXEDO provides a reliable queuing mechanism, known officially as TUXEDO System/Q. This book uses the term /Q when referring to this feature. /Q is an XA compliant resource manager that provides a mechanism to store messages in reliable storage, which will later be forwarded to services for processing.

/Q provides the following capabilities.

- An application interface to enqueue requests and dequeue previously stored requests.
- There is a mechanism to enforce the processing of each message from the queue no more than once.
- Both the application and the administrator can control the order of messages in the queue. The messages can either be stored LIFO, FIFO, time-based, by priority, or some combination of these keys.
- A service is provided by TUXEDO to do the actual enqueuing or dequeuing.
- A service is provided by TUXEDO to dequeue messages and forward them to application services. This service allows using application services written without /Q code to receive /Q requests.
- A number of administrator features for controlling the behavior of queues.

/Q is useful for a number of application functions. If there is a batch type job which can be started from a TUXEDO transaction, the information can be stored in a reliable queue and processed when convenient. The application storing the information can be sure that the elements of the queue will be processed.

Figure 14.1 illustrates how /Q can be used effectively to maintain a secondary copy of data in another database. Suppose that there is an application that updates the customer database. Suppose further that the database has been partitioned such that the information on customers most likely to use a specific branch office is stored locally at the branch office. There is a requirement to maintain an up-to-date copy of the entire customer database at the home office. The application that updates the local customer master can place a copy of the update into a

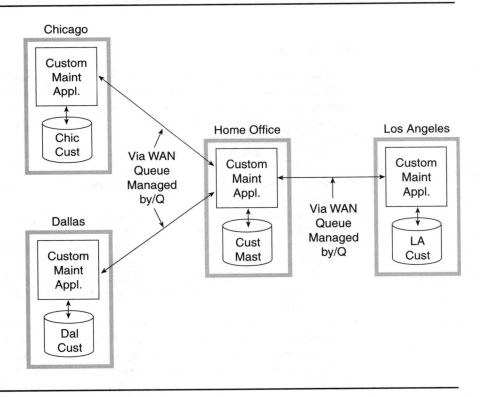

Figure 14.1 Using /Q to maintain a home office customer master.

reliable queue. The queue can be forwarded to the home office via a wide area network, and the updates can be replicated in the home office database. /Q can be used to assure that every update completed at the local office is also completed at the home office.

14.2   HOW /Q WORKS

Figure 14.2 illustrates how /Q works in its simplest form. Both the enqueuing process and the dequeuing process can be a client or a server. The enqueuing process begins a transaction with **tx_begin(3)**. During the processing of the transaction, it enqueues a message with **tpenqueue(3)**. The enqueued message is not made available for dequeuing until the enqueuing process commits the transaction with **tx_commit(3)**. The dequeuing process starts a transaction and in the course of processing the transaction calls **tpdequeue(3)**. **tpdequeue(3)** will deliver a message from the queue. When the **tx_commit(3)** called by the dequeuing process returns successfully, the message has been removed from the queue.

TUXEDO provides a /Q server named TMQUEUE(5). TMQUEUE(5) provides enqueuing and dequeuing services. Arrow (1) in Figure 14.2

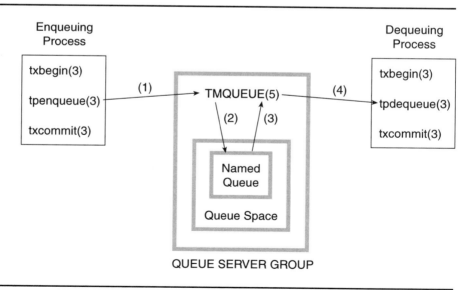

Figure 14.2   A simple view of /Q.

shows that **tpenqueue(3)** sends the message that is to be queued to the enqueuing service provided by **TMQUEUE(5)**, which places the message on the queue named as a parameter in **tpenqueue(3)**. Arrow (2) shows that the enqueuing process places the message on the queue. **tpdequeue(3)**, called by the dequeuing process, invokes the dequeuing service in TMQUEUE(5), which retrieves the message from the queue named by a parameter supplied with **tpdequeue(3)** (arrow (3)) and sends it to the dequeuing service (arrow (4)). The queue space and the queue server group are defined by the administrator.

TUXEDO provides a server called TMQFORWARD(5), which provides a service that will dequeue messages and pass them on to a service not programmed to dequeue /Q messages. This server provides a method to use /Q to invoke services that have been developed to use the standard request/response paradigm. Figure 14.3 illustrates how this feature works.

The application enqueuing process, usually a client, enqueues a message with **tpenqueue(3)** (arrow 1). The message is designated for the queue named Service A. The queuing service in TMQUEUE(5) places the message on the queue Service A. The server TMQFORWARD(5) contains a dequeuing and forwarding service. The service is associated with the queue Service A by the administrator. After the enqueuing process has committed the transaction, the TMQFORWARD(5) dequeuing service starts its own transaction and dequeues the message from Service A (arrow (3)) and forwards the message to application Service A by invoking Service A with a **tpcall(3)** (arrow (4)). TMQFORWARD(5) uses the name of the queue as the name of the service to invoke. Service A processes the data in the message without any knowledge that the message was received via /Q, creates whatever return message it is designed to create, and calls **tpreturn(3)**, which returns the result to the service in TMQFORWARD(5) (arrow (5)).

The service in TMQFORWARD(5) will enqueue the returned message on the reply queue that was named by in the original **tpenqueue(3)** in the enqueuing process (arrow(6)). The enqueuing service will, at some point in time, start another transaction and call **tpdequeue(3)** with the name of the reply queue to retrieve the result of the earlier invocation of Service A via /Q. The **tpdequeue(3)** call causes the dequeuing service to retrieve the reply from the reply queue (arrow (7)) and return it to the enqueuing service (arrow (8)).

During these message exchanges the queue is managed as follows:

1. The original message from the enqueuing process is not available on the queue until the transaction calling **tpenqueue(3)** is committed.
2. TMQFORWARD(5) starts a new transaction before retrieving the

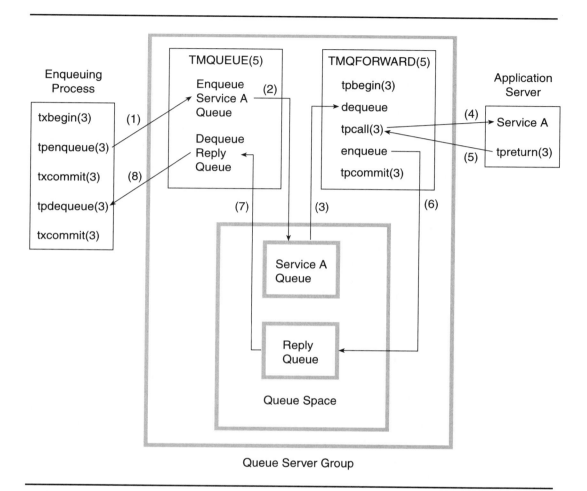

Figure 14.3   Using **TMQFORWARD(5)**.

message from the Service A queue and commits the transaction after Service A has completed successfully. The commit by TMQFORWARD(5) removes the original message from the Service A queue and makes the reply message in the reply queue available.

3. The enqueuing process starts a second transaction where it calls **tpdequeue(3)** to retrieve the response. When the enqueuing process commits the second transaction, the reply message is removed from the reply queue.

Use of TMQFORWARD(5) does not result in high performance, but it does allow using /Q to invoke services that have been developed to work in the normal request/response paradigm.

14.3   DEFINITION OF /Q TERMS

There are three important terms used to refer to entities within /Q: queue device, queue space, and named queue. In the simplest logical sense, the named queue resides within the queue space, which in turn is stored on the queue device. For most practical purposes the simple logical understanding is sufficient. The following definitions provide a more comprehensive look at these ideas. A repeat of the definition of the TUXEDO Universal Device List (UDL) is included for convenience.

Named Queue The *named queue* is the actual queue. It is called a named queue because it must have a name so that applications can reference specific queues. Each queue can have different characteristics. Each named queue resides in a queue space on a queue device. Multiple named queues can be defined within a single queue space.

Queue Device The *queue device* is the device where the queue will be physically stored. Generally the queue device is a UNIX file, but it may be a raw device. The queue device is always specified with a full path name. The queue device is the location of the stable storage used to store named queues. Multiple queue devices may be specified.

Queue Space The *queue space* is the space where named queues reside on the queue device. When the domain is running, the queue space also includes a shared memory segment and a semaphore. Multiple queue spaces may be specified for each queue device.

Universal Device List (UDL) The *universal device list* (UDL) is a list of the devices used by TUXEDO. It contains entries for devices such as the transaction log (TLOG) device and the queue device. Entries in the UDL are created or changed dynamically by using the administration tools. **tmadmin(1)** is used to create and update the entry for the transaction log device. **qmadmin(1)** is used to create and update entries for queue devices.

14.4   /Q ADMINISTRATION

14.4.1   ubbconfig Entries

Since /Q is an XA resource manager, the MACHINES section for each machine where a queue will be used must have a TLOGDEVICE entry as described in Chapter 10.

The following entry must be in the GROUPS section of ubbconfig for each queue space:

```
quegrp    LMID=machine
          TMSNAME=TMS_QM  TMSCOUNT= number
          OPENINFO="TUXEDO/QM: queue_device:queue_space_name"
```

quegrp is the name of the /Q server group. *machine* is the name of the machine where the queues will reside. *number* is the number of copies of the TMS_QM transaction manager server to start. *queue_device* is the device where the queue is stored. *queue_space_name* is the name of the queue space. *queue_device* and *queue_space_name* refer to the names assigned when the queue space is created with **qmadmin(1)**.

The SERVERS section must contain a specification for the TMQUEUE(5) server for each *quegrp*. The best method is to specify the parameters for TMQUEUE(5) in ubbconfig, but it is possible to hard code the parameters by building TMQUEUE(5) with **buildserver(1)**. Normally, TMQUEUE(5) is only rebuilt to add buffer types.

The usual form (see below about server options) of the entry to set the TMQUEUE(5) parameters in ubbconfig is:

```
TMQUEUE   SVRGROUP=" quegrp"
          SRVID= number
          RESTART=Y
          GRACE=0
          CLOPT="-s queue_space_name:TMQUEUE"
```

quegrp is the group name assigned in the groups section to contain the /Q servers. *number* is the server identifier for the TMQUEUE(5) server, and should be set high to allow room for application server identifiers. *queue_space_name* is the name of the queue space the server will manage.

To hard code the *queue_space_name*, use the following command line to rebuild the TMQUEUE(5) server:

```
buildserver -o TMQUEUE -s queue_space_name:TMQUEUE -r TUXEDO/QM \
    f $(TUXDIR)/lib/TMQUEUE.o
```

If TMQUEUE(5) has been rebuilt with **buildserver(1)**, and the **-s** parameter was included with the build as shown above, then the ubbconfig SERVERS entry is:

```
TMQUEUE   SVRGROUP=" quegrp"
          SRVID= number
```

```
                    RESTART=Y
                    GRACE=0
                    CLOPT="-A"
```

Note that TMQUEUE(5) may be rebuilt without the **-s** option when the purpose of the rebuild to support user defined buffer types.

Data dependent routing can be used with TMQUEUE(5) to direct messages to queues based on the data content. To set up data dependent routing for TMQUEUE(5), do the following:

1. Set up queue server groups for multiple queue spaces. The intent is that messages will be queued into different queue spaces depending on the content of the messages. The same queue name will be used in each case.
2. Add the following entry to the SERVICES section of ubbconfig for each service involved in data dependent routing:

```
queue_space_name     ROUTING=criterion_name
```

queue_space_name is the same as explained above. *criterion_name* is the name of the routing criterion.
3. Add the routing criterion using *criterion_name* for identification. See the section on data dependent routing in Chapter 10 for information on how to specify routing criteria.

If queue forwarding is used by the application, a SERVERS section TMQFORWARD(5) entry must be included for each queue group that requires queue forwarding. The usual (see below about server options) form of the entry is:

```
TMQFORWARD     SVRGRP=" quegrp"
               SVID= number
               REPLYQ=N
               RESTART=Y
               GRACE=0
               CLOPT="-A — -q queuename[,queuename...]
                           [-t  trantime] [-i idletime] [-e]
                           [-d] [-n] [-r delay]"
```

quegrp is the group name assigned in the groups section to contain the /Q servers. *number* is the server identifier for the TMQUEUE(5) server, and should be set high to allow room for application server identifiers.

The **CLOPT** parameter provides information and options to TMQFORWARD(5). The options are:

-q *queuename*[,*queuename...*] *queuename* is the name of the queue to be serviced by TMQFORWARD(5). *queuename* must be the same as the service that TMQFORWARD(5) will invoke after dequeuing messages. At least one *queuename* must be specified.

-t *trantime* *trantime* is the timeout value in seconds for the transaction started by TMQFORWARD(5) to dequeue and forward messages. *trantime* defaults to 60 seconds.

-I *idletime* *idletime* is the amount of time TMQFORWARD(5) should wait for additional queue entries after the queues are empty. Before this limit is reached, TMQFORWARD(5) will continually attempt to read the queues. After this limit is reached, TMQFORWARD(5) will wait until there is an entry in a queue before reactivating. A value of zero for *idletime* will cause TMQFORWARD(5) to continually attempt to retrieve messages from the queue. *idletime* defaults to 30 seconds.

-e When this option is specified, TMQFORWARD(5) will exit when idletime is reached. The server will automatically be restarted when messages are again placed on the queue. This feature is discussed in more detail in the section on **qmadmin(1)**.

-d When this option is specified, TMQFORWARD(5) will delete reply messages from services that have failed from the reply queue.

-n When this option is specified, TMQFORWARD(5) invokes the application service with the TPNOTRAN flag set. The **-n** option can be used to forward messages to services that do not use XA resource managers. The **-n** option can also be used to prevent two-phase commit when the application service uses an XA resource manager. To take advantage of this feature, the application service should start a new transaction when invoked. TMQFORWARD(5) waits for a successful return from the application service before committing /Q transaction. If the application succeeds, it returns success with **tpreturn(3)** and TMQFORWARD(5) will commit the queue transaction, thereby deleting the message from the queue. If the application transaction fails, the service should set TPFAIL with **tpreturn(3)**, causing TMQFORWARD(3) to abort the queue transaction, thereby preserving the message.

-f *delay* This option causes TMQFORWARD(5) to use **tpforward(3)** to invoke the application service. *delay* is the amount of time, in seconds, to delay before invoking the service again. *delay* should be specified with some positive value to prevent overloading the system with excessive numbers of messages. *delay* must be specified with this option. If no delay is desired, set *delay* to zero. When this option is used, no reply is expected and as soon as the dequeued message is successfully forwarded (successful return from **tpforward(3)**), the transaction will be committed and the message deleted from the queue.

A typical entry for TMQFORWARD(5) is:

```
TMQFORWARD     SRVGRP=QUEGRP
               SRVID=999
               GRACE=0
               RESTART=Y
               CLOPT="-A — -i 5 -q custupd1, custupd2"
```

Usually the **CLOPT** parameter for TMQUEUE(5) and TMQFORWARD(5) can be used as described above. It is possible to use all the servopts(5) options for each of these servers, but note the following:

- The **-A** option has little effect on TMQUEUE(5) since all services should be specifically defined for TMQUEUE(5) with the **-s** option.
- The **-s** option should always be used for TMQUEUE(5), as shown above.
- The **-n** option should not be used for either TMQUEUE(5) or TMQFORWARD(5), unless the clients and servers associated with them can be allowed the potential delays caused by nicing these servers.

14.4.2   Environment Variables for /Q

The environment for the application using /Q must contain the full path name of the file or raw device that will contain the queue devices in the environment variable QMCONFIG. QMCONFIG must be set before queue devices can be created. The following script was used to set up environment variables for /Q:

```
TUXDIR=/home/tuxdir; export TUXDIR
TUXCONFIG=/home/clh/qapp/qconfig; export TUXCONFIG
PATH=$TUXDIR/bin:/home/clh/qapp:$PATH; export PATH
QMCONFIG=/home/clh/qapp/CUSTQ; export QMCONFIG

FLDTBLDIR=/home/clh/qapp:$TUXDIR/udataobj; export FLDTBLDIR
FIELDTBLS=fmlflds,Usysflds; export FIELDTBLS
```

```
LD_LIBRARY_PATH=$TUXDIR/lib:$LD_LIBRARY_PATH
export LD_LIBRARY_PATH
```

14.4.3   **Creating Queue Devices, Queue Spaces, and Queues**

Queue devices, queue spaces, and queues must be created before /Q can be used. The utility **qmadmin(1)** is used to create these objects. The order of creation must be:

1. Create queue devices
2. Create queue spaces in the devices
3. Create the queues in the queue spaces

It is not necessary to create all devices before creating queue spaces, it is only necessary that the device that contains the queue space is created before attempting to create the queue space. Queues can only be created after the queue space that contains them has been created.

The following interaction with **qmadmin(1)** creates one queue device, one queue space, and two queues:

```
qmadmin - Copyright © 1987 - 1990 AT&T; 1991 - 1993 USL; 1994
Novell. All rights reserved.
QMCONFIG=/home/clh/qapp/CUSTQ
> #  Create a device.
> crdl /home/clh/qapp/CUSTQ 0 200
Created device /home/clh/qapp/CUSTQ, offset 0, size 200 on
/home/clh/qapp/CUSTQ
> #
> # Create a queue space
> qspacecreate
Queue space name: CUSTQSPC
IPC Key for queue space: 23456
Size of queue space in disk pages: 160
Number of queues in queue space: 2
Number of concurrent transactions in queue space: 5
Number of concurrent processes in queue space: 5
Number of messages in queue space: 10
Error queue name: errq
Initialize extents (y or n - default no): y
Blocking factor (default 16):
> #
```

```
> # Open queue space
> qopen CUSTQSPC
> #
> # Create queue CUSTQ
> qcreate
Queue name: CUSTQ
Queue order (fifo, lifo, priority, time): fifo
Out-of-ordering enqueuing (none, top, msgid): none
Retries: 1
Retry delay in seconds: 10
High limit for queue capacity warning ( b for bytes used,
B for blocks used, % for percent used, m for messages): 90%
Reset (low) limit for queue capacity warning: 0%
Queue capacity command:
No default queue capacity command
Queue CUSTQ created
> #
> # Create queue errq
> qcreate
Queue name: errq
Queue order (fifo, lifo, priority, time): fifo
Out-of-ordering enqueuing (none, top, msgid): none
Retries: 0
Retry delay in seconds: 10
High limit for queue capacity warning ( b for bytes used,
B for blocks used, % for percent used, m for messages): 100%
Reset (low) limit for queue capacity warning: 0%
Queue capacity command:
No default queue capacity command
Queue errq created
> #
> # All done so quit
> q
```

14.4.4   More about qmadmin(1)

qmadmin(1) is an interactive utility used to administer /Q. **qmadmin(1)**
may be used at any time, with certain logical limitations on what can be
changed based on the conditions of the referenced queue space and queue.
The previous section illustrated how to create queue devices, queue spaces,
and queues. **qmadmin(1)** provides an extensive set of operations to retrieve information about queue spaces and queues, change characteristics

of queue spaces and queues, and destroy queue spaces and queues. Under some circumstances individual messages can also be retrieved and deleted. Note that even if a device is set in QMCONFIG, there is no usable device until one is created with the **crdl** command as shown above.

qmadmin(1) attaches to a queue device when executed from the command line. If **qmadmin(1)** is entered without specifying a queue device, it attempts to attach to a queue device as specified in the environment variable QMCONFIG. If it is executed with a device specified, **qmadmin(1)** will attach to the specified queue device. The device must be specified with a full path name. A queue device specified on the command line will override the value in QMCONFIG. The following command line will cause **qmadmin(1)** to attach to /home/clh/qapp/otherq:

```
qmadmin /home/clh/qapp/otherq
```

When **qmadmin(1)** is executed from the command line, it displays the copyright notice and the value of QMCONFIG, then displays the command prompt, a greater than sign (>) and waits for a command. The command **help** (or **h**) displays a list of commands with their parameters. Most commands may be entered without parameters and will then prompt for the required information. Queue devices and queue spaces may be addressed directly. Queues may be accessed only after opening a queue space with the command **qopen**. Messages may be accessed in an open queue space only after setting the queue name with the **qset** command.

Some important commands follow:

crdl [device [offset [size]]]: crdl creates a device and registers it in the UDL.

qaddext [queue_space_name [pages]]: qaddext adds disk space to the queue space to allow more messages to be queued.

qclose: qclose closes the queue space that is currently open.

qchange [queue_name [out-of-order [retries [delay [high [low [cmd]]]]]]]: qchange changes the characteristics of a queue. The queue must be open before this command is used.

qcreate (qcr) [queue_name [qorder [out-of-order [retries [delay [high [low [cmd]]]]]]]]: qcreate creates a named queue in the open queue space. A queue space must be open before this command is used.

qdeletemsg (qdltm) [-y]: qdeletemsg deletes a message that was previously selected by the **qscan** command. If the **-y** option is not specified, **qdeletemsg** prompts for confirmation before the message is deleted.

qdestroy (qds) [{-p | -f}] [-y] [queue_name]: qdestroy destroys the named queue. If no options are specified the queue will not be destroyed if there is a message on the queue or if there is a process attached to the queue. If the **-p** option is specified, the queue will be destroyed even if there are messages on the queue, but only if there are no processes attached to the queue. If the **-f** option is specified, the queue will be destroyed unconditionally. If the **-y** option is not specified, **qdestroy** prompts for confirmation before destroying the queue. The queue space must be open before using this command.

qinfo [*queue_name*]: qinfo lists information about queues in the open queue space. If no queue name is specified with the command, the information for all queues in the queue space is listed. The queue space must be open before using this command.

qlist (ql): qlist lists information on messages in a queue. The queue must have been selected by the **qset** command before this command is used.

qopen [queue_space_name]: qopen opens a queue space to allow use of commands that apply to individual named queues.

qscan [{ [-t time1[-time2]] [-p priority1[-priority2]] [-m msgid] [-I corrid] | none}]: qscan selects an individual message on a queue. The queue must be previously selected with the **qset** command. **qscan** does not prompt for selection criteria so the message selection criteria must be set with the command. If multiple criteria are specified, they are and'd together to make the selection.

qset [queue_name]: qset selects a named queue for use in queue specific commands. Each time **qset** is used, any previously selected queues are deselected and the new queue selected. The queue space must be open before using this command.

qspacechange (qspch) [queue_space_name [ipckey [trans [procs [messages [errorq [inityn [blocking]]]]]]]]: qspacechange changes the characteristics of a queue space. All characteristics except the number of queues allowed are changed.

qspacecreate (qspc) [queue_space_name [ipckey [pages [queues [trans [procs [messages[errorq[inityn[blocking]]]]]]]]]]: qspacecreate creates a queue space in the device that **qmadmin(1)** attached to when it was executed.

qspacedestroy (qspds) [-f] [-y] [queue_space_name]: qspacedestroy destroys a queue space. If the **-f** option is not specified, the space will not be destroyed if any messages exist within any queues in the queue space or a process is attached to the queue space. If the **-f** option is specified the queue space is destroyed unconditionally. If the **-y** option is not specified, **qspacedestroy** prompts for confirmation before destroying the queue space.

qspacelist (qspl) [queue_space_name]: **qspacelist** lists the characteristics of a queue space.

quit (q): **quit** shuts off **qmadmin(1)**.

Many of the commands have short forms. The short forms are shown in parentheses.

Some of the commands require that other commands have been previously executed. For instance, the following sequence is required to delete a message from a queue:

1. Open the queue space with **qopen**.
2. Select the queue with **qset**.
3. List the messages with **qlist** to determine the identifying values, unless these are already known.
4. Select the message with **qscan**.
5. Execute **qdeletemsg** to delete the message.

14.5 /Q PROGRAMMING

14.5.1 Overview

Any client or server can enqueue onto and dequeue messages from queues. Messages are enqueued with the function **tpenqueue(3)** and dequeued with the function **tpdequeue(3)**. These functions can be called while the process is in transaction mode, but need not be. Messages enqueued while in transaction mode cannot be dequeued until after the transaction is committed. Messages cannot be enqueued, then dequeued in the same transaction.

If a process is not in transaction mode when **tpenqueue(3)** is called, a separate transaction is started by TUXEDO to do the enqueuing; in this case, when **tpenqueue(3)** returns successfully, the calling process can be sure that the message has been placed on the queue. If a process is not in transaction mode when **tpdequeue(3)** is called, a separate transaction is started by TUXEDO to do the dequeuing and the calling process can be sure that the message has been deleted from the queue when **tpdequeue(3)** returns successfully. In either case, if the calling process fails before the function returns, the only way to determine if the function was successful is by use of **qmadmin(1)** to examine the queues for the message, or by attempting to dequeue it.

If a process calls **tpenqueue(3)** while in transaction mode, the message will be successfully enqueued if the transaction commits successfully. If the transaction aborts, the message is not on the queue. If a process calls **tpdequeue(3)** while in transaction mode, the message will be deleted from the queue when the transaction commits. If the transaction aborts, the message is not deleted. A process can call **tpenqueue(3)** multiple times in the same transaction, with the same rule applied to all messages. If a process calls **tpdequeue(3)** multiple times in the same transaction, each call will return a message from further down in the queue; no message will be returned more than once. If multiple messages have been retrieved in the same transaction, all will be deleted when the transaction is committed.

/Q messages are typed buffers. Any typed buffer provided with TUXEDO may be used to contain or receive a message.

14.5.2   The TPQCTL **Structure**

Both **tpenqueue(3)** and **tpdequeue(3)** include a pointer to a TPQCTL structure. While use of this structure is optional, its use facilitates using queues most efficiently. For instance, the fact that **tpdequeue(3)** failed because the queue is empty is returned in this structure. The fields in the structure are:

long flags The content of **flags** controls action with the queue. Flag values may be combined by or'ing them in the usual way, as long as the combination is valid for the function. The available flags and their meaning is included with the descriptions of **tpenqueue(3)** and **tpdequeue(3)**.

long deq_time The contents of **deq_time** are used to order the queue by time when the queue was created with time as an ordering parameter. The time may be expressed as absolute time by setting flags to TPQTIME_ABS or relative time with flags set to TQPTIME_REL.

long priority If the queue was created with priority as a queue ordering parameter, the value in the field priority is used as the priority. The value in priority may be in the range 1 through 100. If a value is put in this field, set the flag TPQPRIORITY. If the queue was not created with priority as one of the ordering parameters, the value in this field and the flag TPQPRIORITY are ignored.

long diagnostic When **tpenqueue(3)** or **tpdequeue(3)** return with the tperrno set to TPEDIAGNOSTIC, this field is set to show

the actual error. The specific errors are listed in the description of
tpenqueue(3) and **tpdequeue(3)**.

char msgid[32] If flags is set to TPQMSGID, **tpenqueue(3)** places
the message identifier for the retrieved message into msgid.

char corrid[32] The value in corrid is used to match messages with
replies. It may also be used in application specific ways. More information on this identifier is included in the descriptions of **tpenqueue(3)**
and **tpdequeue(3)**.

char replyqueue[16] The contents of replyqueue name the queue
for a reply message. The name of a reply message must be provided
when using the message forwarding feature and a reply is expected.
The flag TPREPLYQ must be set to indicate that a reply is expected.

char failurequeue[16] The value in failurequeue names a queue
where a failure message will be placed if dequeuing the message fails.
The flag TPQFAILUREQ must be set to implement this feature.

CLIENTID cltid When a message is dequeued, the client identifier of the originating client is placed in cltid. The client identifier is
created by TUXEDO.

long urcode urcode may be set by the application process that calls
tpenqueue(3). The value is returned when messages are dequeued.

long appkey appkey is the application authorization key. The
value is created by the authorization service and propagated by
TUXEDO. A service invoked by TMQFORWARD(3) will receive the
appkey in TPSVCINFO. A process that dequeues a message can use
the appkey in TPQCTL to verify authorization.

The pointer to TPQCTL may be set to NULL in both **tpenqueue(3)**
and **tpdequeue(3)**. If NULL is specified, the flags variable is assumed
to be TPNOFLAGS and the values that may be returned in TPQCTL
are not available to the program.

14.5.3   **A Description of** tpenqueue(3)

The form of **tpenqueue(3)** is:

```
int tpenqueue(char *qspace, char *qname, TPQCTL *qctl,
    char *data, long len, long flags)
```

qspace is a pointer to the name of the queue space containing the
queue where the message is to be enqueued. qname is a pointer to the
name of the queue where the message is to be enqueued. qctl is a pointer

to the TPQCTL structure. data is a pointer to the data that is to be enqueued. data must point to a typed buffer and the buffer type must be known to TUXEDO and to TMQUEUE(5). If the forwarding feature is being used, the buffer type must also be known to TMQFORWARD(5). Both TMQUEUE(5) and TMQFORWARD(5) recognize the buffer types supplied with TUXEDO. len is the length of the data. If the data length can be inferred by the buffer type, such as for FML buffers, len is ignored. **flags** can be set with the same meanings as with other ATMI functions. The valid flags for **tpenqueue(3)** are: TPNOTRAN, TPNOBLOCK, TPNOTIME, and TPSIGRSTRT.

    tpenqueue(3) enqueues a message to the queue named by qname in the queue space named by qspace. If the process calling **tpenqueue(3)** is in transaction mode, the message will be successfully enqueued when the transaction is committed successfully. If the calling process is not in transaction mode or the TPNOTRAN flag is set, a new transaction is started, the message is enqueued and the transaction is committed. In this case, when **tpenqueue(3)** returns successfully, the message has been reliably placed on the queue.

    The following values may be set in **flags** in TPQCTL.

TPNOFLAGS This setting means that there are not flags set.

TPQCORRID This value must be set if a correlation identifier is provided in qctl.corrid to enable /Q to use the correlation identifier.

TPQFAILUREQ Set this value when an error queue is named in qctl.failurequeue to enable /Q to use the named error queue.

TPQBEFOREMSGID If this value is set in **flags**, the message will be placed ahead of the message identified in qctl.msgid if the queue was created with a characteristic allowing out of order queuing. TPQTOP and TPQBEFOREMSGID are mutually exclusive and a TPEINVAL error will occur if both are specified.

TPQMSGID If this value is set in **flags**, the message identifier of the queued message will be placed in qctl.msgid when **tpenqueue(3)** returns successfully.

TPQPRIORITY This flag must be set if a value has been placed in qctl.priority to enable /Q to enqueue based on priority.

TPQTOP If this value is set in **flags**, the message will be placed ahead of all messages in the queue if the queue was created with a characteristic allowing out of order queuing. TPQTOP and TPQBEFOREMSGID are mutually exclusive and a TPEINVAL error will occur if both are specified.

TPQREPLYQ This value must be set in **flags** if a reply queue was named in qctl.replyqueue to enable /Q to place the expected reply in the named queue.

TPQTIME_ABS If this value is set in **flags**, the enqueued message will be made available after the time set in qctl.deq_time. See the description of deq_time on how to set the absolute time.

TPQTIME_REL If this value is set in **flags**, the enqueued message will be made available after the number of seconds set in qctl.deq_time, counting from the time the enqueuing transaction is committed.

If the qctl pointer is specified with **tpenqueue(3)**, the following fields in TPQCTL may be populated before calling the function:

flags flags must contain a valid combination of the flags mentioned above.

long deq_time If TPQTIME_ABS is set in **flags**, deq_time must contain the absolute time when the queued message will be made available. Use the C function **mktime()** to load deq_time with the absolute time. If TPQTIME_REL is set in **flags**, deq_time must contain the time in seconds to wait after the message is enqueued and committed before making the message available.

long priority If the queue was created with priority as a queue ordering parameter, the value in the field priority is used as the priority. The value in priority may be in the range of 1 through 100. If a value is put in this field, set the flag TPQPRIORITY. If the queue was not created with priority as one of the ordering parameters, the value in this field and the flag TPQPRIORITY are ignored.

char msgid[32] If TPQBEFOREMSGID is set in **flags**, msgid must contain the message identifier that will immediately follow the current message. If **flags** is set to TPQMSGID, **tpenqueue(3)** places the message identifier for the enqueued message into msgid.

char corrid[32] The value in corrid is used to match messages with replies. It may also be used in application specific ways. If this value is specified, set TPQCORRID in **flags**.

char replyqueue[16] The contents of replyqueue name the queue for a reply message. The name of a reply message must be provided when using the message forwarding feature and a reply is expected. The flag TPREPLYQ must be set to indicate that a reply is expected.

char failurequeue[16] The value in failurequeue names a queue where a failure message will be placed if dequeuing the message fails. The flag TPQFAILUREQ must be set to implement this feature.

long urcode urcode may be set by the application process that calls **tpenqueue(3)**. The value is returned when messages are dequeued.

When **tpenqueue(3)** returns, the following fields in TPQCTL may be populated.

long flags If **tpenqueue(3)** returns successfully, **flags** will contain the value for the actual flags implemented when the message was enqueued. For instance, if TPQTOP was specified, but the queue was defined such that out of order queuing is not allowed, TPQTOP will be off in the flags value returned.

char msgid[32] When **tpenqueue(3)** returns successfully, the message identifier of the enqueued message will be in msgid.

long diagnostic If **tpenqueue(3)** fails with tperrno set to TPEDIAGNOSTIC, diagnostic will contain a value that indicates which error specific to **tpenqueue(3)** caused the failure.

tpenqueue(3) returns 0 for success and –1 for failure. Programs should test for less than zero to determine success or failure. If **tpenqueue(3)** fails, tperrno is set to indicate the type of failure. The usual failure types are returned. TPEDIAGNOSTIC set in tperrno indicates that the actual failure indicator is stored in qctl.diagnostic. The values usually caused by program failure for diagnostic are:

QMEINVAL The value in qctl.flags was invalid.

QMEBADMSGID The flag TPQBEFOREMSGID was specified, but the value in msgid was invalid.

QMEABORTED The transaction that attempted to enqueue the message was aborted. If the calling process was in transaction mode, that transaction is set to abort only.

QMEBADQUEUE The queue named in qname does not exist in the queue space named in qspace.

14.5.4   A Description of tpdequeue(3)

The form of **tpdequeue(3)** is:

```
int tpdequeue(char *qspace, char *qname, TPQCTL *qctl,
    char **data, long *len, long flags)
```

qspace is a pointer to the name of the queue space containing the queue from which the message is to be dequeued. qname is a pointer to the name of the queue from which the message is to be dequeued. qctl is a pointer to the TPQCTL structure. **data is the address of a pointer to the area where the dequeued data is to be. *data must point to an area allocated with **tpalloc(3)**. *len is a pointer to a field containing the length of the data area. len must not be 0. When **tpdequeue(3)** returns successfully, the actual length of the data stored is placed in *len. **flags** can be set with the same meanings as with other ATMI functions. The valid flags for **tpdequeue(3)** are: TPNOTRAN, TPNOBLOCK, TPNOTIME, TPNOCHANGE, and TPSIGRSTRT.

tpdequeue(3) dequeues a message from the queue named by qname in the queue space named by qspace and places it in the data area pointed to by *data. If the process calling **tpdequeue(3)** is in transaction mode, the message will be deleted when the transaction is committed successfully. If the calling process is not in transaction mode or the TPNOTRAN flag is set, a new transaction is started, the message is dequeued and the transaction is committed, causing the message to be deleted. In this case, when **tpdequeue(3)** returns successfully, the message has been deleted from the queue.

The following values may be set in **flags** in TPQCTL.

TPNOFLAGS This setting means that there are no flags set.

TPQGETBYMSGID When this flag is set, **tpdequeue(3)** uses the value in **qctl.msgid** to find the message to dequeue. TPQGETBYMSGID and TPQWAIT are mutually exclusive. If both are specified, **tpdequeue(3)** fails with QMEINVAL set in qctl.diagnostic.

TPQGETBYCORRID If TPQGETBYCORRID is set in flags, **tpdequeue(3)** uses the value in qctl.corrid to find the message to dequeue. TPQGETBYCORRID and TPQWAIT are mutually exclusive. If both are specified, **tpdequeue(3)** fails with QMEINVAL set in qctl.diagnostic.

TPQWAIT If this flag is set, and the queue is empty, **tpdequeue(3)** will wait until another message is available, then dequeue it. If this flag is not set and the queue is empty, **tpdequeue(3)** returns with a QMENOMSG error set in qctl.diagnostic.

TPQCORRID If this value is set in **flags**, the correlation identifier associated with the dequeued message will be stored in qctl.corrid when tpdequeue(3) returns successfully.

TPQFAILUREQ If this value is set in **flags**, the failure queue name associated with the dequeued message will be returned in qctl.failurequeue. The process doing the dequeuing should use this queue name to enqueue failure messages.

TPQMSGID If this value is set in **flags**, the message identifier of the dequeued message will be placed in qctl.msgid when **tpdequeue(3)** returns successfully.

TPQPRIORITY If this value is set in **flags**, the priority of the dequeued message will be placed in qctl.priority when **tpdequeue(3)** returns successfully.

TPQREPLYQ If this value is set in **flags**, the name of the reply queue associated with dequeued message will be placed in qctl.replyqueue when **tpdequeue(3)** returns successfully.

If the qctl pointer is specified with **tpdequeue(3)**, the following fields in TPQCTL may be populated before calling the function.

flags: flags must contain a valid combination of the flags mentioned above.

char msgid[32] If **flags** is set to TPQGETBYMSGID, **tpdequeue(3)** will attempt to retrieve a message with the message identifier equal to msgid.

char corrid[32] If **flags** is set to TPQGETBYCORRID, **tpdequeue(3)** will attempt to retrieve a message with the correlation identifier equal to corrid. If **flags** is set to TPQCORRID, the correlation identifier of the dequeued message is placed in corrid when **tpdequeue(3)** completes successfully.

When **tpdequeue(3)** returns, the following fields in TPQCTL may be populated:

long flags If **tpdequeue(3)** returns successfully, **flags** will contain the value for the actual **flags** implemented.

char msgid[32] If **flags** is set to TPQMSGID, the message identifier of the dequeued message is placed in msgid when **tpdequeue(3)** completes successfully.

char corrid[32] If **flags** is set to TPQCORRID, the correlation identifier of the dequeued message is placed in **corrid** when **tpdequeue(3)** completes successfully.

char replyqueue[16] If TPQREPLYQ is set in **flags** before **tpdequeue(3)** is called and the message was enqueued with a reply queue name, the reply queue name is stored in replyqueue when **tpdequeue(3)** returns successfully.

char failurequeue[16] If TPQFAILUREQ is set in **flags** before **tpdequeue(3)** is called and the message was enqueued with a failure queue name, the failure queue name is stored in failurequeue when **tpdequeue(3)** returns successfully.

long urcode urcode will contain the value placed in urcode when the message was enqueued upon successful return from **tpdequeue(3)**.

long appkey If an authorization key is available and **tpdequeue(3)** returns successfully, appkey will contain the authorization key.

long diagnostic If **tpdequeue(3)** fails with tperrno set to TPEDIAGNOSTIC, diagnostic will contain a value that indicates which error specific to **tpdequeue(3)** caused the failure.

tpdequeue(3) returns 0 for success and –1 for failure. Programs should test for less than zero to determine success or failure. If **tpdequeue(3)** fails, tperrno is set to indicate the type of failure. The usual failure types are returned. TPEDIAGNOSTIC set in tperrno indicates that the actual failure indicator is stored in qctl.diagnostic. The values usually caused by program failure for diagnostic are:

QMEINVAL The value in qctl.flags was invalid.

QMEBADMSGID The flag TPQGETBYMSGID was specified, but no message was found with a message identifier equal to the value in msgid.

QMEINUSE If either TPQGETBYMSGID or TPQGETBYCORRID was set, the selected message has been dequeued by a transaction that has not yet completed. Otherwise, all messages in the queue were in use by a transaction that has not yet completed. This error will occur when **tpdequeue(3)** attempts to retrieve a message that has already been dequeued within the current transaction. If a process is attempting to retrieve all messages on the queue in the same transaction, this error can be used to indicate that all available messages have been retrieved.

QMEABORTED The transaction that attempted to dequeue the message was aborted. If the calling process was in transaction mode, that transaction is set to abort only.

QMEBADQUEUE The queue named in qname does not exist in the queue space named in qspace.

QMENOMSG This value indicates that there are no messages on the queue available for dequeuing.

14.5.5 **Programming Tips**

Use the following rules when programming with /Q.

- Always use the TPQCTL structure, even if nothing is populated so that errors can be detected properly.
- If not using a field can be used as input to **tpenqueue(3)** or **tpdequeue(3)**, populate the field with a 0 or NULL. That is, populate a numeric field with 0 and populate the first character of a string with NULL. Populate **flags** with TPNOFLAG if not using **flags**.
- Always test tperrno for TPEDIAGNOSTIC if the enqueue or dequeue function fails. If TPEDIAGNOSTIC is set, test qctl.diagnostic to determine the actual error.
- If the enqueued message is intended for forwarding, be sure the name of the queue is equal to the name of the service it is intended for.
- If a reply queue is used when forwarding, be sure to dequeue the reply queue in another transaction.
- If an error queue is used, always dequeue the error queue when an error is detected.
- If either **tpenqueue(3)** or **tpdequeue(3)** fails, it is a good idea to wait a second or two, then try again. This can be especially important when enqueuing or dequeuing over a WAN.

If TPQWAIT is set for **tpenqueue(3)**, the enqueuing process will be blocked if TMQUEUE(5) is busy. If TPQWAIT is set for **tpdequeue(3)**, the dequeuing process will be blocked either if TPQUEUE(5) is busy or there are no available messages on the queue. Remember that using TPQWAIT in qctl.flags is not consistent with TPNOBLOCK set in the **flags** parameter of the function. The amount of time that the calling process is blocked by **TPQWAIT** is set by the administrator when defining TPQUEUE(5) in ubbconfig. This time can be overridden by setting the TPNOTIME flag as a parameter when calling the function. TPQWAIT does not prevent transaction timeout, so the program must be written to handle this situation.

14.6 **A SAMPLE APPLICATION**

A potential use of /Q was described in the beginning of this chapter. The discussion in this section will describe the design in more detail. The application as shown has been purposely kept simple in order to best illustrate the use of /Q. There are other applications that use the customer database at each location, and the hooks to them are not shown.

A sample of some of the code for the application is included with other coding samples in Appendix D.

Figure 14.4 is repeated from the earlier description to show the topology of the application. The enterprise maintains branch offices in Chicago, Dallas, and Los Angeles. The home office is in none of those cities. The customer database has been partitioned by location to provide very high performance of the customer maintenance application via a local LAN at each branch office. There is a policy that requires a complete up-to-date copy of the entire customer database at the home office. In reality, there will always be some delay between the time a change is made to a local database and when that same update is made at the home office, but the goal is to minimize that time.

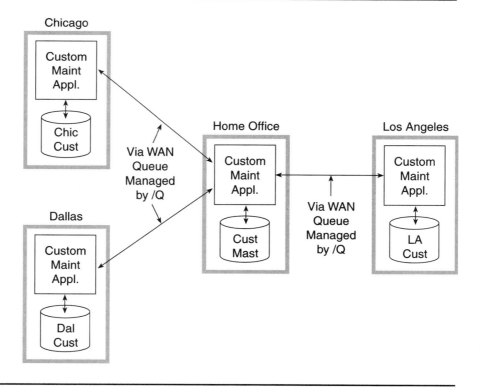

Figure 14.4   Using /Q to maintain the home office database.

Figure 14.5 shows the detail of the design. The customer maintenance client and the customer update service operate in the normal request/response paradigm at a branch office. The customer update service performs the necessary updates to the local customer database in the transaction started by the customer maintenance client. The customer update service uses a **tpacall(3)**, with the TPNOTRAN flag set, to invoke the customer enqueue service with the same request that the client maintenance client sent. The customer enqueue service enqueues the message on the local queue called CUSTQ. At the home office, the native client, customer master client, starts a transaction and invokes the branch office customer dequeue service to retrieve the message, then passes the message to the home office customer update service.

The branch office customer update service uses **tpacall(3)** to invoke a separate enqueuing service instead of calling **tpenqueue(3)** to maintain as high a performance level as possible. The enqueuing is done in a separate transaction to prevent causing a two-phase commit, again to maintain as high a performance as possible. There is no loss of integrity between the update of the database and the enqueuing at the local office because the customer update service retrieves the reply from the customer enqueuing service before doing a **tpreturn(3)**. If the enqueuing process fails, the enqueuing service will return with the TPFAIL flag set, alerting the customer update service of the failure. The customer update service will then return to the customer maintenance client with the TPFAIL flag set, and the customer update service will abort the transaction. The user can then enter the transaction again.

The home office master client includes both the dequeuing service and the customer update service in the same transaction, incurring a two-phase commit. This simpler approach is used because the performance at the home office is not as critical.

Several variations are possible. If it is not required that the home office database be quite so current, the home office master client could be run periodically using the UNIX **cron** mechanism. In this case, the customer dequeue service at the branch office could dequeue blocks of data. Each time the home office client is run, the customer dequeue service would retrieve a block of data and update the home office database in a single transaction per block. The client would run until there was nothing left on the queue and stop. If a daily update is sufficient, the home office client could be run once a day at off-peak hours, so as not to load the WAN while it is being heavily used by daily activities. If there are several branch offices, either a separate home office client could be run for each, or data dependent routing could be used to cycle the requests to the dequeuing service at each branch office in turn.

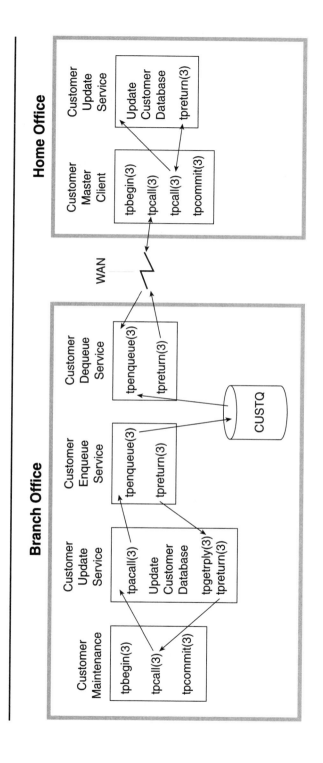

Figure 14.5 Maintaining the home office database.

Another variation of the design would place the enqueue service at the home office. The only problem with this arrangement is that it could adversely affect the performance of the branch office system, perhaps having a negative effect on daily activities. The problem could become especially acute if the WAN failed. In most cases, the queuing should be done locally, to protect the system from communication weaknesses.

The ubbconfig file for this application might look as follows:

```
*RESOURCES
IPCKEY          52617
MASTER          HOMEOFC
MODEL           MP
#
*MACHINES
#
unix1
     LMID = HOMEOFC
     TUXDIR ="/home/tuxdir"
     TUXCONFIG = "/home/clh/qapp/qbkconfig"
     TLOGDEVICE ="/home/clh/qapp/TLOG"
     TLOGSIZE=10
     APPDIR = "/home/clh/qapp"
     ULOGPFX = "/home/clh/qapp/ULOG"


unix2
     LMID = DALLAS
     TUXDIR ="/home/tuxdir"
     TUXCONFIG = "/home/clh/qapp/qbkconfig"
     TLOGDEVICE ="/home/clh/qapp/TLOG"
     TLOGSIZE=10
     APPDIR = "/home/clh/qapp"
     ULOGPFX = "/home/clh/qapp/ULOG"
#
*GROUPS

DALGRP1
     LMID = DALLAS   GRPNO = 1
     TMSNAME=TMS TMSCOUNT=2
QUEGRPD
     LMID = DALLAS   GRPNO = 2
     TMSNAME = TMS_QM TMSCOUNT = 2
     OPENINFO = "TUXEDO/QM:/home/clh/qapp/CUSTQ:DCUSTQSPC"
```

```
#
HOMGRP1
     LMID = HOMEOFC GRPNO = 10
     TMSNAME=TMS TMSCOUNT=2
QUEGRPH
     LMID = HOMEOFC GRPNO = 11
     TMSNAME = TMS_QM TMSCOUNT = 2
     OPENINFO = "TUXEDO/QM:/home/clh/qapp/CUSTQ:HCUSTQSPC"
#
*SERVERS
#
DEFAULT:  CLOPT="-A"
custsv          SRVGRP=DALGRP1
          SRVID=1
          CLOPT="-A - DCUSTQSPC"
deqsv           SRVGRP=DALGRP1 SRVID=2
          CLOPT="-A - DCUSTQSPC"
enqsv           SRVGRP=DALGRP1 SRVID=3
          CLOPT="-A - DCUSTQSPC"


custsv          SRVGRP=HOMGRP1
          SRVID=1
          CLOPT="-A - HCUSTQSPC"
deqsv           SRVGRP=HOMGRP1 SRVID=2
          CLOPT="-A - HCUSTQSPC"
enqsv           SRVGRP=HOMGRP1 SRVID=3
          CLOPT="-A - HCUSTQSPC"


TMQUEUE
     SRVGRP = QUEGRPD  SRVID = 1
     GRACE = 0  RESTART = Y CONV = N
     CLOPT = "-s DCUSTQSPC:TMQUEUE -  "


TMQUEUE
     SRVGRP = QUEGRPH  SRVID = 1
     GRACE = 0  RESTART = Y CONV = N
     CLOPT = "-s HCUSTQSPC:TMQUEUE -  "


*SERVICES
custupd   ROUTING="custrout"
enqsvc    ROUTING="enqrout"
deqsvc    ROUTING="deqrout"
```

```
#
*ROUTING
custrout
     FIELD=location BUFTYPE="FML"
     RANGES="'D':DALGRP1,'H':HOMGRP1"

enqrout
     FIELD=location BUFTYPE="FML"
     RANGES="'D':DALGRP1,'H':HOMGRP1"

deqrout
     FIELD=location BUFTYPE="FML"
     RANGES="'D':DALGRP1,'H':HOMGRP1"
```

This configuration allows using the exact same customer update and enqueuing and dequeuing servers in all branch offices and the home office. Note that the name of the local queue space is passed as a **CLOPT** parameter to these services. The same customer maintenance client may also be used in all branch offices and the home office. Note that if updates are done in the home office, they will be enqueued in the same manner as in the branch offices, and the home office dequeuing client will dequeue from the home office queue in the same way that it dequeues from all other queues.

The data dependent routing will cause updates to the customer database to be routed to the branch office where the customer is normally processed no matter where the customer maintenance client is located.

15

X/Open Transaction
Processing Interfaces

15.1 OVERVIEW

X/Open Company, Ltd. is an independent, worldwide, open systems organization supported by most of the world's largest information systems suppliers, user organizations, and software companies. X/Open provides specifications to support open systems. These specifications become de facto standards to most enterprises.

TUXEDO currently provides compliance with the following X/Open specifications for distributed transaction processing:

- A *Guide, Distributed Transaction Processing: Reference Model Version 2*, which describes the X/Open model for distributed transaction processing.
- The *Preliminary Specification, Distributed Transaction Processing*: *The XATMI Specification* that defines the client/server API.
- *The Preliminary Specification, Distributed Transaction Processing*: The *TX (Transaction Demarcation) Specification* that defines an API to manage transaction boundaries.
- The *Preliminary Specification, Distributed Transaction Processing*: *The TxRPC Specification* that defines an interface to apply transactional semantics to RPC based on OSI-TP protocols. TUXEDO provides a means to use the OSF Distributed Computing Environment (DCE) with TxRPC.
- The *CAE Specification Distributed Transaction Processing: The XA*

specification that defines the distributed transaction model and the API for the interface between the transaction manager and resource managers.

X/Open is currently working on a number of additional distributed transaction processing specifications such as peer-to-peer, extended communications manager functionality, and CPI-C. Novell states that TUXEDO will become compliant to these specifications as soon as practical after the work has reached the point where a preliminary specification is published.

The X/Open model is described in Chapter 2. The diagram of the model is repeated here in Figure 15.1 for convenience and review.

The XATMI provides an interface between the application program and the communication manager (sometimes called the CRM, which stands for communications resource manager). The CRM provides the services and protocols to allow the application program to invoke other application programs as services.

The TX interface allows the application program to manage transaction boundaries and access information about the current status of transactions.

The TxRPC interface provides a means for the application program to use ISO RPC services and DCE, but with transaction semantics added. By using TxRPC, the application program can use distributed remote procedure calls with a managed global transaction.

The XA interface provides the communication between the transaction manager and resource managers to provide coordinated global trans-

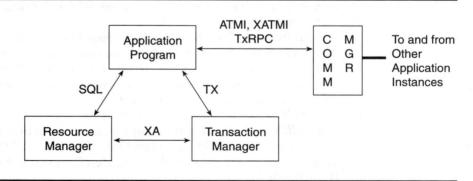

Figure 15.1   The X/Open DTP model.

action completion. The XA interface was discussed in Chapter 4. This chapter will provide some additional information about the XA interface.

15.2 THE XATMI INTERFACE

X/Open chose to adopt a true subset of the TUXEDO ATMI as the XATMI, including the tp*() format. The XATMI provides all necessary functionality to develop an enhanced client/server application, but leaves out a number of useful features provided by TUXEDO. All functions provided by the XATMI are used exactly the same way as previously described. If the application must remain source portable to other equivalent products (such as Top End), the application programs should use only the XATMI functions and buffers. When developing applications for TUXEDO, the TUXEDO reference manual should be used for information about the XATMI calls. The rest of this section provides a description of the differences.

XATMI supports typed buffers, but does not support the equivalent of FML or STRING buffers. The XATMI buffer type X_OCTET is the same as the TUXEDO type CARRAY and is used in exactly the same manner. Types X_COMMON and X_C_TYPE are exactly the same as the TUXEDO type VIEW and are used in the same way, including the use of **viewc(1)** and **viewc32(3)** to provide the C header files for defined buffers. Type X_COMMON is provided specifically for COBOL, though it will work just as well with C and C++ programs. The X/Open specification uses COBOL terms to describe the allowed contents of X_COMMON and uses C terms to describe the contents of X_C_TYPE. Since X_C_TYPE and X_COMMON are TUXEDO VIEW type buffers, data translation works for these buffer types when transmitting messages among heterogeneous platforms.

XATMI supports the request/response and conversational paradigms. If the application limits its use of ATMI to the XATMI supported functions, the application will be source portable to any system that also supports XATMI. XATMI supports the following functions for C and C++ programs:

tpacall(3)	tpcancel(3)	tpgetrply(3)	tpsend(3)
tpadvertise(3)	tpconnect(3)	tprealloc(3)	tpservice(3)
tpalloc(3)	tpdiscon(3)	tprecv(3)	tptypes(3)
tpcall(3)	tpfree(3)	tpreturn(3)	tpunadvertise(3)

When using these functions, use the buffer type X_C_TYPE instead of VIEW and use X_OCTET instead of CARRAY in those functions that require a buffer type parameter. Return codes are the same as for ATMI and error values are returned in tperrno. The program must use the non-XATMI calls, such as **tpstrerror(3)** for error presentation.

The following COBOL functions are provided by XATMI:

TPACALL	TPCANCEL	TPGETRPLY	TPSEND
TPADVERTISE	TPCONNECT	TPRECV	TPSVCSTART
TPCALL	TPDISCON	TPRETURN	TPUNADVERTISE

The return codes and data structures used with these functions is the same as for TUXEDO. Use the buffer type X_COMMON where buffer type is required. Chapter 14 provides information on how to develop TUXEDO applications using COBOL.

15.3   THE TRANSACTION DEMARCATION (TX) INTERFACE

15.3.1   Overview

The TX interface (called the transaction demarcation interface by X/Open) contains the functionality to support application program control of transaction boundaries when using XA compliant resource managers. The interface includes functions to:

- Start and end a transaction
- Open and close a resource manager
- Inquire for transaction information
- Modify transactional behavior

The functions provided by the TX interface roughly parallel the equivalent functions provided by the tp*() versions. In most cases the resultant functionality is identical to the tp*() versions, but the calling method is different. The TX interface also provides the ability to inquire for transaction information and modify transactional behavior; this functionality is not part of the tp*() versions.

Table 15.1 compares the TX versions with the tp*() versions.

The TX interface provides a feature that immediately starts a new transaction when the current transaction is completed by either **tx_commit(3)** or **tx_rollback(3)**. When a new transaction is started in this way, it is a chained transaction. By default, transactions are unchained. The application program can use **tx_set_transaction_control(3)** to the characteristic TX_CHAINED. The details of chaining and unchaining and the implications of each are explained in the sections that follow.

Table 15.1   TX Functions Compared with **tp*()** Transaction Management Functions

TX function	*tp*() function*	*Purpose and comment*
tx_begin(3)	tpbegin(3)	Begin a transaction.
tx_close(3)	tpclose(3)	Close a resource manager.
tx_commit(3)	tpcommit(3)	Commit a transaction.
tx_info(3)	tpgetlev(3)	Return information about a transaction. tpgetlev(3) returns only transaction state.
tx_open(3)	tpopen(3)	Open a resource manager.
tx_rollback(3)	tpabort(3)	Rollback (abort) a transaction.
tx_set_commit_return(3)	tpscmt(3)	Sets commit return point. Overrides setting in configuration file.
tx_set_transaction_control(3)	—	Set transactions to chained or unchained. Feature available only with TX functions.
tx_set_transaction_timeout(3)	—	Sets transaction timeout value. Transaction timeout value is set as parameter in tpbegin(3).

15.3.2   Definitions Used by the TX Interface

The TX interface uses some terms differently than might be expected. The following definitions are provided to clarify the meaning and usage of TX terms.

> **Thread of control:** The thread of control is actually an operating system process. In some environments the term thread is used with a slightly different connotation than process, but for practical purposes thread of control can be used interchangeably with operating system process.

> **Global transaction:** Global transaction is used to describe the work done by multiple processes in the system. The effect is that as soon as more than one process is involved in the transaction, it is a global transaction.

15.3.3   Transaction Boundary Functions

The form of **tx_begin(3)** is:

```
int tx_begin(void)
```

tx_begin(3) starts a transaction. Its logical function in TUXEDO is the same as **tpbegin(3)**. **tx_begin(3)** returns a non-negative value, TX_OK, when it completes successfully. If **tx_begin(3)** fails, it returns a negative error code as follows.

TX_OUTSIDE The program is already in a transaction with a local resource manager. Theoretically, this error will be returned if the program is using a resource manager that has entered its own non-XA transaction, such when it is already accessing a database before starting the global transaction. Experience indicates that not all databases will cause this error.

TX_PROTOCOL_ERROR The program is already running in transaction mode. The current transaction continues and **tx_begin(3)** does nothing. This error is also returned if the program has not called **tx_open(3)** to open the resource manager.

TX_ERROR The transaction manager or a resource manager could not start a transaction at this time. More information is written to ULOG. The transaction is not started.

TX_FAIL The transaction manager or the resource manager has failed. This is a fatal error. More information is written to ULOG.

The form of **tx_commit(3)** is:

```
int tx_commit(void)
```

tx_commit(3) requests the transaction manager to commit the current transaction. If the commit fails, **tx_commit(3)** returns an error as described below. If transaction control indicates chained transactions, a new transaction will be started before **tx_commit(3)** returns.

tx_commit(3) returns the non-negative value TX_OK upon successful completion. The following negative values will be returned upon failure.

TX_NO_BEGIN Transactions are being chained, but the system was not able to begin a new transaction. The current transaction was committed successfully, but no new transaction has been started.

TX_ROLLBACK The current transaction failed and its work has been rolled back. If transactions are being chained, a new transaction has been started.

TX_ROLLBACK_NO_BEGI The current transaction failed and its work has been rolled back. This error occurs when transactions are being chained and the system was unable to start a new transaction after rolling back the current transaction. A new transaction has not been started.

TX_MIXED The transaction was partially committed and partially rolled back. If transactions are being chained, a new transaction has been started.

TX_MIXED_NO_BEGIN The transaction was partially committed and partially rolled back. If transactions are being chained, a new transaction has not been started.

TX_HAZARD This error is returned when the system cannot determine the status of commit and rollback for all resource managers used by the transaction. This failure is usually due to some type of manual intervention occurring during the execution of the transaction. If transactions are being chained, a new transaction has been started.

TX_HAZARD_NO_BEGIN This error is returned when the system cannot determine the status of commit and rollback for all resource managers used by the transaction. This failure is usually due to some type of manual intervention occurring during the execution of the transaction. If transactions are being chained, a new transaction has not been started.

TX_PROTOCOL_ERROR This error occurs because the function was called while the system was in an inappropriate state. The most common cause of this error is when **tx_commit(3)** is called while the program is not in transaction mode.

TX_FAIL A fatal error occurred that prevented the commit from completing. The status of the current transaction is unknown.

Note: If **tx_commit(3)** returns TX_MIXED or TX_MIXED_NO_BEGIN, transaction integrity has been lost. Some data has been modified incorrectly. If this error should occur, the application should immediately notify an administrator and prevent further processing until the situation is corrected.

The form of **tx_rollback(3)** is:

```
int tx_rollback(void)
```

tx_rollback(3) requests the transaction manager to rollback the work done on behalf of the current transaction. If transactions are being chained, a new transaction is started.

tx_rollback(3) returns the non-negative value TX_OK when it succeeds. If **tx_rollback(3)** fails, the following negative error values are returned:

TX_NO_BEGIN Transactions are being chained, but the system was not able to begin a new transaction. The current transaction was committed successfully, but no new transaction has been started.

TX_MIXED The transaction was partially committed and partially rolled back. If transactions are being chained, a new transaction has been started.

TX_MIXED_NO_BEGIN The transaction was partially committed and partially rolled back. If transactions are being chained, a new transaction has not been started.

TX_HAZARD This error is returned when the system cannot determine the status of commit and rollback for all resource managers used by the transaction. This failure is usually due to some type of manual intervention occurring during the execution of the transaction. If transactions are being chained, a new transaction has been started.

TX_HAZARD_NO_BEGIN This error is returned when the system cannot determine the status of commit and rollback for all resource managers used by the transaction. This failure is usually due to some type of manual intervention occurring during the execution of the transaction. If transactions are being chained, a new transaction has not been started.

TX_COMMITTED The transaction was heuristically committed. The most usual cause of this error is manual intervention while the transaction was active. If transactions are being chained, a new transaction has been started.

TX_COMMITTED_NO_BEGIN The transaction was heuristically committed. The most usual cause of this error is manual intervention while the transaction was active. If transactions are being chained, a new transaction has not been started.

TX_PROTOCOL_ERROR This error occurs because the function was called while the system was in an inappropriate state. The most common cause of this error is when **tx_commit(3)** is called while the program is not in transaction mode.

TX_FAIL A fatal error occurred that prevented the commit from completing. The status of the current transaction is unknown. More information is written to ULOG.

Note: If **tx_rollback(3)** returns TX_MIXED or TX_MIXED_NO_BEGIN, transaction integrity has been lost. Some data has been modified incorrectly. If this error should occur, the application should immediately notify an administrator and prevent further processing until the situation is corrected.

15.3.4   Functions to Open and Close a Resource Manager

If the application uses TX functions to begin and end transactions, the application must use **tx_open(3)** and **tx_close(3)** to open and close resource managers. **tx_open(3)** must be in **tpsvrinit(3)** and **tx_close(3)** must be in **tpsvrdone(3)**. The default functions **tpsvrinit(3)** and **tpsvrdone(3)** use **tpopen(3)** and **tpclose(3)**, so they must be replaced by application specific versions to use the TX interface.

The form of **tx_close(3)** is:

```
int tx_close(void)
```

tx_close(3) closes the resource manager associated with the group containing the server using the information in tuxconfig. **tx_close(3)** also disconnects the resource manager from the server. The scope of **tx_close(3)** is limited to the server containing the calling **tpsvrdone(3)** function.

When **tx_close(3)** completes successfully, it returns the non-negative value TX_OK. If **tx_close(3)** fails, it returns one of the following negative values.

TX_PROTOCOL_ERROR The state of the system did not allow closing the resource managers. The usual cause of this error is that a transaction is still in process. No resource managers are closed when this error occurs.

TX_ERROR The transaction manager or a resource manager could not perform the function at this time. More information is written to ULOG. The transaction is not started.

TX_FAIL A fatal error occurred that prevented the transaction manager or the resource manager from completing the operation. The current resource manager status is unknown. More information is written to ULOG.

The form of **tx_open(3)** is:

```
int tx_open(void)
```

tx_open(3) opens the resource manager associated with the group the server is part of, using information from tuxconfig. **tx_open(3)** also connects the resource manager to the server to make it available for use by the services in the server.

tx_open(3) returns the non-negative value TX_OK to indicate success. If **tx_open(3)** fails, it returns one of the following negative values.

TX_ERROR The transaction manager or a resource manager could not perform the function at this time. More information is written to ULOG. The transaction is not started.

TX_FAIL A fatal error occurred that prevented the transaction manager or the resource manager from completing the operation. The current resource manager status is unknown. More information is written to ULOG.

15.3.5   Getting Information about the Current Transaction

The form of **tx_info(3)** is:

```
int tx_info(TXINFO *info)
```

where the *info points to a structure containing information about the transaction after **tx_info(3)** returns successfully. The information contained in *info* is:

```
XID                  xid;
COMMIT_RETURN        when_return;
TRANSACTION_CONTROL  transaction_control;
TRANSACTION_TIMEOUT  transaction_timeout;
TRANSACTION_STATE    transaction_state;
```

If the calling process is currently running in transaction mode, XID will contain the global transaction identifier of the current transaction, otherwise XID will be NULL. All other fields will be populated with the current settings whether the process is in transaction mode or not. See the section in this chapter, Using TX Functions, for details on how to use the values in this structure.

The values in *info* reflect only the values set by the tx_set_*() functions, and are valid only when **tx_info(3)** is called from the same process which called the tx_set*_() functions.

When successful, **tx_info(3)** returns 1 if the calling process is in transaction mode, 0 if not in transaction mode. If **tx_info(3)** fails, it will return one of the following negative values.

> **TX_PROTOCOL_ERROR** The state of the system did contain information about transactions. The usual cause of this error is that **tx_info(3)** was called from a server before **tx_open(3)** has successfully been called.

> **TX_FAIL** A fatal error occurred that prevented the transaction manager from completing the operation. More information is written to ULOG.

15.3.6 Modifying Transactional Behavior

The TX interface provides functions to modify the way a transaction behaves in certain circumstances. The functions act by setting values in the TXINFO structure. The functions are described here, but see the section in this chapter, Using the TX Functions, for more information.

The form of **tx_set_commit_return(3)** is:

```
int tx_set_commit_return(COMMIT_RETURN  when_return)
```

where *when_return* is one of the following values:

> **TX_COMMIT_DECISION_LOGGED** When this flag is set, the transaction manager will return the result of a commit as soon as it has received responses to the prepare request from all resource managers used in the transaction.

> **TX_COMMIT_COMPLETED** When this flag is set, the transaction manager will wait until all resources managers have indicated that they have successfully committed before returning the result of a commit request.

An application program should not use this function except in exceptional circumstances. Normally the return point is set by the administrator in the TUXEDO configuration file.

When **tx_set_commit_return(3)** completes successfully, it returns the non-negative value TX_OK. If **tx_set_commit_return(3)** fails, it returns one of the following negative values.

> **TX_EINVAL** The value of *when_return* was not valid.

> **TX_PROTOCOL_ERROR** The state of the system did contain in-

formation about transactions. The usual cause of this error is that **tx_set_commit_return(3)** was called from a server before **tx_open(3)** has successfully been called.

TX_FAIL: A fatal error occurred that prevented the transaction manager from completing the operation. More information is written to ULOG.

The form of **tx_set_transaction_control(3)** is:

```
int     tx_set_transaction_control(TRANSACTION_CONTROL
control_value)
```

where *control_value* may be one of the following:

TX_UNCHAINED When this value is set, it prevents a new transaction from starting when **tx_commit(3)** or **tx_rollback(3)** complete. When transactions are unchained, new transactions can be started only by calling **tx_begin(3)**.

TX_CHAINED When this value is set, new transactions are started when **tx_commit(3)** or **tx_rollback(3)** complete. When transactions are chained, new transactions are started immediately after a commit or rollback operation, providing a method to leave the process in transaction mode at all times after the first **tx_begin(3)**.

When **tx_set_transaction_control(3)** completes successfully, it returns the non-negative value TX_OK. If **tx_set_transaction_control(3)** fails, it returns one of the following negative values.

TX_EINVAL The value of *control_value* was not valid.

TX_PROTOCOL_ERROR The state of the system did contain information about transactions. The usual cause of this error is that **tx_set_transaction_control(3)** was called from a server before **tx_open(3)** has successfully been called.

TX_FAIL A fatal error occurred that prevented the transaction manager from completing the operation. More information is written to ULOG.

The form of **tx_set_transaction_timeout(3)** is:

```
int     tx_set_transaction_timeout(TRANSACTION_TIMEOUT
timeout_value)
```

where *timeout_value* is the number of seconds to wait before causing a transaction timeout. A *timeout_value* of 0 disables transaction timeout. The valid values of *timeout_value* from 0 through any valid value for a long as defined by the system.

tx_set_transaction_timeout(3) sets the timeout value for the next transaction started after the function is called. If the process is currently in transaction mode, the timeout value will take effect when the next transaction is started from the process calling **tx_set_transaction_timeout(3)**.

When **tx_set_transaction_timeout(3)** completes successfully, it returns the non-negative value TX_OK. If **tx_set_transaction_timeout(3)** fails, it returns one of the following negative values.

TX_EINVAL The value of *timeout_value* was not valid.

TX_PROTOCOL_ERROR The state of the system did contain information about transactions. The usual cause of this error is that **tx_set_transaction_timeout(3)** was called from a server before **tx_open(3)** has successfully been called.

TX_FAIL A fatal error occurred that prevented the transaction manager from completing the operation. More information is written to ULOG.

15.3.7   Using the TX Functions

The following rules must be followed when using TX functions.

- Every process that calls TX functions must first call **tx_open(3)**. Servers must call **tx_open(3)** from **tpsvrinit(3)**. If clients use TX calls, they must also first call **tx_open(3)**. Note that **tx_open(3)** may be called successfully, even if the client or server is not associated with a resource manager.
- The process that calls **tx_commit(3)** or **tx_abort(3)** must be the same process that called **tx_begin(3)**.
- The tx_set_*() functions produce valid results only when called from the same process that has already or will call **tx_begin(3)**. No errors are produced when the tx_set_(*) functions are called from other processes but the results are unpredictable.
- **tx_info(3)** may be called from any process to determine if the process is part of an existing transaction or not, but only the process that has already or will call **tx_begin(3)** will return valid values in *info*.
- Values returned by **tx_info(3)** in info reflect only the values set by previously called tx_set_*() functions. They will not reflect values that may be set in the configuration file.

- Application programs should not call **tx_set_commit_return(3)** except for very exceptional situations. This call overrides the setting made by the administrator and changing it may not be in accordance with enterprise policy.
- Changes made by tx_set_*() functions take affect on the next transaction started by the process and do not affect the current transaction.

Though not always required, it is a good idea to call **tx_close(3)** from every process that calls **tx_open(3)**. Servers should call **tx_close(3)** from **tpsvrdone(3)** and clients should call **tx_close(3)** before calling **tpterm(3)**. Do not mix using TX functions with using the transactional tp*() functions. In some cases no errors will be returned to the program, but the results are unpredictable.

Most application programs should require using only:

```
tx_begin(3)    tx_close(3)    tx_commit(3)    tx_open(3)
tx_rollback(3) tx_set_transaction_timeout(3)
```

The following code fragment shows a typical usage in a client:

```
#include <stdio.h>
#include "atmi.h"        /* TUXEDO  Header File */
#include "tx.h"          /* TX  Header File */

main(int argc, char *argv[])
{

    .
    .
    .

    int ret;
    TXINFO *infoptr;

    .
    .
    .
    /* Attach to System/T as a Client Process */
    if (tpinit((TPINIT *) NULL) == -1) {
        fprintf(stderr, "Tpinit failed\n");
        exit(1);
    }
```

```
        .
        .
        .
    if((ret = tx_open()) < 0)
    {
        /* put error handling code here */
    }
        .
        .

        .
    /* it would be reasonable to put a while not done */
    /* statement here */
    if((ret = tx_begin()) < 0)
    {
        /* put error handling code here */
    }
        .
        .

        .
    if((ret = tx_commit()) < 0)
    {
    /* put error handling code here */
    }
        .
        .

        .
    /* this is a good place to put the last } of the while
*/
    /* not done statement */
    if((ret = tx_close()) < 0)
    {
    /* put error handling code here */
    }

    /* Free Buffers & Detach from System/T */
    /* don't forget to free the buffers !! */
    tpterm();
}
```

The following code fragment shows a typical use in a server when the transaction is controlled from the client:

```c
#include <stdio.h>
#include <ctype.h>
#include <atmi.h>    /* TUXEDO Header File */
#include <xatmi.h>   /* X/OPEN Header File */
#include <tx.h>          /* TX Header File */
#include <userlog.h>     /* TUXEDO Header File */

EXEC SQL begin declare section;
/* define SQL host variables here */
EXEC SQL end declare section;

void tpsvrdone()
{
    int ret;
    userlog("entering tpsvrdone in xaserv");
    if((ret = tx_close()) < 0)
    {
        /* put error handling here */
    }
    return;
}

tpsvrinit(int argc, char *argv[])
{
    int ret; /* place to put return code */

    /* Use args so compiler won't complain. */
    argc = argc;
    argv = argv;

    /* userlog writes to the central TUXEDO message log */
    userlog("xaserv starting");

        if((ret = tx_open()) < 0)
    {
        /* put error handling here */
    }
    return(0);
}

/* This function is the actual service */
```

```
xasvc(TPSVCINFO *rqst)
{

    /* be sure to define your variables */
    /* then retrieve the data, etc. */
    .
    .
    .

    /* do processing of service, which may include SQL
commands */
    /* if using a relational database */

    /* rqst->data is a place holder for the pointer to the
*/
    /* data being returned */
    tpreturn(TPSUCCESS, 0, rqst->data, 0L, 0);
}
```

If the transaction is being controlled from the service, include **tx_begin(3)**, **tx_commit(3)**, **tx_rollback(3)**, and **tp_set_transaction_ timeout(3)** in the appropriate places in the logic in a server structured as shown.

16

Using Multiple Domains

ABOUT /DOMAIN

TUXEDO provides a feature that allows communication between two TUXEDO domains, or between a TUXEDO domain and domains defined by other products, such as Top End, Encina, or CICS 6000, if the other domain adheres to the OSI standard and X/Open specifications. Novell calls this feature TUXEDO System /Domain. This chapter will designate this feature as simply /Domain.

/Domain provides functionality that is transparent to application programs by allowing clients and services in a domain to use services in another domain exactly as if the remote services were local. From the application program viewpoint, there is no difference between using a service in the same domain or a service in another domain.

Domains are defined by the administrator. The administrator also defines how the services in one domain are made available to another domain.

Figure 16.1 shows interdomain communication in its simplest form. The request on Platform 1 and Server 1 are both included in Domain 1. Server 2 is included in Domain 2 on Platform 2. The requestor invokes both Service A and Service B in exactly the same manner, but because the administrator has provided configuration files that direct the requests to different domains, the request for Service B is communicated via /Domain.

Figure 16.2 shows a more realistic use of /Domain. The four domains

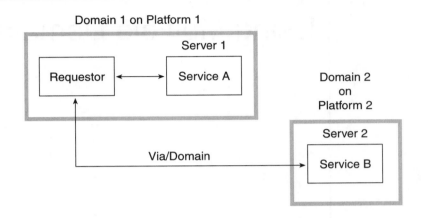

Domain 1 on Platform 1

Server 1

Requestor ←→ Service A

Domain 2 on Platform 2

Server 2

Via/Domain

Service B

Figure 16.1 Simple interdomain communications.

shown are logically separate within the enterprise. Each domain is administered by a separate administrator. The need for intercommunication is obvious, for when the order entry system requires information about customers, it must invoke services in the customer maintenance domain. The order entry system must also use services that reside within the inventory management domain and the accounts receivable domain.

Note the following items about the architecture in Figure 16.2:

- Each domain is administered independently.
- The administrator of each domain can control access from other domains.
- Domains need not be on separate physical platforms (use the network loop back mechanism).
- The order entry system has access to services on all the other domains.
- The accounts receivable system has access only to the customer maintenance domain.
- The customer maintenance system and the inventory management system have no access to other domains.

TUXEDO supports two protocols that can be used to communicate between domains: /TDOMAIN and /OSITP. /TDOMAIN is a proprietary protocol used between TUXEDO domains. /OSITP is an implementation

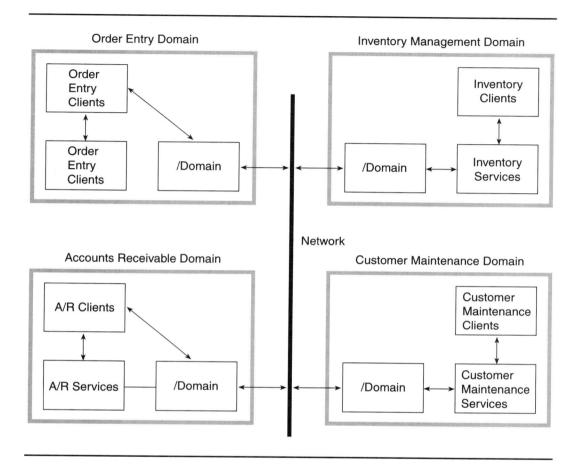

Figure 16.2   An enterprise-wide multiple domain system.

of a protocol defined by ISO. The X/Open Networking and TP working groups are examining this implementation. This chapter will concentrate on the /TDOMAIN protocol. The principles and methods for using /Domain are the same for both protocols. /TDOMAIN provides higher performance than /OSITP; therefore, applications should use /TDOMAIN between TUXEDO domains. An enterprise that wants to set up communication between domains from different vendors should contact the vendors involved to determine how to implement the solution. There are no programming implications for either protocol within TUXEDO.

/Domain provides a runtime administrative utility to maintain the /Domain configuration on a running system.

16.2   SOME SPECIAL DEFINITIONS

A few special terms are used with /Domain. They are defined here for convenience.

Domain: A *domain* is a TUXEDO instance. A domain may have many nodes. What makes it a domain is that it is a single administrative entity, supported by a one configuration definition. TUXEDO documentation has traditionally called a domain an *application*. In this book the word application will be reserved to apply to the set of processes that define user functionality. When comparing discussions in this book with the TUXEDO documentation, the word application and the word domain can be interchanged. A domain may also be an instance of another OLTP or enhanced client/server product.

Domain gateway: The *domain gateway* is the process that communicates with other domains. TUXEDO provides a domain gateway for each of the supported protocols. Enterprises may develop their own customized domain gateway.

Gateway server group: The *gateway server group* is the group defined within a domain that contains the domain gateway server and the /Domain administrative servers.

Local domain: The *local domain*, as defined for /Domain, is the set of services within a domain that are made available for use by other domains. The term *domain gateway group* is sometimes substituted for the term local domain. The local domain referenced in the DM_LOCAL_DOMAINS section of the /Domain configuration file is actually a group within a domain. Technically, a domain is a TUXEDO instance that can contain many groups and many nodes. In other words, a domain is a single administrative entity. /Domain provides a finer breakout, by allowing creation of multiple "local domains," also called gateway server groups. Unfortunately, the TUXEDO documentation and messages used by interactive administration utilities refer to local domains and gateway server groups interchangeably, and do not make a discrimination between the terms.

Remote domain: A *remote domain* is a domain that is accessed using the domain gateway. From the viewpoint of Domain 1, Domain 2 is a remote domain. A remote domain is always a gateway server group (or local domain) in some other domain.

Remote service: A *remote service* is a service that resides on a remote domain and is made available to some other domain. From the viewpoint of Domain 1, services residing on Domain 2, which are available for use from Domain 1, are remote services.

Local service: A *local service* is a service that is made available to another domain. From the viewpoint of Domain 1, services within Domain 1 that are made available to Domain n are local services.

Some of these terms have generic meanings and may be used in different ways when not specifically referring to /Domain particulars. For instance, any service on a domain can be considered a local service because no Domain gateway is used to access them. The context will make the specific meaning clear in these cases.

16.3   HOW /DOMAIN WORKS

Figure 16.3 shows one node of the order entry domain a little closer. When the invoker, which may be a client or a service, invokes a service, the request is routed to the local BBL service, which determines the location of the service. This may be local or on another node in the same domain or in another domain. If the service is local, the BBL service passes the request to the service. When the service is complete, the result is returned directly to the invoker. When the service is complete, the TUXEDO mainline also notifies the BBL service of that fact, though for clarity that is not shown on the diagram.

If the service is on another domain, the BBL service passes the request to the /Domain gateway. The /Domain gateway determines which domain contains the service and routes the request to the proper domain. The /Domain gateway receives the request on the other domain, passes it to the local blackboard where it is passed to the service. When the service is complete, the result is returned via the /Domain gateways, then to the invoker.

The /Domain gateway is multithreaded and passes messages in both directions asynchronously. The /Domain gateway will pass transaction management information between domains in such a manner that transactions are managed logically in the same manner as if they were on a single domain. That is, if some part of a transaction that runs on multiple domains fails in one domain, the entire transaction is guaranteed to fail and thus be rolled back. Also, if a commit request is successful, the transaction was correctly processed on all participating domains.

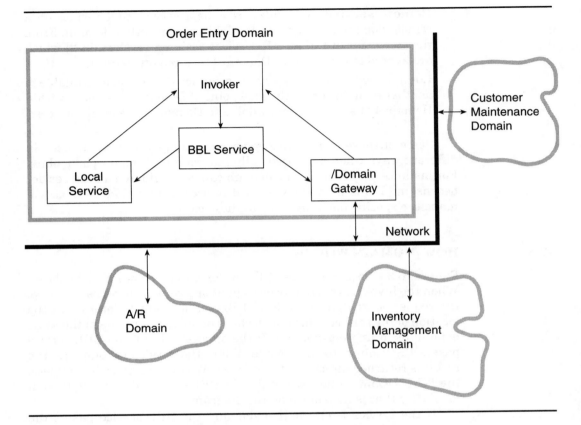

Figure 16.3   How /Domain works.

TUXEDO also provides support that allows application developers to write custom /Domain gateways.

16.4   TUXEDO FEATURES SUPPORTED WITH /DOMAIN

With few exceptions all features of TUXEDO are supported across domains by /Domain. This means that developers design and create clients and services that use /Domain in exactly the same way as if all services were within the local domain. /Domain supports:

- The request/response model
- The conversational model

- Transaction management
- Typed buffers
- The /Q feature, which is discussed later in the book

Clients can attach to only their designated domain. **tpinit(3)** will not be effective across domains.

tpnotify(3) and **tpbroadcast(3)** are not supported across domains. If a service needs to send an unsolicited message to a client that is attached to another domain, the service must invoke a service on that domain that will in turn use **tpnotify(3)** or **tpbroadcast(3)** to send an unsolicited messages to its local clients.

Communication of typed buffers between TUXEDO domains works exactly as it does within the local domain. Communication (using the domain type OSITP) of typed buffers with domains from other vendors are limited by the support provided by the other vendor. Communication with X/Open compliant domains is supported because TUXEDO provides the X/Open buffer types and provides a means to convert FML buffers to VIEW buffers (X/Open X_C_TYPE and X_COMMON).

The /Q feature works the same as it does within a domain for domain type TDOMAIN. /Q does not work with domain type ISOTP. Novell may provide this capability, based on the ISO Queued Data Transfer protocol, at a later time.

16.5   SETTING UP /DOMAIN

/Domain is controlled by a configuration file, known as a dmconfig file. Its format is similar to the ubbconfig file used to define each domain. There is utility, **dmloadcf(1)**, which converts the ASCII version of the dmconfig file into a binary form known as the BDMCONFIG file.

/Domain is set up by adding to the ubbconfig file and by creating a dmconfig file for each domain. The steps required to set up /Domain are:

1. Populate the environment variable BDMCONFIG on each platform that uses /Domain.
2. Define a gateway server group in the ubbconfig for each remote domain.
3. Add the servers DMADM, GWADM, and GWTDOMAIN to the ubbconfig file on each domain where /Domain will be used.
4. Create the new tuxconfig file with **tmloadcf(1)** for each new ubbconfig file.
5. Create a dmconfig file for each domain.
6. Run **dmloadcf(1)** for each dmconfig file to create the binary form.

The environment variable BDMCONFIG must contain the full path name of the BDMCONFIG file associated with the domain.

The ubbconfig file in each domain must contain a definition of a gateway server group for each remote domain that the domain will communicate with. The servers DMADM, GWADM, and GWTDOMAIN must be defined in each gateway server group.

The /Domain configuration is defined in the dmconfig file. The utility **dmloadcf(1)** creates the binary version, called BDMCONFIG. Each domain must have its own BDMCONFIG file as well as a tuxconfig file. Examples and further explanations of these steps are provided later in this chapter.

The discussions in this chapter refer to dmconfig, ubbconfig, and their relationship as if dmconfig and ubbconfig were the active files for a running system. This terminology is used for clarity. Actually the binary forms, tuxconfig for a domain, DBMCONFIG for /Domain, are used by an active system.

16.6 THE DMCONFIG FILE

16.6.1 Overview

The syntax of the dmconfig file is the same as the syntax of the ubbconfig file. There are nine possible sections. Each section begins with a line of the form *name_of_section*. The possible sections are:

DM_RESOURCES: Provides a place to identify the version. This section is not used by TUXEDO, but provides a place for the user to document the version of the dmconfig file.

DM_LOCAL_DOMAINS: This section identifies the local domains and gateway server groups. This section is required.

DM_REMOTE_DOMAINS: This section names the remote domains that the local domain can access. The type of each remote domain is specified in this section. This section is required.

DM_TDOMAIN: This section provides network addressing information for domains that are type TDOMAIN. This section is required for TDOMAIN type domains. Either the DM_TDOMAIN section or the DM_OSITP section must be included, but not both.

DM_OSITP: This section provides information required by the OSI protocol. This section is required for those domains using the OSITP protocol. Either the DM_TDOMAIN section or the DM_OSITP section must be included, but not both. This section will not be discussed further.

DM_ACCESS_CONTROL: This section defines access control lists (ACLs) that specify which domains can access the local domain. This section is optional.

DM_LOCAL_SERVICES: This section provides a list of local services that are made available to other domains. Additional information about each service may also be included. This section is optional. If this section is not included, all services within the local domains named in the DM_LOCAL_DOMAINS section are made available to remote domains.

DM_REMOTE_SERVICES: This section provides a list of services available from remote domains and may name the domain where each service resides. Additional information may also be provided about each service. This section is required if remote services will be accessed from the local domain.

DM_ROUTING: This section provides data dependent routing criteria for the services named in DM_REMOTE_SERVICES. It works similar to the data dependent routing provided in ubbconfig.

16.6.2   The DM_RESOURCES Section

The DM_RESOURCES section contains one entry:

```
VERSION=string
```

where *string* is any set of characters. This parameter is not currently used by TUXEDO. The user can put values in VERSION to identify specific dmconfig files.

16.6.3   The DM_LOCAL_DOMAINS Section

The DM_LOCAL_DOMAINS section names local domains and associates each one with a gateway server group. There must be an entry for each local domain. Each entry has the form:

```
LDOM parameters
```

where *LDOM* is the name of the local domain and *parameters* consists of a set of required parameters and chosen optional parameters.

The required parameters are:

GWGRP = *grpname*: *grpname* is the name of the local gateway server group to associate with the local domain name. The local gateway server group must contain the servers DMADM, GWADM, and GWTDOMAIN. It is possible to define multiple local gateway server groups within one true domain, thus providing a method to have multiple domain names defined on the same domain.

TYPE = *domaintype*: *domaintype* is the type of protocol to use for communication with the named local domain. The valid types are TDOMAIN and OSITP. If TDOMAIN is specified, the section DM_TDOMAIN must be included in dmconfig. If OSITP is specified, the section DM_OSITP must be included in dmconfig.

DOMAINID = *ldomname*: *ldomname* is the name of the local domain. The name must be unique within the local domain and across all domains. It is a good idea to make *ldomname* the same as *LDOM*.

DMTLOGDEV = devname: devname is the full path name of the device used for the /Domain transaction log. It is used by the /Domain transaction manager in the same way that the local transaction manager uses TLOGDEVICE. Multiple local domains can share the same DMTLOGDEV if they are on the same platform, as long as a different DMTLOGNAME is specified for each local domain. The DMTLOGDEV is created by the gateway servers the first time the local domain associated with the dmconfig file is booted.

Some optional parameters are:

AUDITLOG = *aud_log_name*: *aud_log_name* is the name of the audit log. The audit log records all /Domain activity on the local domain when the audit log feature is activated with **dmadmin(1)**. If this parameter is not specified, and the audit log feature is activated, the audit log is recorded on *$APPDIR* with the file name *DMdate.LOG*.

DMTLOGNAME = *logname*: *logname* is the name of a log within the device named by DMTLOGDEV. This parameter is only required when more than one local domain is defined and separate logs are required for each. The individual logs are created with the device by the gateway servers the first time the local domain is booted.

SECURITY=NONE | APP_PW | DM_PW: The **SECURITY** parameter determines the security requirement of interdomain communications. If **SECURITY** is not specified or is specified equal NONE, there is no security requirement established. If **SECURITY = APP_PW** is specified, remote domains are required to supply the password determined by the local tuxconfig file. If **SECURITY = APP_PW** is specified, **SECURITY = APP_PW** must also be specified in the local tuxconfig file. If **SECURITY = DM_PW**, domain password protection is independent of the local tuxconfig requirement. Passwords for the **DM_PW** option must be entered with **dmadmin(1)**.

Other optional parameters allow:

*   Setting a blocking timeout specifically for inter-domain communication.
*   Setting the size of the log.
*   Settings for several maximums.

The defaults are usually appropriate for these parameters. For instance, if blocking time is not set in dmconfig, the value from ubbconfig is used.

16.6.4   The DM_REMOTE_DOMAINS Section

The DM_REMOTE_DOMAINS section lists the remote domains accessible from the local domain. The type of each remote domain is specified. Entries have the form:

```
RDOM parameters
```

RDOM is the name of a remote domain as used in the local domain. All parameters are required.

> **TYPE = *domaintype*:** *domaintype* is the type of protocol used by the remote domain. The valid values are TDOMAIN and OSITP. This value must match the value for the **TYPE** parameter of the DM_LOCAL_DOMAINS section for the remote domain.
>
> **DOMAINID = *rdomname*:** *rdomname* is the name of the local domain. This value must match the value for the **DOMAINID** in the DM_LOCAL_DOMAINS section in dmconfig for the remote domain. It is possible to use a different value for *rdomname* than for *RDOM*, but it is a good idea to use the same value for both.

16.6.5   **The DM_TDOMAIN Section**

The DM_TDOMAIN section provides addressing information. The information must be supplied for all remote domains that will be used from this local domain. The address of local domains that expect to receive information from remote domains must also be provided.

Multiple entries may be made for a single domain in this section. When this is done for remote domains, the first entry will be used to create the connection, if possible. The additional entries act as alternate addresses for remote domains. If multiple entries are made for a local domain, multiple listening ports become available.

Entries in this section have the form:

```
domname parameters
```

domname is the name of a local or remote domain.
The required parameter is:

NWADDR = *address*: *address* is the network address of the local or remote domain named in *domname*. The form of the address must match the type of network used. If the address is a hexadecimal address of form **0x*address value***, it must contain an even number of characters specifying an even number of hexadecimal digits.

Optional parameters are:

NWDEVICE = *dev*: *dev* is the device file name used to bind the listening address. If TLI is used as an interface with the network, *dev* must be the absolute path name of the device file name. If using a sockets interface, this parameter is not needed.

NWIDLETIME = *number*: *number* is the time in minutes allowed for a connection to be idle. If this time is exceeded, the connection will be terminated. If this parameter is not specified, the connection will remain until it is shutdown.

16.6.6   **The DM_ACCESS_CONTROL Section**

The DM_ACCESS_CONTROL section limits those remote domains that can access the local domain. More information on /Domain security is provided later in this chapter. The form of entries in this section is:

```
aclname parameters
```

aclname is the name of an access control list. There is one parameter, ACLIST.

ACLIST = *rdomname*[,*rdomname*]: *rdomname* is the name of a remote domain. The list contains a list of comma separated remote domains. If the wild card character, "*" is used for *rdomname*, it means that all domains named in the DM_REMOTE_DOMAINS section have access to any local service that names this ACL in the ACL parameter in the DM_LOCAL_SERVICES section.

16.6.7   The DM_LOCAL_SERVICES Section

The DM_LOCAL_SERVICES section provides a list of local services that are made available to other domains. This section is optional. If this section is not included, all services within the local domains named in the DM_LOCAL_DOMAINS section are made available to remote domains. If this section is included, only the services named will be available for use from remote domains.

Entries in this section have the form:

```
svcname parameters
```

svcname is the name of a service available to remote domains. All parameters are optional. Some important optional parameters are:

ACL = *aclname*: *aclname* is the name of an access control list named and defined in the DM_ACCESS_CONTROL section. Only the remote domains named in the named access control list can access the service. If **ACL** is not specified, all remote domains named in DM_REMOTE_DOMAINS section will have access to the service.

LDOM = *ldomname*: *ldomname* is the name of the local domain that provides the service. If this parameter is not present, the service will be offered from all local domains that provide the service.

RNAME = *alias*: *alias* is the name by which the service will be known to remote domains. If this parameter is not specified, the name of the service will be used for identification.

16.6.8   The DM_REMOTE_SERVICES Section

The DM_REMOTE_SERVICES section provides a list of services available from remote domains and names the domain where the service resides. The name of the local domain that will access the service may also be provided. If this section is not included, the local domain will not be able to access remote services. The form of entries is:

```
svcname parameters
```

svcname is the name that the service is known by locally; it is the name that will be placed in the local BBL to make it available for local requests. The parameters for the entries in this section are used in a similar manner to the parameters in the SERVICES section of ubbconfig. All parameters are optional.

The important parameters are:

AUTOTRAN = {Y|N}: If **AUTOTRAN = Y** is specified, and the requestor is not already in transaction mode, a transaction will be started when the service is invoked and completed when the service completes. The default is **AUTOTRAN = N**. See description of the **AUTOTRAN** parameter in the SERVICES section of ubbconfig in Chapter 10.

CONV = {Y|N}: If **CONV = Y** is specified, the service is a conversational service. Note that the server supplying the service in the remote domain must be marked **CONV = Y** in the ubbconfig for that domain. The default is **CONV = N**.

LDOM = *ldomname*: *ldomname* is the name of the local domain that will route the request for the service. If this parameter is not specified, all local domain gateways will be enabled to route requests to this service.

LOAD = *number*: *number* represents the load used in the load balancing algorithm when considering when to route to the remote service. If the same service is named locally in ubbconfig, or is offered on multiple remote domains, the load factor helps determine which instantiation of the service should be invoked. The default value is 50.

RDOM = *rdomname*: *rdomname* is the name of a remote domain offering the service. If this parameter is specified, request for the service will be routed to the remote domain name in *rdomname*. If this parameter is not specified and data dependent routing is not specified, TUXEDO will route requests for the service to any domain that offers the service. The domain named in *rdomname* must be the same type as the local domain. Do not specify **RDOM** if data dependent routing is being used with this service.

RNAME = *rname*: *rname* is the name of the service as known to the remote domain. If **RNAME** is not included, then the name in *svcname* will be used.

ROUTING = *criterion_name*: *criterion_name* is the name of a routing criterion specified in the DM_ROUTING section. If this parameter is specified, requests to the service are routed to a remote domain based on the specification in the named criterion.

16.6.9   The DM_ROUTING Section

The DM_ROUTING section provides the criteria for data dependent routing of a service to a remote domain. TUXEDO buffer types FML, VIEW, X_C_TYPE, or X_COMMON support data dependent routing.

The form of the DM_ROUTING section is:

```
CRITERION_NAME parameters
```

where *CRITERION_NAME* is a string that names a specific criterion. All parameters are required for each criterion.

The parameters are:

FIELD = *fldname*: *fldname* is the name of the field to be tested to determine routing. The value of *fldname* must match a field defined in an FML field table file or a viewfile. Note that these files require running **mkfldhdr(1)** for FML field tables or **viewc(1)** for viewfiles before the information they contain is available to TUXEDO.

RANGES = *string*: *string* provides the values to be used for routing and a group that names the location where the request is directed when the specified values match those in the buffer. The form of string is a comma separated list of range and target groups. Each range and associated target group has the form:

```
range:rdomname
```

range may be a single value, a pair of values, or a wildcard character (*). Values in *range* are matched against the value in the field named by FIELD. When a match is found, the request is sent to the service in the server group named by the group. The service chosen in the group is the service that has named *CRITERION_NAME* in its **ROUTING** parameter.

If an element of *range* is a single value, the routing is done when the value in the buffer matches the value of the element. If two values are specified they must be in the form:

```
firstvalue - secondvalue
```

where *firstvalue* is lower in the collating sequence than *secondvalue*. When two values are specified, the routing is done when the value in the buffer is equal to or greater than *firstvalue* and less than or equal to *secondvalue* in the collating sequence for the data type.

The wildcard character (* without quotes) may be specified to provide a default routing when other routing criteria do not match the value in the buffer. The wildcard character may be used only once in each *range* and must be specified last in the *range*.

Numeric values may be of any type allowed for dmcomfig and may be signed with a single plus (+) or minus (–). String values within range must be enclosed in single quotes ('). If a single quote is enclosed in a string it must be preceded by two backslashes (\ \ ). The type of value specified in range must be the same as specified for the field named by **FIELD**. A value may be specified as **MIN** or **MAX**, without quotes. TUXEDO will substitute the lowest value for the data type for **MIN** and the highest value for **MAX**.

rdomname is a name that matches a remote domain name specified in the DM_REMOTE_DOMAINS section. *rdomname* may be specified with the wildcard character (*), in which case a match on the *range* allows TUXEDO to choose the named service from any remote domain which offers it.

BUFTYPE = *string*: *string* is a list of buffer types and subtypes. Within the list, subtypes are listed with each buffer type as a comma separated list and are separated from the buffer type by a colon. The list of types with their subtypes is in turn a semicolon separated list. The form is:

```
type1[:subtype1[,subtype2,...]][;type2[:subtype3
    [,subtype4,...]]...
```

type can be FML, VIEW, X_C_TYPE, or X_COMMON. No **subtype** can be specified with **type** FML.

A criterion in the DM_ROUTING section might be:

```
LOCATE
    FIELD=custloc
    RANGES="'AL - MI':*,'TX':AR1DOM,
        'CA-MO':WESTGRP,*:AR2DOM"
    BUFTYPE="FML"
```

16.7   SECURITY WITH /DOMAIN

16.7.1   Overview

/Domain security is provided at three levels:

1. Each domain provides security for itself as described in Chapter 12. This security limits who can access each domain.
2. Local domains can specify which remote domains have access to local services with the access control list specified in the dmconfig file.
3. Local domains can require a password from each remote domain on every attempt to access local services. This level of security is not currently available for OSITP type domains.

The security of each domain protects the local domain from unauthorized use, but does not protect the local domain from access by remote domains. Since each domain is individually administered, it is possible that the security of a local domain can be bypassed by a remote domain that does not require appropriate security.

Some protection of local services is provided by access control lists defined in the DM_ACCESS_CONTROL section of the dmconfig file and invoked for each service with the **ACL** parameter in the DM_LOCAL_SERVICES section. The dmconfig file is an ASCII file with no encryption, so anyone who can pass the UNIX limitations on file access can determine the required parameters to access local services.

The final level of security is provided by requiring a password from each remote domain each time a local service is invoked from a remote domain. These passwords are encrypted in the tuxconfig and the BDMCONFIG files. Two mutually exclusive methods of specifying the password required from a remote domain can be specified for each local domain.

The password required can be the password entered by the administrator when **tmloadcf(1)** is run. This password is required when the **SECURITY = APP_PW** parameter is specified in the RESOURCES section of the local ubbconfig file. This method is specified for /Domain by setting **SECURITY = APP_PW** in the DM_LOCAL_DOMAINS section of the local dmconfig file. This password is stored encrypted in the tuxconfig file of the local domain.

The local domain can require a different password from each remote domain by specifying **SECURITY = DM_PW** in the local dmconfig file. The passwords are then entered for each remote domain using **dmadmin(1)**. These passwords are stored encrypted in the local BDMCONFIG file.

16.7.2   Access Control Lists

The access control list defined in the DM_ACCESS_CONTROL section of dmconfig lists sets of remote domains that may have access to local services. Multiple lists can be named and defined. The **ACL** parameter in the DM_LOCAL_SERVICES section associates local services with a specific ACL. When a remote domain attempts to access a local service, TUXEDO attempts to find the name of the remote domain in the access control list associated with the local service. If the name of the remote domain is not found in the named ACL, access is denied.

If the remote domain has been protected by proper security and there is sufficient external security that prevents setting up unauthorized domains, this level of security on remote domains may be sufficient.

16.7.3   Remote Domain Passwords

Remote domains are required to provide passwords before gaining access to the local domain by setting **SECURITY = DM_PW** in the DM_LOCAL_DOMAINS section. When this parameter is set, the local administrator uses **dmadmin(1)** to enter a local password–remote password pair for each remote domain. The administrator for each local domain can enter the passwords necessary to allow remote domains to access the local domain. It is not possible for the administrator of the remote domain to enter the password required to allow the remote domain to access the local domain. Local and remote passwords used to allow access between domains are not required to be the same as the local general password.

16.8   USING DMADMIN(1)

16.8.1   Overview

dmadmin(1) is an interactive utility used to perform dynamic administration of /Domain. **dmadmin(1)** runs in two modes: administration and configuration. When **dmadmin(1)** is executed without options, it runs in administration mode by default. When the command line option -**c** is used, **dmadmin(1)** runs in configuration mode.

    dmadmin(1) attaches to the domain that is local to the platform it is executed on. If that domain requires a general password, **dmadmin(1)** will prompt for that password. If the user executing **dmadmin(1)** does not have the administrator UID, use of **dmadmin(1)** will be restricted to inquiry.

    Administration mode allows the administrator to

- Add or change local–remote domain password pairs
- Destroy and restart the audit and transaction logs
- Advertise and unadvertise remote services available to a local domain
- List information about the local domains
- Suspend and resume operation of services offered by the local domain

Configuration mode allows the administrator to

- Add or change local–remote domain password pairs
- Retrieve and list the contents of BDMCONFIG
- Modify values in BDMCONFIG
- Create a new dmconfig from BDMCONFIG

16.8.2   Using Administration Mode

When **dmadmin(1)** is executed with no options, it enters administration mode by default. The **dmadmin(1)** command prompt is a greater than sign (>). The important commands and their descriptions follow.

    advertise (adv) -d *local_dom_name* [**-all** | *svcname*]: **advertise** will mark the local bulletin board of the local domain named by *local_dom_name* that remote services are available for use. If the **-all** option is specified, all remote services will be marked available. If *svcname* is specified, only the named service will be marked available.

    audit -d *local_dom_name* [{**off** | **on**}]: **audit** activates or deactivates the audit trace for the domain named by *local_dom_name*. If neither **off** nor **on** is specified, **audit** toggles between activate and deactivate. If **off** is specified, the audit log is deactivated. If **on** is specified, the audit log is activated.

    config (conf): **config** switches dmadmin to configuration mode.

    default (d) -d *local_dom_name*: Sets the value in *local_dom_name* as the default local domain name. If the default is set, the default will be used by all commands that accept a local domain name as a parameter. The default can be overridden by the **-d** option for these commands.

dsdmlog (dsdlg) -d *local_dom_name* **[-y]**: **dsdmlog** destroys the domain transaction log for the domain named in *local_dom_name*. If **-y** is not specified, **dsdmlog** requests confirmation before destroying the log.

indmlog (indlg) -d *local_dom_name* **[-y]**: **idmlog** reinitializes the domain transaction log for the domain named in *local_dom_name*. If **-y** is not specified, **indmlog** requests confirmation before reinitializing the log.

passwd (passwd) *[-r]* *local_dom_name* **rem_dom_name**: **passwd** sets the passwords for the local–remote domain pair named in *local_dom_name* and *rem_dom_name*. When executed, **passwd** requests the passwords for the local and remote domain. The **-r** option causes the encryption routine to use a new key for encrypting the passwords.

printdomain (pd) -d *local_dom_name*: **printdomain** lists information about the domain named in *local_dom_name*.

printstats (pstats) -d *local_dom_name*: **printstats** lists the statistics for the domain named in local_dom_name gathered since statistics gathering was begun with the **stats** command.

quit (q): Exit dmadmin.

stats (stats) -d *local_dom_name* **[off | on | reset]**: **stats** activates or deactivates gathering of statistics for the domain named in *local_dom_name*. **stats** toggles between activate and deactivate if none of **off**, **on**, or **reset** is specified. If **off** is specified, statistics gathering is deactivated. If **on** is specified, statistics gathering is activated. If **reset** is specified, the values for all statistics are reset to 0 and the gathering status is not affected.

unadvertise (unadv) -d *local_dom_name* **[-all | svcname]**: **unadvertise** will mark the local bulletin board of the local domain named by *local_dom_name* that remote services are unavailable for use. If the **-all** option is specified, all remote services will be marked unavailable. If *svcname* is specified, only the named service will be marked unavailable.

16.8.3   Using Configuration Mode

Configuration mode allows the administrator to modify the values in BDMCONFIG dynamically. Operationally, the configuration mode of dmadmin works the same as tmconfig. When the user requests to modify a section, an editor of choice is started with a temporary file open, allowing entry of required values. When the editor is exited, dmadmin reads the values from the temporary file and attempts to update BDMCONFIG. The environment variable EDITOR must be set to the desired editor before entering configuration mode.

The steps to using **dmadmin(1)** in the configuration mode are:

1. Enter configuration mode by executing **dmadmin(1)** with the **-c** option from the command line or using the **config** command while in administration mode.
2. Select the section to be worked with.
3. Select the desired operation.
4. Enter the editor or not.
5. If in editor, make desired changes and exit editor.
6. Answer prompts until action complete.

As with **tmconfig(1)**, fields can be updated, deleted, or changed dynamically only when the effected section is not in use. For instance, the DOMAINID my not be changed, deleted, or a new one added while any domain gateway is running. To make a change of this type, use **tmdamin(1)** to shut down the gateway servers (the server GWTDOMAIN(5) in each domain) in the system, make the changes, then restart the gateway servers.

The field identifiers used by the configuration mode of **dmadmin(1)** use a TA_ prefix on the names used in dmconfig.

To add a record to a section, choose **ADD**, then answer y when **dmadmin(1)** asks if the editor should be entered. In the editor, create the record. The rules for values in the section are the same as described for dmconfig. Add one record at a time. When the editor is exited, answer y to the question about completing the operation. **dmadmin(1)** will then attempt to complete the operation.

To update a record, first retrieve it by selecting RETRIEVE, then select UPDATE and enter the editor. Make the changes in the editor. When the editor is exited, answer **y** to the question about completing the operation. **dmadmin(1)** will then attempt to complete the operation.

To delete a record, first retrieve it by selecting RETRIEVE, then select DELETE. Do not enter the editor. Answer **y** to the question about completing the operation. **dmadmin(1)** will then attempt to complete the operation.

If there are multiple records in a section, the first retrieval will return the first record in the section. Once the first record is retrieved, use the NEXT option to move through the records in the section until the desired record is found, then update or delete as discussed earlier.

A /DOMAIN APPLICATION

The application described in Chapter 14 can be modified to use /Domain so that each branch office maintains its own TUXEDO domain. The home office also maintains a domain. /Q is still used to maintain synchronization between the branch office and home office customer databases.

Figure 16.4 is repeated from the earlier description to show the topology of the application. The enterprise maintains branch offices in Chicago, Dallas, and Los Angeles. The home office is in none of those cities. The customer data base has been partitioned by location to pro-

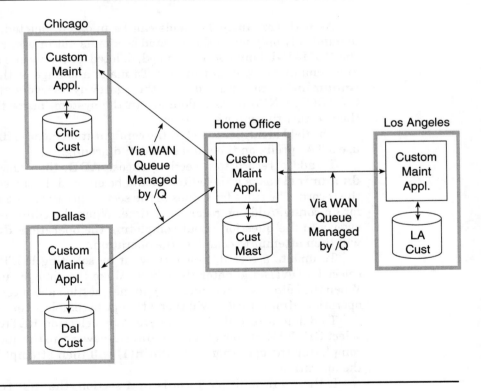

Figure 16.4   Maintaining the home office database.

vide very high performance of the customer maintenance application via a local LAN at each branch office. There is a policy that requires a complete up-to-date copy of the entire customer database at the home office. In reality, there will always be some delay between the time a change is made to a local database and when that same update is made at the home office, but the goal is to minimize that time.

Figure 16.5 shows the detail of design. Each branch runs a separate domain. The customer maintenance client and the customer update service operate in the normal request/response paradigm at a branch office. The customer update service performs the necessary updates to the local customer database in the transaction started by the customer maintenance client. The customer update service uses a **tpacall(3)**, with the TPNOTRAN flag set, to invoke the customer enqueue service with the same request that the client maintenance client sent. The customer enqueue service enqueues the message on the local queue called CUSTQ. At the home office, the native client, customer master client, starts a transaction and invokes the branch office customer dequeue service to retrieve the message, then passes the message to the home office customer update service.

The branch office customer update service uses **tpacall(3)** to invoke a separate enqueuing service instead of calling **tpenqueue(3)** to maintain as high a performance level as possible. The enqueuing is done in a separate transaction to prevent causing a two-phase commit, again to maintain as high a performance as possible. There is no loss of integrity between the update of the database and the enqueuing at the local office because the customer update service retrieves the reply from the customer enqueuing service before doing a **tpreturn(3)**. If the enqueuing process fails, the enqueuing service will return with the TPFAIL flag set, alerting the customer update service of the failure. The customer update service will then return to the customer maintenance client with the TPFAIL flag set, and the customer update service will abort the transaction. The user can then enter the transaction again.

The customer master database at the home office is run as a separate domain from the branches. The home office master client includes both the dequeuing service and the customer update service in the same transaction, incurring a two-phase commit. This simpler approach is used because the performance at the home office is not as critical.

Several variations are possible. If the home office database is not required to be quite so current, the home office master client could be run periodically using the UNIX **cron** mechanism. In this case, the customer dequeue service at the branch office could dequeue blocks of data. Each time the home office client is run, it would retrieve a block of

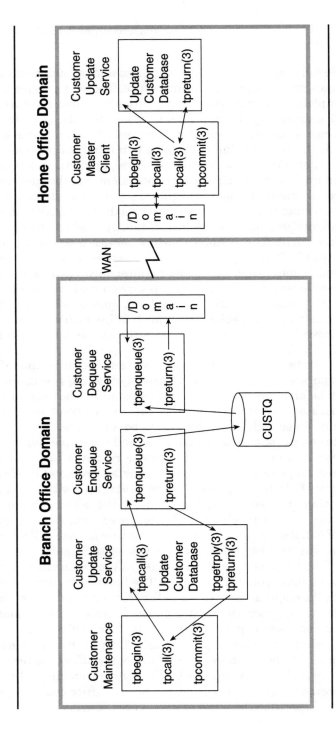

Figure 16.5   Maintaining the home office database with /Domain.

data and update the home office database in a single transaction per block. The client would run until there was nothing left on the queue and stop.

If a daily update is sufficient, the home office client could be run once a day at off peak hours, so as not to load the WAN while it is being heavily used by daily activities.

If there are several branch offices, either a separate home office client could be run for each, or data dependent routing could be used to cycle the requests to the dequeuing service at each branch office in turn.

Another variation of the design would place the enqueue service at the home office. The only problem with this arrangement is that it could adversely affect the performance of the branch office system, perhaps having a negative effect on daily activities. The problem could become especially acute if the WAN failed. In most cases, the queuing should be done locally, to protect the system from communication weaknesses.

This design requires a ubbconfig and a dmconfig file for each domain. For illustration, suppose there is a Dallas branch office and a branch office (called the home branch in this example) physically located in the same building with the home office. The home branch is granted a separate computing platform from the home office. The system uses three domains to support this activity.

The configuration files for the system follow.

```
# Home Office ubbconfig file
*RESOURCES
IPCKEY          123456
MASTER          HOMEOFC
MAXACCESSERS    40
MAXSERVERS      35
MAXSERVICES     75
MODEL           SHM
DOMAINID        HODOM
#
*MACHINES

HOMEOFC
    LMID = HOMEOFC
    TUXDIR ="/home/tuxdir"
    TUXCONFIG = "/home/clh/dombk/hoconfig"
    TLOGDEVICE ="/home/clh/dombk/TLOG"
    TLOGSIZE=10
    APPDIR = "/home/clh/dombk"
```

```
#
*GROUPS
# The home office application group
HOMGRP1
            LMID = HOMEOFC GRPNO = 10
            TMSNAME=TMS TMSCOUNT=2
# The home office domain gateway group
HODGRP      LMID=HOMEOFC GRPNO=22 OPENINFO=NONE
#
*SERVERS

DEFAULT: RESTART=Y MAXGEN=5 REPLYQ=Y CLOPT="-A"
# The server which access the customer database
custsv      SRVGRP=HOMGRP1
            SRVID=1
            CLOPT="-A — NONE"

# The domain gateway servers
DMADM       SRVGRP=HODGRP  SRVID=32
GWADM       SRVGRP=HODGRP  SRVID=30
GWTDOMAIN SRVGRP=HODGRP  SRVID=31

#
*SERVICES
custupd
# End of Home office ubbconfig file
#*************************************************************

# Home office dmconfig file
#
*DM_RESOURCES
#
VERSION=CUSTHO
#
#
*DM_LOCAL_DOMAINS
#
HODOM      GWGRP=HODGRP
    TYPE=TDOMAIN
    DOMAINID="HODOM"
    BLOCKTIME=10
    MAXDATALEN=56
    MAXRDOM=89
```

```
        DMTLOGDEV="/home/clh/dombk/DMTLOGHO"
        SECURITY=DM_PW
#
*DM_REMOTE_DOMAINS
#
HBDOM       TYPE=TDOMAIN
      DOMAINID="HBDOM"
DALDOM      TYPE=TDOMAIN
      DOMAINID="DALDOM"
#
*DM_TDOMAIN
#
HODOM       NWADDR="<put in address of home office>"
HBDOM       NWADDR="<put in address of home office branch>"
DALDOM      NWADDR="<put in address of Dallas branch>"
#
*DM_REMOTE_SERVICES
deqsvc      ROUTING=deqrout
#
*DM_ROUTING
# Routing the dequeue request to the dequeue service to
# either Dallas or the home office branch
deqrout
     FIELD=location BUFTYPE="FML"
     RANGES="'D':DALDOM,'H':HBDOM"
# End of Home office dmconfig file
#*************************************************************

# Home office environment script
TUXDIR=/home/tuxdir; export TUXDIR
TUXCONFIG=/home/clh/dombk/hoconfig; export TUXCONFIG
BDMCONFIG=/home/clh/dombk/BDMHO; export BDMCONFIG
PATH=$TUXDIR/bin:/home/clh/dombk:$PATH; export PATH
LD_LIBRARY_PATH=$TUXDIR/lib:$LD_LIBRARY_PATH; export
LD_LIBRARY_PATH

EDITOR=vi; export EDITOR
# End of Home office environment script
#***********************************************************

# Home office branch ubbconfig
*RESOURCES
IPCKEY          123456
```

```
MASTER         HOMEBR
MAXACCESSERS   40
MAXSERVERS     35
MAXSERVICES    75
MODEL          SHM
DOMAINID  HBDOM
#
*MACHINES
#
HOMEBR
     LMID = HOMEBR
     TUXDIR ="/home/tuxdir"
     TUXCONFIG = "/home/clh/dombk/hbconfig"
     TLOGDEVICE ="/home/clh/dombk/TLOG"
     TLOGSIZE=10
     APPDIR = "/home/clh/dombk"
#
*GROUPS
# The application server group
HBGRP1
          LMID = HOMEBR GRPNO = 10
          TMSNAME=TMS TMSCOUNT=2
# The /Q server group
QUEGRPH
          LMID = HOMEBR GRPNO = 11
          TMSNAME = TMS_QM TMSCOUNT = 2
          OPENINFO = "TUXEDO/QM:/home/clh/dombk/
CUSTQ:HCUSTQSPC"

# The domain gateway group
HBDGRP    LMID=HOMEBR GRPNO=22 OPENINFO=NONE
#
*SERVERS

DEFAULT: RESTART=Y MAXGEN=5 REPLYQ=Y CLOPT="-A"
# The server which accesses the customer database
custsvc        SRVGRP=HBGRP1
               SRVID=1
               CLOPT="-A — HCUSTQSPC"

# The server which will dequeue the customer updates
deqsv          SRVGRP=HBGRP1 SRVID=2
               CLOPT="-A — HCUSTQSPC"
```

```
# The server which will enqueue the customer updates
enqsv           SRVGRP=HBGRP1 SRVID=3
                CLOPT="-A — HCUSTQSPC"

# The domain gateway servers
DMADM           SRVGRP=HBDGRP   SRVID=32
GWADM           SRVGRP=HBDGRP   SRVID=30
GWTDOMAIN SRVGRP=HBDGRP   SRVID=31

# The /Q server
TMQUEUE
    SRVGRP = QUEGRPH   SRVID = 1
    GRACE = 0   RESTART = Y CONV = N
    CLOPT = "-s HCUSTQSPC:TMQUEUE —  "
#
*SERVICES
custupd
enqsvc
deqsvc
# End of Home office branch ubbconfig
#****************************************************************

# Home office branch dmconfig
#
*DM_RESOURCES
#
VERSION=CUSTHB
#
#
*DM_LOCAL_DOMAINS
#
HBDOM     GWGRP=HBDGRP
          TYPE=TDOMAIN
          DOMAINID="HBDOM"
          BLOCKTIME=10
          MAXDATALEN=56
          MAXRDOM=89
          DMTLOGDEV="/home/clh/dombk/DMTLOGHB"
          SECURITY=DM_PW
#
*DM_REMOTE_DOMAINS
#
HODOM     TYPE=TDOMAIN
```

```
              DOMAINID="HODOM"
DALDOM    TYPE=TDOMAIN
              DOMAINID="DALDOM"
#
*DM_TDOMAIN
#
HODOM     NWADDR="<put in address of home office>"
HBDOM     NWADDR="<put in address of home office branch>"
DALDOM    NWADDR="<put in address of Dallas branch>"
#
*DM_LOCAL_SERVICES
custsvc
deqsvc
#
*DM_REMOTE_SERVICES
# Assign an alias for remote access
custsvcr  RNAME="custsvc"      ROUTING=custrout
#
*DM_ROUTING
# Route to the proper branch
custrout
     FIELD=location BUFTYPE="FML"
     RANGES="'D':DALDOM"
# End of Home Office branch dmconfig
#*************************************************************

# Home office branch environment script
TUXDIR=/home/tuxdir; export TUXDIR
TUXCONFIG=/home/clh/dombk/hbconfig; export TUXCONFIG
BDMCONFIG=/home/clh/dombk/BDMHB; export BDMCONFIG
PATH=$TUXDIR/bin:/home/clh/dombk:$PATH; export PATH

LD_LIBRARY_PATH=$TUXDIR/lib:$LD_LIBRARY_PATH;        export
LD_LIBRARY_PATH

EDITOR=vi; export EDITOR
# End of home office branch environment script
#*************************************************************

# Dallas branch ubbconfig
*RESOURCES
IPCKEY         123456
MASTER         DALLAS
```

```
MAXACCESSERS    40
MAXSERVERS      35
MAXSERVICES     75
MODEL           SHM
DOMAINID   DALDOM
#
*MACHINES
#
DALLAS
     LMID = DALLAS
     TUXDIR ="/home/tuxdir"
     TUXCONFIG = "/home/clh/dombk/dalconfig"
     TLOGDEVICE ="/home/clh/dombk/TLOG"
     TLOGSIZE=10
     APPDIR = "/home/clh/dombk"
#
*GROUPS
# Application server group
DALGRP1
          LMID = DALLAS GRPNO = 10
          TMSNAME=TMS TMSCOUNT=2


# /Q server group
QUEGRPD
          LMID = DALLAS GRPNO = 11
          TMSNAME = TMS_QM TMSCOUNT = 2
          OPENINFO = "TUXEDO/QM:/home/clh/dombk/
CUSTQ:DCUSTQSPC"


# domain gateway group
DALDGRP         LMID=DALLAS GRPNO=22 OPENINFO=NONE
#
*SERVERS

DEFAULT: RESTART=Y MAXGEN=5 REPLYQ=Y CLOPT="-A"
# customer database access server
custsv          SRVGRP=DALGRP1
         SRVID=1
         CLOPT="-A — HCUSTQSPC"

# dequeuing server
deqsv           SRVGRP=DALGRP1 SRVID=2
             CLOPT="-A — HCUSTQSPC"
```

```
# enqueuing server
enqsv          SRVGRP=DALGRP1 SRVID=3
               CLOPT="-A - HCUSTQSPC"

# domain gateway servers
DMADM          SRVGRP=DALDGRP SRVID=32
GWADM          SRVGRP=DALDGRP SRVID=30
GWTDOMAIN      SRVGRP=DALDGRP SRVID=31

# /Q server
TMQUEUE
        SRVGRP = QUEGRPH  SRVID = 1
        GRACE = 0  RESTART = Y CONV = N
        CLOPT = "-s DCUSTQSPC:TMQUEUE - "
#
*SERVICES
custupd
enqsvc
deqsvc
# End of Dallas ubbconfig
#*******************************************************

# Dallas dmconfig
#
*DM_RESOURCES
#
VERSION=CUSTDAL
#
#
*DM_LOCAL_DOMAINS
#
DALDOM   GWGRP=DALDGRP
         TYPE=TDOMAIN
         DOMAINID="DALDOM"
         BLOCKTIME=10
         MAXDATALEN=56
         MAXRDOM=89
         DMTLOGDEV="/home/clh/dombk/DMTLOGDAL"
         SECURITY=DM_PW
#
*DM_REMOTE_DOMAINS
#
```

```
HODOM       TYPE=TDOMAIN
            DOMAINID="HODOM"
HBDOM       TYPE=TDOMAIN
            DOMAINID="HBDOM"
#
*DM_TDOMAIN
#
HODOM       NWADDR="<put in address of home office>"
HBDOM       NWADDR="<put in address of home office branch>"
DALDOM      NWADDR="<put in address of Dallas branch>"
#
*DM_LOCAL_SERVICES
custsvc
deqsvc
#
*DM_REMOTE_SERVICES
custsvcr  RNAME="custsvc"        ROUTING=custrout
#
*DM_ROUTING
custrout
     FIELD=location BUFTYPE="FML"
     RANGES="'H':HBDOM"
# End of Dallas dmconfig
#*************************************************************

# Dallas environment script
TUXDIR=/home/tuxdir; export TUXDIR
TUXCONFIG=/home/clh/dombk/dalconfig; export TUXCONFIG
BDMCONFIG=/home/clh/dombk/BDMDAL; export BDMCONFIG
PATH=$TUXDIR/bin:/home/clh/dombk:$PATH; export PATH

LD_LIBRARY_PATH=$TUXDIR/lib:$LD_LIBRARY_PATH;       export
LD_LIBRARY_PATH

EDITOR=vi; export EDITOR
# end of Dallas environment script
#*************************************************************
```

The home office configuration contains the information required to invoke the dequeue service at each branch, then update the home office customer database. The dmconfig file uses data dependent routing to access the correct dequeue service for the branch being processed.

The branch configuration is the same for both branch offices, except that the names have been change to prevent human confusion. Each branch advertises deqsvc as a local service available for use from a remote domain. The branch dmconfig uses an alias for custsvc, custsvcr, to allow using the same service locally and remotely. Data dependent routing in the dmconfig file is used for custsvcr to allow updates to any branch office customer database from any other branch.

Each branch ubbconfig file provides the name of the local queue in **CLOPTS**. The name of the local queue is stored by custsv in **tpsvrinit(3)**, and used by custsvc to enqueue updates to the local queue for retrieval by the home office.

The servers custsv, enqsv, and deqsv are identical. The **tpsvrinit(3)** in the home office custsv will find "NONE" in the name of the local queue space and set a flag indicating that there is no enqueuing.

All branch clients are identical. Each branch work station should store the local branch identifier in an environment variable, or some other globally accessible form so that the branch client can retrieve the local branch identifier. The client will access the customer access service custsvc for local database access and custsvcr for accessing the customer database from a remote domain.

More information on techniques for partitioning is provided in Chapter 5.

17

TUXEDO Release 6.1 Features

17.1   OVERVIEW

The significant features included with Release 6.1 are:

- Addition of an Event Broker that allows an application to post and detect application and system events
- Enhanced security that includes Access Control Lists (ACLs)
- Programmed administration using an administration application programming interface (/AdminAPI)
- A graphical user interface (GUI) administration tool

The Event Broker is a TUXEDO subsystem that allows services and clients to post exception conditions that are then detected by the system. When an event is posted, TUXEDO will notify a client using the unsolicited messaging capability, invoke a service, or put the event information into a reliable queue, depending on how an application program requested notification.

The enhanced security includes the ability to use ACLs to limit access to services, reliable queues, and events. If the administrator has enabled the ACL feature, whenever access is attempted to one of these resources, an associated ACL is checked to determine the access rights of the user.

The programmed administration feature provides the capability of performing administration functions from an application program. Users of administration programs are restricted to those authorized to perform administration.

The GUI administration tool pulls all administration into a single place where standard GUI techniques can be used. Many functions can be performed by a single mouse click. This tool will be especially useful for administration of large multinode systems.

All applications that have been developed for previous releases will run with Release 6.1. Recompiling all application programs from previous releases before running them with Release 6.1 is recommended. Configuration files from previous releases should be recreated with the Release 6.1 **tmloadcf(1)** to convert them to Release 6.1 format.

17.2 THE EVENT BROKER

17.2.1 Overview

The TUXEDO Event Broker provides the capability for posting messages, which are then distributed to processes that have subscribed to receiving event notices. Processes can specify the name of events and a set of rules to specify specific events for subscription. In a way, the Event Broker provides another processing paradigm by providing a method allowing a many-to-many relationship between sending and receiving processes.

The Event Broker provides the following capabilities.

- Any TUXEDO client or service can post events and subscribe to events.
- Events can be subscribed to via three methods:
  - As unsolicited messages by clients
  - As an invocation of a service
  - Via a reliable queue
- The same event can be posted by many processes.
- Many processes can subscribe to the same event, and each subscription can be requested by any of the three methods independently.
- TUXEDO includes a set of system events that can be subscribed to by application processes.

The Event Broker should only be used to handle exception cases. An on-line inventory system can use the Event Broker to notify a person when the stock level of an item falls below a critical level. The person could then check to see why the replenishment has not been completed. A person could also be notified if the delivery of replenishment has not been completed by a prespecified date.

17.2.2   **How the Event Broker Works**

The Event Broker uses two processes: The process that receives notification subscribes to the event by name using the function **tpsubscribe(3)**; the process that creates the specific instance of an event uses **tppost(3)** to create the notification and send the accompanying message. Figure 17.1 shows how event posting and notification work for a client that specifies notification by the unsolicited message method.

The steps as shown in Figure 17.1 are:

1. The client starts and subscribes to the event with **tpsubscribe(3)**.
2. Some process, either another client or a service, posts the event with **tppost(3)**.
3. The subscribing client receives the event and its message with its unsolicited message handler.

The Event Broker for user events is implemented by the TUXEDO server TMUSREVT(5). Services provided by TMUSREVT(5) are invoked by **tpsubscribe(5)** to store the subscription parameters. **tppost(3)** invokes services in TMUSREVT(5) to post the event. If the subscription called for notification by unsolicited message, TMUSREVT(5) services create a message using the data provided with **tppost(3)** and send an unsolicited message to the subscribing client.

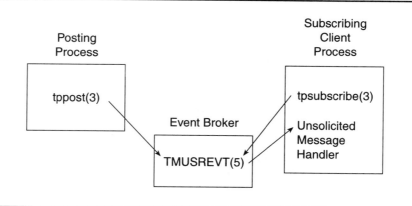

Figure 17.1   Event Broker processing.

17.2.3   **Posting Events**

Application processes post events with the function **tppost(3)**. Any TUXEDO process (client or service) can post an event. The form of **tppost(3)** is:

```
int tppost(char *eventname, char *data, long len, long flags)
```

tppost(3) posts the event identified by *eventname*. If *data* is not NULL, the contents of *data* are provided to subscribers as a message. *len* is the length of *data* and *flags* are the usual TUXEDO function flags. If present, *data* must point to an area allocated with **tpalloc(3)**. *data* may be any buffer type recognized by TUXEDO. *len* is ignored if the buffer type of data provides the length internally, such as with FML and VIEW buffer types. If *data* is NULL, no message is provided when subscribers are notified.

If the process calling **tppost(3)** is in transaction mode and the TPNOTRAN flag is not set, subscribers who called **tpsubscribe(3)** with the TPEVTRAN flag set in ctl->flags will be notified with the posting transaction. Subscribers who called **tpsubscribe(3)** with TPEVTRAN not set will be notified outside of the positing transaction.

If the TPNOREPLY flag is not set, **tppost(3)** returns when all subscribers to the event have been successfully notified with the number of notifications set in tpurcode.

The valid flags for **tppost(3)** are:

TPSIGRSTRT: The flag TPSIGRSTRT should always be specified with **tppost(3)** to be sure that the call is reissued if processing is interrupted by a signal during the execution of the call.

TPNOTRAN: If TPNOTRAN is set the posting is not made on behalf of the callers transaction. If the posting fails, the current transaction is not affected if TPNOTRAN is set.

TPNOREPLY: When TPNOREPLY is set, **tppost(3)** returns immediately after posting the event without waiting for the system to process subscriptions of the event. If **tppost(3)** is called with this flag set, tpurcode is set to 0 upon return, no matter how many processes have subscribed to the event.

TPNOBLOCK: The flag TPNOBLOCK will cause **tppost(3)** to return immediately with the error TPEBLOCK without posting the event if there is a blocking condition, such as when there is no room in the internal buffer used for messages.

TPNOTIME: The flag TPNOTIME prevents a timeout for any reason other than a transaction timeout. This timeout is called the blocking timeout. TPNOBLOCK and TPNOTIME are mutually exclusive. The transaction may still fail due to a transaction timeout.

tppost(3) returns 0 for success and −1 for failure (it is a good idea to look for < 0 to check for failure). When success is returned, tpurcode will contain the number of successful subscribers that have been notified of the event. On failure, tperrno will contain a value to indicate the type of error. The possible errors for **tppost(3)** are:

TPEINVAL: Error TPEINVAL means that the parameters were set incorrectly, such as when an invalid value is placed in *flags*.

TPENOENT: TPENOENT means that **tppost(3)** could not access the TUXEDO Event Broker.

TPETRAN: Error TPETRAN occurs when the posting process is in transaction mode, the Event Broker is not able to function in transaction mode, and the TPNOTRAN flag was not specified.

TPETIME: Error TPETIME indicates that a timeout has occurred. If the process was in transaction mode when the timeout occurred, the error is a transaction timeout. A transaction timeout sets an internal flag that will prevent the transaction from being committed. A transaction that has timed out can only be aborted. If the process was not in transaction mode and the TPNOBLOCK flag was not set, error TPETIME occurs on a blocking timeout.

TPSVCFAIL: The error TPSVCFAIL is set when the Event Broker cannot post the event. If the call was made in transaction mode and the TPNOTRAN flag was not set, the transaction is marked abort only. When this error is returned the number of nontransactional postings completed is returned in tpurcode.

TPSVCERR: The error TPSVCERR is set when the Event Broker is not able to process the posting.

TPEBLOCK: The error TPEBLOCK means that a blocking condition was present, but the TPNOBLOCK flag was set.

TPGOTSIG: Error TPGOTSIG indicates that a signal occurred during process of the function, but the flag TPSIGRSTRT was not set.

TPESYSTEM: The TPESYSTEM error means that there was a failure within TUXEDO. A message describing the problem is written to the log file.

TPEOS: The TPEOS error means that an operating system error has occurred.

tppost(3) is used to post events. The type of notification is determined by use of **tpsubscribe(3)** and is independent of the posting process. When an event is posted, it immediately becomes available to all processes that have subscribed to it.

The following code fragment illustrates use of **tppost(3)**.

```
/* sample to illustrate using tppost(3) */

#include <atmi.h>   /* TUXEDO Header File */
#include "evview.h"
 .
 .
 .

void
POSTSAMP(TPSVCINFO *rqst)
{
     int i, ret;
     long msglen, subhnd;
     char workstr[101];
     char workarea[101];
     struct evview *mypdata;
          .
          .
          .
     /* get data and do service processing */
          .
          .
          .
     if(workstr[0] == 'p') /* test for exception */
     {
          /* get space for posting message */
          msglen = sizeof(struct evview);
          if((mypdata = (struct evview *) tpalloc("VIEW",
"evview",
msglen+1)) == (struct evview *) NULL) {
          userlog("Error allocating msg buffer %d\n", tperrno);
          }

          /* put data into posting message pointed to by
             mypdata here */
```

```
        .
        .
        .
    /* post the event with the msg pointed to by mypdata */
    if(tppost("mypost", (char *) mypdata, 0, 0) < 0)
    {
            /* handle posting error here */
    }
        tpfree(mypdata); /* free up the event message buf */
}
    /* complete the processing for the service */
        .
        .
        .
```

17.2.4   **Subscribing to Events**

Processes detect events by subscribing with the function **tpsubscribe(3)**. The form of **tpsubscribe(3)** is:

```
long tpsubscribe(char * eventexpr, char *filter, TPEVCTL *ctl, long
flags)
```

eventexpr is a NULL terminated string with a maximum length of 255 bytes containing a regular expression that names one or more events. The form of the regular expression is the same as used by the UNIX editors vi() and ed(). For example, **"mypost"** is a regular expression that will select the event named **"mypost"**. The regular expression **my.*** will select all events with names starting with my.

filter is a string containing a boolean rule used to select the specific instance of the event. The filter rule is applied to the message associated with the event. The form of *filter* depends on the type of buffer used for the message. If an FML or VIEW type buffer is used, *filter* is a boolean expression of the form used for conditional testing in C, except that the operators **<<**, **>>**, **|**, **&**, and **?** are not allowed. If a STRING buffer is used, filter is a regular expression as used in **vi()** or **ed()**.

For example, a filter for a VIEW or FML buffer could be **"mystr1 == 'p' || mystr1 == 'y'"**. This example selects events where the field mystr1 contains the value **'p'** or **'y'**. Note that variables used in the filter rule must be the names of fields in the buffer definitions.

ctl points to an event control structure. If *ctl* is NULL, the subscription defaults to using unsolicited notification. The fields in the event control structure are:

```
long flags;
char name1[32];
char name2[32];
TPQCTL qctl;
```

The valid bits for *flags* are:

TPEVSERVICE: TPEVSERVICE indicates that the caller wants to subscribe to events using service notification. If this flag is set, notification is made by invoking the service named in ctl->name1. TPEVSERVICE and TPEVQUEUE are mutually exclusive.

TPEVQUEUE: TPEVQUEUE indicates that the caller wants to subscribe to events using reliable queue notification. TPEVQUEUE and TPEVSERVICE are mutually exclusive. If this flag is set, the name of the queue space must be in ctl->name1 and the name of the queue in ctl->name2. ctl->qctl may be used to control queuing in the same manner as when using **tpenqueue(3)**.

TPEVTRAN: TPEVTRAN indicates that the notification for the event is to be included in the transaction of the poster, if the poster was in transaction mode when calling **tppost(3)**. This flag is not valid when **tpsubscribe(3)** is called from a client. TPEVTRAN may be used together with either TPEVSERVICE or TPEVQUEUE.

TPEVPERSIST: If this flag is set, the Event Broker will save the information on the subscription until errors preventing posting have been corrected. By default, if posting cannot be made because the resource named in the subscription, such as a queue, is not available, the Event Broker deletes the subscription. If this flag is used in combination with TPEVTRAN, and the resource is not available at the time of notification, any transaction attempting notification will be marked abort only, but the subscription will remain.

tpsubscribe(3) will fail with error TPEMATCH if an attempt is made to subscribe twice with the same subscription parameters. The Event Broker uses various factors to determine if a subscription is a duplicate depending on the type of notification requested. No matter the type of notification, the test for duplicates checks *eventexpr*, *filter*, and the type of notification.

If the subscription is requesting unsolicited notification, the callers CLIENTID is included in the check for duplicates. In other words, multiple clients can subscribe to the same event in exactly the same manner by unsolicited notification.

If the subscription is requesting notification by invoking a service (ctl->flags set to TPEVSERVICE), the subscription will be considered a duplicate if the values of *eventexpr*, *filter*, and ctl->name1 are the same.

If the subscription is requesting notification by reliable queue (ctl->flags set to TPEVQUEUE), the subscription will be considered a duplicate if the values of *eventexpr*, *filter, ctl->name1, ctl->name2,* and TPQCOORID are not set in ctl->qctl.flags or if TPQCOORID is set in ctl->qctl.flags and the values in ctl->qctl.corrid match.

The valid bits that can be set in *flags* are:

TPSIGRSTRT: The flag TPSIGRSTRT should always be specified with **tpsubscribe(3)** to be sure that the call is reissued if processing is interrupted by a signal during the execution of the call.

TPNOBLOCK: The flag TPNOBLOCK will cause **tpsubscribe(3)** to return immediately with the error TPEBLOCK without posting the event if there is a blocking condition, such as when there is no room in the internal buffer used for messages.

TPNOTIME: The flag TPNOTIME prevents a timeout for any reason other than a transaction timeout. This timeout is called the blocking timeout. TPNOBLOCK and TPNOTIME are mutually exclusive. The transaction may still fail due to a transaction timeout.

When successful, **tpsubscribe(3)** returns a handle that identifies the specific subscription. The handle can be used with **tpunsubscribe(3)** to remove the specific subscription. If **tpsubscribe(3)** fails, it returns –1 and sets **tperrno** to indicate the specific error. The error that can occur for **tpsubscribe(3)** are:

TPEINVAL: Error TPEINVAL means that the parameters were set incorrectly, such as when an invalid value is placed in *flags*.

TPENOENT: TPENOENT means that **tpsubscribe(3)** could not access the TUXEDO Event Broker.

TPELIMIT: TPELIMIT means that the maximum number of subscriptions allowed by the Event Broker has been reached.

TPEMATCH: TPEMATCH means that the subscription is a duplicate of a subscription already known to the Event Broker.

TPETIME: Error TPETIME indicates that a timeout has occurred. If the process was in transaction mode when the timeout occurred, the error is a transaction timeout. A transaction timeout sets an internal flag that will prevent the transaction from being committed. A transaction that has timed out can only be aborted. If the process was not in transaction mode and the TPNOBLOCK flag was not set, error TPETIME occurs on a blocking timeout.

TPEBLOCK: The error TPEBLOCK means that a blocking condition was present, but the TPNOBLOCK flag was set.

TPGOTSIG: Error TPGOTSIG indicates that a signal occurred during process of the function, but the flag TPSIGRSTRT was not set.

TPESYSTEM: The TPESYSTEM error means that there was a failure within TUXEDO. A message describing the problem is written to the log file.

TPEOS: The TPEOS error means that an operating system error has occurred.

Event subscriptions are removed with **tpunsubscribe(3)**. The form of **tpunsubscribe(3)** is:

```
int tpunsubscribe(long subhandle, long flags)
```

tpunsubscribe(3) removes the event identified by **subhandle** from the event subscription list. If *subhandle* contains the value –1, all nonpersistent subscriptions made by the calling process are removed. Persistent subscriptions (subscriptions made with TPEVPERSIST set in ctl->flags) must be removed using the specific handle returned by **tpsubscribe(3)**.

subhandle must be a valid handle as returned by a previous **tpsubscribe(3)**. Any valid handle can be used even if the subscription associated with the handle was made by another process. The valid bit settings for *flags* are:

TPSIGRSTRT: The flag TPSIGRSTRT should always be specified with **tpunsubscribe(3)** to be sure that the call is reissued if processing is interrupted by a signal during the execution of the call.

TPNOBLOCK: The flag TPNOBLOCK will cause **tpunsubscribe(3)** to return immediately with the error TPEBLOCK without posting the event if there is a blocking condition, such as when there is no room in the internal buffer used for messages.

TPNOTIME: The flag TPNOTIME prevents a timeout for any reason other than a transaction timeout. This timeout is called the blocking timeout. TPNOBLOCK and TPNOTIME are mutually exclusive. The transaction may still fail due to a transaction timeout.

tpunsubscribe(3) returns the number of subscriptions removed in tpurcode (>=0), whether successful or unsuccessful. The number of subscriptions removed will be greater than one only when the wild card (–1) is used for *subhandle*. **tpunsubscribe(3)** will return unsuccessfully if the Event Broker is unable to remove one or more of the selected subscriptions, with tpurcode set to the number of subscriptions actually removed. **tpunsubscribe(3)** returns –1 for unsuccessful completion with **tperrno** set to indicate the specific error. The errors that can be returned by **tpunsubscribe(3)** are:

TPEINVAL: Error TPEINVAL means that the parameters were set incorrectly, such as when an invalid value is placed in *flags*.

TPENOENT: TPENOENT means that **tpunsubscribe(3)** could not access the TUXEDO Event Broker.

TPETIME: Error TPETIME indicates that a timeout has occurred. If the process was in transaction mode when the timeout occurred, the error is a transaction timeout. A transaction timeout sets an internal flag that will prevent the transaction from being committed. A transaction that has timed out can only be aborted. If the process was not in transaction mode and the TPNOBLOCK flag was not set, error TPETIME occurs on a blocking timeout.

TPEBLOCK: The error TPEBLOCK means that a blocking condition was present, but the TPNOBLOCK flag was set.

TPGOTSIG: Error TPGOTSIG indicates that a signal occurred during process of the function, but the flag TPSIGRSTRT was not set.

TPESYSTEM: The TPESYSTEM error means that there was a failure within TUXEDO. A message describing the problem is written to the log file.

TPEOS: The TPEOS error means that an operating system error has occurred.

17.2.5   **Subscribing Using Unsolicited Message Notification**

TUXEDO clients may subscribe to events using the unsolicited message feature. The client program includes the following procedures to subscribe to events using unsolicited message notification:

1. An unsolicited message handler routine
2. A call to **tpsetunsol(3)**

3. One or more calls to **tpsubscribe(3)** with *ctl* set to NULL
4. A call to **tpunsubscribe(3)**

The client must remove all subscriptions it has set by calling **tpunsubscribe(3)** before calling **tpterm(3)**.

The call to **tpsetunsol(3)** must precede any calls to **tpsubscribe(3)** in order of execution.

The message handler must be programmed to accept the type of buffer used by the posting program with the call **tppost(3)**. If multiple buffer types are possible, the message handler should use **tptypes(3)** to determine the type of buffer received. See Chapter 8 for more information on receiving unsolicited messages.

The following code fragment illustrates how a client can subscribe to events using the unsolicited message method.

```c
#include <stdio.h>
#include <sys/types.h>
#include <unistd.h>
#include <stdlib.h>

#include "atmi.h"        /* TUXEDO  Header File */
#include "fml.h"   /* put in by carl */
#include "evview.h"

char *msg;
long msglen;
void msghand(char*, long, long);
void (*msghptr)() = msghand;

main(argc, argv)
int argc;
char *argv[];
{

    int ret, i;
    int done = 0;
    long subhnd;
    uid_t myid;
    char myname[100];
    char myinit[5];
    char *dummy, answ[2];
    TPINIT *initbuf;
```

```
    /* allocate an initialization buffer */
    if ((initbuf = (TPINIT *) tpalloc("TPINIT", NULL, 0)) ==
(TPINIT *) NULL)
    {
        printf("tpalloc fail on tpinit, %d\n", tperrno);
    }
    /* set unsolicited message flag */
    initbuf->flags = TPU_DIP;

    /* put user id string into initialization buffer */
    /* getpw(getuid(), myname); */
    initbuf->usrname[3] = NULL;
    printf("usrname %s cltname %s\n", initbuf->usrname,
initbuf->cltname);

    /* Attach to System/T as a Client Process */
    if (tpinit(initbuf) == -1) {
        fprintf(stderr, "Tpinit failed %d\n", tperrno);
        exit(1);
    }

    /* set up ready for an unsolicited message */
    (*tpsetunsol) (msghptr);

    if((subhnd = tpsubscribe("my.*", NULL, NULL, 0)) < 0)
    {
        printf("subscribe failed %d", tperrno);
    }
    /* loop waiting for unsolicited message */
    while(!done)
    {
    if(tpchkunsol() < 0)
    {
        printf("tpchkunsol failed %d\n", tperrno);
        exit(1);
    }

    sleep(5);
    printf("continue y or n?\n");
    dummy = gets(answ);
    if(answ[0] == 'n' || answ[0] == 'N')
    {
```

```
            done = 1;
        }
    } /* end of while not done */

    tpunsubscribe;
    tpterm();
} /* end of main */

void msghand(char *msg, long msglen, long flags)
{
    char workstr[200];

    printf("entering message handler\n");
    printf("rec msg: %s %s\n", msg);
    return;
}
```

17.2.6   Subscribing Using Reliable Queues

The steps to using reliable queues for posting events are:

1. Call **tpsubscribe(3)** with ctl->flags set to TPEVQUEUE in a server **tpsvrinit(3)**. Be sure the correct queue space and queue name are set in ctl->name1 and ctl->name2 before calling **tpsubscribe(3)**.
2. Post events with the name used in the subscribe. Events may be posted from any TUXEDO process.
3. Dequeue the events from the reliable queue from any TUXEDO process.
4. Remove the subscription with **tpunsubscribe(3)** using the handle returned by **tpsubscribe(3)**. If the subscription is valid for the entire time the domain is running, use **tpunsubscribe(3)** in the **tpsvrdone(3)** of the same server that called the **tpsubscribe(3)**.

If multiple instances of the server subscribing to the event are started, the event will be subscribed to only when the first instance is started, and will return a **TPEMATCH** error for each additional instance. In some circumstances it is desirable to provide a special server to subscribe and remove subscriptions.

TPEVCTL includes TPQCTL, so it is possible to use queuing options in the same manner as when calling **tpenqueue(3)**. See Chapter 14 for more information on queuing and dequeuing messages.

The following server code illustrates how to subscribe to an event using a reliable queue.

```
#include <stdio.h>
#include <ctype.h>
#include <Uunix.h>
#include <atmi.h>    /* TUXEDO Header File */
#include <userlog.h>      /* TUXEDO Header File */
#include "evview.h"

long subhnd;

tpsvrinit(int argc, char *argv[])
{
     TPEVCTL ctl;

     /* note that server is starting and report arguments */
     userlog("The evsub server is starting");

     memset(&ctl, 0, sizeof(ctl));
     ctl.flags = TPEVQUEUE;
     strcpy(ctl.name1, "EVQSPC");
     strcpy(ctl.name2, "EQ");
     if((subhnd = tpsubscribe("mypost", NULL, &ctl, 0)) < 0)
     {
          userlog("subscribe failed %d", tperrno);
     }
     return(0);
}

void tpsvrdone()
{
     userlog("entering tpsvrdone in evsub");

     if(tpunsubscribe(subhnd, 0) < 0)
     {
          userlog("unsubscribe failed %d", tperrno);
     }
     return;
}
/* dummy service */
```

```
void
evsubsvc(TPSVCINFO *rqst)
{
    /* Return with no buffer. */
    tpreturn(TPSUCCESS, 0, NULL, 0L, 0);
}
```

17.2.7   **Subscribing to Events by Invoking a Service**

To invoke a service when an event occurs, call **tpsubscribe(3)** with
ctl->flags set to TPEVSERVICE and the name of the service in
ctl->name1. It is best to include the call to **tpsubscribe(3)** in a server
tpsvrinit(3). Be sure to call **tpunsubscribe(3)** using the handle
returned by **tpsubscribe(3)** to remove the subscription. If the subscription will be active the entire time the domain is running, call
tpunsubscribe(3) in the **tpsvrdone(3)** of the same server that set the
subscription. The service invoked by the event may be in the same
server that calls **tpsubscribe(3)** or may be a service in any other server.

If multiple instances of the server that subscribes to the event are
started, the event will be subscribed to only when the first instance is
started, and will return a TPEMATCH error for each additional instance. In some circumstances it is desirable to provide a special server
to subscribe and remove subscriptions.

The following code illustrates how to subscribe to an event by invoking a service.

```
#include <stdio.h>
#include <ctype.h>
#include <Uunix.h>
#include <atmi.h>    /* TUXEDO Header File */
#include <userlog.h>     /* TUXEDO Header File */
#include "evview.h"

long subhnd;

tpsvrinit(int argc, char *argv[])
{
    TPEVCTL ctl;

    /* note that server is starting and report arguments */
    userlog("The evsub server is starting");
```

```
                memset(&ctl, 0, sizeof(ctl));
                ctl.flags = TPEVSERVICE;
                strcpy(ctl.name1, "evsvc");
                if((subhnd = tpsubscribe("mypost", NULL, &ctl, 0)) < 0)
                {
                        userlog("subscribe failed %d", tperrno);
                }

                return(0);
        }

        void tpsvrdone()
        {
                int ret;
                userlog("entering tpsvrdone in evsub");

                ret = tpunsubscribe(subhnd, 0);
                if(ret < 0);
                {
                        userlog("ret %d", ret);
                        userlog("unsubscribe failed %d", tperrno);
                }
                return;
        }
        /* dummy service */
        void
        evsubsvc(TPSVCINFO *rqst)
        {
                /* Return with no buffer. */
                tpreturn(TPSUCCESS, 0, NULL, 0L, 0);
        }
```

17.3   SECURITY

17.3.1   Features

TUXEDO Release 6.1 provides five levels of security and also provides means to add additional security such as Kerberos. The enterprise desiring to use Kerberos or another security package with TUXEDO should get information about the product and how to use it with TUXEDO from the product vendor. It is also possible to use security services developed by the enterprise. The levels of security are:

Level one: Level one security, provided by the usual UNIX security, is called operating system security. This security places restrictions on who can use clients and who can boot the system. This level of security is available with all releases of TUXEDO.

Level two: Level two security, called application password security, is provided with TUXEDO. This level requires the user of a client to enter a valid password before the client is allowed to attach to TUXEDO. This level of security is available with TUXEDO Release 4.2 and later.

Level three: Level three security, called user authentication, provides an authentication service that checks for the combination of user identification, password, and client name before the client is allowed to attach to TUXEDO. The authorization service provides a ticket that can be used in services to further restrict the user. This level is available with Release 5 and later.

Level four: Level four security, called optional access control lists, provides a means to use an optional access control list (ACL) to control access to services, reliable queues, and events. This level of security requires authentication of the user in the same manner as for level three. A service, queue, or event can be associated with an ACL to limit access to these resources by users and groups of users. If no ACL is associated with the resource, access is available to everyone, hence the appellation of "optional." This level is available with Release 6.1 and later.

Level five: Level five security, called mandatory access control lists, is similar to level four, except that an ACL must be associated with every resource to allow access. This level is available with Release 6.1 and later.

Application programming for Release 6.1 security is the same as described in Chapter 12.

17.3.2   **Security Administration**

The security level for a domain is determined by the entry in the **SECURITY** parameter in the RESOURCES section of the configuration file. The **SECURITY** parameter for Release 6.1 has the form:

```
SECURITY NONE | APP_PW| USER_AUTH | ACL | MANDATORY_ACL
```

The value NONE indicates level one security. The value APP_PW indicates level two security. For compatibility with previous releases, if APP_PW is specified and a value is provided with **AUTHSVC**, security is raised to level three. The value USER_AUTH indicates level three. The value ACL indicates level four. The value MANDATORY_ACL indicates level five. If USER_AUTH, ACL, or MANDATORY_ACL are specified, the name of the authorization service must be provided with the parameter **AUTHSVC**.

The RESOURCES section parameter **MAXACLGROUPS** must be if USER_AUTH, ACL, or MANDATORY_ACL is set for **SECURITY**. The default is 16K groups, causing TUXEDO to attempt to allocate sufficient memory to store that many ACL groups. The form is:

```
MAXACLGROUPS numeric_value
```

numeric_value should be set to the maximum number of expected ACL groups.

If security is set to level three (USER_AUTH), **tpaddusr(1)**, **tpmodusr(1)**, and **tpdelusr(1)** may be used to create, modify, and delete users as explained in Chapter 12, but the new Release 6.1 utilities or the graphical user interface administration tool should be used to manage users for Release 6.1. The Release 6.1 user authorization utilities are described in the following paragraphs.

> **tpusradd(1)**: **tpusradd(1)** is used to add new users to the TUXEDO security authorization file. A user can be associated with a client name, a numeric user identification, and a numeric group identification. The user identification and group identification are for use by TUXEDO security and are independent of the UNIX uid and gid, but can be assigned the same values. The file $APPDIR/tpusr is used to store information about users. **tpusradd(1)** will create $APPDIR/tpusr if it does not already exist.

> **tpusrmod(1)**: **tpusrmod(1)** modifies the values for a user in the authorization file $APPDIR/tpusr. It is possible to modify all values for the user including the user sign on value.

> **tpusrdel(1)**: **tpusrdel(1)** deletes all entries for a user from the authorization file $APPDIR/tpusr.

ACLs may be managed with a set of utilities or by using the GUI administration tool (preferred). The utilities used for managing users are used with ACLs to maintain the list of authorized users. When ACLs are used, the administrator must:

- Maintain a list of authorized users, and associate each user with a group.
- Maintain a list of groups.
- Maintain a list of associations between groups and individual resources.

The list of users and their associations with groups are managed with the utilities noted previously.

The list of groups is managed with the utilities **tpgrpadd(1)**, **tpgrpmod(1)**, and **tpgrpdel(1)**.

The list of associations between groups and individual resources is managed with **tpacladd(1)**, **tpaclmod(1)**, and **tpacldel(1)**.

17.4   PROGRAMMED ADMINISTRATION

Programmed administration (/AdminAPI) makes it possible to create custom administrative interfaces. /AdminAPI allows performing any administrative task, including:

- Defining a new domain
- Modifying the definition of an existing domain
- Starting and stopping servers in an active domain
- Activating a domain
- Modifying the definitions of an active domain

Programmed administration makes it possible to write programs that react to system and application events (using the Event Broker) and dynamically modify the domain configuration. For instance, a program could be written that migrates selected servers when problems are detected with an active domain node.

The components of the programmed administration feature are:

- A set of TUXEDO objects, called the Management Information Base (MIB).
- A new function, **tpadmcall(3)**, that can be used to modify domain definitions.
- A TUXEDO core service called .TMIB that can be invoked from

properly authorized clients to perform modify MIBs and execute administrative functions.

The MIB contains objects for the components of TUXEDO. Administrative programs manage the system by manipulating the values in the appropriate MIB components.

tpadmcall(3) is provided primarily to create and modify domain definitions on an inactive system, but can be used with active systems.

The service .TMIB can be invoked with **tpcall(3)** like any other TUXEDO service to modify the characteristics of an active system. The messages exchanged between the administrative program and .TMIB use FML32 buffers. The message sent to .TMIB contains instructions about the action to take. The result is returned in an FML32 buffer. Client programs that invoke .TMIB must use special TUXEDO client names tpsysadm or tpsysop to gain access to the service. Users of these clients must have security access to these client names.

Programmed administration allows designers to cooperate with administrators to design systems that dynamically modify their own configuration in response to changing system conditions. People developing administrative programs must fully understand TUXEDO administration and how MIBs can be used to modify system behavior.

17.5   ## THE GRAPHICAL USER INTERFACE ADMINISTRATION TOOL

A running TUXEDO domain uses a binary file, called the tuxconfig file, to store current configuration definitions. Prior to Release 6.1, it was necessary to create a text version of the configuration file, called the ubbconfig file, which was then compiled into the **tuxconfig** file using the TUXEDO command line utility **tmloadcf(1)**. Even though TUXEDO Release 5 provided enhanced capabilities for modifying the configuration directly to the tuxconfig binary version, it was very helpful to the administrator to maintain a recent copy of ubbconfig for human interpretation. Indeed, many times when working with the TUXEDO configuration for Release 5 and earlier, it was so difficult to make changes directly to tuxconfig that many administrators modified the ubbconfig using their favorite programming editor, then rebuilt tuxconfig from it. The changes then took place the next time the system was booted.

With the advent of the GUI administrative tool it is no longer necessary to maintain the ubbconfig, since all information required by the administrator can be displayed in color in a TUXEDO administration window. The tool is powerful enough to provide for making all necessary changes to the configuration without resorting the ubbconfig or using the command line utilities. It is probable that with the advent of further releases of TUXEDO, the use of ubbconfig will cease, being replaced entirely by the GUI tool.

Chapters 10 and 11 present TUXEDO administration in the terms of the ubbconfig file for several reasons:

- There will continue to be many installations that do not use Release 6.1 for some time to come and this information is essential to the administrators at these installations.
- Programmers will continue to use ubbconfig to define small test configurations, even where the GUI administration tool is available, since it is much easier to do it that way.
- The best way to presen the concepts required for full understanding of TUXEDO administration is by discussing the points in terms of ubbconfig parameters. These concepts do not change with Release 6.1, and in fact, a solid grounding in the basics is a necessity to using the GUI tool.

This book is essentially about how to design and develop applications that run using TUXEDO as the client/server manager. Administration is included primarily so that TUXEDO design and development people can work with the TUXEDO administrator knowledgeably to develop sound, user friendly, and robust applications.

The GUI administration tool runs on any native TUXEDO Release 6.1 platform that supports "X" type windowing systems such as Motif. The tool allows administrators to create and modify domains, boot and shutdown domains, tune domains while they are active, manage user authorization lists, manage ACLs, and so on. The tool allows administration of both remote and local domains. Enterprises using Release 6.1 should use the GUI administration tool for all administration tasks for production domains. The GUI administration tool combines in one place administration of local domains, /Domain, /Q, security, and so on.

To properly use the GUI tool, the administrator should fully understand the configuration of TUXEDO as presented in Chapters 10 and 11. The screens used by the tool will be readily understood in terms of the parameters defined in the ubbconfig file. Figure 17.2 shows the main menu screen of the tool. The config button will first present the RESOURCES section of the configuration (called domain by the tool).

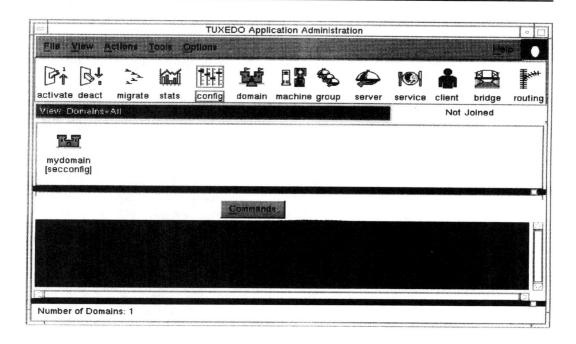

Figure 17.2   GUI administration tool main menu.

There are also buttons for some of the sections of the configuration, such as domain, machine, group, server, and service.

Figure 17.3 shows the screen that appears when the config button is clicked once. The buttons Security, Limits, and Timers refer to parts of the domain (or RESOURCES) section. The object selection button in the figure shows that the screen is showing domain-wide parameters. A single click on this button will show a list of the various object classes that can be accessed, such as Machine, Server, Service, and ACL. A click on the object will produce a screen that allows working with the object.

The buttons on the bottom of Figure 17.3 show the typical actions that can be performed. The Change button will change the values in the configuration file. The New button will present a screen that allows creation of a new configuration of the object. The Delete button will delete the version of the object being presented. The Dismiss button will

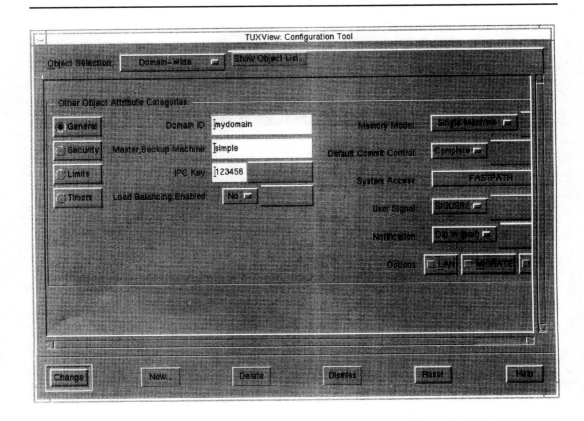

Figure 17.3   The configuration screen.

cancel the screen. The Reset button will reset the parameters of the object to their original value.

Once an administrator has mastered the relatively simple process of navigating through the tool, administration of TUXEDO becomes much easier than the method of modifying ubbconfig with an editor, running **tmloadcf(1)**, and so on, or using **tmconfig(1)** and **tmadmin(1)**.

APPENDIX A

Adding New Buffer Types

The buffer types provided with TUXEDO are sufficient for most applications. The steps listed here are required when new buffer types are added or new functions, such as data encryption, are added to existing buffer types.

TUXEDO does not encrypt buffers for transmission. If encryption is desired, define some of the buffer switch functions as described in the following list. Remember that data encryption is incompatible with data compression and translation.

It is also possible to enhance data dependent routing by redefining the buffer switch functions.

The steps required to add or delete buffer types or modify buffer switch functions are:

1. Code new buffer switch functions as required.
2. Make a copy of the existing tmtypesw.c file for backup. This file is in $TUXDIR/lib.
3. Modify tmtypesw.c.
4. Compile the new functions to create object modules.
5. Compile tmtypesw.c to create an object module.
6. Link all the functions named in tmtypesw.c with the tmtypesw.c and place the resulting object module in a shared library on all platforms used.

When these steps are completed, the new buffer definitions are available for use by application programs.

The order of the list of functions in tmtypesw.c must be maintained. The time when the function will be called is determined by the location of the function entry point in the list. To redefine a function, replace the existing function name with a new function name. There must be an entry for each function listed in the supplied tmtypesw.c. An entry may be NULL.

For more information, consult the *TUXEDO Administrator's Guide,* and the buffer(3I) section in the *TUXEDO Reference Manual.*

TUXEDO Related Products

There are a number of development tools and other products available that can be used to build TUXEDO applications. Some of these vendors are listed here, along with other information about various vendors of TUXEDO and related products. This list is not necessarily complete. The listing here does not imply an endorsement by the author or the publisher of this book.

Decision Support, Inc.

Correspondence:	Decision Support, Inc.
	170 Kinnelon Road, Suite 16
	Kinnelon, NJ 07405
Voice phone:	201-492-9393
FAX:	201-492-5677

Decision Support, Inc., publishes the printed TUXEDO as provided by Novell, Inc.

DYNASTY

Correspondence:	Dynasty Technologies
	600 Rockmeed, Suite 200
	Kingwood, TX 77339
Voice Phone:	713-358-2764

DYNASTY provides an object oriented tool for developing applications with or without TUXEDO. It operates on the popular UNIX and PC platforms and on the IBM mainframe.

Four Seasons Software

Correspondence:	Four Seasons Software
	2025 Lincoln Highway
	Edison, NJ 08817
Voice phone:	908-248-6667
FAX:	908-248-6675

Four Seasons Software sells the product SuperNOVA. SuperNOVA is a 4GL development tool that works with or without TUXEDO. SuperNOVA runs on most popular platforms and can access legacy data from IBM mainframes and minicomputers through a gateway to the EDA/SQL and ODBC products.

Information Management Company (IMC)

Correspondence:	IMC
	P.O. Box 6446
	130 Campus Drive
	Edison, NJ 08818
Voice phone:	908-346-3100
	800-4-OPEN-TP (800-467-3687)

IMC provides TUXEDO on a variety of platforms. IMC also provides an interconnectivity product, called Open TransPort, that will connect TUXEDO to several OLTP platforms, including CICS and IMS. IMC provides certified training courses on TUXEDO and TUXEDO consulting services.

JYACC

Correspondence:	JYACC
	55 William Street
	Wellesley, MA 02181
Voice Phone:	617-431-7431

JYACC sells the product JAM. JAM is an application development tool that has been used successfully for a number of years. A version of JAM, known as JAM/TP*i* is now available. JAM/TP*i* provides the ability to use JAM tools to build TUXEDO clients and servers.

Magna Software Corporation

Correspondence: Manager, Marketing
Magna Software Corporation
275 Seventh Avenue
New York, NY 10001
Voice Phone: 212-691-0300
email info@magna.com

Magna Software Corporation provides a product called MAGNA X. MAGNA X provides a development tool for developing TUXEDO servers and software that provides two-way communication between TUXEDO and CICS via SNA.

The MAGNA X development tool generates TUXEDO servers written in Micro Focus COBOL. The tool provides interfaces to enable clients developed with several development tools, including PowerBuilder, Visual Basic, and JAM.

MAGNA X is available on all popular platforms.

Micro Focus Incorporated

Correspondence: Micro Focus Incorporated
2465 East Bayshore Road
Palo Alto, CA 94303
Voice phone: 415-856-4161
800-872-6265
FAX: 415-856-6134

Micro Focus provides a popular COBOL compiler for use on UNIX, Windows, OS/2, and other platforms. Micro Focus also provides a product, called BridgeWare, that links 4GL GUI and CICS applications with Micro Focus COBOL applications. The sample COBOL programs in this book were tested using Micro Focus COBOL.

Nat Systems

Correspondence: Nat Systems
100 rue La Fayette
75010 Paris
France

Nat Systems
300 Winston Drive #722
Cliffside Park, NJ 07010

Voice phones:	(33) 1 40 22 95 94
	201-886-0660
FAX:	(33) 1 40 22 95 92
	201-886-0629

Nat Systems provides a CASE tool that helps build TUXEDO applications. The tool will generate both clients and servers in C.

O2 Technology

Correspondence:	O2 Technology
	2685 Marine Way #1220
	Mountain View, CA 94043
Voice phone:	415-969-2333

O2 Technology provides an object oriented database, called O2, that supports the XA interface. O2 operates with any transaction manager which supports the X/Open XA specification, including TUXEDO.

PROMARK

Correspondence:	PROMARK
	8 Campus Drive
	Parsippany, NJ 07054
Voice phone:	201-540-1980
FAX:	201-540-8377

PROMARK provides a testing product, called Rhobot/Client-Server, that can be used to create testing scripts to test many client/server applications, including TUXEDO applications. PROMARK also provides testing consulting services.

tangent INTERNATIONAL

Correspondence:	tangent INTERNATIONAL
	30 Broad Street
	New York, NY 10004
Voice phone:	212-809-8200
FAX:	212-968-1398

Tangent provides the Distributed Computing Integrator (DCI) product, which allows developers using standard PowerBuilder code to build Distributed Application clients. DCI functions with CICS, TUXEDO, and TOP END. Though PowerBuilder can be used without DCI to build TUXEDO clients, it requires additional code written in C or Visual Basic to do so. DCI eliminates the need for any special coding.

In addition to these companies, UNISYS, Sequent, and other hardware manufacturers provide TUXEDO and TUXEDO services for their own UNIX platforms.

For more information on TUXEDO from Novell, Inc., contact:

Director, TUXEDO Marketing
Novell, Inc.
180 Park Ave., Bldg. 103
Florham Park, NJ 07932-0949
Voice phone: 201-443-6000

Installation Hints

The installation guide that comes with TUXEDO from Novell, Inc. is very clear and comprehensive. The suggestions here highlight some of the problems that have been encountered after TUXEDO is installed.

The most common problem is caused by inadequate provision for UNIX IPC resources. TUXEDO makes extensive use of UNIX message queues, shared memory, and semaphores. The default size of these resources is seldom adequate on most UNIX platforms. To determine the requirement for a specific TUXEDO domain, run the following command:

```
tmloadcf -c ubbconfig
```

where ubbconfig is the specific ubbconfig file for the domain. The numbers produced reflect only the resources required by TUXEDO for the specific domain. Add any further resources required for databases and other products which may also be running on the platform. In some cases, it is a good idea to provide very large numbers for the IPCs in anticipation of additional TUXEDO domains.

If possible, make separate copies of TUXEDO available for production and development. In large installations, development should be done on separate platforms from production.

Be sure that all system resource parameters are set sufficiently high. Some key parameters are: **ULIMIT**, **NOFILES**, **MAXUP**, **NPROC**, **NREGION**, **NUMTIM**, and **NUMTRW**. Be sure that all of these resources parameters are set high.

TUXEDO administration privileges for development domains should be given to individual developers, so that each individual can test clients and services in their own domain without affecting other domains.

On-line documentation should be made available to all developers for reference. If possible, printed books, such as this one, should also be made available to developers.

Be sure to run at least two sample applications that come with the installation package: simpapp and bankapp. There are several sample applications. After running simpapp and bankapp, the installer should run additional sample applications that test the features to be used by the enterprise. All sample applications are stored in directories under $TUXDIR/apps.

The directories are:

CSIMPAPP: Simple COBOL application.

STOCKAPP: A more complex COBOL application that uses a database.

bankapp: The standard C application that uses a database.

creditapp: A complex C application to test /Domain.

qsample: A complex C application to test /Q.

simpapp: A very simple C application.

ws: The directory ws contains work station client programs that work with the servers provided in bankapp.

Follow the directions in the README file in each directory to set up and run the samples.

The database samples run with an undocumented database provided with TUXEDO, called TUXEDO/SQL.

Sample Programs

These sample programs implement a customer database maintenance system similar to the one suggested in Chapter 14. The ubbconfig file and other files are also included here. The programs were tested using the TUXEDO/SQL database. TUXEDO/SQL is the database used by bankapp. If the TUXEDO system came from a vender other than Novell, Inc., TUXEDO/SQL may not be present. This sample system can be run on any site by:

1. Changing the database OPENINFO string in the ubbconfig.
2. Changing the directory paths in the ubbconfig and the environment file scripts.
3. Replacing the TUXEDO/SQL database definition script with one for the local database.
4. Replace the precompiler esql with the precompiler for the local database in the compile script.
5. Run the environment script.
6. Run **tmloadcf(1)** to create the tuxconfig.
7. Use **qmadmin(1)** to create the queues.
8. Use **tmboot(1)** to boot the system.
9. Run the system. Customer maintenance is done with the program custmnt. The program custdeq is a client that invokes deqsvc to dequeue the branch messages and apply them to the home office.

```
/*************************************************************
* custmnt.c                                                 *
* client to do customer maintenance at branches             *
*                                                           *
* services invoked: rtrvcust, chgcust                       *
*                                                           *
* Application Functions:                                    *
*   allocbuf - acclocate buffers                            *
*   attch - attaches to TUXEDO                              *
*   displcust - display customer info to user               *
*   dtach - disconnects the client from TUXEDO              *
*   dosvc - "do service" - sets up the buffers and invokes  *
*                          the chgcust service              *
*   freebufs - frees the buffers                            *
*   getdata - gets customer info from user                  *
*   getpass - gets passwords from dumb terminal             *
*   rtrv - retrieves customer from database                 *
*                                                           *
* Requests function for user and does it. Functions are:    *
* (r)etrieve (d)elete (u)pdate (n)ew                        *
*                                                           *
* Loops thru request for function and action until user     *
* signals done by making no entry to function request.      *
*                                                           *
* custmnt expects chgcust to run AUTOTRAN=Y                 *
*                                                           *
* This program gives a hint of how to structure a client that*
* has most of its code usable both in native clients and    *
* /WS clients. It can be done better.                       *
*************************************************************/

#include <stdio.h>
#include <string.h>
#include <termio.h>
#include "atmi.h"        /* TUXEDO  Header File */
#include "fml.h"         /* FML header          */
#include "custhdr.h"     /* Application header  */
#include "sampflds.h"    /* output from mkfldhdr */

main()
{
```

```
    FLDLEN worksze; /* length of field for FML functions */
    struct custstruct *cstructptr; /* ptr to cust data   */

    /* security fields */
    char usrname[10], genpasswd[10], authpasswd[10];
    char errstr[100]; /* error message holder */
    long sendlen, rcvlen; /* buffer sizes */
    int ret, i;
    int dun; /* program sw */

    /* misc work areas */
    char ucustno[7], ufunc[2], answ[2];
    char *strptr;

    /* get space for customer structure */
    cstructptr = (struct custstruct *)malloc(sizeof(struct
custstruct));
    if(cstructptr == (struct custstruct *)NULL)
    {
        printf("could not get space for custstruct\n");
        exit(1);
    }

    /* have user sign on */
    if(usersignon(usrname, genpasswd, authpasswd, errstr) < 0)
    {
        printf("user signon failed\n");
        printf("%s\n", errstr);
        exit(1);
    }

    /* attach to TUXEDO */
    if(attch(usrname, genpasswd, authpasswd, errstr) < 0)
    {
        printf("failed to attach to TUXEDO\n");
        printf("%s\n", errstr);
        exit(1);
    }

    /* allocate send and receive buffers */
    if(allocbuf(cstructptr, errstr) < 0)
```

```
    {
        printf("failed to allocate buffers\n");
        printf("%s\n", errstr);
        freebufs(cstructptr);
        exit(1);
    }

    /* work with customer maintenance until done */
    dun = 0;
    while(dun == 0)
    {

    printf("press enter with no entry to end session\n");

    /* get function the user wants to do */
    ufunc[0] = NULL;
    printf("what function? (r)etrieve (u)pdate (d)elete (n)ew ");
    strptr = gets(ufunc);
    if(strlen(ufunc) == 0)
        break;
    strcpy(cstructptr->actsw, ufunc); /* setup action for service
*/

    /* get customer number to use */
    ucustno[0] = NULL;
    printf("enter customer number ");
    strptr = gets(ucustno);
    if(strlen(ucustno) == 0) /* don't go any further */
        continue;

    /* put custno into struct */
    strcpy(cstructptr->custno, ucustno);

    /* get customer location */
    printf("enter location where customer is serviced ");
    strptr = gets(cstructptr->loc);

    /* retrieve information about customer */
    /* If new customer don't try          */
    if(ufunc[0] != 'n' && ufunc[0] != 'N')
    {
        if((ret = rtrv(cstructptr, errstr)) != 0)
```

```
     {
          if(ret == NOTFOUND)
          {
               printf("cust nbr %s not found\n", ucustno);
               continue;
          }
          else
          {
               printf("Fatal error on cust retrieve\n");
               printf("%s\n", errstr);
               break;
          }
     }
displcust(cstructptr); /* show information to user */
}

switch(ufunc[0])
{
     case 'r': /* retrieve customer data */
     case 'R':
     {
          break; /* already did so don't try again */
     }
     case 'u':
     case 'U': /* update database */
     {
          getdata(cstructptr); /* get data from user */
          /* dosvc invokes the service chgcust */
          if((ret = dosvc(cstructptr, errstr)) > 0)
          {
               printf("%s %d\n", errstr, ret);
               break;
          }
          if(ret < 0)
          {
               printf("customer update failed\n");
               printf("%s\n", errstr);
               break;
          }
          break;
     }
     case 'd':
```

```
        case 'D': /* delete */
        {
                printf("Are you sure you want to delete this
customer? (y)es (n)o ");
                strptr = gets(answ);
                if(answ[0] == 'y' || answ[0] == 'Y')
                {
                        if(dosvc(cstructptr, errstr) < 0)
                        {
                                printf("customer delete failed\n");
                                printf("%s\n", errstr);
                                break;
                        }
                        break;
                }
                printf("not deleting the customer\n");
                break;
        }
        case 'n':
        case 'N': /* create new customer */
        {
                getdata(cstructptr); /* get cust info from user */
                if((ret = dosvc(cstructptr, errstr)) != 0)
                {
                        if(ret == DUPLICATE)
                        {
                                printf("duplicate cust\n");
                                break;
                        }
                        printf("fatal error adding cust\n");
                        printf("%s\n", errstr);
                        break;
                }
                printf("customer %s added\n", cstructptr->name);
                break;
        }
        default:
        {
                printf("invalid function\n");
        }
} /* end of switch on ufunc */
```

```
        } /* end of while(!dun) */

        /* all done, so clean up and stop */
        freebufs(cstructptr);
        dtach();
        exit(0);
} /* end of main */

/* usersignon is a function that retrieves the user
     name and passwd */

int usersignon(char *usrname, char *genpasswd, char *authpasswd,
char *errstr)
{
        char *usrptr;

        /* get user id and password */
        printf("enter user id ");
        usrptr = gets(usrname);
        printf("\nenter SECURITY APP_PW password ");
            if(getpass(genpasswd) < 0)
            {
                strcpy(errstr,"getpass failed");
                return(-1);
            }
        printf("\nenter application password ");
            if(getpass(authpasswd) < 0)
            {
                strcpy(errstr,"getpass failed");
                return(-1);
            }
        return(0);
}

/* getpass gets passwords without displaying them as they are typed
*/

int getpass(char *password)
{
        struct termios attrs;
        int c, handle;
```

```c
    FILE *file;
    long flags;

    /* Open the terminal */
    if ((file = fopen("/dev/tty", "r")) == NULL)
        return (-1);

    /* Set unbuffered IO */
    setbuf(file, NULL);

    /* Get the file handle */
    handle = fileno(file);

    /* Get the current terminal attrs */
    (void)tcgetattr(handle, &attrs);

    /* Save the attributes */
    flags = attrs.c_lflag;

    /* Disable echo bits */
    attrs.c_lflag &= ~(ECHO | ECHOE | ECHOK | ECHONL);

    /* Set the new attributes */
    (void)tcsetattr(handle, TCSAFLUSH, &attrs);

    /* Prompt and enter password */
    /* (void) fputs("Enter the password: ", stdout); */
    while ((c = getc(file)) != EOF && c != '\n')
        *password++ = (char)c;
    (void) putc('\n', stdout);
    *password = '\0';

    /* Restore the old terminal attributes */
    attrs.c_lflag = flags;
    (void) tcsetattr(handle, TCSAFLUSH, &attrs);

    /* Close the terminal device */
    (void)fclose(file);

    /* Return success */
    return (0);
} /* end of getpass */
```

```
/* attch attaches the client to TUXEDO */

int attch(char *usrname, char *genpasswd, char *authpasswd, char
*errstr)
{
    int ret;
    long initbufsz; /* size of initialization buffer */
    char *errwords; /* error work area              */
    TPINIT *initbuf; /* pointer to init buf          */

    /* allocate space for init buffer */
    initbufsz = sizeof(struct tpinfo_t) + 100;

    if ((initbuf = (TPINIT *) tpalloc("TPINIT", 0, initbufsz)) ==
(TPINIT *) NULL)
    {
        errwords = tpstrerror(tperrno);
        strcpy(errstr, errwords);
        return(-1);
    }

    strcpy (initbuf->usrname, usrname);
    strcpy (initbuf->passwd, genpasswd);
    strcpy ((char *)&initbuf->data, authpasswd);
    strcpy (initbuf->cltname, "custmnt");

    /* Attach to System/T as a Client Process */

    if (tpinit(initbuf) < 0) {
        errwords = tpstrerror(tperrno);
        strcpy(errstr, errwords);
        return(-1);
    }
    return(0);
} /* end of attch */

/* allocbuf allocates the send and receive buffers */
/* the buffer pointers are placed in custstruct     */
int allocbuf(struct custstruct *cstructptr, char *errstr)
{
    char *errmsg;
    FBFR *sendbuf;
```

```
    FBFR *rcvbuf;

    /* set sendbuf size */
    cstructptr->bufsize = Fneeded(10, 100);

    /* Allocate the request buffer */

    if((sendbuf   =    (FBFR   *)   tpalloc("FML",   NULL,
cstructptr->bufsize)) == (FBFR *) NULL)
    {
        errmsg= tpstrerror(tperrno);
        strcpy(errstr, "allocating sendbuf ");
        strcat(errstr, errmsg);
        return(-1);
    }
    cstructptr->sendbuf = sendbuf;

    /* allocate the receive buffer */
    if((rcvbuf   =    (FBFR   *)   tpalloc("FML",   NULL,
cstructptr->bufsize)) == (FBFR *) NULL)
    {
        errmsg= tpstrerror(tperrno);
        strcpy(errstr, "allocating rcvbuf ");
        strcat(errstr, errmsg);
        return(-1);
    }
    cstructptr->rcvbuf = rcvbuf;
    return(0);
} /* end of allocbuf */

/* rtrv invokes the service rtrvcust to get the customer
    by custno */
int rtrv(struct custstruct *cstructptr, char *errstr)
{
    char *errmsg; /* error work area */
    int ret, retcode;
    FLDLEN worksze; /* size of each receive field */

    /* put location into buffer */
    ret   =   Fchg(cstructptr->sendbuf,   LOC,   0,   (char
*)cstructptr->loc, 0);
    if(ret < 0)
```

```
      {
           errmsg = Fstrerror(Ferror);
           strcpy(errstr, "putting loc into buffer");
           strcat(errstr, errmsg);
           return(-1);
      }


      /* put customer number into FML buffer */
      ret = Fchg(cstructptr->sendbuf, CUSTNO, 0, cstructptr->custno,
   0);
      if(ret < 0)
      {
           errmsg= Fstrerror(Ferror);
           strcpy(errstr, "putting custno into buffer ");
           strcat(errstr, errmsg);
           return(-1);
      }


      /* Request the service rtrvcust waiting for a reply */
      ret = tpcall("rtrvcust", (char *) cstructptr->sendbuf, 0,
   (char**) &cstructptr->rcvbuf, &cstructptr->bufsize, (long)0);

      if(ret < 0) {
           errstr = tpstrerror(tperrno);
           return(-1);
      }
      if(tpurcode != 0)
      {
           retcode = tpurcode; /* probably a not found */
           return(retcode);
      }


      /* get each field from buffer to custstruct */
      worksze = sizeof(cstructptr->name);
      ret = Fget(cstructptr->rcvbuf, CUSTNME, 0, cstructptr->name,
   &worksze);
      if(ret < 0)
      {
           if(Ferror == FNOTPRES)
           {
                cstructptr->name[0] = NULL;
           }
```

```
        else
        {
            errmsg= Fstrerror(Ferror);
            strcpy(errstr, "getting name from buffer");
            strcat(errstr, errmsg);
            return(-1);
        }
    }

    worksze = sizeof(cstructptr->addr1);
    ret = Fget(cstructptr->rcvbuf, CADDR1, 0, cstructptr->addr1,
&worksze);
    if(ret < 0)
    {
        if(Ferror == FNOTPRES)
        {
            cstructptr->addr1[0] = NULL;
        }
        else
        {
            errmsg= Fstrerror(Ferror);
            strcpy(errstr, "getting addr1 from buffer");
            strcat(errstr, errmsg);
            return(-1);
        }
    }

    worksze = sizeof(cstructptr->addr2);
    ret = Fget(cstructptr->rcvbuf, CADDR2, 0, cstructptr->addr2,
&worksze);
    if(ret < 0)
    {
        if(Ferror == FNOTPRES)
        {
            cstructptr->addr2[0] = NULL;
        }
        else
        {
            errmsg= Fstrerror(Ferror);
            strcpy(errstr, "getting addr2 from buffer");
            strcat(errstr, errmsg);
            return(-1);
```

```
        }
    }

    worksze = sizeof(cstructptr->addr3);
    ret = Fget(cstructptr->rcvbuf, CADDR3, 0, cstructptr->addr3,
&worksze);
    if(ret < 0)
    {
        if(Ferror == FNOTPRES)
        {
            cstructptr->addr3[0] = NULL;
        }
        else
        {
            errmsg= Fstrerror(Ferror);
            strcpy(errstr, "getting addr3 from buffer");
            strcat(errstr, errmsg);
            return(-1);
        }
    }

    worksze = sizeof(cstructptr->st);
    ret = Fget(cstructptr->rcvbuf, CUSTST, 0, cstructptr->st,
&worksze);
    if(ret < 0)
    {
        if(Ferror == FNOTPRES)
        {
            cstructptr->st[0] = NULL;
        }
        else
        {
            errmsg= Fstrerror(Ferror);
            strcpy(errstr, "getting custst from buffer");
            strcat(errstr, errmsg);
            return(-1);
        }
    }

    worksze = sizeof(cstructptr->zp1);
    ret = Fget(cstructptr->rcvbuf, CUSTZP1, 0, cstructptr->zp1,
&worksze);
```

```
    if(ret < 0)
    {
        if(Ferror == FNOTPRES)
        {
            cstructptr->zp1[0] = NULL;
        }
        else
        {
            errmsg= Fstrerror(Ferror);
            strcpy(errstr, "getting custzp1 from buffer");
            strcat(errstr, errmsg);
            return(-1);
        }
    }

    worksze = sizeof(cstructptr->zp2);
    ret = Fget(cstructptr->rcvbuf, CUSTZP2, 0, cstructptr->zp2,
&worksze);
    if(ret < 0)
    {
        if(Ferror == FNOTPRES)
        {
            cstructptr->zp2[0] = NULL;
        }
        else
        {
            errmsg= Fstrerror(Ferror);
            strcpy(errstr, "getting custzp2 from buffer");
            strcat(errstr, errmsg);
            return(-1);
        }
    }

    worksze = sizeof(cstructptr->consis);
    ret = Fget(cstructptr->rcvbuf, CCONSIS, 0, (char
*)&cstructptr->consis, &worksze);
    if(ret < 0)
    {
        errmsg= Fstrerror(Ferror);
        strcpy(errstr, "getting cconsis from buffer");
        strcat(errstr, errmsg);
```

```
            return(-1);
    }

    return(0);
} /* end of rtrv */

/* dosvc invokes chgcust to change the customer database */
int dosvc(struct custstruct *cstructptr, char *errstr)
{
    char *errmsg;
    int retcode, ret;

    retcode = 0;

    /* put action code into buffer */
    ret = Fchg(cstructptr->sendbuf, ACTSW, 0, cstructptr->actsw,
0);
    if(ret < 0)
    {
        errmsg = Fstrerror(Ferror);
        strcpy(errstr, "putting actsw into buffer");
        strcat(errstr, errmsg);
        return(-1);
    }

    /* put location into buffer */
    ret    =    Fchg(cstructptr->sendbuf,    LOC,    0,    (char
*)cstructptr->loc, 0);
    if(ret < 0)
    {
        errmsg = Fstrerror(Ferror);
        strcpy(errstr, "putting loc into buffer");
        strcat(errstr, errmsg);
        return(-1);
    }

    /* put customer number into FML buffer */
    ret = Fchg(cstructptr->sendbuf, CUSTNO, 0, cstructptr->custno,
0);
    if(ret < 0)
    {
```

```
            errmsg = Fstrerror(Ferror);
            strcpy(errstr, "putting custno into buffer");
            strcat(errstr, errmsg);
            return(-1);
    }

    ret = Fchg(cstructptr->sendbuf, CCONSIS, 0, (char
*)&cstructptr->consis, 0);
    if(ret < 0)
    {
            errmsg = Fstrerror(Ferror);
            strcpy(errstr, "adding consis to buffer");
            strcat(errstr, errmsg);
            return(-1);
    }

    /* if action is delete no need to load rest of buffer */
    if(cstructptr->actsw[0] != 'd' && cstructptr->actsw[0] != 'D')
    { /* no indent so things fit on page!! */

    ret = Fchg(cstructptr->sendbuf, CUSTNME, 0, cstructptr->name,
0);
    if(ret < 0)
    {
            errmsg = Fstrerror(Ferror);
            strcpy(errstr, "adding name to buffer");
            strcat(errstr, errmsg);
            return(-1);
    }

    ret = Fchg(cstructptr->sendbuf, CADDR1, 0, cstructptr->addr1,
0);
    if(ret < 0)
    {
            errmsg = Fstrerror(Ferror);
            strcpy(errstr, "adding addr1 to buffer");
            strcat(errstr, errmsg);
            return(-1);
    }

    ret = Fchg(cstructptr->sendbuf, CADDR2, 0, cstructptr->addr2,
0);
```

```
    if(ret < 0)
    {
        errmsg = Fstrerror(Ferror);
        strcpy(errstr, "adding addr2 to buffer");
        strcat(errstr, errmsg);
        return(-1);
    }

    ret = Fchg(cstructptr->sendbuf, CADDR3, 0, cstructptr->addr3,
0);
    if(ret < 0)
    {
        errmsg = Fstrerror(Ferror);
        strcpy(errstr, "adding addr3 to buffer");
        strcat(errstr, errmsg);
        return(-1);
    }

    ret = Fchg(cstructptr->sendbuf, CUSTST, 0, cstructptr->st, 0);
    if(ret < 0)
    {
        errmsg = Fstrerror(Ferror);
        strcpy(errstr, "adding state to buffer");
        strcat(errstr, errmsg);
        return(-1);
    }

    ret = Fchg(cstructptr->sendbuf, CUSTZP1, 0, cstructptr->zp1,
0);
    if(ret < 0)
    {
        errmsg = Fstrerror(Ferror);
        strcpy(errstr, "adding zip1 to buffer");
        strcat(errstr, errmsg);
        return(-1);
    }

    ret = Fchg(cstructptr->sendbuf, CUSTZP2, 0, cstructptr->zp2,
0);
    if(ret < 0)
    {
        errmsg = Fstrerror(Ferror);
```

```
            strcpy(errstr, "adding zip2 to buffer");
            strcat(errstr, errmsg);
            return(-1);
        }

    } /* end of if not delete */

    /* Request the service rtrvcust waiting for a reply */
    ret = tpcall("chgcust", (char *) cstructptr->sendbuf, 0,
(char**) &cstructptr->rcvbuf, &cstructptr->bufsize, TPNOTRAN |
TPSIGRSTRT);

    if(ret < 0) {
        errmsg = tpstrerror(tperrno);
        strcpy(errstr, errmsg);
        return(-1);
    }
    /* if tpurcode comes back not zero there was a problem */
    /* most likely with the consistency value            */
    if(tpurcode != 0)
    {
        strcpy(errstr, "non=zero urcode");
        retcode = tpurcode;
        return(retcode);
    }

    return(0);
} /* end of dosvd */

/* freebufs frees the buffers which have been allocated
    for services */
freebufs(struct custstruct *cstructptr)
{
    tpfree((char *) cstructptr->sendbuf);
    tpfree((char *) cstructptr->rcvbuf);
    return;
} /* end of freebuf */

/* dtach detaches the client from TUXEDO */
dtach()
{
    tpterm();
} /* end of dtach */
```

```
/* displcust prints customer information on users terminal */
displcust(struct custstruct *cstructptr)
{
     printf("customer number  %s\n", cstructptr->custno);
     printf("         name    %s\n", cstructptr->name);
     printf("         address %s\n", cstructptr->addr1);
     printf("                 %s\n", cstructptr->addr2);
     printf("                 %s\n", cstructptr->addr3);
     printf("         state   %s\n", cstructptr->st);
     printf("         zip             %s-%s\n", cstructptr->zp1,
cstructptr->zp2);
} /* end of displcust */


/* getdata gets the data for a customer from the user */
getdata(struct custstruct *cstructptr)
{
     char * strptr;

     printf("enter customer information\n");
     printf("for customer number %s\n", cstructptr->custno);
     printf("enter customer name ");
     strptr = gets(cstructptr->name);
     printf("enter customer address line 1 ");
     strptr = gets(cstructptr->addr1);
     printf("enter customer address line 2 ");
     strptr = gets(cstructptr->addr2);
     printf("enter customer address line 3 ");
     strptr = gets(cstructptr->addr3);
     printf("enter customer state ");
     strptr = gets(cstructptr->st);
     printf("enter customer 5 digit zip ");
     strptr = gets(cstructptr->zp1);
     printf("enter customer zip + 4 ");
     strptr = gets(cstructptr->zp2);
} /* end of getdata */


/**************************************************************
 * retrvsv.ec server to retrieve customer data               *
 *                                                           *
 * Service provided: retrvcust                               *
 *                                                           *
 * retrvcust uses the custno and loc values as keys to       *
 * retrieve customer information. The entire row is          *
```

```
* returned to the invoker. If the the row is not found,    *
* retrvcust returns TPSUCCESS with recode set to NOTFOUND. *
*                                                          *
* The tx inferface is used for transaction management.     *
*                                                          *
* The tpsvrinit calls tx_open(3)                           *
*                                                          *
***********************************************************/

#include <stdio.h>
#include <ctype.h>
#include <Uunix.h>
#include <atmi.h>          /* TUXEDO header        */
#include <userlog.h>       /* TUXEDO header        */
#include <sqlcode.h>       /* TUXEDO/SQL header    */
#include <tx.h>            /* TX header            */
#include "fml.h"           /* FML header           */
#include "sampflds.h"      /* output from mkfldhdr */
#include "custhdr.h"       /* application header   */

/* SQL DECLARE section for SQL host variables */
EXEC SQL begin declare section;
static char loc[2];
static char custno[7];
static char custnme[31];
static char caddr1[31];
static char caddr2[31];
static char caddr3[31];
static char custst[3];
static char custzp1[6];
static char custzp2[5];
static int cconsis;
EXEC SQL end declare section;

/* really dont't need tpsvrdone, but if its here its easier to
modify */
void tpsvrdone()
{
    int ret;

    userlog("chgsv has been shutdown");
    return;
}
```

```
/* a custom tpsvrinit to call tx_open(3) */
tpsvrinit(int argc, char *argv[])
{
     int ret;
     char *errmsg;

     /* open the database */
     if((ret = tx_open()) != TX_OK)
     {
          userlog("txi_open failed %d", ret);
          return(-1);
     }
     return(0);
}
/* the function rtrvcust is the code for the service rtrvcust */
void
rtrvcust(TPSVCINFO *rqst)
{

     int i, ret;
     FBFR *bufptr; /* pointer to data area for FML buffer */
     FLDLEN worksze; /* size of fields */
     char *errmsg, errstr[100];
     int urcode, retcode;

     urcode = 0;
     retcode = TPSUCCESS;
     bufptr = (FBFR *) rqst->data; /* get location of data */

     /* get required fields to local host variables */
     /* location value */
     worksze = sizeof(loc);
     if(Fget(bufptr, LOC, 0, loc, &worksze) < 0)
     {
          userlog("getting location failed");
          errmsg = Fstrerror(Ferror);
          userlog("%s", errmsg);
          urcode = NOFLD;
          tpreturn(retcode, urcode, rqst->data, 0L, 0);
     }

     /* customer number */
     worksze = sizeof(custno);
```

```
if(Fget(bufptr, CUSTNO, 0, custno, &worksze) < 0)
{
      userlog("getting custno failed");
      errmsg = Fstrerror(Ferror);
      userlog("%s", errmsg);
      urcode = NOFLD;
      tpreturn(retcode, urcode, rqst->data, 0L, 0);
}

/* use a cursor to select on loc and custno */
EXEC SQL
      declare getcust cursor for
            select
                  LOC,
                  CUSTNO,
                  CUSTNME,
                  CADDR1,
                  CADDR2,
                  CADDR3,
                  CUSTST,
                  CUSTZP1,
                  CUSTZP2,
                  CCONSIS
            from cust
            where
                  LOC = :loc
                  AND CUSTNO = :custno;

   EXEC SQL
      open getcust;
      if(SQLCODE != SQL_OK)
      {
            userlog("sqlcode from open getcust is %d", SQLCODE);
            retcode = TPFAIL;
            tpreturn(retcode, urcode, rqst->data, 0L, 0);
      }

   if(urcode == 0)
   {
      EXEC SQL
            fetch getcust into
                  :loc,
```

```
                  :custno,
                  :custnme,
                  :caddr1,
                  :caddr2,
                  :caddr3,
                  :custst,
                  :custzp1,
                  :custzp2,
                  :cconsis;
     if(SQLCODE == NOTFOUND)
     {
          urcode = NOTFOUND;
          EXEC SQL
              close getcust;
          tpreturn(retcode, urcode, rqst->data, OL, 0);
     }
     if(SQLCODE != SQL_OK)
     {
          userlog("sqlcode from fetch is %d", SQLCODE);
          retcode = TPFAIL;
          EXEC SQL
              close getcust;
          tpreturn(retcode, urcode, rqst->data, OL, 0);
     }
}

EXEC SQL
     close getcust;

/* put data into buffer area */

/* put location into buffer */
ret = Fchg(bufptr, LOC, 0, loc, 0);
if(ret < 0)
{
     errmsg = Fstrerror(Ferror);
     strcpy(errstr, "putting loc into buffer");
     strcat(errstr, errmsg);
     userlog("%s", errstr);
}

/* put customer number into FML buffer */
```

```
ret = Fchg(bufptr, CUSTNO, 0, custno, 0);
if(ret < 0)
{
    errmsg = Fstrerror(Ferror);
    strcpy(errstr, "putting custno into buffer");
    strcat(errstr, errmsg);
    userlog("%s", errstr);
}

/* put consistency value into FML buffer */
ret = Fchg(bufptr, CCONSIS, 0, (char *)&cconsis, 0);
if(ret < 0)
{
    errmsg = Fstrerror(Ferror);
    strcpy(errstr, "adding consis to buffer");
    strcat(errstr, errmsg);
    userlog("%s", errstr);
}

/* put customer name into FML buffer */
ret = Fchg(bufptr, CUSTNME, 0, custnme, 0);
if(ret < 0)
{
    errmsg = Fstrerror(Ferror);
    strcpy(errstr, "adding name to buffer");
    strcat(errstr, errmsg);
    userlog("%s", errstr);
}

/* put customer address lines into FML buffer */
ret = Fchg(bufptr, CADDR1, 0, caddr1, 0);
if(ret < 0)
{
    errmsg = Fstrerror(Ferror);
    strcpy(errstr, "adding addr1 to buffer");
    strcat(errstr, errmsg);
    userlog("%s", errstr);
}

ret = Fchg(bufptr, CADDR2, 0, caddr2, 0);
if(ret < 0)
```

```
{
    errmsg = Fstrerror(Ferror);
    strcpy(errstr, "adding addr2 to buffer");
    strcat(errstr, errmsg);
    userlog("%s", errstr);
}

ret = Fchg(bufptr, CADDR3, 0, caddr3, 0);
if(ret < 0)
{
    errmsg = Fstrerror(Ferror);
    strcpy(errstr, "adding addr3 to buffer");
    strcat(errstr, errmsg);
    userlog("%s", errstr);
}

ret = Fchg(bufptr, CUSTST, 0, custst, 0);
if(ret < 0)
{
    errmsg = Fstrerror(Ferror);
    strcpy(errstr, "adding state to buffer");
    strcat(errstr, errmsg);
    userlog("%s", errstr);
}

ret = Fchg(bufptr, CUSTZP1, 0, custzp1, 0);
if(ret < 0)
{
    errmsg = Fstrerror(Ferror);
    strcpy(errstr, "adding zip1 to buffer");
    strcat(errstr, errmsg);
    userlog("%s", errstr);
}

ret = Fchg(bufptr, CUSTZP2, 0, custzp2, 0);
if(ret < 0)
{
    errmsg = Fstrerror(Ferror);
    strcpy(errstr, "adding zip2 to buffer");
    strcat(errstr, errmsg);
    userlog("%s", errstr);
```

```
    }

    /* customer number and location are already in buffer */

    /* Return the modified buffer to the requestor. */
    tpreturn(retcode, urcode, rqst->data, 0L, 0);
}

/***************************************************************
* chgsv.ec server to make changes to the customer database *
*                                                          *
* Service provided: chgcust                                *
*                                                          *
* chgsv.ec receives requests to add a new customer, update *
* a customer or delete a customer.                         *
*                                                          *
* The service enqsvc is invoked with a tpacall(3) for each *
* request to place the request message on a queue for      *
* later dequeuing by the home office                       *
*                                                          *
* The tx interface is used for transaction management.     *
*                                                          *
* A custom tpsvrinit is used to get a parameter which tells*
* chgsvc whether or not to enqueue requests. The tpsvrinit *
* also calls tx_open(3)                                     *
*                                                          *
***************************************************************/

#include <stdio.h>
#include <ctype.h>
#include <atmi.h>           /* TUXEDO Header File */
#include <userlog.h>        /* TUXEDO Header File */
#include <fml.h>            /* TUXEDO header File */
#include <tx.h>             /* X/Open header file */
#include <sqlcode.h>        /* TUXEDO/SQL header file */
#include "sampflds.h"       /* Application FML field definitions */
#include "custhdr.h"        /* Application header file */

/* SQL DECLARE section for SQL host variables */
EXEC SQL begin declare section;
static char loc[2];
```

```
static char custno[7];
static char custnme[31];
static char caddr1[31];
static char caddr2[31];
static char caddr3[31];
static char custst[3];
static char custzp1[6];
static char custzp2[5];
static int cconsis;
EXEC SQL end declare section;

/* storage enqueue switch value */
char qsw[2];

/* a custom tpsvrinit to pick up arguments */
tpsvrinit(int argc, char *argv[])
{
     int ret, argno, userarg;
     char *errmsg;

     argno = optind; /* get index of first user argument */
     userarg = argc - optind; /* get loc of user arguments */

     /* Get arguments from ubbconfig. */
     if(userarg > 0)
     {
          strcpy(qsw, argv[argno]); /* get enqueue sw value */
     }
     else
     {
          strcpy(qsw, "N"); /* default sw to none */
     }
     /* log the enqueue switch being used */
     userlog("chgsv running with q option %s", qsw);

     /* open the database */

     if((ret = tx_open()) != TX_OK)
     {
          userlog("tx_open failed %d", ret);
          return(-1);
```

```
    }

    return(0); /* use a C return for tpsvrinit(3) */
}

/* chgcust is the service which makes changes to the
   customer database */
void
chgcust(TPSVCINFO *rqst)
{

    int i, ret;
    char actsw[2]; /* used for deciding what action to do */
    char *errmsg, errstr[100]; /* format and log errors */
    FBFR *bufptr; /* pointer to data area for FML buffer */
    FBFR *qrplybuf; /* enqsvc reply buffer */
    FLDLEN worksze;
    int retval, urcode, cd;
    long bufsize;

    retval = TPSUCCESS; /* assume no failure for now */
    urcode = 0; /* assume no user return code for now */
    bufptr = (FBFR *) rqst->data; /* get location of data */

    /* invoke the enqueue service to enqueue the orig request */
    /* if queue switch is set to 'Q' */
    if(qsw[0] == 'Q')
    {
        if((cd = tpacall("enqsvc", (char *)bufptr, 0L, TPSIGRSTRT)) < 0)
        {
            userlog("tpacall to enqsvc failed %d", tperrno);
            retval = TPFAIL;
        }
    }

    /* update local database */
    /* get all fields to local host variables */
    worksze = sizeof(loc);
    if(Fget(bufptr, LOC, 0, loc, &worksze) < 0)
    {
        userlog("getting location failed");
        errmsg = Fstrerror(Ferror);
```

```
      userlog("%s", errmsg);
      urcode = NOFLD;
}

worksze = sizeof(custno);
if(Fget(bufptr, CUSTNO, 0, custno, &worksze) < 0)
{
      userlog("getting custno failed");
      errmsg = Fstrerror(Ferror);
      userlog("%s", errmsg);
      urcode = NOFLD;
}

worksze = sizeof(custnme);
if(Fget(bufptr, CUSTNME, 0, custnme, &worksze) < 0)
{
      userlog("getting cust name failed");
      errmsg = Fstrerror(Ferror);
      userlog("%s", errmsg);
      urcode = NOFLD;
}

worksze = sizeof(caddr1);
if(Fget(bufptr, CADDR1, 0, caddr1, &worksze) < 0)
{
      userlog("getting address 1 failed");
      errmsg = Fstrerror(Ferror);
      userlog("%s", errmsg);
      urcode = NOFLD;
}

worksze = sizeof(caddr2);
if(Fget(bufptr, CADDR2, 0, caddr2, &worksze) < 0)
{
      userlog("getting address 2 failed");
      errmsg = Fstrerror(Ferror);
      userlog("%s", errmsg);
      urcode = NOFLD;
}

worksze = sizeof(caddr3);
if(Fget(bufptr, CADDR3, 0, caddr3, &worksze) < 0)
```

```
{
     userlog("getting address 3 failed");
     errmsg = Fstrerror(Ferror);
     userlog("%s", errmsg);
     urcode = NOFLD;
}

worksze = sizeof(custzp1);
if(Fget(bufptr, CUSTZP1, 0, custzp1, &worksze) < 0)
{
     userlog("getting zip 5 failed");
     errmsg = Fstrerror(Ferror);
     userlog("%s", errmsg);
     urcode = NOFLD;
}

worksze = sizeof(custzp2);
if(Fget(bufptr, CUSTZP2, 0, custzp2, &worksze) < 0)
{
     if(Ferror != FNOTPRES)
     {
          userlog("getting zip 4 failed");
          errmsg = Fstrerror(Ferror);
          userlog("%s", errmsg);
          retval = TPFAIL;
     }
}

worksze = sizeof(custst);
if(Fget(bufptr, CUSTST, 0, custst, &worksze) < 0)
{
     if(Ferror != FNOTPRES)
     {
          userlog("getting state failed");
          errmsg = Fstrerror(Ferror);
          userlog("%s", errmsg);
          retval = TPFAIL;
     }
}

worksze = sizeof(cconsis);
if(Fget(bufptr, CCONSIS, 0, (char *)&cconsis, &worksze) < 0)
```

```
{
    userlog("getting consistency value failed");
    errmsg = Fstrerror(Ferror);
    userlog("%s", errmsg);
    urcode = NOFLD;
}

worksze = sizeof(actsw);
if(Fget(bufptr, ACTSW, 0, actsw, &worksze) < 0)
{
    userlog("getting action switch failed");
    errmsg = Fstrerror(Ferror);
    userlog("%s", errmsg);
    retval = TPFAIL;
}

/* choose proper action and execute it */
/* note use of the consistency column  */
switch(actsw[0])
{
    case 'd':
    case 'D':
    {
        EXEC SQL
        delete from cust
            where LOC = :loc
            and CUSTNO = :custno
            and CCONSIS = :cconsis;
        if(SQLCODE != SQL_OK)
        /* if it fails it probably did not match the
           consistency value                       */
        {
            userlog("sqlcode from del is %d", SQLCODE);
            urcode = NOTFOUND;
        }
        break;
    }

    case 'n':
    case 'N':
    {
        cconsis = 0; /* init consistency value */
```

```
                EXEC SQL
                insert into cust
                (LOC,
                 CUSTNO,
                 CUSTNME,
                 CADDR1,
                 CADDR2,
                 CADDR3,
                 CUSTST,
                 CUSTZP1,
                 CUSTZP2,
                 CCONSIS)
                values (
                     :loc,
                     :custno,
                     :custnme,
                     :caddr1,
                     :caddr2,
                     :caddr3,
                     :custst,
                     :custzp1,
                     :custzp2,
                     :cconsis);
                if(SQLCODE != SQL_OK)
                {
                     userlog("sqlcode from insert is %d", SQLCODE);
                     retval = TPFAIL;
                }
                break;
        }

        case 'u':
        case 'U':
        {
            EXEC SQL
            update cust
                set CUSTNME = :custnme,
                    CADDR1 = :caddr1,
                    CADDR2 = :caddr2,
                    CADDR3 = :caddr3,
                    CUSTST = :custst,
                    CUSTZP1 = :custzp1,
```

```
                    CUSTZP2 = :custzp2,
                    CCONSIS = CCONSIS + 1
                where LOC = :loc
                  and CUSTNO = :custno
                  and CCONSIS = :cconsis;
            if(SQLCODE != SQL_OK)
            /* if it fails it probably did not match the
               consistency value                          */
            {
                userlog("sqlcode from upd is %d", SQLCODE);
                urcode = NOTFOUND;
            }
            break;
        }

        default:
        {
            userlog("actsw not received correctly %s", actsw);
            retval = TPFAIL; /* fail the transaction */
        }
    } /* end of switch on actsw */

    /* get reply from tpacall to be sure it enqueued ok */
    if(qsw[0] == 'Q')
    {
        /* allocate a reply buffer */
        bufsize = Fneeded(5, 1);
        if((qrplybuf = (FBFR *) tpalloc("FML", NULL, bufsize)) ==
(FBFR *) NULL)
        {
            errmsg= tpstrerror(tperrno);
            strcpy(errstr, "allocating sendbuf ");
            strcat(errstr, errmsg);
            userlog("failed to allocate qreply buffer");
            userlog("%s", errstr);
            retval = TPFAIL; /* fail transaction */
        }
        if(tpgetrply(&cd, (char **)&qrplybuf, &bufsize, TPGETANY
| TPSIGRSTRT) < 0)
        {
            userlog("tpgetrply to enqsvc failed %d", tperrno);
            retval = TPFAIL; /* fail transaction */
```

```
        }
        tpfree((char *) qrplybuf);
    }

    /* Return the result to the requestor. */
    tpreturn(retval, urcode, rqst->data, 0L, 0);

} /* end of chgcust */

/**************************************************************
* enqsv.c server to enqueue to branch queues              *
*                                                          *
* Service provided: enqsvc                                 *
*                                                          *
* enqsvc enqueues messages to the queue space named in     *
* the ubbconfig.                                           *
*                                                          *
* The name of the queue is always CUSTQ, but that could be *
* a ubbconfig parameter also.                              *
*                                                          *
* The tx interface is used for transaction management.     *
*                                                          *
* A custom tpsvrinit is used to get a parameter which tells*
* enqsvc the name of the queue space. The tpsvrinit        *
* also calls tx_open(3)                                    *
*                                                          *
**************************************************************/

#include <stdio.h>
#include <ctype.h>
#include <Uunix.h>
#include <atmi.h>          /* TUXEDO Header File */
#include <userlog.h>       /* TUXEDO header file */
#include <fml.h>           /* FML header file    */
#include <tx.h>            /* X/Open TX header   */
#include "sampflds.h"      /* output of mkfldhdr */
#include "custhdr.h"       /* application header */

/* storage for name of q space */
char qspcname[20];
tpsvrinit(int argc, char *argv[])
```

```
{
     int argno,userarg, ret;
     char *errmsg;

     argno = optind; /* get index of first app arg */
     userarg = argc - optind; /* get number of app args */

     /* Get arguments from ubbconfig. */
     if(userarg > 0)
     {
          strcpy(qspcname, argv[argno]);
     }
     else
     {
          userlog("qspcname not specified, killing server");
          return(-1);
     }
     userlog("enqsv running with q space %s", qspcname);

     /* set up to work with tx transactions */
     if((ret = tx_open()) != TX_OK)
     {
          userlog("txopen failed %d", ret);
          return(-1);
     }
     return(0);
}

/* service to enqueue requests for customer database changes */
void
enqsvc(TPSVCINFO *rqst)
{

     int ret, retval;
     long urcode;
     TPQCTL qctl;
     FBFR *bufptr;

     retval = TPSUCCESS;
     urcode = 0;
     bufptr = (FBFR *) rqst->data; /* get location of data */
```

```
     /* setup TPQCTL */
     qctl.flags = TPQMSGID; /* in order to get msgid returned */
     qctl.msgid[0] = NULL;

     /* enqueue the modified message */
     ret = tpenqueue(qspcname, "CUSTQ", (TPQCTL *)&qctl,
rqst->data, 0, TPSIGRSTRT);
     if(ret < 0)
     {
          userlog("tpenqueue failed %d", tperrno);
          retval = TPFAIL;
     }

     /* Return to the requestor. */
     tpreturn(retval, urcode, rqst->data, 0L, 0);
}


/****************************************************************
* custdeq.c                                                   *
* client to do customer maintenance at branches              *
*                                                             *
* Invokes services: chgcust, rtrvcust and deqsvc.            *
*                                                             *
* custdeq.c invokes enqsvc at a branch office to dequeue      *
* customer database changes and then invokes chgcust to      *
* do the same changes to the home office master.             *
*                                                             *
* enqsvc is first invoked with a tpcall(3) to start the       *
* process. In the loop, a tpacall is used to invoke enqsvc   *
* to allow updating the home office database while waiting    *
* for the next message from the queue.                       *
*                                                             *
* The dequeuing and updating is done for all messages in one *
* transaction. In production, commit every 10 or so messages.*
*                                                             *
* The services retrvcust and chgcust are the same code as the*
* services used in the branches. Data dependent routing is   *
* used to direct the requests to the correct service.        *
*                                                             *
* This version is designed to run as a native client         *
****************************************************************/
```

```
#include <stdio.h>
#include <string.h>
#include <termio.h>
#include "atmi.h"        /* TUXEDO  Header File */
#include "fml.h"         /* FML header file    */
#include "sampflds.h"    /* output from mkfldhdr */
#include "custhdr.h"     /* application header file */

main()
{

     FLDLEN worksze; /* length of field for FML functions */

     /* security values entered by user            */
     char usrname[10], genpasswd[10], authpasswd[10];

     char errstr[100], *errwords; /* format and log errors */
     long sendlen, rcvlen, initbufsz, bufsize;
     int ret, i;
     int dun; /* program switch */
     int cd; /* handle for tpacall(3) */
     char *strptr;
     struct custstruct *cptr;
     TPINIT *initbuf; /* initialization buffer */
     char *errmsg; /* more error stuff */
     FBFR *qbuf; /* buffer for dequeuing */
     FBFR *getbuf; /* buffer for retrieving from database */
     FBFR *updbuf; /* buffer for updating database */

     /* fldlist is used to delete all fields from an FML buf */
     F  L  D  I  D       f  l  d  l  i  s  t  [  ]        =
{LOC,CUSTNO,CUSTNME,CADDR1,CADDR2,CADDR3,CUSTST,CUSTZP1,CUSTZP2,C
CONSIS,ACTSW,BADFLDID};
     FLDID *listptr; /* pointer to fldlist */

     /* have user sign on */

     /* get user id and password */
     printf("enter user id ");
     strptr = gets(usrname);
     printf("\nenter SECURITY APP_PW password ");
```

```
        if(getpass(genpasswd) < 0)
        {
          printf("getpass failed");
    }
    printf("\nenter application password ");
        if(getpass(authpasswd) < 0)
        {
          printf("getpass failed");
    }

    /* allocate space for init buffer */
    initbufsz = sizeof(struct tpinfo_t) + 100;

    if ((initbuf = (TPINIT *) tpalloc("TPINIT", 0, initbufsz)) ==
(TPINIT *) NULL)
    {

        errwords = tpstrerror(tperrno);
        printf("%s\n",errwords);
        exit(-1);
    }

    strcpy (initbuf->usrname, usrname);
    strcpy (initbuf->passwd, genpasswd);
    strcpy ((char *)&initbuf->data, authpasswd);
    strcpy (initbuf->cltname, "custdeq");

    /* Attach to System/T as a Client Process */
    if (tpinit(initbuf) < 0) {
        errwords = tpstrerror(tperrno);
        printf("%s\n",errwords);
        exit(-1);
    }

    /* must call tx_open(3) before calling tx_begin(3) */
    ret = tx_open();
    if(ret < 0)
    {
        printf("txopen failed %d\n", ret);
    }

    /* get space for customer info structure */
```

```
    if((cptr  =  (struct  custstruct  *)malloc(sizeof(struct
custstruct))) == NULL)
    {
        printf("can't get working space\n");
        exit(1);
    }

    /* set updbuf size */
    bufsize = Fneeded(10, 100); /* too large, but good enuf */

    /* Allocate FML buffers to work with */
    /* The buffer used to update        */
    if((updbuf = (FBFR *) tpalloc("FML", NULL, bufsize)) == (FBFR
*) NULL)
    {
        errmsg= tpstrerror(tperrno);
        strcpy(errstr, "allocating updbuf ");
        strcat(errstr, errmsg);
        printf("%s\n", errstr);
        exit(-1);
    }

    /* The buffer used to retrieve from the database */
    if((getbuf = (FBFR *) tpalloc("FML", NULL, bufsize)) == (FBFR
*) NULL)
    {
        errmsg= tpstrerror(tperrno);
        strcpy(errstr, "allocating getbuf ");
        strcat(errstr, errmsg);
        printf("%s\n", errstr);
        exit(-1);
    }

    /* The buffer used to retrieve from the queue */
    if((qbuf = (FBFR *) tpalloc("FML", NULL, bufsize)) == (FBFR *)
NULL)
    {
        errmsg= tpstrerror(tperrno);
        strcpy(errstr, "allocating qbuf ");
        strcat(errstr, errmsg);
        printf("%s\n", errstr);
        exit(-1);
```

```
    }

    listptr = fldlist; /* set address of fldlist */
    dun = 0; /* set to !dun */

    /* start a transaction */
    ret = tx_begin();
    if(ret < 0)
    {
        printf("erron on begin %d\n", ret);
    }

    /* Request the service deqsvc waiting for a reply */
    /* this tpcall starts the process by getting the first
message */
    ret = tpcall("deqsvc", (char *)qbuf, 0, (char**)&qbuf,
&bufsize, (long)0);
    if(ret < 0) {
        errmsg = tpstrerror(tperrno);
        strcpy(errstr, errmsg);
        printf("%s\n", errstr);
        dun = 1;
    }

    /* deqsvc sets the rcode to QEMPTY and returns success when
        the queue goes empty */
    if(tpurcode == QEMPTY)
    {
        dun = 1;
    }

    /* dequeue until queue empty */
    while(!dun)
    { /* not indenting because of long lines */

    /* get data from qbuf to updbuf */
    if(Fcpy(updbuf, qbuf) < 0)
    {
        errmsg= Fstrerror(Ferror);
        strcpy(errstr, "copying fields from qbuf");
        strcat(errstr, errmsg);
```

```
        printf("%s\n", errstr);
}

/* delete all values from qbuf to shorten message */
if(Fdelete(qbuf, listptr) < 0)
{
    errmsg= Fstrerror(Ferror);
    strcpy(errstr, "deleting fields from qbuf");
    strcat(errstr, errmsg);
    printf("%s\n", errstr);
}

/* use tpacall to start request for next message
   from queue */
if((cd = tpacall("deqsvc", (char *)qbuf, 0L, TPSIGRSTRT)) < 0)
{
    errmsg = tpstrerror(tperrno);
    strcpy(errstr, errmsg);
    printf("tpacall to deqsvc failed ");
    printf("%s\n", errstr);
    dun = 1;
    continue;
}

/* change the location in the recv buffer to homeoffice */
cptr->loc[0] = 'H';
if(Fchg(updbuf, LOC, 0, cptr->loc, worksze) < 0)
{
    errmsg= Fstrerror(Ferror);
    strcpy(errstr, "getting addr1 from buffer");
    strcat(errstr, errmsg);
    printf("%s\n", errstr);
    exit(1);
}

/* retrieve the current database */
/* first copy the request to the get buffer */
/* NOTE: it is better for the network to Fget the
   custno from the incoming buffer and put it into getbuf */
/* but this illustrates an easy way to move data
   between buffers */
```

```
     Fcpy(getbuf, updbuf);

     /* Need to retrieve the row from the home office database
        to get the consistency value.                         */
     /* use the same retrieve as the branches do */
     ret = tpcall("rtrvcust", (char *)getbuf, 0, (char**)&getbuf,
&bufsize, (long)0);
     if(ret < 0) {
          errmsg = tpstrerror(tperrno);
          strcpy(errstr, errmsg);
          printf("%s\n", errstr);
          dun = 1;
     }
     /* if its not found, the first change should be a new */
     if(tpurcode == NOTFOUND)
     {
          cptr->consis = 0;
     }
     else
     {
          /* if its found move the consistency value */
          worksze = sizeof(cptr->consis);
          if(Fget(getbuf, CCONSIS, 0, (char *)&cptr->consis,
&worksze) < 0)
          if(Ferror == FNOTPRES)
          {
               printf("custno  %s does not have consis - assigning
0\n", cptr->custno);
          }
          else
          {
               errmsg= Fstrerror(Ferror);
               strcpy(errstr, "getting CCONSIS from buffer");
               strcat(errstr, errmsg);
               printf("%s\n", errstr);
               exit(1);
          }
     }

     /* put the home office consistency value in update buf */
     worksze = sizeof(cptr->consis);
```

```
    if(Fchg(updbuf, CCONSIS, 0, (char *)&cptr->consis, worksze) <
0)
    {
        errmsg= Fstrerror(Ferror);
        strcpy(errstr, "putting CCONSIS into buffer");
        strcat(errstr, errmsg);
        printf("%s\n", errstr);
        exit(1);
    }


    /* Request the service chgcust to update the database */
    ret = tpcall("chgcust", (char *)updbuf, 0, (char**)&updbuf,
&bufsize, (long)0);
    if(ret < 0) {
        errmsg = tpstrerror(tperrno);
        strcpy(errstr, errmsg);
        printf("%s\n", errstr);
        dun = 1;
    }


    /* If consistency does not match, someone else updated
       the database since the retrieve. In production, this
       code would be more sophisticated.                  */
    if(tpurcode != 0)
    {
        printf("chgcust failed urcode is %d\n", tpurcode);
    }


    /* Get response from deqsvc waiting for a reply */
    if(tpgetrply(&cd, (char **)&qbuf, &bufsize, TPGETANY |
TPSIGRSTRT) < 0)
    {
        errmsg = tpstrerror(tperrno);
        strcpy(errstr, errmsg);
        printf("%s\n", errstr);
        dun = 1;
    }


    if(tpurcode == QEMPTY)
    {
        dun = 1;
```

```
                continue;
        }

        } /* end of while(dun == 0 */

        /* commit the transaction */
        ret = tx_commit();
        if(ret < 0)
        {
                printf("erron on commit %d\n", ret);
        }

        /* all done, so clean up and stop */
        ret = tx_close();
        if(ret < 0)
        {
                printf("tx_close failed %d\n", ret);
        }

        tpfree((char *) qbuf);
        tpfree((char *) getbuf);
        tpfree((char *) updbuf);
        tpterm();
        exit(0);
} /* end of main */

/* getpass gets passwords without displaying them as they are typed
*/

int getpass(char *password)
{
        struct termios attrs;
        int c, handle;
        FILE *file;
        long flags;

        /* Open the terminal */
        if ((file = fopen("/dev/tty", "r")) == NULL)
                return (-1);

        /* Set unbuffered IO */
        setbuf(file, NULL);
```

```
    /* Get the file handle */
    handle = fileno(file);

    /* Get the current terminal attrs */
    (void)tcgetattr(handle, &attrs);

    /* Save the attributes */
    flags = attrs.c_lflag;

    /* Disable echo bits */
    attrs.c_lflag &= ~(ECHO | ECHOE | ECHOK | ECHONL);

    /* Set the new attributes */
    (void)tcsetattr(handle, TCSAFLUSH, &attrs);

    /* Prompt and enter password */
    /* (void) fputs("Enter the password: ", stdout); */
    while ((c = getc(file)) != EOF && c != '\n')
        *password++ = (char)c;
    (void) putc('\n', stdout);
    *password = '\0';

    /* Restore the old terminal attributes */
    attrs.c_lflag = flags;
    (void) tcsetattr(handle, TCSAFLUSH, &attrs);

    /* Close the terminal device */
    (void)fclose(file);

    /* Return success */
    return (0);
} /* end of getpass */

/**************************************************************
 * deqsv.c server to dequeue from branch queues              *
 *                                                           *
 * Service provided: deqsvc                                  *
 *                                                           *
 * deqsvc dequeues messages from the queue space named in    *
 * the ubbconfig and passes the message as a whole back      *
 * to the invoker                                            *
 *                                                           *
 *                                                           *
```

```
 * The name of the queue is always CUSTQ, but that could be *
 * a ubbconfig parameter also.                              *
 *                                                          *
 * The tx interface is used for transaction management.     *
 *                                                          *
 * A custom tpsvrinit is used to get a parameter which tells*
 * deqsvc the name of the queue space.        The tpsvrinit *
 * also calls tx_open(3)                                    *
 *                                                          *
 ***********************************************************/

#include <stdio.h>
#include <ctype.h>
#include <Uunix.h>
#include <atmi.h>           /* TUXEDO Header File */
#include <userlog.h>        /* TUXEDO Header File */
#include <fml.h>            /* FML header file    */
#include <tx.h>             /* X/Open TX header   */
#include "sampflds.h"       /* Output from mkfld hdr */
#include "custhdr.h"        /* application header */

/* storage for name of q space */
char qspcname[20];

tpsvrinit(int argc, char *argv[])
{
     int argno, orgargc, orgopti, userarg;
     int ret;
     char arg1[30], arg2[30];

     argno = optind; /* get index of user arguments */
     userarg = argc - optind;
     strcpy(arg1, "initial-arg1");
     strcpy(arg2, "initial-arg2");

     /* Get arguments from ubbconfig. */
     if(userarg > 0)
     {
          strcpy(qspcname, argv[argno]);
     }
     else
     {
```

```
            userlog("qspcname not specified, killing server");
            return(-1);
    }
    /* log the queue space being used */
    userlog("deqsv running with q space %s", qspcname);

    /* Need to call tx_open(3) to make the server part of the */
    /* tx transaction, even though the server does not        */
    /* directly use any resource manager.                     */
    if((ret = tx_open()) != TX_OK)
    {
            userlog("tx_open failed %d", ret);
            return(-1);
    }

    return(0); /* use a C return in tpsvrinit */
}

/* service to dequeue requests for customer database changes */
void
deqsvc(TPSVCINFO *rqst)
{

    int ret, retval; /* retval is used for rval in tpreturn */
    int urcode; /* used for rcode in tpreturn(3)          */
    long bufsize; /* size of buffer */
    char errstr[100], *errmsg;
    TPQCTL qctl; /* pointer to /Q control area */
    FBFR *rcvbuf; /* FML buffer pointer */

    retval = TPSUCCESS;
    urcode = 0;

    /* set buf size */
    bufsize = Fneeded(10, 100); /* a good guess */

    /* buffer to receive response from TMQUEUE */
    if((rcvbuf = (FBFR *) tpalloc("FML", NULL, bufsize)) == (FBFR
*) NULL)
    {
            errmsg= tpstrerror(tperrno);
            strcpy(errstr, "allocating rcvbuf ");
```

```
                strcat(errstr, errmsg);
                userlog("%s", errstr);
                retval = TPFAIL;
        }

        /* setup TPQCTL */
        qctl.flags = TPQMSGID; /* so can get message id */
        qctl.msgid[0] = NULL; /* clear it so it doesn't confuse */

        /* denqueue the message */

        ret = tpdequeue(qspcname, "CUSTQ", (TPQCTL *)&qctl, (char **)
&rcvbuf, &bufsize, TPSIGRSTRT);
        if(ret < 0)
        {
                if(tperrno == TPEDIAGNOSTIC && (qctl.diagnostic ==
QMENOMSG || qctl.diagnostic == QMEINUSE))
        {
                urcode = QEMPTY; /* assume any error means this */
        }
        else
        {
        /* fatal error */
        userlog("Can't dequeue\n");
        userlog("tperrno = %d\n", tperrno);
        userlog("diagnostic = %d\n", qctl.diagnostic);
        retval = TPFAIL; /* fail the transaction */
        }
        }

        /* Return to the requestor. */
        tpreturn(retval, urcode, (char *)rcvbuf, 0L, 0);
}


/**************************************************************************/
/* custhdr.h                                                            */
/**********************************************************************/

/* custstruct stores customer information and other data needed
   by custmnt and custdeq                                              */
struct custstruct
{
```

```
    char loc[2];          /* location value  */
    char custno[7];       /* customer number */
    char name[31];        /* customer name   */
    char addr1[31];       /* 3 lines of addr */
    char addr2[31];
    char addr3[31];
    char st[3];           /* state           */
    char zp1[6];          /* five digit_zip  */
    char zp2[5];          /* four digit zip  */
    int consis;           /* consistency value */
    /* action switch (n)ew (d)elete (u)pdate */
    char actsw[2];
    /* storage for buffer size and buffer pointers */
    long bufsize;
    FBFR *sendbuf;
    FBFR *rcvbuf;
    TPINIT *initbuf;
};

/* application error defines */
#define NOTFOUND 100      /* same value as database returns */
#define DUPLICATE 101     /* application value */
#define NOFLD 102         /* no occurrence in buffer */

/* misc defines */
#define QEMPTY 1          /* queue is empty */


#************************************************************
# ubbsamp - ubbconfig file for sample customer maintenance
# system using /Q to implement database replication
$************************************************************

*RESOURCES
IPCKEY          52617
MASTER          DALLAS
# change SYSTEM_ACCESS to FASTPATH for production
MODEL           SHM
SYSTEM_ACCESS   PROTECTED
SECURITY   APP_PW
AUTHSVC         "AUTHSVC"
#
*MACHINES
```

```
#
unix1
     LMID = DALLAS
     TUXDIR ="/home/tuxdir"
     TUXCONFIG = "/home/clh/bkapp/bkconfig"
     TLOGDEVICE ="/home/clh/bkapp/TLOG"
     TLOGSIZE=10
     APPDIR = "/home/clh/bkapp"
     ULOGPFX = "/home/clh/bkapp/ULOG"
#
*GROUPS

DALGRP1
     LMID = DALLAS   GRPNO = 1
     TMSNAME=TMS_SQL      TMSCOUNT=2
     OPENINFO="TUXEDO/SQL:/home/clh/bkapp/dbdev:custdb:readwrite"

HOMEOFC
     LMID = DALLAS   GRPNO = 2
     TMSNAME=TMS_SQL      TMSCOUNT=2
     OPENINFO="TUXEDO/SQL:/home/clh/bkapp/mastdb:custdb:readwrite"

QUEGRPD
     LMID = DALLAS   GRPNO = 3
     TMSNAME = TMS_QM TMSCOUNT = 2
     OPENINFO = "TUXEDO/QM:/home/clh/bkapp/CUSTQ:CUSTQSPC"
#
*SERVERS
#
DEFAULT:  CLOPT="-A"
retrvsv          SRVGRP=HOMEOFC
          SRVID=10

chgsv            SRVGRP=HOMEOFC
          SRVID=20
          CLOPT="-A - N"
AUTHSVR          SRVGRP=HOMEOFC
          SRVID=99
          RESTART=Y
          GRACE=0
          MAXGEN=2
          MIN=2
```

```
             MAX=5
             CLOPT="-A — -f /home/clh/bkapp/passwd"

retrvsv          SRVGRP=DALGRP1
             SRVID=10

chgsv            SRVGRP=DALGRP1
             SRVID=20
             CLOPT="-A — Q"

deqsv            SRVGRP=DALGRP1 SRVID=30
             CLOPT="-A — CUSTQSPC"

enqsv            SRVGRP=DALGRP1 SRVID=40
             CLOPT="-A — CUSTQSPC"

TMQUEUE
             SRVGRP = QUEGRPD   SRVID = 1
             GRACE = 0   RESTART = Y CONV = N
             CLOPT = "-s CUSTQSPC:TMQUEUE — "

*SERVICES
chgcust          AUTOTRAN=Y
             ROUTING=chg

rtrvcust  AUTOTRAN=Y
             ROUTING=rtrv

enqsvc
deqsvc

#
*ROUTING
chg  FIELD="LOC" BUFTYPE = "FML"
     RANGES="'D':DALGRP1,'H':HOMEOFC"

rtrv FIELD="LOC" BUFTYPE = "FML"
     RANGES="'D':DALGRP1,'H':HOMEOFC"

# This is the FML field definition file for the application
# name   fld-id type flag comment
*base 200
```

```
LOC       0    string    -    customer location
CUSTNO    1    string    -    customer number
CUSTNME   2    string    -    customer name
CADDR1    3    string    -    customer address line 1
CADDR2    4    string    -    line 2
CADDR3    5    string    -    line 3
CUSTST    6    string    -    state
CUSTZP1   7    string    -    zip 5
CUSTZP2   8    string    -    zip 4
CCONSIS   9    long      -    consistency check column
ACTSW     10   string    -    'u' update 'd' delete 'n' new
```

```c
/* This is the output from mkfldhdr */
/*    fname       fldid        */
/*    ─           ─            */
#define   LOC      ((FLDID)41160) /* number: 200  type: string */
#define   CUSTNO   ((FLDID)41161) /* number: 201  type: string */
#define   CUSTNME  ((FLDID)41162) /* number: 202  type: string */
#define   CADDR1   ((FLDID)41163) /* number: 203  type: string */
#define   CADDR2   ((FLDID)41164) /* number: 204  type: string */
#define   CADDR3   ((FLDID)41165) /* number: 205  type: string */
#define   CUSTST   ((FLDID)41166) /* number: 206  type: string */
#define   CUSTZP1  ((FLDID)41167) /* number: 207  type: string */
#define   CUSTZP2  ((FLDID)41168) /* number: 208  type: string */
#define   CCONSIS  ((FLDID)8401)  /* number: 209  type: long */
#define   ACTSW    ((FLDID)41170) /* number: 210  type: string */
```

```sh
#*******************************************************************
# Script to set environment
#*******************************************************************
# set TUXEDO home directory
TUXDIR=/home/tuxdir; export TUXDIR
# configuration file full path name
TUXCONFIG=/home/clh/bkapp/bkconfig; export TUXCONFIG
# put application execution path in PATH for convenience
PATH=$TUXDIR/bin:/home/clh/bkapp:$PATH; export PATH
# full path name of queue device
QMCONFIG=/home/clh/bkapp/CUSTQ; export QMCONFIG

# location and name of FML definitions
# Usysflds required to use ud(1) and sql
FLDTBLDIR=/home/clh/bkapp:$TUXDIR/udataobj; export FLDTBLDIR
FIELDTBLS=sampflds,Usysflds; export FIELDTBLS
```

```
# The dynamic load libraries
LD_LIBRARY_PATH=$TUXDIR/lib:$LD_LIBRARY_PATH;
     export LD_LIBRARY_PATH


# Name editor for tuxconfig(1) and dmconfig(1)
EDITOR=vi; export EDITOR


# The following variables are used by TUXEDO/SQL
# Logical block size; Database Administrator must set this variable
#
BLKSIZE=1024
#
# Set database name
DBNAME=custdb
#
# Set to allow access to database by everyone
#
DBPRIVATE=no
#
# Set Ipc Key for the database; this MUST differ from
# the UBBCONFIG *RESOURCES IPCKEY parameter
#
DIPCKEY=80953
#
# Null out FSCONFIG. Not needed for TUXEDO.
FSCONFIG=
export DBNAME DBPRIVATE DIPCKEY FSCONFIG


# This script is used to define the branch database using
# TUXEDO/SQL. Note use of tmadmin to define a device
#
FSCONFIG=/home/clh/bkapp/dbdev; export FSCONFIG
# Create device list
#
tmadmin -c <<!
crdl -z ${FSCONFIG} -b 2560
!

if [ ${?} -ne 0 ] ; then
     echo "tmadmin failed to created device list."
     exit 1
fi
#
```

```
# Create database files, fields, and secondary indices
#
sql <<! >sqltemp
create database custdb with ( DEVNAME='${FSCONFIG}',
    IPCKEY=${DIPCKEY},       LOGBLOCKING=0, MAXDEV=1,
    NBLKTBL=200,   NBLOCKS=2048, NBUF=70,   NFIELDS=80,
    NFILES=20,     NFLDNAMES=60, NFREEPART=40, NLCKTBL=200,
    NLINKS=80,     NPREDS=10,    NPROCTBL=20,  NSKEYS=20,
    NSWAP=50, NTABLES=20,    NTRANTBL=20,   PERM='0666',
    STATISTICS='n'
)\g

create table cust (
    LOC           char(2) not null,
    CUSTNO        char(7) not null,
    CUSTNME       char(31),
    CADDR1        char(31),
    CADDR2        char(31),
    CADDR3        char(31),
    CUSTST        char(3),
    CUSTZP1       char(6),
    CUSTZP2       char(5),
    CCONSIS       integer not null,
    primary key(LOC, CUSTNO)
) with (
    FILETYPE='hash',    ICF='PI', FIELDED='FML',
    BLOCKLEN=${BLKSIZE},      DBLKS=8,  OVBLKS=2
)\g

\q

FSCONFIG=; export FSCONFIG

# This script is used to define the home office database using
# TUXEDO/SQL. Note use of tmadmin to define a device
#
#
# Create device list
#
FSCONFIG=/home/clh/bkapp/mastdb; export FSCONFIG
tmadmin -c <<!
crdl -z /home/clh/bkapp/mastdb -b 2560
!
```

```
if [ ${?} -ne 0 ] ; then
    echo "tmadmin failed to created device list."
    exit 1
fi
#
# Create database files, fields, and secondary indices
#
sql <<! >sqltemp
create database custdb with ( DEVNAME='/home/clh/bkapp/mastdb',
    IPCKEY=90876,        LOGBLOCKING=0, MAXDEV=1,
    NBLKTBL=200,    NBLOCKS=2048,  NBUF=70,  NFIELDS=80,
    NFILES=20,      NFLDNAMES=60,  NFREEPART=40,  NLCKTBL=200,
    NLINKS=80,      NPREDS=10,     NPROCTBL=20,   NSKEYS=20,
    NSWAP=50, NTABLES=20,    NTRANTBL=20,   PERM='0666',
    STATISTICS='n'
)\g

create table cust (
    LOC         char(2) not null,
    CUSTNO          char(7) not null,
    CUSTNME         char(31),
    CADDR1          char(31),
    CADDR2          char(31),
    CADDR3          char(31),
    CUSTST          char(3),
    CUSTZP1         char(6),
    CUSTZP2         char(5),
    CCONSIS         integer not null,
    primary key(LOC, CUSTNO)
) with (
    FILETYPE='hash',    ICF='PI', FIELDED='FML',
    BLOCKLEN=${BLKSIZE},     DBLKS=8,  OVBLKS=2
)\g
\q
FSCONFIG=;export FSCONFIG

#*********************************************************
# this script allows interactive access to the branch
# customer database
#*********************************************************
FSCONFIG=/home/clh/bkapp/dbdev; export FSCONFIG
sql
FSCONFIG=; export FSCONFIG
```

```
# This script is used for TUXEDO/SQL databases
# to invoke interactive sql on the home office
# database.
FSCONFIG=/home/clh/bkapp/mastdb; export FSCONFIG
sql
FSCONFIG=; export FSCONFIG

#*********************************************************
# this script builds compiles and links the programs
#*********************************************************
# pre-compiler for TUXEDO/SQL
esqlc -c 30 chgsv.ec
# compile server which makes changes to database
buildserver -o chgsv -f chgsv.c -s chgcust -r TUXEDO/SQL
# compile server which dequeues for home office
buildserver -o deqsv -f deqsv.c -s deqsvc -r TUXEDO/SQL
# compile server which enqueues changes to branch database
buildserver -o enqsv -f enqsv.c -s enqsvc -r TUXEDO/SQL
# compile client that user uses to make changes to database
buildclient -o custmnt -f custmnt.c
# compile client used at home office to get changes from branch
buildclient -o custdeq -f custdeq.c
# compile server used to retrieve information from database
esqlc -c 30 retrvsv.ec
buildserver -o retrvsv -f retrvsv.c -s rtrvcust -r TUXEDO/SQL
```

Standards

There are two types of standards: Those written by a recognized standards body and de facto standards that recognize the reality that everyone uses a certain convention. This appendix will discuss only written standards. The discussion will be in the form of a quick description of some of the standards and how they got that way.

This discussion will be limited to those standards that specifically concern client/server applications. Database and programming language and other such standards are not discussed.

E.1 STANDARDS FROM INTERNATIONAL STANDARDS ORGANIZATION (ISO)

E.1.1 ISO Open Systems Interconnect (OSI) Reference Model

ISO-OSI is referenced by all people working with networks. This is the well known seven-layer model:

> Application
> Presentation
> Session
> Transport
> Network

Data Link

Physical

Information flows up from the physical media (coaxial, twisted pair, microwave, etc.) and down from the application layer. The application layer is not necessarily the actual application as seen by the end user, but includes anything that receives the information from the network, such as a database or a system like TUXEDO.

The presentation layer provides services that prepare the data and present it to the application layer. It does *not* have anything to do with presenting the information to people.

The rest of the layers manage the transmission of information to assure that what is received is exactly what was sent.

TCP/IP provides everything from the transport layer down. Most current networking systems do not include an active presentation or session layer.

LU6.2 provides the equivalent of all layers, including the application layer.

UNIX provides a transport layer interface (TLI), which provides a sort of presentation layer, and isolates the application layer from the lower layers. Using TLI, an application layer system can be connected with any networking system that provides a transport layer without regard for the underlying networking system.

E.1.2   ISO Distributed Transaction Processing

The ISO standard *Information Processing Systems - Open Systems Interconnection - Distributed Processing*, is a high level standard for distributed transaction systems. It includes a standard model, a set of protocols, and a set of services. There is no application interface (API) included, and others, such as X/Open, are creating the APIs. The ISO distributed processing standard is placed in the application layer.

E.1.3   ISO Two-phase Commit

The ISO standard *Information Processing Systems - Open Systems Interconnection - Service Definition for the Commitment, Concurrency and Recovery Service Element* (CCR), includes an application layer standard for two-phase commit and recovery capability. Again, no API is provided, just a protocol and capability definition. The ISO CCR has been implemented by most database vendors and is a required integral part of all distributed transaction processing systems.

E.2   ## X/OPEN DISTRIBUTED TRANSACTION PROCESSING SPECIFICATIONS

X/Open Company, Ltd. is an independent, worldwide, open systems organization supported by most of the world's largest information systems suppliers, user organizations, and software companies. X/Open provides specifications to support open systems. These specifications become de facto standards to most enterprises.

The document *Distributed Transaction Processing: the XA Specification* published by X/Open is the first of several specifications relating directly to distributed processing and client/server processing. This specification defines the distributed transaction model and the API for the interface between the transaction manager and resource managers.

Future specifications from X/Open are expected to define:

- An API providing the capability of transaction start and stop (transaction demarcation) for the application program
- An API to support peer-to-peer distributed and cooperative computing
- An expanded XA specification, sometimes called XA+

The bibliography lists the documents from X/Open that are applicable to TUXEDO.

E.3   ## OPEN SOFTWARE FOUNDATION

The Open Software Foundation (OSF) was formed to develop open systems platforms. It is supported by many major information systems vendors. OSF develops and sells open systems products to its members. For distributed processing and client/server, OSF provides the distributed computing environment (DCE), which provides many services required for these environments.

TUXEDO supports DCE via the TxRPC interface. OSF also provides Motif, a graphical user interface based on X/Windows.

Glossary

This glossary defines some of the more important terms peculiar to client/server, distributed processing, and TUXEDO. This book is written with the assumption that the reader knows the common terms used in information processing, so these are not included here. All definitions are made in the context of TUXEDO. Many have more general meanings. Consult the literature for the more general meanings.

Abort   *Abort*, in information processing, means to cease a process and remove all interim affects of the process. If a transaction has updated a database and is then aborted, the database is restored to exactly the state it was before the start of the transaction. Abort is sometimes called *rollback*.

ACID properties   Transaction processing standards define a transaction by requiring that any processing must meet the *ACID properties* to be called a transaction. The ACID properties are:

Atomicity—Each transaction is a complete entity; that is, all the work is either done or not done.

Consistency—Any changes to the system that remain at the end of the transaction must be consistent with the rules of processing. Changes made to a database must be consistent with the rules within the database. Consistency implies that every time the same information is processed the result will be the same.

Isolation—Changes made by a transaction are not affected by changes made by any other transaction running at the same time. Isolation implies that changes made during the processing of a transaction are not seen by any other transaction until the first transaction commits.

Durability—All changes made during a transaction become persistent once the transaction commits. This means that once a transaction commits, changes made to a database must remain until further changes are made by another transaction.

Atomic   *Atomic* in the general sense means the smallest possible object. In a more mathematical sense, atomic refers to a process or object that is complete in itself. An atomic object may be broken down into smaller pieces under certain circumstances, but its completeness may never be compromised. A transaction is atomic, in the sense that it must be either all completed or all effects of its interim operations must be erased.

Authentication   *Authentication* is the security process that verifies that the person using the system is who they say they are. Authentication includes checking passwords and preparing the system for secure use.

Authorization   *Authorization* is the security process that assures that users have access only to the data and processes they are supposed to. Authorization includes granting *privileges* to users. For instance, a user may have the privilege of reading certain data, but not have the privilege of updating it.

Bandwidth   *Bandwidth* indicates the amount of information that can be sent over a network in a given amount of time. The term is defined from the fact that as more information is put on the line in a given amount of time, it requires a wider frequency handling capacity, or bandwidth. Higher bandwidths carry more information than lower bandwidths.

Baud   A *baud* is a measure of the bandwidth in terms of the amount of information that can be sent. In this book and in most applications in the 90s, *baud* is used to mean *bit rate*, though it has not always meant exactly that. For example, a 9600 baud modem has the capacity to transmit 9600 bits per second.

BBL   The *BBL* is the name given to the TUXEDO administration service that manages the TUXEDO bulletin board. Sometimes the bulletin board itself is called the BBL. The bulletin board stores the TUXEDO configuration and certain dynamic information while a domain is running. Every TUXEDO node has a bulletin board and a BBL.

Bit rate   A *bit rate* is a measure of the bandwidth in terms of the number of bits that can be sent in a second. WANs can have as little bandwidth as 56 thousand bits per second, written 56Kb. LANs often have a bandwidth capacity for 10 million bits per second, written 10Mb. Sometimes 56Kb and 10Mb are mistaken to mean 56 thousand and 10 million bytes per second. A byte is 8 bits, so actually a 56Kb WAN can transmit 7 thousand bytes per second.

The actual amount of application data that can be transmitted is decreased by the number of bits the transmission protocol uses to assure accuracy of transmission. On a LAN this can be up to 30 percent of the bandwidth. On a WAN 10 percent is reasonable.

Client/Server The term *client/server* (considering software clients and servers) refers to a protocol which has a rule that there can be only one exchange of messages between two programs. The first program, called the client, sends a message requesting a service to another program, called the server. The server can only respond once, presumably with the results of performing the service.

Commit *Commit* is the process by which the effects of a transaction are made permanent. When a DBMS commits, it writes the updated information to disk in the permanent storage area.

Conversational *Conversational* protocols set rules that allow two programs to send messages back and forth until one of them terminates the conversation. Between two programs, if the protocol allows either of them to initiate the conversation, the programs are said to be *peers*, and the protocol is called *peer-to-peer*. Some systems have a protocol that allows only one of the two programs to start the conversation; these systems provide conversational mode processing, but not peer-to-peer.

Daemon A *daemon* is a process that is always running, waiting to detect a condition to which it must respond and begin processing. Software servers and network listeners are daemons. The name dates back to the beginnings of UNIX when people were fond of anthropomorphizing the computer. The spelling is from Old English.

DBBL The *DBBL* is the distinguished bulletin board server that runs on the MASTER platform. The DBBL is responsible for everything the BBL handles plus the DBBL runs the heartbeat of the system to check for system partitioning and other failures. All administrative activity must take place on the MASTER platform using the DBBL. If changes are made to the bulletin board on the master using TUXEDO dynamic administration tools, the DBBL propagates the changes to all BBLs in the domain.

Distributed database A *distributed database* is a database that has its data spread over more than one platform, transparent to the application. Distributed database and distributed processing are vastly different and should not be confused.

Distributed processing   *Distributed processing* means that the processing of an application can proceed on more than one platform. A distributed processing application may use the various platforms in parallel or serially, depending upon the application requirements. Sometimes the term *cooperative processing* is used to describe the distributed processing technique where the processes of the application communicate with each other and work together to complete a transaction.

Domain   A *domain* is a TUXEDO instance. A domain may have many nodes. What makes it a domain is that it is a single administrative entity, supported by a one configuration definition. TUXEDO documentation has traditionally called a domain an *application*. In this book the word application will be reserved to apply to the set of processes that define user functionality. When comparing discussions in this book with the TUXEDO documentation, the word application and the word domain can be interchanged.

Found set   A *found set* is the set of rows that are the result of an SQL SELECT. If the SELECT is against a single table, then all the rows are from that table. If the SELECT creates a join or other type operation that results in a new table, then the found set is the resulting table with the selection criteria applied.

Kernel   A *kernel* is the central part of an operating system. This term is usually used only in reference to UNIX and means the nonremovable part of UNIX.

Listener   In a network, the *listener* is a background process, always running, that detects that the network has information for the platform.

MASTER platform   The *MASTER platform* is where the active DBBL resides. TUXEDO allows definition of a backup MASTER. If the platform running as MASTER fails, the backup will automatically assume the function of MASTER. The administrator can use TUXEDO administration tools to switch masters at any time.

Native client   A *native client* is a TUXEDO client that runs on the same platform where a full TUXEDO node also resides. Since TUXEDO usually is built on UNIX, a native client is usually a UNIX program. Discussions in this book assume that a native client is running on a UNIX platform with a full TUXEDO node. Note that a client running on a UNIX platform that is connected to TUXEDO via the /WS feature is not a native client.

Node   The term *node* in this book is used in its traditional sense, with the added concept that in some types of multiprocessor computers, each processor may be treated as a node. The terms node, platform, and machine are used interchangeably when discussing TUXEDO configurations.

Paradigm   A *paradigm* is a pattern, an example. In general usage, a paradigm is defined as a way of doing things. In this book the way of doing things with the mainframe is contrasted with the way of doing things with open systems, especially UNIX.

Peer-to-peer   *Peer-to-peer* communications is a protocol between two programs that allows either program to initiate a conversation and exchange messages.

Platform   A *platform* is a local computing environment. A platform consists of hardware and the operating system software. If a computer runs more than one operating system at the same time, each operating system is a platform.

Prepare   *Prepare* is the term often applied to the first phase of two-phase commit. When a resource manager, such as a database, responds with an OK vote, it is said to have completed the prepare phase. At this point, the database must be ready, or prepared, to either rollback or commit any changes made by the transaction under any circumstances.

Protocol   A *protocol* is a set of rules that must be followed to accomplish a desired result. In a client/server environment, there may be several protocols: the transmission protocol, the transaction management protocol, the client-to-server protocol, and so on. Systems enforce protocols by checking that the rules are followed and rejecting any request that does not follow the proper protocol. Usually, an application program need not be aware of the protocols it is using. A notable example where the application must be carefully programmed to follow the proper protocol is advanced peer-to-peer communications.

Recovery   *Recovery*, in this book, refers to the process of completing in-doubt transactions after a system failure. Transaction managers and DBMSs usually provide utilities for recovery, which are effective when used with two-phase commit.

Remote procedure call (RPC)   A *remote procedure call* (RPC) is a method whereby a program can invoke a subroutine on another platform as if that subroutine were local. Ideally, a program should not be aware that it is using RPC, but many RPC systems require that the program perform certain actions and include special parameters in an RPC. There continues to be considerable discussion among technical people about how to implement RPCs in various environments. RPC usage by itself does not assure transaction integrity.

Request/Response paradigm   The *request/response paradigm* speci-

fies that the server responds only to requests for service. Request/
response services receive a request, perform the requested service,
and either return the result to the requestor or forward the partial
result to another service for more processing. TUXEDO servers can
process only one service request at a time, even if several services are
part of the server.

Resource manager   The *resource manager* is the component that manages a computer's shared resources. The resource manager has many
responsibilities, including proper implementation of two-phase commit,
managing the resource to assure its integrity, and the like. In many
systems, the DBMS is the only resource manager, but a resource manager may manage any resource, such as a money vending machine.

Rollback   See *Abort*.

Saturation   *Saturation* of a network occurs when the network capacity for carrying data is approached. Saturating a network may decrease the total data throughput of the network, and in severe and
prolonged cases may cause the network to become inoperative.

Symmetrical multiprocessing (SMP)   *Symmetrical multiprocessing* is a method of managing multiple processors that allows any
application to run on any processor. An SMP system will run efficiently without requiring special programming, though use of appropriate distributed processing systems will aid SMP in providing
the best performance.

Transaction   A *transaction* is any group of processes that must complete, including updates to resources, in its entirety or leave no traces
of ever having been attempted. A transaction is completed successfully by committing the transaction. A transaction may be aborted.
TUXEDO applications programs may be involved in local transactions or global transactions, but not both. By definition, if a program
uses transaction management facilities of the resource manager, the
program is participating in a local transaction. If a program uses
TUXEDO transaction management facilities, the program is participating in a global transaction. For instance, if the program executes
the SQL COMMIT WORK statement, the program was in a local
transaction. If the program calls **tpbegin(3)** or **tx_begin(3)**, or is a
service invoked within such a transaction, the program is participating in a global transaction.

Transaction integrity   *Transaction integrity* is the term applied to
the fact that work done during a transaction was done in accordance with transaction rules. If transaction integrity is lost, then
the user can no longer be certain that either all updates are completed or all updates have been rolled back. In more technical terms,

loss of transaction integrity means that the ACID properties have been lost.

Transaction manager   In its purest sense, the *transaction manager* is that part of the system that maintains transaction integrity on a transaction. Many people refer to the entire transaction processing system as a transaction manager. Care must be used to understand the context where this term is used.

Transaction semantics   *Transaction semantics* refers to providing transaction management to processes. Most RPC systems do not include transaction semantics, which means they do not provide a transaction manager.

Universal device list (UDL)   The *universal device list* (UDL) stores the location of transaction logs and queues.

Bibliography

Distributed Transaction Processing: The Peer-to-Peer Specification. Berkshire, UK: X/Open Company Ltd., 1992.

Distributed Transaction Processing: Reference Model Version 2. Berkshire, UK: X/Open Company Ltd., 1993.

Distributed Transaction Processing: The TX (Transaction Demarcation) Specification. Berkshire, UK: X/Open Company Ltd., 1992.

Distributed Transaction Processing: The TxRPC Specification. Berkshire, UK: X/Open Company Ltd., 1993.

Distributed Transaction Processing: The XA Specification. Berkshire, UK: X/Open Company Ltd., 1991.

Distributed Transaction Processing: The XATMI Specification. Berkshire, UK: X/Open Company Ltd., 1993.

Gray, J., and A. Reuter. *Transaction Processing: Concepts and Techniques.* San Mateo, CA: Morgan Kaufmann, 1993.

Hall, C.L. *Technical Foundations of Client/Server Systems.* New York: John Wiley & Sons, Inc., 1994.

Ozsu, M.T., and P. Valduriez. *Principles of Distributed Database Systems.* Englewood Cliffs, NJ: Prentice-Hall, Inc., 1991.

TUXEDO Administration Guide. Decision Support, Inc., 1995.

TUXEDO Programmer's Guide, Volume 1. Decision Support, Inc., 1995.

TUXEDO Programmer's Guide, Volume 2. Decision Support, Inc., 1995.

TUXEDO Reference Manual. Decision Support, Inc., 1995.

TUXEDO System Message Manual (2 Volume Set). Decision Support, Inc., 1995.

Index